ABA Biography Series

ABA

Defending Liberty
Pursuing Justice

Lawyers Pursuing Justice

The March for Civil Rights
The Benjamin Hooks Story

Dr. Benjamin L. Hooks
with Jerry Guess
Foreword by Dennis W. Archer

CONTENTS

Dedication

Jerry Guess was an NAACP regional director when I came on board. I was impressed with him and asked him to be my administrative assistant. In that job, he performed miracles while handling a wide range of responsibilities. He retired when I did and worked with me on this book. Back and forth he came to Memphis to research, quiz me and write. Finally, he completed the job and sent the papers to me. I was so exhausted by that time, I did not proceed. Then, I came into contact with the ABA and Adrienne Cook, and we went forward. Thanks, Jerry, and thanks also to your lovely wife, Marjorie, and darling daughter, apple of your eye, Jackie.

To Almighty God for life and its infinite possibilities;

To my daughter, Pat, for her invaluable and immeasurable contributions;

To my loving family;

To Greater Middle Baptist Church, Greater New Mount Moriah Baptist Church, my Masonic organizations, the Pythian, Calanthe, and Omega Psi Phi families, and my NAACP family;

To the sainted memory of Roy Wilkins, American civil rights icon whose legendary achievements and splendid leadership still shine, and whose shoes I was called on to fill;

And, finally, to my wife, Frances, critic, lover, devoted companion for over 50 years ... my leader and my follower—what more can I say that I haven't said so many times before. The river is wide and I can't step it. I love you, honey, and I can't help it.

Foreword

It is with great pride that I pen the foreword for the biography of a remarkable man and cherished friend. Lawyer, judge, pastor, civil rights activist, trailblazer, and great humanitarian, Benjamin Hooks knocked down the walls and cleared the way for so many men and women of color in this country.

As the grandson of one of the first black women in the United States to attend college, Benjamin Hooks had instilled in him the importance of higher education. He is the product of a supportive and loving family—far more typical in the black community than is often portrayed in the media—that encouraged him to succeed despite the racism and barriers that would dog him at every turn. And succeed he did.

His achievements can be attributed not only to his solid foundation, but to his irrepressible faith—in himself, in his people, and in God. Discouraged at the outset from entering the ministry, he did the next best thing—he chose the law. This choice was not as far a cry from his initial vocation as one may think. I often liken lawmakers to ministers. As stated in Romans 13:4, a lawmaker is considered "the minister of God to thee for good," as well as "a revenger to execute wrath upon him that doeth evil."

Thus, Benjamin Hooks became a "minister of justice," a healer of the wounds of injustice. And his challenges were great.

Barred from white bar associations and often degraded in court, he nevertheless persevered. He became an honorable judge, a prominent businessman, a longtime leader of the NAACP, and, yes, a minister. Often I had the pleasure of hearing him preach at the Greater New Mount Moriah Baptist Church in Detroit. His voice echoed the spirit of the days when he walked side-by-side with Dr. Martin Luther King, Jr. and worked with the Southern Christian Leadership Conference organizing sit-ins at restaurants and boycotts of services that discriminated against blacks.

He made history in 1972 when he became the first black appointee to the Federal Communications Commission. He was among the first to bravely speak out against the lack of representation of minorities at the executive levels of television and radio station management. He spoke out against the derogatory image of blacks in the media. More minorities were employed in broadcasting than had ever been employed before his tenure as FCC commissioner.

As leader of the NAACP for 15 years, Benjamin Hooks oversaw the organization's position on affirmative action and federal aid to the poorer neighborhoods of American cities. He participated in dialogues with the governments of South Africa and in hundreds of domestic issues affecting minorities in the United States.

A staunch advocate for self-help, Benjamin Hooks preaches responsibility and accountability, and calls for a "moratorium on excuses." He urges the black community to strengthen the family unit and impels those who have succeeded to reach out and help their brothers and sisters. Unity in community is essential, he suggests, for blacks to participate in the American dream.

America indeed is a better place for African Americans than before Benjamin Hooks. With the knowledge of a lawyer and judge, the voice of a preacher, the position at the FCC, and the power of the NAACP, he opened doors and remedied injustice in a way that extended opportunities for generations to come.

I am grateful for his work, support, and, more than anything, his friendship. His legacy will live long.

Dennis W. Archer
President
American Bar Association, 2003/2004

Preface

This book was written to tell what I believe to be an important story of breaking down barriers and building bridges. The book chronicles my experiences as a young black boy growing up in the South during one of the most racially oppressive and economically disastrous periods in our nation's history.

My story is not unique in some respects. Millions of African Americans grew up in the South during the '30s and the '40s. They too had to overcome unspeakable odds and obstacles. They too shook off society's imposed chains of social, political, educational, and economic "second classness"—and went on to make significant contributions to their communities, their families, and their nation.

My story is different in a number of important respects, however. I was blessed to have the opportunity to help change the judiciary in Memphis, as the first African American to serve on a court of record in the South since Reconstruction. As the first black on the Federal Communications Commission (FCC), I helped shape the nation's policies as they related to bringing greater fairness in our communications industries. Finally, as the chief executive officer of the nation's largest and oldest civil rights organization, the NAACP, I helped to set the agenda for the national civil rights struggle for more than one and one-half decades.

This book, therefore, gives the reader a bird's-eye view of what it was like, as a black person of the World War II generation, to work on the inside to change the social, economic, and political fabric of America.

I believe it is important that this story, if it is to have credence and legitimacy, be told by one who has been instrumental in shaping the history of this period. I have attempted to be objective, straightforward and honest. I have refused the temptation to inject controversial materials for controversy's sake. That would be a disservice both to me and to those whose contributions forever altered the landscape of race relations in this nation.

My objective is to share with my readers a story of faith—a story that portrays the magnificence of the indomitable spirit of African Americans.

Despite the many shortcomings of America, this is the one of the few nations on the face of the globe where the age-old "cripplets" of ignorance, poverty, and intolerance can be nonviolently overturned by the oppressed. The road from slavery to freedom has been a long and arduous one. There have been many bumps in that road. Chasms had to be bridged by the sheer faith and determination of African Americans. Our Constitution, that same Constitution that made my ancestors three-fifths of a person, ultimately became the indispensable vehicle that we used to get to freedom's door. We have not yet entered the inner chambers, but we are closer than at any other time in our history to the banquet table of equality.

With this book, I will take you on a guided tour through one of the most turbulent periods in the history of race relations. I will share with you the flavor, the excitement, and the frustrations of that period. I want the reader to get a peek into the decision-making process in the halls of power. A glimpse will forever change the way you view the struggle for dignity and respect by black people in America.

Acknowledgments

I would like to thank Jerry Guess, my friend, co-worker, and co-author, without whose help this book would never have been written. I would also like to thank his wife, Marjorie, and his daughter, Jacqueline.

Many thanks to the American Bar Association for publishing this book and thanks to a newfound friend, Adrienne Cook, without whose editorial insight, steely determination, and perseverance, we would not have completed this project.

I am grateful also to Courtland Malloy and Chester Higgins for their assistance.

For their help and insight, for reading discussing, editing, supplying needed information, and filling missing gaps, I thank particularly Julia, Raymond, Mildred, Bessie, Frances, Pat, Robert III, Ronnie, Fred, Michael Sr., Michael Jr., Carole, Margie, Anita, Arlie, Charlie, Reece, Archie Mae, Doug, David, Howard, John, Donald, Jed, Jeanne, Pitt, Barbara, Carla, Beverly, Beverly, Art, Bill, Kenneth, Alberta, Gwen, Macy, Linda, David, Donald, Jackie L., Jackie T., Leonard, Earlene, Evelyn D., Evelyn M., H.T., Russell, Odell, Vasco, Maxine, Johnnie Mae, Allegro, Hal, Jo, Arlelia, and the list goes on.

CHAPTER 1

DEEP ARE THE ROOTS: "THE ANGEL OF BEALE STREET"

The year was 1876. The guns of war had long been silenced. Soldiers from both the North and South had returned home. But things would never be the same. Many who left to fight lay beneath white markers in national cemeteries. Others were buried in haste in shallow unmarked graves. The wounded had stumbled home, many with missing limbs and far more with broken spirits.

More than 200,000 black men who had joined the Union Army to help bring an end to the diabolical practice known as slavery returned to conditions that were changed but still repressive. The back of the plantation system had been broken. Massive estates that had hundreds of slaves providing free labor were now decimated by the fires of General William T. Sherman's troops, or by the slow but methodical advances of General Ulysses S. Grant's victorious army.

Throughout the South, former slaves sought work wherever it could be found, walking from one white farmer or merchant to another in quest of acquiring the dignity of a day's work for a day's pay. The peonage system was alive and well. America had fought a war that had ended slavery but created a feudal system and a class of serfs. The noble dream of Frederick Douglass, President Lincoln, and Harriet Tubman that the wounds of the nation would soon heal, and that blacks would be afforded the dignity of full citizenship, had faded like the early-morning dew on a hot summer day.

There was an uneasy peace, but no justice. America's era of slavery had ended, and apartheid-like discrimination had emerged in its stead.

1

Black men, many who had fathered children only to watch help-lessly as they were sold to a distant plantation owner, searched desper-ately for their families. There are recorded cases of black men walking 300 miles in hopes of uniting with their families and marrying the women they were forbidden to marry during the days of slavery.

The Civil War had been over for less than 11 years when my grand-mother, Julia Britton, arrived in Memphis, Tennessee. The South was still under federal control; the Hayes-Tilden Compromise had not yet been struck. That fateful compromise in 1876 ended Reconstruction in the South and aborted the fleeting dreams of the abolitionists and black citizens, especially in the South.

Memphis was a sleepy city nestled along the banks of the Missis-sippi River. Here federal troops had earlier encamped. Slaves had once toiled in the cotton mills and in manufacturing plants, enriching some of the most prominent and respected citizens of the city. Now Mem-phis, like so many other cities, lay nearly in ruins, its economy shat-tered, its collective spirit broken, and its future in serious doubt.

Into this quagmire came a young black woman, the daughter of a free black man and a fair-skinned woman, who had grown up in a privileged household in Kentucky. Her parents had been house ser-vants. While they were spared the unspeakable hardships of working in the field, they shared the collective, excruciating indignities that all blacks were forced to endure.

Julia Britton, born in 1852, was among the fortunate. She and her brothers and sisters were born free. Her parents were Henry and Laura Marshall Britton. She had three sisters, Mary, Amanda, and Susan, and four brothers, Robert, James, Joseph, and Tommy.

While most blacks were relegated to picking cotton, tending horses, cultivating tobacco, and tilling the field, she was fortunate to attend William Gibson School, a private school in Louisville. There were no schools for colored children in Lexington, Kentucky, where she and the family lived.

Uniquely talented in music, Julia, at the tender age of nine, had received widespread acclaim as an accomplished pianist. One of the contemporary newspapers in Lexington called her "Kentucky's little musical prodigy."

After completing the William Gibson School, Julia was able to attend Berea College. She became the first black woman to attend that school.

There was something deep down in my grandmother's very being that caused her to refuse to accept the egregious mistreatment of blacks and flagrant discrimination. That trait, which dominated her life until she died in 1942 at the age of 89, would set her apart from those who obsequiously bowed to the persistent perversity of the denial of basic human rights.

While she was an excellent student, one who competed successfully with some of the best and brightest minds of her day, she was restless. Berea was known for its tough curriculum and exceptional students. She was so talented that she was asked to teach music while still a student. She took great pride in her work and was an excellent teacher.

Nevertheless, Julia Britton managed to get into trouble. Her stubborn streak, like that of Harriet Tubman before her and Fannie Lou Hamer years later, propelled this relatively tiny woman with a huge fighting heart to stand up against injustice wherever it raised its ugly head.

Berea College, while offering opportunity to blacks, maintained separate social functions for black and white students. If she had been willing to accept these conditions, there would have been no problem. But my grandmother had a very strong sense of right and wrong. Right was to be followed and emulated, wrong was to be avoided at all costs. So Julia Britton led a protest against the college's policy of holding separate proms. Her clarion cries for racial justice did not endear her to many at Berea, but it did force the administration to change the policy.

Satisfied that she had chosen the right course, Julia packed her bags and headed south to Greenville, Mississippi. She had met Sam Werles, a teacher and preacher from Greenville, and they had become engaged a year earlier. In 1872, they were married. Tragically, he died a year later in an epidemic of yellow fever that struck Greenville and a number of other areas in Mississippi. They did not have any children.

She had been offered a teaching position earlier by Benjamin Kellogg Sampson, assistant superintendent of colored schools in Memphis. After the death of her husband, she decided to accept Sampson's offer. When she arrived, she was offered a teaching position at the Monroe Street School. Many of her students could attend school only during the five-month period when crops were not being planted, cultivated or harvested. Some did not attend during the cold of winter because they lacked coats or shoes.

In the summer of 1878, sanitation in Memphis was nonexistent. There was no system for the disposal of garbage or ashes. The streets were filthy. There was no sewer system; privies emptied into the Gayso Bayou, which divided the city. The preceding year there had been a

drought, which continued into the summer of 1878. This caused the
bayou to become sluggish and covered with a thick, greenish slime.

Dead animals floated in parts of the bayou. Boards from roads built
of wooden planks also made their way into the stagnant waters, thus
exacerbating an already critical situation. It was only a matter of time
before some waterborne or airborne viral infection would explode. That
was what happened in the summer of 1878, two years after Julia arrived.

People began to get sick. Death started its seemingly endless march
throughout the city. No class, race, or gender remained unscathed. The
death wagons rolled down the streets and through narrow alleys picking up the dead at night. A state of emergency was finally declared by
the Memphis City Council on August 13. The city admitted what
everybody by now knew: Memphis was in the midst of a devastating
yellow fever epidemic.

Once the fears of the citizens of Memphis were confirmed, panic
broke out. People began to flee the city like rats deserting a sinking
ship. By the end of August, less than half of the city's inhabitants remained. Most of those who stayed did so because they had no place
else to go. Of the 20,000 who remained, 14,000 were black.

A Citizens Relief Committee was organized to provide aid to the
poor. My grandmother worked endless hours, according to the record
and the accounts that she shared with me, as a nurse's aide at various
hospitals. She also dispensed food, clothing, and medicine to the needy.
There was no other entity doing this grueling work at this critical time.
As the epidemic wore on, when people saw her coming, they referred
to her as the Angel of Beale Street. The name stuck with her until her
death.

As the epidemic raged, a pall of pessimism and despair hung like a
deep fog over the city. Memphis was desolate by day and eerie at night.
Banks, schools, and businesses were closed. No work was being done
at the once busy Mississippi River front. The sounds of children playing were absent. Even the birds seemed to have lost their urge to sing.
The one sound that was predictable and constant was the clattering of
the wheels of the death wagons. Human bodies were unceremoniously
piled on the wagons like firewood. Many entire families were wiped
out by the dread fever. Others became widows, widowers, and orphans.

As fate would have it, it was in the midst of these gloomy conditions that my grandmother met my grandfather, Charles Hooks. Their
mutual concern for the suffering of others brought them inextricably

together. Their compassion for the downtrodden led to a mutual affection that required no deciphering.

My grandmother often told the story of how she was trying to find the children of one of her dying patients while working for the Citizens Relief Committee. There was this handsome, genteel, and exceptionally polite gentleman. He was a porter who was volunteering during the crisis. The man knew that the children she was looking for had been taken to an orphanage. He told my grandmother where they could be found. That informal, fortuitous encounter became the antecedent of a long and loving partnership.

They were quite different in upbringing and in experiences. Both were the byproducts of mixed racial heritage. My grandfather had limited formal education; however, he could read and write well. On the other hand, my grandmother had the advantage of private primary and secondary education, and had attended college. Julia was a professional black woman, which was unique in the 1800s. My grandfather was a hardworking laborer, and soft-spoken. Julia Britton was outgoing and engaging.

I remember, while growing up in the same house with my grandmother, seeing the sparkle that came into her eyes and hearing the glee in her voice whenever she talked about him. The differences in their socioeconomic conditions never stood in the way of the genuine affection and mutual respect that they obviously had for each other.

In late October of 1878, the temperature dropped and the epidemic began to wane. By this time, the nation's attention was riveted on Memphis. Word of the yellow fever's devastation had been trumpeted in the daily newspapers of every major city. Even the Congress was moved from inaction to find ways of eliminating the fever. Late in December 1878, there was a meeting at the Greenlaw Opera House, where a plan to surrender the city's charter was adopted. On January 31, 1879, the Tennessee legislature abolished the corporate charter of Memphis.

Schools did not reopen until March 1879. With the city's economy in ruins, it was not even known if the teachers would get paid. This did not prevent my grandmother from pressing Benjamin Sampson, the black principal, for improved conditions, and for more books and school supplies.

In December, after the school's Christmas recess, Charles Hooks proposed to Julia Britton. She accepted, and they were married. A year and a half later, on July 22, 1881, their first child, Henry Alfred Hooks, was born. He was given the name of his maternal grandfather. Robert, my father, was born on October 22, 1890. Another child born to my grandparents, Charles, Jr., died as a young child.

Julia Britton Hooks met and befriended Ida B. Wells, a noted activist, writer, and one of the founders of the National Association for the Advancement of Colored People (NAACP). My grandmother, my grandfather, and Ida Wells went to hear Frederick Douglass when he spoke in Memphis at the Greenlaw Opera House. This was a fortuitous coincidence. The impassioned speech for racial justice by Douglass and the arrival of Wells coincided with an official move on the part of the power structure of Memphis to resegregate many areas of public life in Memphis. Among the most repugnant to my grandmother was the resegregation of the theaters in Memphis.

The Memphis Theater, on Jefferson Street, had advertised a comedy in three acts to be presented in early April. My grandmother and a friend made plans to see the show when it opened. When she and her friend entered the theater after purchasing a full-price ticket, they were led to a center orchestra section that was occupied entirely by whites. Shortly after they were seated, an usher approached and ordered them to move to the balcony. They refused to comply. The usher then left and returned with two uniformed white police officers. They were forcibly removed from the theater, given tickets for disorderly conduct, and instructed to appear before the magistrate the following morning.

The next day, in court, the manager of the theater admitted that blacks had not been segregated before the 1878 season. He did not deny that Julia had taken a seat in the section of the theater where she usually sat. However, he stated that they should have moved when ordered to do so by an usher on duty. The judge ruled in favor of the theater. My grandmother and her friend were found guilty and fined five dollars each.

Grandmother was outraged, but her indignation turned into consternation when she heard her friend apologize to the court: "We were wrong, I know that, Your Honor. This will never happen again." From that day forward, Julia Hooks would go to the theater alone and pay whatever penalty might be imposed on her for refusing to "sit in her place."

When Ida Wells came to Memphis, they began to go to the theater together. They always sat in the orchestra section and forced the theater personnel to either make them move or leave them alone. The two decided that when told to change seats they would do so, since neither could afford to continue to pay the court-imposed fines.

The following year, in May 1883, Ida Wells was forcibly removed from a train when she refused to move to the smoking car to make room for a white passenger. The smoking car was designated for blacks whether they smoked or not. Ida B. Wells was to challenge the railroad's policies and actions in court. As hard as it might be for some today to believe it, she prevailed in court and was awarded a $500 judgment—an enormous sum for that day. *The Memphis Daily Appeal* reported the story on page 4 under the headline, "A Darky Damsel Obtains a Verdict for Damages Against the Chesapeake & Ohio Railroad." Julia was angered by the racial reference, but she was inspired by her friend's courage and legal victory.

Ida B. Wells would turn out to be a powerful abolitionist, journalist, and newspaper publisher. She was eventually run out of Memphis after a lynch mob burned down her newspaper office. This came as a result of a series of editorials that she wrote for *Free Speech* after my grandfather, Charles Hooks, and other blacks were falsely arrested in the wake of an attempt by the black community to protect a black store. Two of the men imprisoned with Charles Hooks were taken out of jail by a mob, carried to the outskirts of town, and lynched. Ida Wells's forcible removal from Memphis was given impetus by the series of articles she wrote in her paper assailing the lynching of black men falsely accused of raping white women.

Ida was not only an excellent writer, but she encouraged Julia to try her hand at publishing some of her writings. Among the articles that my grandmother wrote was one whose title she said came to her while watching children on the playground. It was called "Duty of the Hour." The article struck a chord in the black community more clearly than any concert she had ever performed. It sparked debate and serious deliberations by leaders and the common black residents of Memphis as never before.

My grandmother wrote in part:

I believe that character should be considered the "Duty of the Hour." Morality must be instilled in our children, as well as mathematics. I am convinced that in too many homes it is neglected as the result of ignorance. There is in every child a divine principle awaiting development, a precious germ awaiting unfolding; duty requires that this principle be divinely developed, that this germ be properly enfolded.

The Negro race of America needs to be thoroughly aroused not only to the necessities of character building, but also to the means of perfecting a better system of education, compulsory and universal.

The chief factor of an advancing civilization is a sound system of instruction which every child, no matter his color or nationality, may receive. Let us make it the duty of the hour to garnish with art, strengthen with acquirement, and elevate with eloquence and good character, the great and transcendent theme which command so many true and willing votaries throughout the whole dominion of the civilized world, which by the grace of our great Creator, can marshal in its defense a mightier and more invincible host than has ever responded to Crusader's rally cry. All hail the auspicious day when the dark sons and daughters of the South shall arise to conquer wrong. He who would cure must first cure himself.

Inspired by my grandfather, Julia and a group of women established the Colored Old Folks and Orphans Home. The inspiration for this effort came apparently from my grandfather's recognition of the dire need for someone to do something to assist the "pathetic old folk" who had no one to care for them, and from my grandmother's desire to have a safe place for orphans and children who had been abandoned by their parents.

Julia Britton Hooks never ceased teaching. Not long after the children came along, she opened the Hooks Cottage School and the Hooks Musical School. Among her students was William Christopher (W.C.) Handy, to whom she taught harmony. She and my grandfather also administered the first juvenile detention home in the city of Memphis for colored youth. Tragically, it was a young man in that youth detention home who my grandparents had tried to help who shot and killed Charles Hooks.

Unfortunately, there was never a thorough investigation to determine why or how he was killed. The irony of this situation was that a kind and caring man, reaching out to help people in trouble, had his life ended by one of those he had sought to help. My grandmother never talked about her tragic loss. Until her death, however, every day of her life, she remembered him by dressing in black.

To this day, among those who recall her, she is remembered fondly as the "Angel of Beale Street," a fighter, a musician extraordinaire, and as being very active during the early days with the Memphis Branch of the NAACP.

Unquestionably, both she and my grandfather—whom I never knew—had a profound impact on me. Their notoriety in the city of my birth served as a catalyst for my desire to change a system of "second-classness." Whenever I was tempted to throw up my hands and say, "I have done enough," my roots, which run deep, told me to struggle on.

Chapter 2

GROWING UP IN MEMPHIS

I grew up in Memphis in the late 1920s and '30s. As a child, life for me was very enjoyable. I was the fifth of seven children. My father, Robert Britton Hooks, Sr., was born in 1890. Family records indicate that my great-grandfather was a white man. I never knew his name, but I heard my grandmother refer to him as "Old Dr. Hooks." It is possible that he was a physician, but that is not really known.

My father was a photographer by trade. He graduated from LeMoyne Institute, a private high school that later became LeMoyne College. Years later I attended LeMoyne as a 16-year-old freshman. Since then, it has become LeMoyne-Owen College. When my father attended LeMoyne, it was one of the best private schools in the nation for blacks. Latin, Hebrew, Greek, chemistry, geometry, physics, biological science, the classics, and history were requirements for graduation.

Dad's dream was to become a surgeon. That dream was destroyed while he was working in the print shop at LeMoyne when his right thumb was crushed by a press. I often think, with the many medical advances that are commonplace today, had my father come along later, his thumb could have been repaired and probably his dream could have been realized. But that was not to be. My father's thoroughness, unquestioned fine mind, scientific knowledge, and inquisitiveness would have made him an excellent surgeon. Instead, he used those attributes in his photography studio.

My Uncle Henry was a photographer, and he and my father established the Hooks Brothers Studio in 1907. For years this was the only black photography studio in Memphis. Their advertising slogan was, "Where there is beauty, we take it; where there is none, we make it." Other black photographers basically worked out of their houses.

Daddy was an articulate, well-bred gentleman of the old school. He was approximately 5 feet 6 inches and about 145 pounds. Daddy was not tall, but I would have sworn when I was young that he was the biggest man around. He was really the opposite of his outgoing and highly vocal mother. He was soft-spoken and, to some extent, an introvert.

His passion was his family and his work. He enjoyed the time he spent with his family, and he enjoyed talking and laughing with my mother. If any two people were ever in love, they were. That love lasted for more than 61 years of marriage. My father also loved his children. He had a particular fondness for girls, like most fathers. He loved my brothers and me, and he made sure that we knew how to do things right. He was meticulous in everything that he did. In his photography studio he was king. Everything had to be done to his specifications. No shortcuts were allowed. His dress was also meticulous. His shoes were always shined to gleaming perfection; he wore a well-pressed shirt every day, and often a tie. He walked with his head up and his shoulders erect. He did not own a car. He either walked to work or used public transportation.

My father distanced himself from white people. As much as possible, dealings with the photo studio supply companies, finishing labs, and other businesses were done by one of his sons or Mr. Butler, an old man who worked for him. He gave everyone respect and he demanded the same for himself. He encouraged each of us to decide for ourselves if we wanted to be social activists. He was proud of Julia when she became active in the Memphis branch of the NAACP. When I became a lawyer and became active in the movement in Memphis, I knew he was proud. He said so, often. As I grew older, I learned to appreciate his unconditional love and openness more than ever.

My mother was Bessie White Hooks. She was born in Huntsville, Alabama. Her mother died when she was a very young child, and she went to live with her grandmother. My mother was one of two children. At some point when she was still young, she came to Memphis to live with her father, Jackson White. Her father was a resourceful working man who provided a good life for his family. I never knew if my mother's father had any brothers and sisters or if he was a native of Huntsville, Alabama.

My mother was a homemaker who was devoted to my father and her children. She was soft-spoken and quiet. Although she did not graduate from high school, her English was flawless. I never heard her make a grammatical mistake in speaking, nor did I ever find one error in the countless letters she wrote to me over the years. Mama had beautiful penmanship and a marvelous way with words. Her letters were poetic as well as inspiring.

I do not remember my mother visiting or going anyplace except church, her neighborhood club, and to PTA meetings. Her concern about the education of her children caused her to become active at both Porter School and the Booker T. Washington High School, where my brothers and sisters and I attended.

Mama was very active in her church, St. Andrew's African Methodist Episcopal Church. That was her true love outside of the home. She rarely missed a Sunday morning worship service. She was not a very emotional person, but from the slight swaying of her head or the light tapping of her feet one could tell that she enjoyed the worship experience. She was a very active member of the Women's Missionary Society at St. Andrew's. Her friend, Miss Lee, would pick her up and take her to the Missionary Society's meeting. During the later years of her life, she was a steward at St. Andrew's. It was unusual for a woman in that day to hold the office of steward in the AME Church.

My mother was an excellent wife and a superb mother. We were poor, like most of our neighbors during the Depression, but my mother never let us feel poor. She made us think that a meal of cornbread, molasses with butter, and cold buttermilk was a special treat. I later discovered that sometimes that was all she had to serve the family.

While her love was unlimited, my mother made sure that we learned to obey and assume responsibility. You had to do your chores. You had to make up your bed. You had to take off your school clothes as soon as you got home, and hang them up. Failure to comply with the rules of the house would subject one to having "the board of education" applied to the "seat of knowledge." My brothers and sisters and I have our mother to thank for much of what we have become. Our values and compassion were learned early at our home around her knees.

I do not have any childhood horror stories to tell about growing up in poverty. My family were, by that day's standard, members of the working middle class. My father made a good living as a well-known and respected photographer, and my mother stayed at home and took care of the children. What we did not have, we did not miss. We didn't have a car, but few people in my neighborhood had a car. With a few very rare exceptions, most blacks lived in a racially identifiable community. Our neighbors were all black except for a few whites who lived over community stores for a while during the period that I was growing up. We had families whose principal wage earners worked in cotton gins or as porters downtown. But we also had doctors, lawyers, schoolteachers, postal workers, and railroad men who lived in the community. Segregation restricted where you could live if you were black. So regardless of one's socioeconomic status, if you were black, you lived in the community with other blacks.

During this period people did not move as much as they do today. As a result, not only did you know your neighbors, but you knew members of their extended family—aunts and uncles, grandfathers and grandmothers, and even distant relatives. Consequently, there was a real sense of neighborhood and community.

In the 1930s the nation was in the grip of the Depression. Most of the children that I came in touch with during the early years were also poor. We were a little better off than most. We lived in a very nice house, there was always some food on the table, and we all had adequate clothes to wear. Having three older brothers, I found myself often wearing hand-me-downs. Today, some people frown on the notion of younger children wearing clothes that older sisters and brothers had outgrown. People were not wasteful back then. Each dollar, each penny counted.

My mother was an expert at stretching a dollar and making the most out of the limited resources she had at her disposal. I remember how she constantly took a little and made it enough. Her father, Jackson White, was a waiter at a hotel in Memphis. The service industry was one where a frugal black person could make a good living, largely off the tips from their patrons. Many blacks bought houses, sent their children to boarding school or college, purchased automobiles, and helped other members of their family who were trapped on the farms of the rural South.

My maternal grandfather, Jackson White, was a creative financier. While supporting his family, he managed to purchase a couple of pieces of property in Huntsville, Alabama, which we rented out during the Depression. He also bought three or four lots on South Parkway in

Memphis. If we had been able to hang onto them until today, they would be worth a fortune. I do not know exactly how much he paid for the Huntsville property, but it did provide his family with extra income during the harsh days of the Depression. We are not talking about any huge sum of money. Maybe it amounted to $10 or $12 a quarter. Nonetheless, those few dollars went a long way during hard times. Years later, I was called upon to dispose of the property. I reflected upon my grandfather's ability to take pennies, nickels, and dimes that he made in tips and purchase an asset that would provide additional income for my family during one of the most difficult periods in our nation's history.

Among the other items left by my grandfather was an old trunk. Like so many others, my grandfather did not have a lot of confidence in banks. The old trunk was his bank. I am told that when he would come home after a hard day's work, he would take some of the tip money he had earned and toss it into the trunk. Eventually, there was probably $100 in quarters, half-dollars, silver dollars, nickels, dimes, and pennies. The trunk was passed on to my mother. She would open the lid on that well-worn trunk during hard times, take out the clothes on the top, and reach down and take out a few cents, a nickel, a dime, or a quarter. She would send us to the store to get something that we needed.

You have to remember that a nickel went a long way during the Depression. It was possible to buy a jar of molasses from the local grocery store for a nickel. You would bring your own jar. There was a barrel of molasses from which the grocer would pump your jar full. You could get a quart of buttermilk for a few pennies. The buttermilk was so thick that it could be mixed with a quart of water. Now you had two quarts of buttermilk. On Fridays, my mother would often prepare a special corn bread treat. It was cooked like a flapjack, made of meal, water, and eggs, and fried on the top of the stove. Butter and molasses were poured on top. Add a glass of buttermilk—and we thought we were in heaven. This was probably the least expensive meal that she could have made. To us young children, this was better than steak and lobster or prime rib and lamb.

Our house had been the place where our family enjoyed so many holidays, where we played, laughed, and cried. It had become for us, each in his or her own way, a security blanket that we held onto when conditions were bleak. My father and his brother had run the Hooks Brothers' Photography Studio for years. Before the Depression set in, they made a good living. They were an anomaly in Memphis. Their work was outstanding, and the quality of their services was unsurpassed. Most of their advertisements were by word of mouth, which in a business is the best form of advertisement. A satisfied customer is better than a billboard touting one's proficiency.

Like so many other nonessential businesses, the studio suffered during the Depression. Photographs are luxuries. During hard times people wisely cut out luxuries before they have to cut out necessities. These were hard years, especially for African Americans. More than 50 percent of the adult males were unemployed. The special work programs of the New Deal—the Works Progress Administration (WPA), the Civilian Conservation Corps (CCC), and a host of others—went a long way in easing the pain and the impact of the Depression, but not far enough to affect my father's business.

The major concern of his clientele was keeping a roof over their heads and food on the table. I watched my father going to work day after day, hoping that the new day would generate some business. He would go to the studio on Sundays after church on the chance that someone would stop in to have a picture taken. He followed every conceivable lead and put in unbelievable hours. He was a proud and industrious man who wanted to be in a position to take care of his family in every way possible. It was not to be. All of his efforts were to no avail.

I had heard bits and pieces of conversations between my parents that should have signaled to me that all was not well. The fact is, my father had lost the house due to foreclosure. But back then parents kept trouble away from the children. They talked a lot in code or in private. It is one thing to be told that you are going to move. It is another to be forced to move.

My father was one of the proudest men I had ever known. He did not talk pride, he walked it. He was self-assured, not arrogant. Fate had dealt him a poor hand. Now he was losing the house that had been in his family for so long. It must have been devastating to him. What I remember from this period was his unfettered optimism, at least outwardly. He never allowed despair to consume him. He stoically stood up in the midst of life's reversals and pressed forward. He assured us that things would get better.

Years later, when I was to have my own personal and financial reversals, I took a page from his book. If one does not allow oneself to become consumed by the clouds of withering pessimism, things can improve. In most instances they do. My father continued to work with what he had. Sure enough, things did improve for him and the rest of the family.

Our grandmother did not take the loss of the house as dispassionately as did my father. They had different personalities and temperaments. Additionally, my grandmother was much older, and her future, from her perspective, was much more fragile. She refused to accept the reality of the eviction. Her life and her memories revolved around that building at 578 South Lauderdale Street. She had reared her children there, given piano lessons, watched the grandchildren play and romp through its rooms, and had some of her fondest memories of family events there. She had lived in the house for more than 50 years. Now, she was seeing her possessions being put out on the street. Nothing could be more devastating to a proud old lady. It is perhaps ironic that my grandmother then went to live in the Hooks-Edwards Rest Home, a beautiful home she had established years before. She died peacefully there in 1942.

Our mother was crestfallen, but stoic. She was reluctant to show emotions during difficult times. She did all that she could to keep our spirits up and our hopes alive. Not once did she make my father feel that there was anything more he could have done to forestall or avoid the unfortunate events that had befallen the Hooks family. My mother had never taken a course in psychology, but she was using the right psychological techniques to lift the spirits of the entire family.

My brothers and sisters were also hurt by the loss. When I discovered we had lost the house, I was hurt too, but I quickly rebounded. When Robert said he had found another place to live, I went to this location and peeped through the windows. It was an old house, but it had nice linoleum floors, a remodeled kitchen, and a real bathroom with a bathtub. It also had a hot water tank and a refrigerator. In the old house, water had to be heated on top of the stove. It dawned on me that I would no longer have to go to the icehouse, cut wood, or take out ashes. It also meant that for the first time in my life, at age 14, I would have a bathtub and not have to take my bath in a tin washtub. I discovered then it's not so bad to have to move if you have somewhere else to go.

After that, we lived on McLemore in a 2-bedroom brick bungalow. Twelve of us lived there, happy as could be—mother and father in one bedroom; my brother Robert, his wife Estelle, and their two children in another bedroom; my older brother, Charlie, on a sofa in the living room; and five of us in the dining room: the three sisters in a bed, and

Raymond and I on a couch. Strangely, we did not feel dispossessed, but were happy we could live comfortably there. So, another lesson learned. Attitude is sometimes more important than physical circumstances.

Later, we moved to the Foote Homes Public Housing Project where we would remain for the next ten years, 1940-1949. Public housing back then was light years from what it later became. In those days, it was a stop, not a destination. People moved into public housing on their way to something better. Public housing was often far better than where the residents had previously lived.

In Memphis, we had a slogan: "Private Housing by way of Public Housing." In 1939, public housing was not relegated to the poor and destitute, or second- and third-generation inhabitants. The projects were segregated, as was private housing. There were a lot of upwardly mobile black people who lived in the Foote Homes. They shared the same values of making your apartment your home. You were expected to keep your apartment spotless. We planted flowers; children were controlled by their parents; we looked out for one another, and obeyed to the letter the rules of the housing authority.

The common areas were the responsibility of everybody. An ice cream wrapper on the ground was simply picked up. No garbage was set out except in the containers and on the dates set aside for that purpose. Children obeyed the instructions of adults. We were as careful in talking to our adult neighbor as we were to our own parents. There were the normal fistfights among young boys, but even that was not condoned. Children played games together. Parents left in the morning to go to their varied jobs. With the exception of the old or infirm, adults worked, or were out looking for work.

Public intoxication and the use of profanity were prohibited, as was any form of public gambling. Those who violated the rules of the housing authority were put out. As a result of these sensible requirements and the determination of the residents, it was possible for people to raise families that had values, ambition, and hope. Many of the children I remembered from the projects grew up and built successful careers. Today some live in gated communities in huge houses with swimming pools and three-car garages. The projects were not then, and need not be today, mere breeding grounds for despair, hopelessness, and spiritual and moral decay.

The Foote Homes was a safety net for my family. It was the ladder that we used to regroup and rebuild from economic dislocation. After I returned to practice law in 1949, my father, my brother Charlie, my sister Julia, and I had managed to save enough money to jointly buy a beautiful three-story house with a full basement at 664 Vance Avenue.

Between 1941 and the time that we were able to purchase another house, however, we managed to have a wonderful home. My mother fixed up the apartment; we celebrated birthdays and graduations and weddings, and commiserated with one another during times of bereavement and grief. Although we lost our house on Lauderdale, we were never out of a home.

In those days, people had a positive attitude about things. We didn't complain about things that we didn't have. We used Norman Vincent Peale's psychology before he did. We exercised positive thinking. It was this philosophy that enabled us to survive. It became an important factor in how I learned to cope with the challenges that life presented me over the next six decades. Take the resources that life gives you and build upon them. We never wallowed in the mud of "I don't haveism."

We had to be creative and innovative to find happiness with what would be viewed today as so little. What we lacked in material possessions we made up for with our vivid imaginations. I do not believe that youngsters today enjoy themselves as much as we did when we grew up. We played for hours with rudimentary homemade toys. We had horses—no, not the kind that you had to groom and breed. We had the kind that you made. We would take a broomstick and tie a string around it. To make sure that the string did not slip, you would cut a little notch around the broom handle and tie the string around the notch as tight as possible. Once you had finished this, you would straddle the broomstick and ride it like a horse.

For hours at a time we would run up and down the street whipping the broomstick horse as we went along with a string or a piece of rope. We would give our horses names and tie them up when we went into the house. A broomstick, a string, a little notch, and a good imagination, and we had hour upon hour of fun.

While it was true that all of the public facilities in Memphis were segregated, that did not prevent us from having organized fun. Robert, who was seven years older than I, was one of the most creative persons I have ever known. He organized a basketball and a softball team. He called the organization the Hooks Brothers' Athletic Club. He turned our backyard into a tennis court, a basketball court, and then into a softball diamond. We had a league where the competition for the neighborhood youngsters was just as fierce as the N.Y. Knicks vs. the Chicago Bulls encounter today.

I would like to say that I was a terrific athlete, but that was not the case. I lacked good eye and hand coordination, which is essential for most team sports. Raymond, on the other hand, was a tremendous athlete. He was hell on wheels on the basketball court. He could dribble the ball, shoot, pass, and do it all. Watching him make jump shots from the corners was a real thrill. In those days, you did not need to be 6'8" or 7 feet to play basketball.

When the time came to select players for teams, I was always the last to be chosen, but Robert saw to it that I was always included. I was more often than not given the privilege of serving as referee. Before long, I was given a nickname by the boys that I was to later receive at the Shelby County Courthouse, "Judge." Robert also put me in charge of selling the hot dogs and the cold drinks at the games. This gave me a tremendous sense of self-worth, or self-esteem, as we like to call it today.

My older brother Charles was not around that often. He was thirteen years older and working most of the time with my father by the time I was seven or eight years old. Charles finished high school in 1931 and immediately went to work with my father and uncle at the Hooks Brothers' photo studio. Later he got a job working for one of the cotton firms on Front Street. I remember how proud we were of Charles—he was earning $15 a week! That was good money then. Robert used his spare time, when he could have been doing so many other things, to create fun opportunities for many young boys in the neighborhood.

Reading was a way of life in the Hooks home. It was always a source of endless enjoyment. Like most youngsters, I started out reading the comics. The *Commercial Appeal* and the *Press Scimitar* were delivered to our house every day. The *Press Scimitar* was considered the more liberal of the two newspapers and was preferred by most blacks. In any event, both of these newspapers had a comics section. My sisters, Mildred and Bessie, and I would fight over who would get the comics first. The Sunday *Commercial Appeal* had a large comics section. What a treat! I enjoyed beating my sisters to the comics on Sundays. Charles brought the *New York Sunday News* and *The Sunday Mirror* to our house on Saturday nights. I would grab my favorites and read them first. I had comic strips running out of my ears on the weekends. There were the *Katzenjammer Kids, Bringing Up Father,* and *Flash Gordon. Dagwood and Blondie* were favorites during that period, as well as *Dick*

Tracy and *Little Orphan Annie*. There were no black characters in the comics back then.

After we got through with the comic section, I went on to the sports pages. I still remember the names of the teams in the Southern League—the Knoxville Smokies, the Nashville Volunteers, the Memphis Chicks, the Little Rock Travelers, the Chattanooga Lookouts, the New Orleans Pelicans, the Birmingham Barons, and the Atlanta Crackers. I also followed the National and American League baseball teams. All of the players were white, but that was the way it was back then. The black teams, such as the Birmingham Black Barons and the Memphis Red Sox, were not covered in the white press.

We got our news regarding what was happening in the black community from the weekly *Memphis World*. The *Memphis World* came out twice each week, Tuesdays and Fridays. The *World* covered every facet of black life imaginable: socials, sports, wedding, funerals, political events, church affairs, and education. You found out who got married, what student won the spelling bee, the progress in the civil rights struggle, and the latest local gossip.

One of the first paying jobs I had was selling the *Memphis World*. I cannot recall now how much it sold for back then, maybe a nickel. I had to pay probably three cents for the paper and made two cents for every paper I sold. I remember hounding my father to advance me 30 or 40 cents. Believe it or not, that was a sizable amount of money in those days. More than the money, the experience of interacting with older people had a great impact on me.

As long as I can remember, there were always newspapers laying around at my father's studio. In those days, it was not uncommon for one person to pass along a newspaper to another after he had finished with it. In any event, I remember seeing and reading on a weekly basis *The Chicago Defender* and *The Pittsburgh Courier*. Both of these newspapers had widespread national appeal in the '30s and '40s. One could get a very good fix on state and national issues and find out what was happening in the North and the Midwest by following the articles that appeared in those papers.

The Pittsburgh Courier and the *Chicago Defender* had excellent writers. There were a few writers who stand out in my memory. P.L. Prentiss, Langston Hughes, George Schuyler, Robert Vann, and Robert Abbott were among them. Schuyler, as I recall, was a very conservative person whose column was also in the white press. I was also influenced early in my life by reading the works of Westbrook Pegler, Raymond Clapper,

Ernie Pyle, Walter Lippman, and many others. There were others whose names I cannot recall whose writings had an impact on my intellectual and philosophical development.

The written word was the primary source of learning available to people of my generation. We did not have TV, radio was limited, and the Internet was not even a figment of anyone's imagination. Reading was not only a method of learning, but also a source of entertainment. I loved reading. To me it was a passion.

As a child, I remember that there were always plenty of books in the house. In our front room, which doubled as a family room, we had a bookcase that we called the library. It probably held 30-35 books, but to me, growing up, it was huge. Among the books that I remember in our little brown bookcase were *Uncle Tom's Cabin; Robinson Crusoe; the Bible;* books written by my pastor, T.O. Fuller, titled *20 Years in Public Life 1890-1910, Baptists in West Tennessee,* and *A Pictorial History of the American Negro*; and other publications of interest to working- or middle-class black families. I read them all before completing the eighth grade.

Across the street from my grammar school was a church-related facility that we called the Bethlehem Center, where you could play basketball in the tiny courtyard, play ping-pong, or just read in the library. The library was really just a little room with a lot of books. I spent countless hours there reading as the time just flew by. There were a lot of Tom Swift books at the center, and I read every one of them I could get my hands on. The hero always came out on top. The villain was always punished. Tom Swift would remind me of Horatio Alger, an American hero who always succeeded at whatever he did.

I also read the pulp magazines: *The Shadow, Phantom, Operator Five, The Spider,* and others. *The Shadow* was my favorite. It was a small magazine that contained a single story theme. Lamont Cranston was the Shadow. A month did not pass when I did not read one or two of them. The book cost a dime. There was a place on Main Street where you could take the book back when you had finished reading it and get another one for a nickel.

Old habits die hard. Over the years I must have read thousands of paperbacks. I read them at airports, on trains and planes, in hotels, at home, and while I'm being driven around. To this day, I carry a paperback in my briefcase. It offers me an escape from the many stresses of life. I can be transported to anyplace that the author's imagination can take me.

If I had five dollars for each paperback that I read since childhood, I could furnish a nice house in one of the swanky neighborhoods of Washington or New York City. However, I could not enjoy it as much as I have enjoyed reading over the past 60 years.

My father died on February 27, 1974, and my mother died exactly three weeks later. At the time of her death she had no obvious signs of sickness. We all thought later that Daddy's death perhaps ended her desire to live. The only time I heard my mother make any public utterance after dad's death was at the graveside. She cried out, "Robert, you have left me!"

Chapter 3

THE SCHOOL YEARS

From the time that I was a year old until I was 14, my family lived at 578 South Lauderdale Street, next door to a grocery store, not far from Main Street in downtown Memphis. There were a variety of businesses in my neighborhood: dry goods stores, grocery stores, cleaners, beauty parlors, barber shops, and service stations. Of course, our community was segregated, as were most communities in the South in the 1930s. Except for a few whites who lived above their stores, the community was all black. There were black communities and white communities—as separate as the fingers on one's hand. As was the case with black communities all over the nation, our community had common laborers living in the same block with professionals, blue-collar workers, and white-collar workers.

I do remember the pride that permeated my neighborhood. Our neighbors were meticulous. They swept their porches and kept well-manicured flower gardens, and vegetable gardens were the pride and joy of those who planted them in the early spring. Children played with reckless abandon, unplagued by fear of crime or abuse from strangers.

My mother was an excellent housekeeper. "Cleanliness was next to godliness" was an expression that I heard often. Everything had its place, and everything had to be in its place. When we got home from school, we had to hang up our school clothes and put on our play or work clothes. We each had to pick up after ourselves. We all had chores, and my mother insisted that we do them right. There were no "prima donnas" in the Hooks household. Love and responsibility were dispensed with even-handed fervor. My mother expected each of us to be both independent and responsible.

We were all taught how to wash clothes and dishes, iron, cook, mend, and do those things vital to being a responsible adult. My mother was soft-spoken, but firm. She did not ask us to do anything more than once. We did what she asked, not out of fear of what would happen if we disobeyed, but because we did not want to disappoint the person who had come to represent the epitome of self-sacrifice and unconditional love. I often wonder, as I see the way young people treat their parents today, how we lost that sense of respect and reciprocal love that was commonplace during my youth.

While we had some well-off families in our modest neighborhood, we were not rich. In fact, as I look back, we might be considered poor by today's standards. Early on, my mother taught us the importance of frugality. People made do with what they had. They were creative. We did not complain about what we did not have; we merely worked with what was available to us. Today, there are sociologists and academicians who would look at our plight and conclude that we were indeed poor and disadvantaged. This disregards the fact that poverty—or being poor—is not just a state of economic or sociological condition. It is a state of mind.

There were always some who had larger homes, wore better clothes, and had their choice of meals, but they were few and far between. There were others who had far less than we had. I remember many in my neighborhood who did not have a coat for the cold Memphis winters. Some did not have enough food to eat from time to time. My siblings—Julia, Charlie, Mildred, Robert, Raymond, and Bessie—and I thought that we were blessed, never impoverished.

Today I see children in economically disadvantaged neighborhoods with new sneakers, designer jeans, tee shirts, and jackets out playing on the streets. I wonder if their parents have any idea how much money they are wasting by not insisting that their children follow the pattern that served our families so well. A dollar saved is still a dollar earned.

Sunday at the Hooks household was a special day. As was the custom throughout the South, especially among blacks, the Sunday meal was a special occasion. This was the one day out of the week that we always had "meat, vegetable, and starch" for dinner. Frequently it was chicken, peas with mashed potatoes, macaroni and cheese, and homemade ice cream. We would sit around the table for hours and laugh and talk. My father particularly enjoyed the give and take of the children. My mother, who was the best cook I have ever known, seemed to take great pride in watching the family savor her cooking.

In those days, families spent more time together. I believe that TV has been a blessing in the sense that it has expanded our horizons and brought current events into our living rooms. On the other hand, because of TV, many family members do not talk to one another, even at suppertime. Each person is watching TV in a different room. We used to sit around the table as a family and talk about everything imaginable. My mother and father would find out from each child what had happened that day at school or at work. Each of us had an opportunity to be heard. We discussed current events and things that we had read about that day in the newspapers.

This early exchange of ideas gave me a greater appreciation of the intellectual abilities of women. My sister Julia was brilliant. She had an uncanny ability to assess a situation and get to the root of the problem. She and my sisters Mildred and Bessie were also gifted academically. They would challenge the boys. I hate to admit it, but we were never really a match for them. Robert, Charlie, and Raymond were all blessed with sharp and analytical minds. As a boy I enjoyed watching them engage in mental games. Robert, extremely articulate even as a boy, could weave words and phrases like few I have met before or since.

These experiences also gave me an appreciation of the importance of people reasoning together. Many situations discussed at our dinner table that we thought of as problems turned out to be challenges laden with possibilities. I also learned the importance of strong families. We were able, again and again, to deal with difficulties as a family that would have been impossible for us to deal with as individuals.

School

When I arrived at the Porter Elementary School on my first day, I was petrified. Everything seemed big. The classroom, the hallways, the teachers, and some students appeared huge. As the youngest boy, but not the youngest child, I must admit to having been somewhat sheltered and overly protected. It did not take long for me to make the adjustment, however. Unlike many of my classmates, I could read and write before I entered school. My mother and sisters had seen to it that I got an early start. In those days there were no nursery schools or kindergartens. Therefore, most children came to school not knowing their alphabets or their numbers. Many parents were illiterate and could not teach their children the basics.

We walked to Porter Elementary School, which was only a short distance from my house on Lauderdale Street. Porter, built about 1926, was an imposing structure to me. It was one of the few schools in the city at that time, for blacks or whites, that had a cafeteria and an auditorium built at the time it was originally constructed. We had extravagant May Day celebrations, a number of sports teams, and a large regulation-size softball diamond. The school had a huge front and back yard. The principal was L.E. Brown, a resourceful educator who made the most of segregated conditions.

At Porter we began each day with the singing of what was known as the Negro national anthem: "Lift Ev'ry Voice and Sing." It was mandatory that we knew all of the words. To this day I can recite all of the verses of that song. It was followed by the Lord's Prayer and then by a Christian hymn.

We had excellent teachers at Porter. It was said that the principal, Mr. Brown, managed to recruit and hire some of the best teachers in Memphis. He recruited the daughters of the city's most prominent families. There were 30 teachers at Porter. All were female except the principal and another male teacher who doubled as the gym teacher and hall monitor. Black history was an integral part of our education. Throughout the year we were taught about black heroes and heroines: Phyllis Wheatley, Peter Salem, Harriet Tubman, Frederick Douglass, Toussaint L'Ouverture, and many others. We certainly had a full dose of black history during Negro History Week. We also learned that Thomas Jefferson owned slaves at the time he wrote the Declaration of Independence, that George Washington only allowed blacks to fight in the Revolutionary War after the British started paying Negroes to fight in their army, and that Abraham Lincoln did not believe in the full equality of black people early during the Civil War period. These lessons were taught early and often.

It did not take me and other classmates long to really start enjoying school. Unfettered by the handicap of having to catch up because of a poor start, and blessed with a good analytical mind, I excelled. I became an "A" student from the first grade on. I got along well with most of my classmates. Having older brothers, a well-known father, and a grandmother who most of the students had heard of because of her juvenile probation officer work did not hurt. I spent most of my time reading every book that I could get my hands on.

Then one day something happened that would alter my life forever. I was skipped from the sixth to the seventh grade. The principal came by my sixth-grade classroom. I was being taught by Miss Mae Della Reeves, one of the best teachers ever to walk into a classroom. Mr. Brown called out six or seven names, mine among them. Within minutes, I was a seventh-grader in a new classroom. At that time, the public schools had a way of equalizing classes through irregular promotions. People moved around a lot during that period working on farms, looking for jobs or seeking new housing, and children had school years interrupted because of this. Later that year, I was promoted once again. This meant that I finished high school at 16, and by the time I was drafted into the army at age 18, I had already finished two years of college.

However, there was a downside to being promoted twice in one year. I was well adjusted socially to the students of my own age. At that age, a year's difference in age is significant. For instance, when I finished eighth grade I was 12 years old. There were students who had started school late who were 14 or even 16 in eighth grade. I am sure that I became more introverted and less secure because of this experience. I began to have problems with the boys who wanted to show the girls who was top dog.

There was another burden that I had to bear. I was light-skinned with curly hair. Here I was, far younger than many, light-skinned and with curly hair. Some of my classmates resented me for matters that God ordained. Color never bothered me. It was not an issue in my family. Unfortunately, there were some blacks then who disliked light-skinned blacks, as is still the case to this day.

We learned invaluable lessons while at Porter. Our teachers taught us that we had to learn how to survive in a system that was stacked against us. We were blacks in a world where whites had most of the power. They controlled the government. They controlled the judicial system and the financial markets. We learned that we had to find ways to change the system by surviving within it. They taught us the rules of the game so that we could compete. They taught us to address white people by titles, Mr., Mrs. or Miss. We were to say, "yes, sir" and "no, ma'am." Those were necessary survival skills for blacks living in Memphis and in the South in the 1930s. It was a part of the culture then, and most people complied.

That is not to suggest that our teachers were "Uncle Toms" or "Aunt Nellies." They certainly were not. Their militancy was focused. For instance, I had a teacher who used to brag about the fact that even though she was "colored," she found subtle and not so subtle ways to strike back at the system within the parameters of what was possible. She would go to Goldsmith's department store, in downtown Memphis, for special sales or discount days and do battle with white customers. She gleefully told us of an occasion when she found a neat pair of shoes on a sales table. A white customer reached over for the same pair of shoes. Our teacher told us how she yanked them away from her. Sometimes the white sales clerk would allow a black to get away with this. This was a small victory for her. It may not look so today, but it was indeed a victory then.

Many of our teachers told us that we had to learn how to maneuver within the white system. You had to be twice as smart and competent. That was the lesson that our parents taught us. I cannot recall the number of times that I heard repeated in my house, "You got to be twice as good as a white person if you are to get half the opportunities they have. You have to work harder, longer, smarter, and do whatever it takes to succeed."

After I finished Porter, I went on to Booker T. Washington High School. Again, I was fortunate to have had an exceptional facility to attend. The school was built in 1927. It was not a hand-me-down school built for whites and turned over to blacks after the whites had used it for years. It was a beautiful, three-story structure with a gigantic auditorium that seated approximately 1,800 people. There was a large stage for plays, assemblies, and other events. There was also a cafeteria in the basement and modern classrooms on the upper floors. Unlike its predecessor, Kortrecht High, which only went to the 11th grade, Booker T. Washington went to the 12th grade. It was a first-class school with an excellent academic environment. There was one catch, however. There was an incinerator nearby where the city of Memphis burned its garbage. The incinerator adjoined the football stadium, which was next door to the school. I am sure that the choice of location for the city's incinerator was no accident. Years later, when I heard people talking about environmental racism as if it were something new, I had to laugh. The system has always placed the least desirable facilities in our communities.

I was elected class treasurer during my senior year and worked on the yearbook and on the school newspaper. My family encouraged me to do well in school. Most of my energies were devoted to my schoolwork. However, no one told me that I was going to be a doctor or a lawyer. In those days it was very rare for a black male to aspire to be anything other than a teacher or a preacher. At one time I thought that maybe I would become a teacher.

In the early 1930s a teacher earned between $60 and $80 per month. A postman made $175 per month. Somehow, teaching had more prestige. If given an option, most people, black and white, would choose teaching. There was a reverence for teachers that we would do well as a society to restore today.

Booker T. Washington had an asset that was just as important as the building. It had Blair T. Hunt, the principal. He was an extremely articulate, handsome, highly intelligent and brilliant manager of people. Hunt always carried a bell as he walked the halls and was the best disciplinarian that I ever met or ever heard of. Like light, he appeared to be everywhere at once. When students heard the bell ring, they would stop in their tracks like videotape suddenly thrown into a freeze position. "Where are you going?" from the booming voice of Blair Hunt was enough to strike terror in the hearts of Booker T. Washington's 2,200 students.

If Mr. Hunt walked into a classroom, there would be a deafening silence. Not a soul would say a word. God forbid you should ever be called to his office; it was like a convicted man being advised that the governor had refused to grant a stay of his execution. Stark terror would encompass the student. I made sure I never had that experience. Ironically, Blair Hunt was not a brutal man. On Sundays he was the pastor of the Mississippi Boulevard Christian Church. He was a well-trained theologian, a compassionate pastor, and an excellent public speaker.

When I graduated in May of 1941 from Booker T. Washington, there were 450 graduating seniors and a student body of more than 2,200. Booker T. Washington High remained for years one of the premier high schools of the South. It was at Booker T. Washington that I was exposed to the political system and to a number of loving and caring teachers who would have a lasting impact on my life and personal development.

I had many fine teachers. One of my history teachers was Nathaniel D. Williams, who was also a columnist for the *Memphis World*. For a Beale Streeter, that was some accomplishment. Mr. Williams was one of the only teachers in the school who openly discussed how some white southerners were using the KKK and lynching to maintain racial dominance.

Mr. Williams wrote in one of his columns, "I know what it means to play with a bunch of kids, white and black . . . and then have yourself singled out one day and be designated 'nigger.' I know the saying, 'If you're white, you're right; if you're brown, stick around; if you're black, get back.'" I remember hearing people talking about that column for years. The observations of Mr. Williams had a lasting impact on my thinking. I am sure that many others benefited from them. I would always leave his class fired up. There was little that we could do to change the conditions of the wider society, but there was a lot we could do to change our attitudes on the matter of skin color. But I remember most of all the drilling, the rehearsals, the repetition, and learning Latin, algebra, history, and English—basic high school subjects. Most of the faculty were excellent teachers.

Booker T. Washington High served me, and most of the other students who attended it, well. We learned lessons beyond the classrooms, the books, or the library. We learned how to be responsible men and women—black men and women, if you will—in a racially stratified society. We learned how to resist injustices and how to demand of ourselves the best that was within us. The foundations for my academic life were laid within her walls. The men and women who taught us live through our accomplishments and those of our children. They were role models. They were heroes and heroines.

On to College

After high school I knew that I wanted to go to college. I would be the first in my family to go. My sisters and brothers were among the brightest and the best academically prepared individuals that I knew. All of them, if conditions were different, could have excelled in college. Unfortunately, the family resources were not there when their time came. My sister Julia took a job; so did my brothers Charlie, Robert, and Raymond. Money was tight. The Depression had not ended yet.

There were no Pell grants, no student loans, no financial aid of any kind available to students in the 1940s. There was, in Memphis, what is now Memphis State University. The tuition was cheap. That was the up side. The down side was that blacks could not attend. Going out of the city required room and board, so that was out of the question. Thank God there was another option, LeMoyne College, a small, private black college in Memphis. I applied, was accepted, and enrolled for the fall of 1941. I was 16 years old. I worked with my father, lived at home, and went to school during the day.

The transition to LeMoyne was not difficult. I had taken college preparatory courses at Booker T. Washington. I had Latin, math, algebra, chemistry, English, biology, history, geography, physics, and a variety of other prerequisite courses necessary to do well in college. Our teachers at Booker T. Washington had been some of the best. LeMoyne was and is an excellent academic institution. Again, I came in contact with another fine educator. Hollis Price was my economics instructor and also the dean of the college. Dean Price later became the first black president of the institution and did an outstanding job.

Chapter 4

THE CALL TO DUTY: MILITARY EXPERIENCE

I turned 18 on January 31, 1943, registered for the draft, and was promptly drafted in July of that same year. The war in both Europe and Asia was at a white-hot fever pitch. News accounts left no doubt that the Axis powers were in the war for the duration. Reminders of the stark horrors of the war were in evidence everywhere. Every community in the nation had been stripped of many, if not most, of its able-bodied men. Among those I knew who had been called to active duty were my brother Raymond, friends that I had gone to school with, neighbors, and college colleagues.

This was also a period of almost universal patriotism. Most Americans, black and white, felt that fighting for one's country was the right thing to do. The attack on Pearl Harbor on December 7, 1941, left no doubt about why America had entered the war. Unlike subsequent police actions and undeclared wars, America's participation in World War II had very few detractors.

The South was a very patriotic region. Many military bases and training camps were located there. Blacks in Memphis were just as patriotic as the white citizens. Frankly, I do not recall having conversations with anyone who suggested that because we did not enjoy first-class citizenship, or because of segregation and discrimination, blacks should not fight. I am sure there were persons who felt that way, but I never encountered them. It should also be remembered that the nation was just coming out of a crippling depression. Blacks were limited as far as job opportunities were concerned. Many jobs were not open to them. Military service was just viewed differently then.

Before entering the armed services, I took a written test and received a score high enough to be included in the Army's Specialized Training Program (ASTP). This meant that after basic training I would report to Howard University in Washington D.C., where I would receive accelerated training, as outlined in detail in the chapter on education. The ASTP program was later ended except for its medical component. Hundreds of men who were enrolled in the medical department became physicians.

I was assigned to Fort Benning, Georgia, for basic training. I was one of 13 black soldiers who trained with some 200 white soldiers. This was my first experience being away from home for any length of time. It was an unsettling yet positive experience. First, one had to get accustomed to doing without the conveniences of home and the dependence on family and friends. On the other hand, military training forces a young person to develop an independence and the camaraderie that are essential in developing unit cohesion. Under these circumstances, one grows up quickly. The learning curve was short and the instruction intensive. Learning to accept the barking of orders by superiors was one of the most demeaning experiences that soldiers faced during basic training.

Many who have never had a military experience believe that the physical training requirements are the most demanding. However, those who have served will confide to their listeners that it is the psychological transformation from thinking like an individual to thinking like a group that is the most excruciating. I was an introvert. I had relied upon my own counsel and that of family and a few close friends all of my life. Now I found myself relying on others, men I did not know, white men I did not trust, and superiors who were often my intellectual inferiors. Many drill sergeants had not finished high school. But that is the nature of the military. Servicemen are taught to obey the orders of superiors based upon rank and not on cognitive proficiency.

There was one bright spot. I was pleasantly surprised when I learned that Wilson Hunt, the son of Blair Hunt, my high school principal, was among those with whom I would train. Blair Hunt had married my second cousin. From this union was born three sons. Wilson, one of his sons, was my third cousin.

I was one of a group of 13 black soldiers in my training unit of more than 200 men. All the blacks were housed together in Hut 13. Fortunately I was not superstitious. The U.S. Army was still segregated in 1943 and remained so throughout the war. As one who was raised in the South, being segregated in 1943 was the norm, not the exception. I did resent not being able to use many of the facilities on and off the base. It was offensive to us, as American soldiers, wearing the uniform of our nation, yet not being able to use all the facilities.

That was life in 1943. Some officers and trainees were openly racist, but most were not. There was an invisible social line that blacks were not to cross. This strange dichotomy existed between creed and deed. Here we were training to defend America against the Japanese, the Italians, and the Germans. We were being asked to defend democracy abroad. At the same time, we were being discriminated against for no reason other than the color of our skin. The slogans of defending democracy rang hollow to the men in Hut 13 and in similar training encampments around the nation.

Just stop and think about it. We were good enough to shed our blood, but not good enough to share a Coke or a beer with someone whose life on the battlefield might depend on our actions. White Americans who served during this war could never relate to "fight for the right to fight with dignity." Except the Japanese Americans, who were interned during the war, no other group of Americans has had the experiences that black Americans endured. America has formally apologized to its Japanese American citizens for its abominable behavior. It has never apologized to African Americans who served by the millions during this pivotal period in our history. Some say that no apology is necessary. That view is held by those who did not have to endure the indignities that we endured in defending our nation's freedoms.

It is a prevailing principle of life that all adverse conditions are laden with hidden possibilities and unintended consequences. Although the military brass figured out how to practice segregation, the army was not equipped to be fully segregated by race. Remember, at this time we had 12 million men in training, drilling, fighting, and being transported on planes, trains, ships, and trucks. It was not possible for the U.S. military to maintain complete segregation, no matter how desperately the civilian command or military commanders may have wanted to do so.

For instance, while you could maintain segregated facilities at the training centers, it was impossible to avoid the breakdown of barriers when the men were brought in for preparations for and during actual combat. How do you segregate toilets, washing facilities, and the like? There were a limited number of facilities available. If we had to relieve ourselves, we had to use the facilities. We had to shower and shave, drink water, get medical attention, and buy supplies from the commissary. The nature of the military is to bring soldiers together, not to keep them separate. Social barriers were broken every day. Men getting ready to fight or to die were less interested in old, tired customs and discredited mores. Unlike civilian life, under the stresses of war we were forced to interact frequently across the racial divide.

Later, when we deployed in Europe, black units relieved white units and white units relieved black units. I was in one of the few black combat units in Europe. Fewer than 2 percent of the black soldiers served in the infantry during the war. In the natural order of things, friendship and bonding occurred. Black soldiers and white soldiers, even those from the South, realized that we had more in common than we realized. We discovered that we enjoyed the same food, the same movies, the same music, and had similar feelings toward our families and neighbors that we had left behind.

This was my first experience with integration, and it confirmed what I already knew. There were some good white people and some evil white people. There were some good black people and some evil black people. There were some black people who were smart and some who were not. Some white people were smart and some were not. As one who wrote well, I was asked by many soldiers—many of them illiterate, others with undecipherable handwriting—to write letters for them to girlfriends and loved ones back home. Through these experiences, I came to understand that people are essentially the same. We all had fears and moments of extreme confidence. We had our "up" moments and our "down" moments. We had our hopes and our dreams, our likes and our dislikes, and our faiths and our doubts. I understood that, stripped of the old habits and group pressures, people are basically good, decent, and understanding. Reinhold Niebuhr explained in his book, *Moral Man and Immoral Society,* the dynamics that cause so much hatred and the wanton disregard for the well-being of others.

I can remember sitting around some days just wondering why, since we have so much in common, we have these schisms between the races. Why, in Memphis and most of America, was race such a determining factor? Since we all bleed red blood when shot and die when mortally wounded, "why," in words echoed by Rodney King years later, "can't we just get along?" These were the thoughts of a young man who could not fathom why Americans allow race to loom so large in our national psyche.

My unit, the 92nd Infantry Division, fought in Italy during the war. Along with the 93rd Infantry Division, it was one of only two black combat units in the U.S. Army at that time. The 92nd Division was known as the Buffalo Division. It had won acclaim during the Civil War. There were some who believed that blacks lacked both the courage and the ability to fight. The 92nd Division won the respect and admiration of military experts and historians during the subsequent Indian and frontier wars and in World War I for its valor and fighting spirit.

General Pershing, known as Black Jack, had commanded the division at one time. Our units were completely segregated. We had white line officers, officers with the rank of major or above, some of whom showed both admiration and respect for our fighting ability, loyalty, and patriotism. We had black officers with the rank of lieutenant and captain. There were a few blacks who rose to the rank of major. I rose to the rating of staff sergeant before the end of the war.

I do not like to talk about the blood and gore that we experienced as we fought our way up the "boot" of Italy. For those who advocate war as a means to resolving international problems, I say the world must find a better way to deal with conflicts. The stench of death still lingers with me after all these years. I cannot forget the faces of dead American soldiers, frozen forever in agony, bodies we crawled over on the battlefields of Italy. I can still see the bloated bodies of innocent civilians scattered across the placid landscape of that nation. I shiver when I hear in my memory the anguished cries of wounded men for whom morphine could not ease their pain. General Sherman was right; war is hell. Those who think otherwise have not experienced war.

We completed the campaign in Italy a short while before the war was won in Europe. We were scheduled to go to the Pacific theater to help end the war there. Unquestionably, many units would have been sent to fight. I am convinced that would have been a costly battle if it became necessary to invade the Japanese homeland. I am aware that there are some enterprising modern historians and revisionists who criticize President Truman's decision to drop the atomic bombs at Hiroshima and Nagasaki. I have read many of their arguments why it should not have been done. They cite theories of how many Americans would have had to be sacrificed if the President had made another decision.

As one who had fought in and saw the horrors of war in Europe, I am not in a position to criticize President Truman's decision. No one alive knows what information President Truman had and what his actual thoughts were regarding that information.

One of the saddest days in my life was sitting in a foxhole in Italy and reading in *The Stars and Stripes* that President Roosevelt had died. He was the only president I knew of and it shook me to hear he was no longer alive. One of the happiest days of my life was when I learned that the war in Europe was over. Another was when I learned that the war was finally over in the Pacific. I am sure that the men and women who had been in service as long as or longer than I were also relieved to know that they would soon be going home.

I was not discharged until February of 1946. We were discharged based upon seniority. It was impossible to discharge everybody at one time; it had to be done in stages. During this period after the war was over, black and white soldiers found themselves in the same quarters. I developed some relationships, although not necessarily friendships, with a number of white soldiers from the South. I detected that their experiences had forever altered both their lives and their attitudes in a positive way. I got the feeling that they also wanted to see America changed. They, like the black soldiers, knew that things would never be the same once we returned home. I had no way of knowing how difficult the task would ultimately be, but I knew deep within my very being that that day would come in my lifetime. It did.

Chapter 5

LAW SCHOOL, CIVIL RIGHTS ACTIVITIES, AND FAMILY

By the time I got back to Memphis, got settled, and cleared my head, it was too late to finish my academic requirements for that semester at LeMoyne in Memphis. From February through May, I basically stayed at home. I was unwinding from a war that was so violent and tragic as to boggle the minds of those who have never seen firsthand wanton human destruction. I did what many GIs did: I hung out with my friends, and worked from time to time at my father's studio. The routine of sleeping late and hanging out at night soon lost its luster. I had never been the kind of person who could wander about aimlessly without a specific purpose. One day it came to me that I needed to do something with the rest of my life.

The government instituted, after World War II, a GI Bill of Rights. Among its provisions were educational benefits for those who had served their country during the war. This provision, more than any before or since, helped to transform America. It certainly opened new vistas for veterans who would not otherwise have gotten training and education. Without the GI Bill, they would have languished, and the nation would have been poorer for it. Thousands of veterans became physicians, lawyers, accountants, teachers, architects, engineers, college professors, and members of the clergy.

Many purchased houses under the GI Bill, which required a small or no down payment. The government underwrote and guaranteed low interest payments to make housing available for them. This factor alone created a boom in the economy of unparallel proportions, and provided the necessary housing for millions of men who were starting their families after being away from home for as long as five years.

    This was the most successful affirmative action program in our nation's history. It is one that both conservative and liberal politicians all agree was necessary, and it worked better than anyone then could have anticipated. What America said to veterans was, "We know that you made a sacrifice for our nation. You risked your life and gave invaluable time to the cause. This was done while others who did not serve in the military stayed at home on their jobs. They bought homes and built farms and businesses. You were in uniform. Therefore, our society owes you something. We will compensate you with educational and other benefits!" This was an aggressive affirmative action program for service veterans.

    I decided that if I were to have a future, I would have to go back to school. There were no law schools in Tennessee that would admit black students in 1946. It did not matter that I was a veteran who fought in Europe for freedom. An ex-German or Italian solider could be admitted to law school in Tennessee, but I could not. I had a simple choice. If I wanted to become a lawyer, which by now I had basically decided to do, I had to leave not only Memphis but the state of Tennessee. My brother Robert was in Chicago. I had been there. It was an exciting place. Certainly, there was more freedom there than I had ever experienced in Memphis, and there were excellent law schools in that city. I got in touch with Robert, who was delighted to learn that his baby brother was thinking seriously about coming to Chicago to go to school. Robert could not have been more encouraging. He told me that he had a number of people who could possibly help me. Additionally, he told me that I was welcome to stay with him. My brother was very resourceful. If anyone knew his way around Chicago, it was Robert.

    When I left home in 1946, I was still torn between finishing my undergraduate work or going straight to law school. At that time, it was possible to be admitted to law school with two years of undergraduate credits. The year that I had skipped in sixth grade made it possible for me to have this choice. If I had not gotten that promotion, I would not have had an option. I would have had to go back to undergraduate school.

    Frank Reeves, a brilliant teacher, had told me about Roosevelt College. He was in his mid-60s when I met him at the University of Florence in Italy, where we made our headquarters while I was there. They had recruited some of the best minds and top instructors from all over the country. Frank Reeves was one of them. The army had instituted college courses at the University of Florence. The purpose was to occupy the time and attention of the troops until they were deployed to Japan. I was enrolled as a student there.

When I arrived in Chicago, I had my mind half set on going to Roosevelt College. I know that it will not make sense to some, but when I got to the campus, something just did not feel right about it. I did not go to the admissions building. Instead, I turned around and went back home and began to read the newspapers. There were a number of ads in the papers for Loyola University and DePaul. They were both Catholic institutions.

I went to Loyola and I didn't get the "feeling" that this was right for me either. Finally, I went down to DePaul. There was a certain "right" feeling about the place. DePaul's law school was at the top of a 16-story building located at 64 East Lake Street. Without my being too mystical, I looked at the building and just went on in. I filled out an application and was admitted. At that time students could be admitted with two years of college.

My brother Robert and his family invited me to move in with them. I got a job as a cab driver and started law school. School was difficult, but I managed to finish a three-year program in two by going year-round. I enjoyed DePaul. Subsequently, I have spoken at commencement exercises and received an honorary degree from DePaul. I was later asked to consider a deanship to the law school in 1977, which I did not accept.

While I was in law school, I was struck by the political and social difference between Chicago and Memphis. Chicago was "heaven" for blacks. We lived on the South Side. It was a black community. The only whites there were selling goods or running some small shops. We could sit wherever we wanted when riding the streetcars. I would go down to the courthouse and see black clerks working. There were blacks in the state legislature, and a black U.S. representative. Blacks were members of the city council. I could eat anyplace I wanted. I later discovered that this was a façade, because places I could afford to go were coffee shops and the department stores. Some upscale restaurants and clubs were not integrated, and I was refused admission to one where the late, legendary Josephine Baker was a featured singer.

The North Side, however, was as racist as any place in the Deep South, according to Martin Luther King, Jr. At that time I had no knowledge of that side of Chicago's personality. What I saw of the city was a vast improvement over what we had to endure in the South.

I was excited and thrilled at seeing ordinary black people in positions of authority. I had heard people who had returned to Memphis from New York, Pittsburgh, and Chicago talking about the important positions they held. You would hear a black person from one of the northern cities say, "I'm a detective," or "I'm a fireman," or "I'm a streetcar operator." It was simply unfathomable for those of us who had never seen blacks in those positions to believe them. I could hardly believe my eyes. My brother

Robert was a streetcar motorman in Chicago. In order to make some extra money, I bought a big, black 1941 Chrysler and converted it into a "jitney" cab. A jitney is a licensed, unmarked car that responds to requests for taxi cab-type services.

As a non-official taxi owner-driver, I was only supposed to answer calls. However, like all other jitney drivers at that time, I picked people up on the street and took them to the Cook County Hospital and downtown. I could charge a pretty penny for those trips. I was trying to make as much money as possible. I needed it not for tuition, but for living expenses. The GI Bill was paying my tuition and giving me $65 per month.

My jitney business was doing quite well financially, but I would get sleepy while working long hours. One particular night I fell asleep at the wheel. It was raining in torrents, like I had never seen before. I was barreling down State Street, nodding from the lack of sleep. I was in class all day and had studied late after I returned from the previous day's work. I must have driven through three or four feet of water that was standing in the street. Fortunately, some water splashed onto my window and woke me up, just in time to jerk the steering wheel and avoid hitting a steel post. I ran through a clump of trees and collided with a lamppost. The car was totaled. I did not get hurt, but that was the end of my cab-driving days.

My cab-driving experience was also instructive. Without that experience I would not have gotten a flavor of what life was really like for the average working black in Chicago in the middle to late 1940s. It also gave me an opportunity to get a firsthand appreciation of the extent to which blacks had succeeded in both business and the political life of the city.

I was truly amazed. I drove past the black-owned Supreme Liberty Insurance Company and Johnson Publishing Company, the publisher of *Ebony* and *Jet* magazines. John Johnson, one of the great business success stories, had great influence in the entire black community. S.B. Fuller, another major black company, had recently purchased a 15-story building that housed chemicals for Fuller Hair Products.

My address was 3644 South State Street, the heart of the black community. You could tell from both the construction and the architecture of the buildings in the neighborhood that it had once been a fashionable community. It was well along the way to decline, caused largely by overcrowding and neglect by absentee landlords. There were 50 blocks of storefronts, and my building was black, dark, and dank. On muggy Chicago summer nights, people could take their mattress and sleep right out on the grass in the median strip of the wide and stately streets or go to the park. People may have been poor, but they were safe.

My brother Raymond moved to Chicago and stayed with Robert and me. We bought some inexpensive paint and painted the apartment. We bought some curtains and hung them at the windows and replaced the linoleum. This not only cleaned and brightened up the apartment but made it very fashionable.

Estelle, Robert's wife and my sister-in-law, was a great housekeeper, neat as a pin. She had a number of babies to care for, one born right after the other. I really do not know how she managed without help when Robert was at work. There was simply a limit to how much she was able to do in terms of housework. Robert was working very hard just trying to make ends meet. Raymond and I did what we could around the apartment to help keep it clean and livable for the entire family. We wanted to give Estelle and Robert some relief from the burden of having additional people staying with them. My mother had taught us how to do domestic work. That knowledge came in handy.

I tended to be more "churchy" than most people. I enjoyed hearing the singing of a good choir. Chicago had its share of great choirs and outstanding soloists. I also liked to hear good, well-prepared, and thoughtful sermons. I spent more time than the average young man in church, particularly at night services. I would usually sleep late Sunday mornings. It was a day when I did not have classes, and frankly, I did not get in from my Saturday night outings until late.

I especially enjoyed a preacher named Clarence Cobb. He pastored a spiritualist church called the First Church of Deliverance. Reverend Cobb was from Memphis, and most Memphians and everybody in Chicago knew him. He had a huge radio audience. The church had one of the greatest choirs that I have ever heard. I made it a point to be at his church every Sunday night at 11 to hear that great choir and to listen to Reverend Cobb make his pronouncements. If I missed church, I could always hear the service on the radio. I also attended Pilgrim Baptist Church, pastored by the Reverend J.C. Austin, one of the great preachers of his day; T.M. Brown at the Progressive Baptist Church; Bishop W.M. Roberts at 40th Street Church of God in Christ; and Woodlawn A.M.E. Church, pastored by Reverend Archibald Carey, who was also one of my favorites because Reverend Carey was not only a great preacher but an outstanding lawyer who later became a judge. In many ways, he served as a role model for me. It was not unusual for me to sometimes attend two or three church services on Sundays.

I also enjoyed going to the movies. They did not segregate the theaters in Chicago, which made it even more enjoyable. I went to movies during the week. Although the White Sox baseball park was only four blocks from where I lived, I did not go to the ballgames. I did not have money to spend on baseball tickets.

During one of my visits downtown, I happened to run into Dr. J.B. Martin, a good friend of my family from Memphis. Dr. Martin owned a drugstore. He had succeeded Robert Church, Jr., as the black head of the Republican Party in Shelby County. After Church left Memphis, some said he was run out of town by E.H. "Boss" Crump. Crump then ran Dr. Martin out of town.

Life is strange. There are things that happen to all of us that we do not understand. My being promoted and sent to a class where the students were older caused me a lot of discomfort. However, that was what made it possible for me to finish two years of college before being drafted. This factor alone forever changed my life. Likewise, chasing Dr. Martin from Memphis to Chicago was like throwing a rabbit into a briar patch. Dr. Martin was a brilliant businessman. He became one of the principal owners of the Chicago American Giants, one of the premier teams of the Negro Baseball League. More important, he was a member of the board of the Cook County Sanitation Commission. This was a top job in the entire country at that time, and he exercised tremendous clout.

Dr. Martin was relatively new to Chicago. However, he was not new to the Republican political intrigue and politics. The Republican Party was trying desperately to hold on to some of the black vote. The once solid Illinois Republican black vote had been eviscerated by the successful policies of the Roosevelt years. Blacks, like most other Americans, had benefited immensely from the Works Progress Administration, the Civilian Conservation Corps, and other New Deal programs. The Republicans needed a black on the ticket. Dr. Martin became that man.

Dr. Martin and I had a discussion that I remember well. He told me that if I stayed in Chicago after I got my law degree, with his help, I would have a great future. Dr. Martin had the ability to open doors for a young man with the right credentials. He said, "Doc, you really don't want to leave Chicago. There's a great future for you here. If you go back to Memphis, you will not have the opportunities that are open to blacks here."

I thought long and hard about his offer. There was no black in Memphis who could do for me what Dr. Martin could do for me in Chicago. Also, I had a girlfriend and had made additional friends. Then there were many people I knew who had migrated from Memphis to Chicago. Many of them knew my father and uncle. The Hooks Brothers' Studio made all of the high school pictures, covered many weddings, and was really the only black photography studio in town. My grandmother had taught music to many musicians who had then moved to Chicago. My brothers,

Raymond and Robert, and I were well known. It was almost impossible for us to walk down 47th Street without someone from Memphis stopping us to ask about somebody in Memphis. I really had the best of both worlds—the relative freedom of Chicago and a Memphis community in that city.

I decided to accept Dr. Martin's offer. But almost immediately, something told me that this was not the thing to do. If I had not been black, but white, Chicago would have been the best place for me. The more I thought about it, the more some inextricable force urged me to return to Memphis. I cannot explain this somewhat mystical experience. All I know is that I saw, in my mind's eye, black police officers and detectives, black lawyers and judges, blacks on the Memphis City Council and the board of Shelby County Commissioners. I saw black women sitting where they wanted on the streetcar and black and white children going to school together. I saw the colored water fountains gone and blacks treated with dignity and respect at Goldsmith's Department Store and the Peabody Hotel.

With that vision in mind, of blacks exercising political power, I packed my bags and headed for Memphis. I had no definitive plan in mind, no long-range plan written out, just a vision of a changed Memphis. I saw a more equitable Memphis, a more just Memphis, a free Memphis.

In October 1948, I took the Illinois bar examination and was notified in November that I had passed. So, I went down to Springfield, Illinois, and was sworn in as a member of the Illinois Bar. In those days, as is the case in some instances today, a member of the bar of one state could apply for reciprocity in another. The second state would accept the certification and the license of the other. This was what I did; I never had to take the Tennessee bar examination. With little more than a law degree and hope, I moved back to a little-changed Memphis and started my practice four days after receiving my license to practice law.

I moved back with my parents in the Foote Homes public housing project until we later purchased the large house on Vance Street. I opened my office in the building where my father and uncle had maintained their photography studio, at 164 Beale Street. When I started, there was only one other black lawyer practicing in Memphis. Memphis had a population of 500,000 in 1949. Roughly 40 percent of that population was black.

Setting up a law practice was much more involved than I had initially expected. Law school prepares you in the theory of law, not the practice of law. Law students learn the theory of deeds, not how to research a property title or how to file a deed. We were not taught how to set up an office, file motions, set up books, or bill clients.

My first task was to get the office straight. I.W. Marshall had occupied the office for years, and it needed a lot of work. The floors had not been stained, varnished, or shellacked for decades, if ever. They were in awful shape. I wanted my office to make a statement when my clients walked in. I believe that people often make determinations of one's professionalism based on the surroundings in which one works. I was determined to transform this dingy office into one that sparkled.

The floor was in such bad shape that I had to prime it with paint. After I painted the floor, I bought a piece of linoleum and put it in the center of the room. In those days most people used linoleum instead of carpeting because carpeting was expensive to purchase and hard to maintain. In any event, I bought a beautiful piece of linoleum and tacked it down in the center of the room. Then I took some brown paint and painted around the borders of the linoleum. After the floor was finished, I painted the walls and had new furniture delivered.

One other important housekeeping chore had to be done. I had to get a sign. No office could exist, I reasoned, without a sign. All of the businesses on Beale Street had signs, some simple and some very elaborate. There were a number of regional peculiarities in the South in those days. Very few blacks liked to be called by their first names. If you put your first name on a sign, white people would call you by your first name. Even white deliverymen would take it upon themselves to address you as Benjamin rather than Mr. Hooks or Attorney Hooks, as they would with white lawyers.

When I was growing up, this was a big issue with most older blacks I knew, including my own parents. It may be a small thing today, but back then it was a tactic used by whites to demean blacks. To this day, I do not like people who do not know me to address me by my first name. I never use the first name of anyone with whom I do not have a personal relationship. I call them Mr., Mrs., Reverend, Doctor, Professor, or whatever title is appropriate. Therefore, I decided to use B.L. Hooks on my sign. My cousin was an artist and sign painter. He was so sure that I would become a lawyer that he had already painted two lovely signs for my new office. I put one sign downstairs and the other on the door of my office. I was now in business: B.L. Hooks, Attorney at Law.

Local politics and civil rights soon became my focus. I was a different person from the young man who had left the city along the Mississippi in 1943. The new Ben Hooks had experienced war. I had seen unspeakable horrors and fighting on distant battlefields. I faced death in defense of rights that my family and I did not enjoy. I had witnessed personally the indignity of guarding Italian prisoners of war who could be served in restaurants where the black soldiers guarding them were not allowed to eat. With my own eyes I had seen the great amount of freedom enjoyed by blacks in Chicago and marveled at how many positions they occupied in government and in the private sector. I was not willing to sit back obsequiously and just practice law in some comfortable office on Beale Street without challenging the system. I knew that I wanted desperately to change the status quo.

I did not know how it was to be done, but I was certain that it would happen. There were many young black men who returned from Europe or the Pacific who promised themselves that they would not be supplicants to an evil social order. Even those who did not fight in the war got caught up in the belief that things could not remain the same. No, we would not be anesthetized by the tempting siren calls from those who urged that we ought to just be patient, that time would solve all problems. Some warned young people like me against stirring the pot of racial animosity by trying to change things too fast. I became active in everything that I could. I joined the Memphis Negro Chamber of Commerce, the Lincoln League (a Republican political organization), and the NAACP. I was heavily involved in voter registration. My experiences in Chicago and what I had observed there convinced me that one of the keys to social change was the exercise of the ballot.

Politically, the infamous Boss Crump was still in power in Memphis in the early 1950s. Blacks were wanted and welcomed to keep the Crump machine formidable, but they were not expected to share power. We had just gotten our first black policemen three years before. These policemen had limited powers; they could arrest "Negroes," but they were powerless when it came to dealing with whites. If a black police officer saw a white person violating the law, he had to call for a white policeman to make the arrest.

The NAACP in Memphis had been pushing hard for voter registration and voting. In 1951, Dr. J.E. Walker, the founder of Universal Life Insurance Company and a real power in the city, decided to run for a seat on the Board of Education. There was nothing unusual about a powerful man running for elective office. What was unusual was that Dr. Walker was black. It is hard for those who have no feeling for the temperament of the times to appreciate the temerity, the audacity, and the courage that it took for a black man to run for office in Memphis in the early Fifties. It must be remembered that although Memphis was relatively progressive for a southern city, it was still, after all, a southern city. It was still an integral part of the "Old South."

When Dr. Walker decided to run for one of the five positions on the school board, by that very act he was striking a major blow for racial equality. His candidacy was a powerful message being sent to both the black and the white communities. To the black community, this was an act of defiance of an old order. It was a clarion call for blacks to rise up politically. To the white community, Walker's candidacy was a testament to the reality that things were forever changed. The genie could not be put back into the bottle.

Dr. Walker chose me as his co-campaign manager. I was only 26 years old. That was an extremely young age for a person to be tapped to head up a historic citywide effort. Taylor Hayes, one of the most prominent undertakers, worked with me. My first challenge was to put together a team of influential people from across the social and political spectrum of the black community. There was some reluctance to become involved on the part of some black people in the city who were employed by the government and feared retaliation. There were some members of the clergy who felt that politics and religion did not mix. Fortunately, they were in the minority. I managed to get the Memphis black leadership on board. It was helpful that Dr. Walker had universal respect throughout the black community.

There were no templates available for me to use in organizing and putting together a strategy to register additional voters and to get out support for Dr. Walker. There was no postcard or mail registration. Voters had to go to City Hall and register. The daily hours for voter registration, 9 to 5, were inconvenient, and the registration office was closed on Saturdays. Despite these handicaps, we were able to add a phenomenal 17,000 new black voters to the registration rolls.

I ran from meeting to meeting, from group to group, whipping up support for Dr. Walker. We needed much more than words. We needed black voters to go to the polls on election day. Dr. Walker had a lot of trust in me. Despite the fact that I was young enough to be his own son or grandson, he never second-guessed me. He allowed me the freedom to run the campaign. We decided on a plan to maximize the impact of the black vote. We knew that the white voters would not vote for a black man, period. Therefore, the only votes we could count on were the blacks who went to the polls to vote.

Since we could not count on getting any white votes, if we were to have any chance of winning (and our objective was to win, not to make a statement), blacks would have to "bullet vote." It was sometimes called "single-shot voting." Since there were five other candidates and Dr. Walker, we knew that the five top vote-getters would be elected. If the black voters voted for four of the five or three of the five white candidates, that candidate would have all of the white votes that he received, plus our votes. Therefore, it was important that the message be clear: Vote for Dr. Walker and Dr. Walker only.

Interest in the campaign was high. There was a new pride in the black community in the city. Everywhere, people were talking about the Walker candidacy. In beauty parlors, barbershops, offices, at church and social club meetings, on street corners, and around dinner tables, the talk was about the election. Black people were enthusiastic about their newfound option. They were happy, for at last they would be able to vote for a black man.

It did not take long for the Crump machine to discover that they had a real problem. If Dr. Walker, a black man who was unapproved by the Crump machine, got elected, the machine would be revealed as severely weakened. Crump struck back on the eve of the election. He had a flyer printed and distributed. Political flyers were nothing new. The Crump people customarily put out a flyer telling their supporters whom they should vote for. This flyer had a new format. It contained a photograph of each of the candidates. There were five white candidates' pictures and Dr. Walker's. They made sure that every white voter in the city knew that Dr. Walker was a "Negro." His picture was so dark that it was hard to recognize him. We laughingly called it an ink spot.

Far more whites were registered to vote than blacks. We hired a young lady, Ms. Tweze Twyman, to direct the campaign. We registered 17,000 black voters during the campaign, bringing our total to 25,000. This was tremendous. Dr. Walker received only a handful of votes in white precincts. He won overwhelmingly the black vote, but that was not enough. Dr. Walker came within a few hundred votes of upsetting the powerful Crump machine in the 1951 election. My role in the Walker campaign gave me citywide recognition and compelled me into a position of leadership in Memphis. To this day, I run into people who remind me of the 1951 election. Perhaps because of my involvement in this campaign, I was quite often called on by Dr. King to come to Montgomery and speak at the weekly church meetings. This election remained a source of pride for the pioneers of the political revolution of the second half of the century.

The beginning of my professional career was also one of the most important and pivotal times in my personal life. It was during this time that I met Frances Dancy, who would later become my wife and partner for life. We had seen each other, knew each other's family, and had mutual friends. Growing up in Memphis in the '30s and '40s, most blacks knew somebody who knew somebody you knew. Frances was a strikingly attractive beauty. Three years my junior, she was the oldest of three children. Her father and mother were well known in Memphis. Her mother had been a schoolteacher and her father was a bellman at one of the city's leading hotels. Her family was very active in the African Methodist Episcopal Church, as was my mother.

Frances was and remains a no-nonsense person. I was the opposite. I had several girlfriends. Some would say that I was somewhat of a playboy. Frances had just started her teaching career. She had agreed to help out on a part-time basis at the fairgrounds of the Tri-State Colored Fair. Frances was always working, and if she could have three or four different jobs simultaneously, she was happy. I remember first seeing this very fashionable, extremely articulate, and exceptionally attractive young lady at the Fair. I was struck with her beauty and with her dynamic personality.

I was happily married to Frances on the 20th day of March in 1951. As of this writing in July 2003, we have been married 52 years. We were not blessed with children of our own, but through adoption we have one of the best daughters one could ever ask for, Patricia Louise Hooks Gray. Pat was living with us. She was the daughter of my brother Robert and his former wife, Estelle. They agreed to the adoption. My sister Bessie had a son, Michael, and at that point we intended to and indeed did file adoption papers for both of them, Pat and Mike. The adoption of Michael was never completed, but we still love him as a son. Pat has been as much a daughter of ours as if she had been our natural child, and she has given us years and years of happiness and support, as has Mike.

In fact, Pat was an unusual child. During the time that my mother, her grandmother, was raising her, from the age of five until we adopted her, we never had to worry about corporal punishment. My mother did use a switch very well on Pat's five brothers and sisters she was also raising, but Pat was not the type of child who needed that kind of discipline, thank God. Sweet and unselfish, unspoiled, unbought, and unbossed, she has made life extremely comfortable for us and we love her dearly, along with her two sons, Carlos and Carlton, children of her marriage to Carlos Gray, Sr., who she met and married while attending Fisk University. (Frances had graduated from Fisk in 1949 with her B.S. and Tennessee State University with an M.S. in 1958.)

After graduating from Fisk, Pat moved to Cincinnati (Carlos's home) and taught in the Princeton City school district for 31 years. She also has been an adjunct professor at Xavier University in Cincinnati for some 19 years. Pat is the grandmother of Amberly, Bryanne, Carlos III, Sierra, Shyanne, and Cherie, and the mother-in-law of Angela. One of the joys in my life was to deliver the commencement address at the graduation of our grandson, Carlton, when he strutted across the stage from Winton Woods High School in 1989.

We did have the opportunity to have Carlos and Carlton and family with us at many wonderful occasions while at the NAACP, and at the Pythian and Baptist conventions. One of the downsides of public service, however, is the loss of time for family activities. Thank God Pat and Frances worked together to make sure we had some quality hours together.

I look back with great fondness on visits to Disney World, Canada, and NBA games, and playing games of Scrabble, checkers, Monopoly, and so on with the family. I must confess that on some trips, when I was trying to lecture to the boys regarding the grandeur of the peaks and valleys of places visited, they were much more interested in the recreational equipment like pinball machines.

With family, we have enjoyed many a great Thanksgiving, Christmas, Fourth of July, and other holidays, plus parties and festive occasions. Our collective families are known to be great cooks, thus, we have all enjoyed eating food "fit for a king." Bessie, Mildred, Julia, Buddy, Lil, Charlie's wife, and Mrs. Gray have gone out of their way to have joyous family occasions. I cannot forget Juanita, Frances's aunt, her excellent cooking, and her constant invitations to dinner to my family. The joy of the family is central in my life and has sustained me across the years. I recommend it to all.

Every Christmas Pat packed those boys up along with their Uncle Rodney and off to Memphis they came, from the time they were born until they had finished college. It reminded me of my sister-in-law, Anita, who lived in Beaumont, Texas, with her husband, Dr. Charles. They had five children, and for 20 years Anita and her husband and their children came to Memphis to spend Christmas. It was a great celebration, and some of those years I physically lived at my mother-in-law's house at 685 Edith. I enjoyed my relationship with Anita, Charles, and their family. I love those nieces and nephews now as dearly as anybody could love a child. And we have all been closely knit together. Frances and I; Anita and her children, Charles, Jr., Crystal, Vicki, Cheryl, and Andrew; Frances and Anita's brother, Andrew, and his wife, Arlie, and their four children, Andrew, Anthony, Amber, and Andrea, continue to be a close-knit family. Andrew died in 1999. My brother Raymond and his wife, Margie, have four children: Karen, Vicki, Ray, Jr., and Denise. Robert had six children who were raised by my mother—Carol, Robert III, Walter, Fred, Pat, and Ronnie—and a seventh child, Barry, by Robert's second wife, Ernestine.

What a marvelous family I married into. What a marvelous family Frances married into; what a marvelous relationship these families have had. We love all of our nieces and nephews dearly.

I think I made it clear that my mother and father as far as I was concerned were among the best parents who ever lived in the world. Mr. and Mrs. Andrew J. Dancy, Sr., were among the best parents-in-law any son-in-law ever had.

Frances has been a great wife, and I thank God I have not had to discipline her too often, that she has been obedient and helpful, that she has been highly respectful of my authority, and therefore I have not had to spend a lot of time making her toe the line. If I said do it, she did it; if I said don't do it, she didn't do it; if I said jump, she said how high. My slightest wish has been her command . . . and obviously, if you believe this, Mother Goose still lives. But thank you, Frances. You have been a loyal, loving, caring, concerned, devoted wife and friend. Do your best to give me another 52 years and I will do my best to do the same. God has blessed our marriage and our family; God has blessed you and has blessed me, and I am thankful.

My thoughts turn to Frances and our cherished years together every time I recall perhaps the most harrowing day of my life. It was a hot Saturday in July in the early 1960s, and it was a day that I almost lost my life in pursuit of civil rights.

Russell Sugarmon, A.W. Willis, and I were sitting around our law office that day when the phone rang. It was a call from some NAACP people in Somerville, Tennessee, east of Memphis in adjacent Fayette County. The gist of the conversation was that some young black students had gone into the drug store on the square in Somerville to buy a soft drink. They had been arrested, were now in jail, and trouble appeared to be brewing. We were asked to come and provide legal assistance. The three of us decided to go and, in the meantime, contacted Rev. Jim Lawson, an outstanding civil rights leader and pastor of Centenary Methodist Episcopal Church in Memphis. He agreed to go with us. I drove my wife's brand new Plymouth station wagon.

When we got to Somerville, I knew we were in for trouble. White people, especially young men and boys, were up in trees, hanging from posts, looking out of second floor windows, and standing in every storefront and all along the street. Cars were there in large numbers. It looked as if the population of Somerville had swollen 10 or 20 times. We made it to the sheriff's office and discussed the matter with him for hours without any progress being made. Finally, late at night, it was agreed that the students would be released and safe passage afforded them to their homes. The sheriff said, "It's a little dangerous out there, so I am going to lead you back to Shelby County, but I don't want you to take the main highway. I want you to take the back road. I will have a deputy in front and I will be right behind you to make sure you are safe."

We started back to Shelby County. A.W. was sitting in the front seat, Jim Lawson and Russell Sugarmon in the back seat. After being on the road for a mile or two, we turned a curve going down a hill and Jim exclaimed, "Ben I wish you could see back here, there are 15 or 20 cars following us. They look loaded with people and I can see shotguns and rifles hanging out of their cars." At this point, the deputy was in front of us and the sheriff was just behind us. After some three or four miles, the sheriff blew his horn for us to stop. He got out and explained to us that his deputy was having car trouble, could go no further, and would be forced to stop leading us. "But don't worry," he said, "I am still behind."

We started again. But moments later, Jim and Russell both exclaimed seemingly simultaneously, "Ben, all those cars are still behind us and every time we turn a curve, or go down a hill, we can see rifles, and guns hanging out." With only a few minutes to go before reaching the Shelby County line, the sheriff blew his horn again and stopped us. This time he said, "I am having trouble with my car, I can't go any further, but you don't have far to go. I think you can make it all right." With that he left us on this desolate backroad.

I resumed driving and Russell immediately said, "Ben, cars are still behind us." I asked A.W. and Jim if I should go slowly, as the sheriff had advised, but neither of them responded. That was their subtle cue for me to pick up speed. I was doing 45 or 50 miles an hour when I turned a curve and a shot rang out from the right side of the road. The bullet crashed across my windshield, causing glass to shatter. I heard A.W., who was sitting next to me, groan. I looked over at him and saw glass crumbled in his lap. Luckily, he wasn't hurt at all. When I asked them this time about speeding up, the resounding response was "YES!" So I started driving 75 to 90 miles an hour with my head still lowered. Luckily and blessedly, we made it back to Shelby County. We filed the proper reports with the state, local, and federal authorities, but nothing was ever done.

That Sunday at the Friendship Baptist Church at a 3 P.M. service, I was notified by phone that we had to go back on Monday morning. I was in the pulpit, preparing to preach at an afternoon service. I choked up when I realized that I was being called on to go back. Earlier that day, my mother and other members of the family and my friends had called and warned me not to go back under any circumstances. Frances, as usual, discussed it, but left the decision up to me. With conflicting emotions, I prepared to preach. The choir started singing, "I've seen the lightning flashing, I've heard the thunder roll, He promised never to leave me, never to leave me alone."

At that moment I decided I had to go back. In fact, all four of us went back on Monday morning and argued our case before a justice of the peace who lectured us and our clients on how wrong we were, but let the students go with a small fine. I thank God that we had the courage to stay the course. Of course, in my position, I've been threatened many times—in person, by telephone, by mail, and in calls to authorities. I have been guarded and my house has been kept under police surveillance for days at a time. My office in Baltimore had to have 24-hour protection on several occasions. Through it all, I have maintained my faith in God and have fought the good fight of faith. As the song says, "I heard the voice of Jesus telling me still to fight on. He promised never to leave me, never to leave me alone."

Chapter 6

THE JUDGESHIP: BREAKING BARRIERS IN MEMPHIS

In the 1950s and before, those of us who practiced law and whose skin was black were reminded constantly, and in many different ways, of the unfairness of the court system in the South. Black lawyers walked into criminal courtrooms every day and saw 20 prisoners/defendants sitting together, dressed in blue denim prison uniforms. On a typical day, three-quarters of the prisoners were black. Looking around, we saw that everyone in a position of authority was white—the judge, the clerk, the bailiff, the deputy sheriff, and the court recorder. Those who dispensed justice were white. Those who had justice administered upon them were mostly black. The civil courts also had no black authority figures.

In Memphis, we began to agitate for the appointment of some black public defenders. After years of constantly insisting on having a black in the public defender's office, the county court, the governing body for Shelby County, agreed. It was decided that I was to be the first assistant public defender appointed. Frankly, I was not interested in the position. It was a hard job. The pay was not commensurate with the amount of work that was required, and the position demanded an inordinate amount of evening and weekend work to defend the large number of indigent clients that a public defender or assistant public defender had to represent. The pay was, in 1961, $150 per month.

I had no choice but to accept the position. After all, I had been one of the chief proponents in the fight to have a black serve as a public defender. Eventually, I bowed and accepted. I worked hard and gave every case my best effort. Being the first has decided disadvantages. The first black at anything had to be superhuman. On that person's shoulders were the future hopes and aspirations of others who would follow in those footsteps.

Although I worked late at night, and spent some entire Saturdays interviewing clients whose cases I had to argue the following week, I enjoyed it. Most of the black men imprisoned had never seen a black lawyer before. To see the expressions on some of their faces when they met me for the first time was more rewarding than most people can imagine.

There were, however, a number of unpleasant experiences. I remember one day when a police officer, testifying against my client in city court, said this "nigger" did this, and that big "nigger" over there did that. I was livid. How in God's name could a person expect justice when a law enforcement officer felt free to use the pejorative term "nigger" in open court? I leaped to my feet and thundered my objection. The judge in this case merely said, "Move on, move on."

In another court, where Judge Ingram presided, another police officer did essentially the same thing. The judge immediately admonished the police officer not to use that name again in his court. The fact that there was an assistant public defender who was black in his courtroom, I am sure, made a difference. There is no question in my mind that having blacks in positions throughout society makes a difference in the way people conduct business. If there is a black judge in a meeting of judges, the conversations are different. Having a black person on the board of a major corporation will often change the tenor of the discussion. If there had been a high-level black executive in the room with the Texaco executives who were taped making disparaging remarks about blacks, those comments would not have been made. In the case of Judge Ingram, he benefited from his sensitivity toward blacks. He received tremendous support from the black voters in his next election.

My caseload and that of others in the public defender's office became increasingly heavy over time. Eventually, the county court decided to appropriate funds so that there would be two assistant public defenders in each courtroom. Not long after this happened, the chief public defender came to me and said, "Mr. So-and-so will be in charge of your courtroom." I was a little suspicious because I had never heard that name before. By this time, I knew most of the lawyers who were practicing in Memphis at that time. His name did not ring any bells. I did some research, and much to my chagrin and utter consternation, I discovered that the young man who was to be my boss had been out of law school for less than a year. He had just passed the bar exam and gotten his license to practice law.

The young lawyer had never tried a case in any court, yet he was to be my superior; he would make more money, give me instructions, and have the use of a part-time secretary. Meanwhile, here I was, a black lawyer with 15 years of extensive experience. I had argued cases in all of the courts in the state of Tennessee—civil, criminal, appellate, and the Tennessee Supreme Court. I had practiced in the federal courts. Yet I was to be supervised by a young man whom I was expected to train. I was furious. Mind you, I did not become angry, I became mad as hell. Now I could empathize with those who wanted to throw bricks and stones at the courthouse. It is difficult to believe that when you are faced with unmistakable, raw, insidious racism and callous discrimination, you are expected to just roll over and take it. My blood still boils at the thought.

I tried to pray, but I could not even get my thoughts together enough to do that right. I realized that I had to say NO to this assault on my personal dignity. I had been made, after all, the victim of the sophisticated segregation practices of the South. I was also a preacher, and I realized that I could not preach—that God took care of the Hebrew boys in the fiery furnace and protected Daniel in the lion's den and then said, in effect, He could not take care of me in Memphis. The line was drawn in the sand. I sat down, took my pen, and wrote my resignation, in which I gave the reasons why I could not serve. My mother and father had taught me when I was a child, and Dr. King had reminded us later, never, never compromise with evil.

A few weeks later, early one morning in 1964, I got a call from Governor Frank G. Clement of Tennessee. He told me he intended to appoint a Negro to the bench and that would be me. I was shocked. It was unbelievable that a Negro would be appointed to a court of record in the South in 1964. It was easier to conceive of a man going to the moon than to imagine a black sitting on the bench with a black robe as a judge in the South. Underscored in my detractors' outcries was the subtle, or not so subtle, belief that no black lawyer was truly qualified for the position. Before I left the bench, even my worst detractor had to concede that I was not only qualified for the position, but well qualified for it.

Even as I received the call, my mind flashed back to 1949 when I returned to Memphis to practice law. There was only one black lawyer practicing in the county, A.A. Latting. Mr. Latting was thoroughly competent and one of the most brilliant lawyers I have ever met. There had been other very prominent black lawyers in Memphis, but by 1949 all of them were dead or retired. The Memphis and Shelby County Bar Association had just prepared a small pamphlet which I was told contained, among other things, a fee schedule. I needed that badly. I finally was able to obtain one. When I opened this little book, the first thing I read was: *Membership in this Memphis and Shelby County Bar Association shall be open to all white lawyers practicing in this vicinity.* I read again *all white lawyers.* This was my introduction to the Bar Association. But progress has been made at the local and national level. One of our most talented, brilliant lawyers, Dennis Archer, is now president of the American Bar Association, and in the wings stands another fine black lawyer, Robert Grey, and black lawyers are to be found in prominent positions throughout the ABA structure. I am thankful to God for the progress that we have made and the political system that made it possible. In Memphis, we have had a black president, Prince Chambliss. I had the privilege of installing him as president of the local bar association.

In 1949, we started our political march, and when the '50s dawned, we organized the Tennessee Voters' Council, whose purpose was to increase voter registration participation. This organization was headed by Charles F. Williams, who was the Grand Master of Masons in Tennessee. At that time, they were some 15,000 strong and had lodges in every nook and corner of the state. It would be too much to name the strong people in Nashville, Knoxville, Chattanooga, Jackson, Memphis, and all those in between who put this organization on the map.

We were able to start voter participation in rural West Tennessee, in a time when blacks could be lynched for trying to vote in that part of the country. We got the black community to vote all over the state and to support the candidate endorsed by the Tennessee Voters' Council. We finally reached a high in our voter registration of approximately 150,000 to 200,000, which constituted in many instances 15-20 percent of the total number of registered voters.

Hence, when Governor Buford Ellington and all the succeeding governors in those years appointed blacks to office and pushed blacks' participation in all forms of government, there was a reason. And that reason is and continues to be the holy grail of politics. We have the votes to support you if you are willing to support us.

Probably one of the most historic days in my life was the day when I took the oath of office to become the judge of Criminal Court Division IV. The date was September 1, 1965. It was a Monday morning, a hot and muggy late summer day in Memphis. I was to be sworn in by Criminal Court Judge Perry H. Sellers at 9:30 A.M. in the courtroom formerly presided over by the late Judge Sam D. Campbell. The reason for using this particular courtroom was because it was the largest courtroom in the courthouse. Because of the symbolic importance of the day's events, and the number of people anticipated to attend the event, it was decided to use this courtroom.

I had been appointed by Governor Frank G. Clement to the bench. The post was created by the legislators to handle the increasing caseload of Shelby County. I was aware of the historical nature of that day's events. I was to be the first African American to serve in a court of record in the history of my state. I would also be the first ever to hold such a position in the South since Reconstruction.

There was a great sense of pride as I prepared myself for the ceremony that was to take place that day. This was more than just a day of personal pride in accomplishment. My mother and father were alive at that time. I knew that neither they, nor any of their generation, ever thought they would see the day when a black man would put on a judicial robe and take his place on a judicial bench in Memphis or Shelby County, Tennessee.

My wife, Frances, and my daughter, Pat, were running around the house, wound up with nervous energy, each helping the other and trying to get me ready. I must admit, I could hardly find anything I was looking for. I was probably the most nervous of the entire group. I had gotten very little sleep the night before. The telephones rang incessantly. There were calls from family, from Memphis NAACP leaders, from the press, from the church folk—a delegation had come from Mt. Moriah Baptist Church in Detroit, where I was also serving as a pastor, to witness the swearing-in ceremony. There were members from Middle Baptist in Memphis. Then there were hundreds of citizens, the great and the not so great, and all in between, just ordinary people who wanted to wish me well.

We were not going to be late, I thought to myself, even if I had to go with my socks and shoes not matching. If black folk had to wait 100 years after the Civil War for me to get on a criminal court bench, the least I could do was to be on time for the swearing-in ceremony. We arrived at the courthouse in plenty of time. I saw elderly black people making their way to the courthouse. Their smiles and their reaction to seeing me spoke legions. I went up to the judge's chambers and put on my robe. Never has a robe seemed so heavy and weighty as did that black robe on that day.

As we entered the courtroom, I saw a sea of familiar faces. There was standing room only in the courtroom and the hallways. My eyes focused first on my mother and my father. They were seated in the jury box with other members of my family. By now they had been married more than 50 years. They had raised seven children and lived through the Depression, through World War I and World War II. They had lived with Jim Crow and his sister Shirley Crow all of their lives. They had to endure indignities that no race of people should have had to tolerate. But on this day, one of their sons was to take the oath of office and become a judge in their city. What a day it must have been for them. Silently I said to myself, what a mighty God we serve.

Frances and Pat knew better than most how much I had given to the struggle and the abuse that I suffered, often at the hands of those that I tried to help. They and many others knew that the honor was well overdue, not for me but for the race. My sisters and brothers, I am sure, must have had flashbacks of my less than stellar behavior as a young boy in the back of their minds when they saw me come into the courtroom. Charles, Julia, Robert, Raymond, Mildred, and Bessie were there.

My NAACP family, led by my good friends Jesse Turner, A.W. Willis, Russell Sugarmon, H.T. Lockard, Maxine and Vasco Smith, Ben Jones, Arthur Bennett, and Odell Horton, Larry Turner, and my in-laws, Andrew, Georgia, Buddy, A.A. Latting, and Juanita, I am sure, felt vindicated for having had the faith to work within the system for change.

The church members from both Memphis and Detroit were elated by the history-making event. The outstanding clergy of the city was present. At precisely 9:30 A.M. the ceremony began. Judge Perry Sellers, a man who looked like someone cast by Hollywood for the part, made a brief statement and then began to administer the oath of office as my wife, Frances, held the Bible.

As I got to the last words of the oath, "so help me God," the finality of the occasion hit me. I was now a member of the judiciary. I signed the oath as is required by custom. I had prepared a few formal remarks. When I was asked to speak, I acknowledged my family and friends and promised to administer justice without fear or favor. I praised my teachers who were present. I promised to follow the Biblical injunction, and quoted the words of Micah, "What doth the Lord require of thee, but to do justly, to love mercy, and to walk humbly with thy God."

Ironically, the first man to appear before me was the Chief Public Defender. He addressed me, "If Your Honor please." He was as gracious and courteous then, and afterwards, as anybody possibly could be. Never, ever, in his courtroom appearances or outside the courtroom did he or any other lawyer show any sign of disrespect. To this day, most of the older lawyers in Memphis still call me Judge whenever and wherever they see me.

After a brief recess, I went back into my chambers. No sooner had I taken off my robe and sat down when the bailiff came in. He said, "Judge, you need to open court." I recall flinching when I heard the word judge used when referring to me. I had never been called judge before. I was not yet comfortable with the title. I slipped on my robe and walked back to the courtroom. I had heard the opening cry of the bailiff before on countless occasions in the criminal and civil courts of Shelby County. I had heard the bailiff open the Tennessee Supreme Court and the Federal District Court, but on that day it sounded different. As I walked through the door, I heard the bailiff intone, "Hear ye, hear ye. This honorable Criminal Court of Shelby County, Tennessee, Division Four is now opened for business pursuant to adjournment. All persons having business before this court, draw nigh, and you shall be heard. The Honorable Ben L. Hooks presiding. Be seated please."

This was an awe-inspiring moment. Here I was, a black who grew up in segregated Memphis, could not go to law school in the state of Tennessee, and was passed over for the position of public defender—and now I was a judge presiding over a court in Memphis, in the very courtroom where I had been denied the right to serve as the head public defender not long before.

When I heard the words "Be seated please," I said to myself, that's right— be seated. For now I am in charge. In spite of any past grievances, justice will prevail in this courtroom. There will be no more discrimination based upon race. There will be no color test used to determine how people are treated when they stand before the bench in my courtroom.

My first days on the court afforded me an opportunity to learn the ways of the bench. I was determined to be not just a good judge, but an exceptional one. Like all other African Americans who were "firsts" in one area or another, I had to carry the whole race on my shoulders. This is a burden that white Americans never have to consider.

A few days before being sworn in, I received a phone call from Jesse Turner, Sr., my close friend and the president of the Memphis NAACP. I had really anticipated the conversation being a congratulatory one. Instead it became an ultimatum. Jesse said, in short, "Now, Hooks, you know the NAACP has long held that the current jury selection system in Memphis and Shelby County discriminates against Negroes. We expect that you will take immediate steps to ensure that future jury panels are consistent with the population in their compositions." I said, "Jesse, I will work on it." He said, "We don't mean work on it, we mean do it." I said, "Jesse, I just got here!" Jesse said, "Hooks, we have been waiting for a hundred years. You just do it or we will picket your home!" After having his say, Jesse promptly hung up on me.

To be frank, I was a little shocked, but I should not have been. That was Jesse's nature, to be frank and blunt. Jesse was a no-nonsense person. World War II army combat captain that he was, he did not believe in taking prisoners. He believed that you had to use it or lose it. He wanted me to move, and move right then. I wanted to believe that maybe Jesse was merely putting me on notice. Maybe this was just posturing by Jesse, I thought.

Not long after that, I ran into my friend H.T. Lockard, told him what had happened, and suggested that he go with me to talk to Jesse and see what we could do about his unreasonable position. Lockard said, "Ben, you don't have a problem. Jesse said he would like to see a jury panel

system that reflects the population makeup. That's simple! Just do it."
With that, he was finished. My friend Ben Jones said the same thing,
and they all were right. Thank God for men like them.

The exclusion of blacks from the Shelby County jury pool, a practice that was widespread throughout the South, would have to be addressed. Originally, blacks were simply kept out of the pool. When
that policy became politically untenable, subterfuge was used—jurors
were selected from only white areas or neighborhoods. Unless an occasional black resident lived on a block where the other neighbors were
white and was selected by accident, the jury would be all white.

My friends and fellow freedom fighters expected me to fight harder
from the inside than I had fought earlier from the outside. Our struggle,
a very different struggle, had made my elevation to the bench possible.
It was not for my comfort and convenience, but for the well-being and
progress of a people that I wore the judicial robe. It was my job to carry
the ball without hesitation, equivocation, or flinching.

After researching the jury selection process, and when I was satisfied
that I had all of the facts, I planned my personal strategy and wrote a
little speech. My plan was to bring the issue up at our next judicial
council meeting.

There were 22 state court judges at that time. We did in fact, as a
group, have charge of the jury master list. All that was required to
change the jury composition was decisive action by the judges. Judge
Wilson, the same judge who presided over the case of the protestors
that I mentioned earlier, was presiding at the council meeting. Each
year the judges elected one of their own to preside at their meetings,
and this year was Judge Wilson's turn.

I was all prepared to bring up the matter of the jury panels and I had
my speech in my hands. I was rehearsing in my mind exactly what I
would say. Judge Battle, a judge who served on the bench with me and
whom I had come to respect and admire, began to speak. He was one
of the most brilliant men I have ever known. I heard him speaking and
I thought he said that we ought to have more Negroes on the jury
panels, and that they should be in the same proportion as Negroes in
the population. My God, that was precisely what he had said! Judge
Battle had preempted my speech.

I could not believe what my ears were hearing and my eyes were
seeing. These white judges were doing voluntarily what I had come
prepared to struggle for. They had come prepared to make this major
change on that day. Judge Battle made the motion. It was seconded,
and passed unanimously. I was stunned with the swiftness of the action

and sat motionlessly for a while just looking at the crumbled speech notes that I held in my hands.

I thanked my colleagues for dealing forthrightly with this important question. They then turned to me and suggested that I be given a budget and the authority to carry out the intent of the motion just passed.

The major impediment to having more blacks on the jury panels was the jury commissioner. He was an elderly man who had made a lot of friends over the years. He knew all of the lawyers and judges in town. He was not necessarily an overt racist, but had grown accustomed to functioning in an environment where blacks were excluded and racism flourished. The judges were prepared to work around him, but they were not prepared to get rid of him.

I was authorized to hire an assistant, a black, whose job it would be to make sure that blacks were included in the jury pools. I chose Reverend H.C. Nabrit, who was the pastor of First Baptist Church Lauderdale and who was my co-chairman of the NAACP's Freedom Fraud Commission a few years earlier. Reverend Nabrit was completing his law studies and had a good understanding of the court system.

The jury commissioner was an interesting old man. He was as nice as he could be, but was a throwback to an earlier time. He was not mean-spirited by any stretch of the imagination; he was just caught up in old customs and past practices. He testified often why there were no blacks on a given jury. He would state clearly and loudly that he did not discriminate. He just took a city directory and went down a whole street. What he failed to say was that the streets he chose were basically streets where only whites lived. There might be a few blacks living in a house or two, but the majority of the persons living on the selected street were white. That was the only reason why we had a few blacks included in the jury pool.

The new system worked well. Reverend Nabrit developed a good working relationship with the jury commissioner, and soon the jury pool began to have more and more blacks. Before long, the jury pool in Memphis reflected the racial composition of the city. This illustrates my belief of how important it is to have blacks in major positions. Their mere presence makes all the difference.

There is no experience that compares with sitting in judgment on one's fellow humans. It has a way of humbling any person. To see some rejects of society, or some good people who somehow got caught up in an illegal situation, being sentenced to long prison terms serves as a reminder of how vulnerable the human spirit really is. Most of the men and women who appear in criminal courts are those who have benefited the least from the fruits of society. Some never learned to read or to write, others were never socialized, and some are completely unaware of right and wrong. I always believe that a delicate balance must be reached, or we are doomed to sink into the abyss of hopelessness and despair.

When I came to the bench, suspended sentences were rare. Judges just imposed the prescribed sentences for a given offense, whether violent or nonviolent. It applied to black and white, the learned and unlearned, the rich and the poor. I took the position that there was a vast difference between nonviolent offenders and career and violent criminals. Many nonviolent offenders need only someone to take an interest in them, to counsel them, and to give them concrete direction. Most of the people who appeared before me in court were young men. There were very few women or older men. Many were first-time offenders, charged with driving under the influence and resisting arrest, trespassing, disturbing the peace, shoplifting, or other petty offenses. Of course, others were guilty of more serious crimes, or were hardened criminals.

I was a great believer in the concept of suspended sentences. I had seen as both a lawyer and pastor scores of people who just needed a little help, people who made one mistake. This does not mean that I believe that those who commit violent crimes should not be put away, or that those who repeatedly commit violent offenses should not be locked up for an extended period of time.

During the first month that I was a judge, I granted more suspended sentences than all of the other judges had given in the past 10 years. I gave as many suspended sentences to whites as I did to blacks. I was an equal opportunity sentence suspender. I can say with pride that with the exception of one or two offenders, none of those given suspended sentences committed additional offenses during my time on the bench. I did not just hand out suspended sentences without asking several responsible members of the community to spend some time counseling and assuming some responsibility for the offender. I told them that if they could spend the time to come to court and testify as a character witness, I knew that they would be willing to spend some time helping these people get their lives back on track.

I remember there was this outstanding pastor of Bellevue Baptist Church and president of the Southern Baptist Convention, Dr. Pollard, who lived in Memphis. He, like many other pastors, would come to court on behalf of members of his church. He would say something like this: "Judge, this is a good kid. He made a mistake. I am sure that if you give him another chance, maybe a suspended sentence or probation, he will not get into trouble again."

I would say, "Pastor, I am glad you said that. Do you think that this man could and will do better? Pastor, do you believe in suspended sentences for others like this fine young man who, for some reason, just got caught up doing the wrong thing, or do you believe in a suspended sentence just for him?" What is he to say? Then I would ask him, "Pastor, I know you are a busy man, but could you agree to give this young man, who you have said needs just a little help, an hour a month for the next twelve months? Would you do that?" Of course, the only possible answer was "Yes, your honor." That system worked in my court. Judge Odell Horton continued it and improved it. Judge Otis Higgs, his successor, got a grant and really improved it. Later, all of the judges started utilizing the concept of suspended sentences. So, the presence of a black man on the bench expanded a system that still flourishes.

During my years on the bench, I presided over a number of important criminal cases. The most difficult for me were those where the death penalty had to be imposed. I was, and am now, opposed to the death penalty. My major objection is that no man-made system is flawless. There is always a possibility of an innocent person being condemned by a jury. Unquestionably, our system of justice works better for the rich than for the poor, better for whites than for blacks, and better for the politically and socially connected than for those who are not. Next, even the best evidence is fallible. Then, once imposed, the death penalty is irreversible. If a mistake is made, society cannot give the wrongfully executed person his life back.

I will never forget the first time I was obligated to pronounce a death sentence upon a man convicted of first-degree murder. After a long but not complicated trial, the jury found the defendant guilty and sentenced him to death. Under Tennessee state statutes, I had to pronounce the sentence. I had no flexibility in sentencing persons convicted of these offenses. When the time came for sentencing, I had to read a prepared statement that caused me great pain. Standing before me was a human being, found guilty by a jury of his peers, but still a human being—a person perhaps hated by the victim's family, but still a human being. I watched as the defendant physically shook with fear. Then, in a voice full of emotion, I read the following words: "(John Doe), having been found guilty, by a jury of your peers, of the offense of murder in the commission of a felony; it is the judgment of this court that you will be delivered by the sheriff of Shelby County to the warden of the State Penitentiary at Nashville, Tennessee; there on the 8th day of June 1967, you are to be shocked with sufficient volts of electricity until you are dead. And may God have mercy on your soul." What a wave of emotion passed over me. I knew then that I never wanted to do this again, and fortunately I was never again called upon to do so.

In the case cited above, I discovered that errors had been committed in the conduct of the trial that required me to grant a new trial. I did not preside at the second trial. The defendant was again found guilty, and was given the death sentence for the second time. However, he was never executed.

There is one final experience I want to convey on the subject of my presence as a Criminal Court judge. We had monthly meetings of the Criminal Court judges. At one of the meetings in Judge Sellers' chambers, Judge Sellers, Judge Battle, Judge Faquin, Judge Colton, and I were present. We were dealing with matters involving administrative procedure in our courtrooms. A representative from the public defender's office was also there and was sitting next to me and from time to time was patting me on the knee. He started off on a long, involved discussion.

His conversation began with, "You know this nigger, big black buck nigger, smells bad, looks bad, don't you recall . . ." and about that time a look of dismay, apprehension, and worry began to appear on the faces of the other judges, and a shuffling of feet was heard. The public defender looked at me, and the expression on his face was hard to describe: disbelief, confusion.

He stopped talking. He stuttered. He changed color. I thought, "What am I to do? What am I to say? How am I to approach this?" I thought. The representative stumbled through to another subject and the meeting was soon adjourned. I was convinced that this experience would cause this man, who had been doing this all of his life without a thought, never to be the same again. Was I right? Was I wrong? Well, the fact is that things did begin to change in that public defender's office and all over the courthouse with my presence on the bench.

Do you think that the nasty remarks made by the Texaco representatives would have been made if a black had been present? Do you think that all of the nasty anti-women jokes that have been told as a matter of routine would have continued if women could have been present? I hold to the theory that we have to change our culture, our folklore, our method of dealing with people. Certain remarks have to be withheld, not given public acceptability, and the best way to do that is through the diversity of having people of all races and creeds together.

Chapter 7
THE KING I KNEW

One of the great privileges of my life was to have known Martin Luther King, Jr. It was during the Montgomery boycott that I first met Dr. King. When we were first introduced, there was nothing out of the ordinary about that meeting or him as a person. We were around the same age. We were both preachers, and both of us had a pathological hatred for racial discrimination and segregation.

During the days of the bus boycott, I was invited on a number of occasions to come to Montgomery to speak at public meetings. Back then we often had speakers from other parts of the country who experienced difficulty in offering words of encouragement. I had developed a technique—an ability to deliver, in a short span of time, rousing speeches that touched all of the necessary bases. At mass public meetings where some speakers drone on and on, this was a well-appreciated talent. For that reason I was invited often to give remarks. I made the most of those opportunities.

Dr. King was an unassuming, relatively soft-spoken man. He was short in stature and muscularly built. King had a beautiful baritone voice. Most people do not realize it, but King loved to sing. Black people, especially black men, sang more than they do now. We would often sit around singing one song after the other, harmonizing without musical accompaniment. King also had a sense of humor; he loved to tell stories and jokes. Each of us would try to outdo the other.

Since most of the people with whom we associated were preachers, we relished the opportunity to bounce sermon ideas off of each other. None of us was above "borrowing" sermon ideas that we heard at these sessions.

Shortly after Dr. King organized the Southern Christian Leadership Conference in 1957 (August 15, 1957), I was asked by King to serve on his board of directors. Soon after, I became extremely active with the SCLC. It was my great fortune to have been involved in every SCLC campaign in which Dr. King was involved, with the exception of Albany, Georgia, and St. Augustine, Florida.

There seems to be consensus among those who knew and worked with Dr. King to describe him with the same adjective. He was brilliant. Dr. King had a first-class mind. His intellectual acumen was thorough and comprehensive. He was well read. He was familiar with, and could cite from memory, the works of the great philosophers of Egypt, ancient Greece, Rome, Italy, England, Scotland, India, Spain, and others. He was a humble man who was also an excellent listener.

King's leadership style was to set the course of the discussion, then allow everybody to express their views regardless of how off-base they might appear to others. Then, King would cut through all of the rhetoric and synthesize and distill all that had been offered. After having the input of his colleagues, King would make up his mind as to the course of action he would take. With that, he would move forward.

King was honest to a fault. His word was sacred and his commitment to the fight for justice was almost fanatical. He was self-effacing, and he had a characteristic that most great leaders possess: the ability to laugh at himself. He did not take himself too seriously, and never became caught up in his own importance.

It was my privilege to preach for him at his church in Atlanta. My church in Memphis, Middle Baptist Church, hosted an Annual Meeting of SCLC. I can remember as if it were yesterday joining him in Selma in 1965 at the Brown Chapel African Methodist Episcopal Church, before the March from Selma to Montgomery.

The Southern Christian Leadership Conference was truly a southern Christian organization. Dr. Gardner Taylor and Dr. Sandy Ray of Concord and Cornerstone Baptist Churches, respectively, in New York and a number of other northern preachers were active in SCLC. There were preachers like Dr. Thomas Kilgore and Bishop H.H. Brookins of Los Angeles, Reverend Hoover of Cleveland, and the renowned C.L. Franklin of Detroit (fabled father of Aretha Franklin, most imitated preacher of his day, and one of the strongest supporters King ever had). A number of midwestern preachers were also pillars of the SCLC; however, the base of the organization was in the South.

SCLC did not have chapters; it had affiliates. The affiliates consisted of local churches or organizations that served as the coordinators of SCLC activities in a given city. Some affiliates were more effective than others. Dr. King, early on, wanted to build a national membership base of his organization. He recognized the advantage of having a mass-based organization from his experiences with the NAACP. I came up with the bright idea of building a membership base by having membership application forms distributed at the public meetings where Dr. King was the speaker.

King was speaking to huge audiences. Sometimes he spoke to overflow audiences of up to three thousand people. We would ask for $1.00 from each adult. I thought, why not ask subscribers to fill out the card and return it, and they would keep their portion as a membership card. The other portion of the application would go to the national office of SCLC in Atlanta.

The idea never worked. People would give in public offerings, but they would not fill out the membership applications. Some were reluctant to belong to anything that could possibly jeopardize their employment. People were fearful of membership lists finding their way into the hands of the wrong people (their employers), who were often hostile to civil rights causes. Others were more than willing to help and to support, but they did not want to join anything.

In early 1968, while in the midst of planning for his Poor People's Campaign that was scheduled to begin on April 22, 1968, in Washington, D.C., Dr. King was asked by Rev. James Lawson, Rev. Ralph Jackson, and Rev. Henry Starks to come to Memphis to support the sanitation workers, who were locked in a bitter battle for union recognition, better working conditions, and better pay. The Memphis sanitation workers were all black.

The workers began their strike on February 12, 1968. The men were working under horrendous conditions, unfit for human beings in a civilized nation. Despite their backbreaking work, the workers did not earn enough to support themselves, much less their family. The work was not only hard, but it was dangerous. Accidents happened with ever-increasing frequency.

The strike was sparked by the death of two workers who were accidentally crushed when they took shelter inside the rear of their truck during a hard rain and the machinery malfunctioned. Garbage workers, as they were called, were not allowed to seek cover in the cabs of their trucks, or in stores and other facilities in the neighborhoods in which they were working. It was felt that if Dr. King came to Memphis and lent his prestige to the fight, maybe the recalcitrant Mayor, Henry Loeb, would agree to the simple demands of the workers: union recognition and a living wage.

From the beginning of his career 12 years earlier in Montgomery, Dr. King was asked repeatedly to come to this city or that town to lend his support to some worthy effort or another. King had a weakness. He was too accommodating. He tried to help everyone who called on him for assistance. I saw him on many occasions change his plans and squeeze in an engagement here and one there when he was dead tired. Regrettably, people never hesitate to call upon giving people like King.

Mayor Loeb, when he was first elected as Commissioner of Public Works in 1952, was seen by the black community as a progressive leader. However, he had become very unpopular by 1968. He was elected mayor despite almost unified opposition of the black community. He was now appealing to some of the more extreme elements in the white community. He was determined not to sign an agreement that would end the strike. He claimed that the strike was illegal.

The city council, which at this time had three blacks, voted to approve a contract or agreement between the union and the city. We had managed to get enough white support on the city council to accomplish this. Mayor Loeb decided to veto the legislation. With no agreement in hand, the men were out of work and increasingly losing hope.

King came to Memphis on March 19. He spoke that evening to an audience of more than 10,000 people that filled Mason Temple. He was scheduled to return on March 22 for a march in support of the workers, but that march was canceled by a late spring snowstorm. The march was rescheduled for Thursday, March 28. King's plane was late, and the march was late getting started. When King and Abernathy arrived, the march of more than 20,000 people began. The leaders were in the front row, followed by other marchers and a few march marshals.

Some young black men who did not understand the nature of the struggle and the principles of nonviolence positioned themselves near the end of the march. They began to break windows. In my opinion, the police overreacted. They waded into the crowd swinging nightsticks, shouting and beating indiscriminately the innocent marchers. If the police had merely contained the disorderly young men and arrested them, the march could have gone forward.

The results were disastrous. Scores were injured and hundreds were arrested. The people at the front of the march had no way of knowing what was happening at the rear of the march. Suddenly, Dr. King was pushed, by people who wanted to protect him, into a car and rushed to the Rivermont Holiday Inn.

Dr. King now faced a major dilemma. He had come to lend his support to a march that ended in violence. It did not matter that neither he nor SCLC had organized the march; in the eyes of the media it was King's March. Never before had Dr. King led a demonstration that ended in violence by demonstrators. When there was violence, it normally came from law enforcement personnel or white detractors. Questions were being raised: If King could not lead a demonstration in Memphis without violence, how could he be expected to lead thousands of demonstrators to the nation's Capitol for the "Poor People's March"?

The television footage of Dr. King being sped off gave the impression that Dr. King had fled, leaving the demonstrators at the mercy of the Memphis police department. King did not want to leave the march when the violence erupted. But all parties agreed that it was in the best interest of the movement to get him to safety. After all, King was the most visible and the preeminent black leader in America at that time.

The media made a big issue of King being housed at the fabulous, plush Rivermont Holiday Inn. The press portrayed King as a hypocrite for staying at a plush white hotel when there was a well-known and well-appointed black hotel where most blacks visiting Memphis traditionally stayed. Ordinarily when King came to town he stayed at the Lorraine Motel, which was black owned and operated. King was a big supporter of black businesses. This move into the Rivermont Holiday Inn suggested that somehow King had set himself above the people he led.

I was on the bench at that time, but called King to just cheer him up. Never had I heard him so despondent. He was devastated by the violence that had occurred. He knew he had to prove that nonviolence was still possible. To him, there was no other way. The struggle for racial equality in America was to be either nonviolent or chaotic. I assured him that no one in his right mind would blame him for what a few irresponsible young men did. And really, it was the Memphis police who had overreacted.

I did not get to see Dr. King that night. He assured me that he would probably have to return to Memphis to demonstrate that it was still possible to have a nonviolent demonstration. The next morning Dr. King left Memphis.

After the march and the attendant violence, the mayor dug in his heels. He would not give in to violence or the threat of violence. If the mayor had settled the strike even at this point, there would not have been a need for Dr. King to come back to Memphis.

A man of his word, Dr. King returned to Memphis on April 3. This time, he brought most of his top executive staff with him. He was to lead another march on Friday, April 5. King held a series of meetings with his staff, met with the press, and made sure that security was set up for the march. This time SCLC would make sure that the demonstration had the necessary marshals (volunteers served as marshals).

King was served with an injunction by U.S. District Judge Bailey Brown banning the march. It was not unusual for opponents of the movement to get injunctions from the courts in an effort to deny the right to march. In this case, King immediately put his lawyers on the case to have the injunction lifted. That evening a mass meeting was planned at Mason Temple. Mason Temple was the largest black facility in the city of Memphis at that time. The church had been built by the legendary founder of the Church of God in Christ, Bishop Mason. Mason Temple was a huge facility that could seat some 5,000 people. At that time, J.O. Patterson, Sr. was the presiding bishop.

That night a terrible storm passed through Memphis. The torrential rains fell like the waters of Niagara. Lightning danced in the spring skies, and thunder sounded like exploding cannons roaring on a thousand distant battlefields. Nature was itself warning us of trouble yet to come. The atmosphere was one of foreboding and fear. Charles Turner, the chairman of my deacon board at Middle Baptist Church, and I were to go over to the meeting, but first we had to attend the funeral service of a dear friend, Marshall Alexander, at 8:00 P.M.

After the funeral, it was late and we decided to go home. As we were driving, both of us remarked almost at the same time, "This storm is really something. There are not going to be many people there tonight." Then we simultaneously said to each other, "If Dr. King could come all the way from Atlanta to Memphis to deal with our problem with the sanitation workers, the least we can do is to be in the audience. If there is a small crowd, there would be two additional people, the two of us!"

We turned and headed for Mason Temple. When we got to the church, the storm had not abated. If anything, it had grown worse. We went in, and much to our surprise there was a nice crowd. More than 3,000 people had made their way out in the midst of the terrible storm to support the sanitation workers, but also to hear Dr. King. Ralph Abernathy was up speaking when we walked in.

I was told later that King had sent word to the church for Ralph Abernathy to give the main speech. He was not feeling well. Abernathy sent word back that there was a great crowd of people who had come for the express purpose of hearing him speak. Ralph Abernathy told King, "The people came to hear you. You better get over here, Martin," he pleaded. King got dressed and made his way over to the church.

I had heard Abernathy introduce King on dozens of occasions, but never the way he did that evening. There was something different, uniquely different, in Ralph's introduction. Abernathy "touched every base," as we preachers call it. He was poetic and profound in his introduction. He likened King to historical and biblical characters. He talked about King's sacrifices, his passion for justice, and his love of freedom. In Southern Baptist vernacular, Ralph waxed eloquently.

As Abernathy was introducing King, there were these tremendous claps of thunder. Every now and then there would be the banging of a shutter. When King rose, the audience exploded in thunderous applause. Without making many introductory comments, he began to speak. Many of King's colleagues were there who had heard him speak before over the years. We all agreed that King was struggling to come to terms with the premonition of his own death. His speech-sermon was not morbid or depressing. It appeared as if King was standing outside of himself—speaking from a paradisiacal celestial elevation, prophetically addressing those of us who were at Mason Temple and all subsequent generations of black people in this troubled land.

King talked about how he would choose that period of history to live in over all others. He related how he had been stabbed in Harlem. King pointed out that the newspapers had reported that the knife blade had come so close to his aorta, the main artery of the heart, that if he had sneezed he would have died. King then related how he had received hundreds of letters and telegrams while recuperating in the hospital.

He said that he did not recall what the letters from the governor and the mayor of New York said, but he remembered a letter written by a little girl. She said simply, "Dr. King, I am a student at the White Plains High School. While it should not matter, I am a white girl. I read in the papers about your pain and your suffering. Dr. King, I read that if you had sneezed you would have died. Dr. King, I want you to know that I'm so happy that you didn't sneeze." Dr. King said to his cheering audience, "I too am happy that I didn't sneeze."

Finally, he talked about going to the mountaintop and looking over and seeing the promised land. King's voice, now cracking with emotion, said, "I may not get there with you, but I want you to know tonight, that we as a people will get to the promised land." He concluded by saying, "So tonight, I am not worried about anything; I am not fearing any man. Mine eyes have seen the glory of the coming of the Lord." With those words, the 20th Century Prophet, the Apostle of Non-Violence, turned around and walked to his seat. As he did, tears began to roll down his cheeks. King was by nature stoic. In all of the years I had known him, I had never seen him moved to tears before.

We realized then and there that we had witnessed a unique historical event. I do not believe that any of us realized that we were hearing Dr. King's last public address on the earth. But we did realize that we had heard a speech unlike any that we had heard before or would likely hear again. When the meeting was over, I hugged Martin, shook his hand and engaged in some normal preacher banter. I told him that I would not be able to be with him at the march because of my duties on the bench. We promised to get together the next day. I went home knowing that something seemingly of cosmic proportions had happened or was about to happen. I did not know what, but I knew that it was something important.

Because of the tension that existed from the previous march with the outbreak of violence, the Director of Public Safety dispatched a police squad car to every fire station in the city. This was done to provide rapid response in the event of a disturbance occurring anywhere in the city.

On the morning of the 4th of April, the rain clouds of the night before had given way to bright sunshine. There was a strange calm on that spring day. The city was split on the march, largely along racial lines. Tension was in the air while flowers bloomed and birds sang. Little did we know that tragedy would collide with fate in Memphis, and that a single bullet would alter the history of the world.

Late that afternoon, I was just returning to my chambers after going to a Bar Association meeting at the Peabody Hotel. Suddenly, a white lawyer came rushing from across the street shouting, "Judge, Judge Hooks, Dr. King has been shot." He told me that he had been shot at the motel. I knew that King was staying at the Lorraine Motel, and I rushed there. It was only minutes away from the courthouse.

When I arrived, I discovered that King had already been taken to St. Joseph's Hospital. From the reactions on the faces of many that I saw whom I had known for years, I knew that things did not look promising. The hurt that was written on the faces of black people who were milling around near the motel spoke louder than any words. Now, I am sure that King was clinically dead when he fell on the balcony at the Lorraine Motel in front of room 306. Not long after I arrived at the hospital, the dreaded announcement was made. *Dr. Martin Luther King, Jr. was dead.*

Word of Dr. King's death hit me like being struck in the chest by a two-by-four. The blow was devastating. I had just seen him, promised that we would get together that evening, and now he was gone! Word had gotten out that a white man was seen fleeing the scene. The search for the culprit was on. Little did anyone realize then that the assassin would not be caught until June 8, some two months later, when the funeral train bearing the body of Senator Robert Kennedy, who himself was assassinated in Los Angeles on June 5, was slowly making the sad journey from New York to Washington, D.C. James Earl Ray, the accused assassin, was arrested in London, England, early that day.

I went over to the R.S. Lewis Funeral Home, where King's body had been taken. The Lewis Funeral Home was one of the best in the Southeast. It was here that I saw the unprepared remains of King. The marks of the bullet and of the autopsy that had been done by the medical examiner were unmistakably evident. Without going into the gory details, I will just say that it was shocking.

I was constrained in what I could do because I was a jurist, and it was possible that matters surrounding the assassination might come before me as a criminal court judge. I talked to Andy Young, Ralph Abernathy, "Samuel" Billy Kyles, and other intimate associates of both Dr. King and myself, later that night. Arrangements had not been made. Coretta, King's wife, had decided to stay with the children after rushing to the Atlanta airport in hopes of getting to Memphis to be with Martin. She was intercepted at the airport along with Juanita Abernathy, who was with her, and told that King had died. After realizing that there was nothing she could do in Memphis, Coretta returned home to tell their four small children that their father was gone. Coretta—what a great and marvelous woman she is! We should ever be grateful for the tremendous contribution she has made to the movement, both before and after Dr. King's death.

We were certain that the funeral services would be held in Atlanta at King's church, Ebenezer Baptist Church on Auburn Street. I joined other members of the board of the Southern Christian Leadership Conference and more than 200,000 other mourning Americans at King's funeral a few days later. Coretta was marvelous. Her strength gave us strength. Her quiet dignity and regal bearing gave comfort to the millions of black Americans who felt deeply the pain of Dr. King's assassination.

Now, more than 30 years after the assassination, there is still an ongoing debate as to whether James Earl Ray was the shooter. Many conspiracy buffs contend that King was shot by army intelligence officers, by FBI agents, by Memphis or state police, or even by aliens. I have seen the evidence, read the testimony and reports issued by investigative entities. I have seen materials that the general public is unaware of. There is no doubt in my mind that Ray was the shooter. I believe that he may have been paid and financed by racist forces. Who they were and what ties they had will remain a mystery.

Centuries from now, scholars will still debate who was responsible for the killing of Dr. King. Too much time has passed, too many people who were in Memphis that fateful day have passed from the scene. Too many memories have become clouded, and too many tracks have been wiped out by the sands of time.

Knowing this, I am happy that fate and destiny allowed me to know and to work with Martin. He was one of those unique characters who walked upon the stage of history and transformed forever a flawed social order. He is much larger in death than he was in life. His life was dedicated to others. The way he died merely brought his life's work and sacrifices to the attention of a world that has to be shocked before it can sit up and take notice. King's legacy is one of love and hope. What a legacy! What a man!

It was April 4, 1968, and Martin Luther King had been killed on the streets of Memphis. I was sitting as a judge in the criminal court of Shelby County. I was disturbed, I was sad, I was upset and angry, and yet I recognized that the world had to go on. One of my best and dearest friends was Jed Dreifus. He and his wife, Jeanie, had contributed much to the progress of Memphis. His mother, Myra, was an early pioneer in black community relations work long before it became acceptable. His father, Fred, supported his wife. My wife, Frances, had worked with Jed and Myra in setting up a model daycare center (which, by the way, still exists). Jed and I were talking. What could we do?

Over the next few days, as we continued to meet and talk about the tragedy, we decided to convene a meeting of outstanding citizens of Memphis, black and white. We would try to make the meeting monthly. All of us—Jed and I and Frances and Jeannie—reasoned that we did not want this to be an action group, but rather a group in which we could think, learn, and grow. So we called the first meeting. Attending were the editors of the two local newspapers, the CEOs of the three local television stations, the presidents of three major local banks, the president of the University of Memphis, two or three prominent white city officials, including the sheriff, and an equal number of outstanding black citizens. This literary group was in existence for several years and was known informally as the Judge Ben Hooks Study Group.

At that very first meeting, I made it clear that in order for Negroes or African Americans or black people to survive in this nation, they not only had to understand black folks, but they had to understand white folks. Likewise, it was possible for a white person to have the highest office in the land and never really have any concept of what black folks wanted or stood for or believed in. Many prominent white citizens had lived and died and, other than the conversation with their cook, maid, chauffeur or houseboy, had never spoken to a black person. So we decided we would initially read and report on some books.

The first books we read were usually printed together and sold as a trilogy. First, *The Souls of Black Folk,* by W.E.B. DuBois, eminent black leader of the early century, founder of *The Crisis* magazine in 1910, first black Ph.D. graduate of Harvard, and one of the most respected black leaders of all times. Second was *Up From Slavery,* by Booker T. Washington, founder of the Tuskegee Institute of Tuskegee, Alabama, a premier black leader in America from 1890 to 1915, a man for whom black schools have been named all over the nation, including Booker T. Washington High School in Memphis. And third was *Autobiography of an Ex-colored Man,* by James Weldon Johnson, author of "Lift Every Voice and Sing," the Negro national anthem.

We assigned one of the white men to read and give a book report. In other words, the white movers and shakers of Memphis read about the black folk: what we read, what we ate, what we thought, how we reacted, who we were. Later in this group, we read books by Martin King, *Why We Can't Wait, Chaos or Community.* We read and discussed *A Letter from a Birmingham Jail,* the famous letter published by King, written during his arrest in Birmingham, Alabama. I saw these white men stand up and openly state that when King was killed in 1968, they had, to that point, never really listened to what he had to say. He was more or less a disturbing presence, but those men looked at each other and said King loved America. King wanted to see America do better. King understood this and that, and stood for this and that.

We tried to make this group conscious for perhaps the first time in their lives and understand that people are people, be they black, white, red, yellow or brown, uneducated, overeducated, or mis-educated. We hoped this background would then give them a better understanding of modern-day problems.

Chapter 8

BUSINESS VENTURES

It was impossible for a black person to grow up in Memphis in the late '20s and '30s without being aware of the Jim Crow practices that were etched indelibly into the landscape of the entire South. We instinctively knew that something was wrong with the picture, but these were the only conditions we had ever experienced.

A cursory look at the rabidly segregated conditions in Memphis during that period, and indeed through the 1950s, made one aware of the fact that to be born black then was to be saddled with a stigma of inferiority. We never accepted the stigma, but it was omnipresent in the relationship between the races.

The neighborhoods in which most of the 400,000 or so residents of Memphis lived were segregated by race—not class, but race. There were parks restricted to whites only; movie theaters had side or back entrances for blacks, who had to sit in the balconies. We rode on the back of the streetcars and drank from "colored only" water fountains. Blacks had to call young whites "Mr." and "Miss" and witness old black people being denied the customary titles of Mr. and Mrs. In general, blacks were relegated to second-class status.

I cannot say exactly when I first became aware of Jim Crow. Black adults and parents sheltered their children as best they could from the effects of racism. Admittedly, it was impossible to immunize those of us who grew up during this period, but they tried to spare us the stings of discrimination and the pains of racism as long as possible.

Memphis was a little more progressive on matters of race than were many cities in the "Old South." Blacks voted in elections, and there were nice schools for black children to attend. These schools were not as nice as the white schools, but compared to what one saw for blacks in other places, they were nice. We had our own parks and even two or three swimming pools. Some streets were paved and had curbs; there were black businesses; and there was a solid black middle class with college-trained professionals. Despite these symbols of progress, I learned early the importance of becoming a successful businessman. Actually, among the factors I considered in choosing a life's profession in law was that I would be working for myself. As such, I could go as far as my talents and fate took me.

I had many ideas about the importance of black-owned businesses. I saw black people owning the means of production and services as a way out of the quagmire of second-class citizenship. We had always been consumers, not producers of anything. To me this was not some esoteric theory; it was just simply common sense. If we could establish our own grocery stores, operate our own dry cleaners and most of the retail stores that provided goods and services to our people, we could employ a lot of other black people. I had seen in Chicago how different ethnic groups used retailing as a ladder to climb to economic self-sufficiency. If they could do it, why couldn't we?

In 1952, my brother Robert moved back to Memphis from Chicago. He was an insurance salesman, but I knew he was not very happy with his job. I thought to myself, suppose Robert and I opened a grocery store! We could give the community exceptional service and fine products. In exchange, we could hire a number of people and make some money for our efforts. We decided that we would take a crack at it. We would open what we called a "super ready." This was a term given to a store that was larger than a corner grocery store, but smaller than what we now know as a supermarket. (This was before the chain stores took complete control.) Our store was called Hooks Brothers' Supermarket. I envisioned it would have all of the grocery items that the average family would need. It would have the staples: vegetables, fruit, canned goods, paper items, laundry and cleaning products, frozen food items, a bakery section, and a professional butcher on duty to provide quality cuts of meats.

I bought a two-story building with a store on the first floor and an apartment on the second floor. I spent a lot of money getting the place prepared. It had an old-fashioned meat counter, a walk-in meat freezer, and a lot of space for displays and shelves. We made sure that our store was as well appointed as any that could be found in the entire city of Memphis. Our store was self-service—the customers would take a basket and pick out the items they wanted. They did not have to depend on someone behind the counter to get an item for them. We took into consideration many of the marketing techniques that later became standard industry practice: creative display of products, fresh produce, stocking only exceptional and choice meats; and we provided wide aisles, good lighting, efficient service, and courteous floor and checkout personnel who treated each customer with the utmost respect. We made sure that every person was called by courtesy titles and that there were no long lines at the checkout counters.

My brother immersed himself in the business. My wife, Frances, came out as often as possible to work the cash register. I got up early in the morning and put in a couple of hours before I left for my law office. I arrived at six or seven o'clock in the morning. We trained people from the community and put them to work.

Not long after we opened our store, with a lot of fanfare and ethnic pride, I began to notice a shocking phenomenon. I saw children that I had come to recognize from the community walking past our store and going to the store that was operated by whites down the street. I would then see them walking back with a bottle of milk and a loaf of bread. Why would they pass by us to buy items that we had readily available? These items were delivered by the same truck on the same day. We sold our milk and bread for the same price as the other store. A quart of milk was 19 cents and a loaf of bread was 21 cents. We carried the same brands as the other store. Therefore, I knew it was neither price nor brand preference. It had to be something else.

I discovered that the children were given instructions by adults to buy grocery items from the white store. This was a shocking revelation! The extent to which our people had been brainwashed into believing that anything sold by blacks was inferior was mind-boggling. Self-hatred born out of years of perverted values and prejudices had taken its toll. Within a year we had to close our doors.

Later, I read a book titled *Looking Back to Harlem*, by Claude McKay. McKay raised a profound and significant question near the end of the book. Why was it that in Spanish Harlem the Spanish people owned and operated the corner stores, the delicatessens, and the other little retail businesses, while in black Harlem, black people owned no businesses except a tavern or two? That question was not posed by McKay in 1953 or in 1999, but in 1931, when Harlem was indeed the cultural and economic capital of black America, when the so-called "Harlem Renaissance" was in full bloom.

I believe that economic empowerment is the one great barrier remaining to be conquered. I can only imagine how much progress we could make as a people if we supported each other in business as well as we do in politics. I intend on spending the rest of my remaining years devoted to tearing down this barrier. I will never lose hope. That is why I am so glad that at that little store I put all my little nephews and nieces (Robert, Carole, Fred, Walter, Pat, Ronald, and Michael) to work, along with my three sisters, so we could work together as a family in business.

My grocery store experience forced me to consider a number of realities that I would never have otherwise considered. After years of being indoctrinated by a society and a culture to believe that black is inferior, there will always be those who believe that the other man's ice is colder, his wood catches fire quicker, his coal burns longer, his hamburgers taste better, and that if there is competition between a white man and a black man, the white man will always win.

We see this situation again and again to this very day. Black savings and loans and banks in New York City and other major metropolitan areas are closing their doors despite the growing pool of middle-class and upper-income blacks. Black insurance company executives complain of the difficulty they confront in selling insurance to blacks. Many blacks refuse to use the services of black lawyers and accountants. Others will not go to a black physician or dentist.

Rather than becoming embittered by my grocery store experience, I became even more convinced that if we give up on those who have been misguided and misdirected, then in a sense we have bought into the cycle of failure and despair that we abhor. As we move through the new millennium, I can honestly say that there are encouraging signs that the pathologies that created the carousel of self-loathing and self-hatred are giving way to black people becoming more interested in doing business with one another. It has been, and will continue to be, a slow and laborious process, but there is progress being made in small increments.

Tennessee had two black-owned and -operated financial institutions. One was the Tri-State Bank, which was the brainchild of Dr. J.E. Walker, who had also founded Universal Life Insurance Company. Dr. Walker was listed in the April 1955 issue of *Our World* magazine as one of the 10 most powerful Negroes in America. Tri-State was celebrating its tenth anniversary at the time. The Walker establishments were the largest black-owned businesses in the state of Tennessee.

There were over 400,000 blacks in Memphis in the mid-'50s, so there was plenty of room for another financial institution. Most blacks, the working class, did not have bank accounts. Not just in Memphis but throughout the country many hourly workers were paid in cash. Many companies that paid by check also arranged to cash the checks for their employees as a courtesy. Blacks, like others in increasing numbers, were beginning to open accounts with financial institutions. Most who did so had no alternative but to bank with white savings and loans. There were fewer than 100 black-owned and -operated financial institutions in the nation.

In 1956, A.W. Willis, my law and business partner, and I decided to organize a federal savings and loan association. These associations were designed to facilitate and encourage savers to deposit their funds and for the savings and loan institution to make mortgage loans. The institution would be depositor-owned, in that each person who invested money in it became a part of it. C.C. Sawyer, who was a phenomenally successful real estate agent in Memphis, was our financial backer. Neither A.W. nor I had much disposable income to invest. Our contribution was our labor. We would put the whole thing together. Sawyer would help supply the money necessary for setting up the business.

There were a number of hurdles that we had to overcome. The first obstacle was the mountain of paperwork—forms that had to be completed and filed with the federal agencies. We had to gather demographic information, business plans and projections, and background information on the principals. The next hurdle was to get commitments from depositors. We needed a minimum of $250,000 in commitments. That would be the equivalent of $3-4 million today.

Willis and I burned the midnight oil getting the paperwork done. We went to Atlanta to meet with the black group operating the savings and loan in that city. They were very helpful, pointing out pitfalls and roadblocks that we would have to overcome. We met with key black business, religious, civic, and fraternal leaders in Memphis. We were encouraged by the response that we received. Of course, there were many who were skeptical of the venture. In addition to these challenges, we had to build and furnish a headquarters, hire a staff, and advertise and plan our grand opening.

The building was erected at 588 Vance Street in Memphis. It was brick, with a number of well-appointed offices and a beautiful main lobby where depositors were served. The front was glass, which allowed light to cascade into the main lobby. The Mutual Federal facility was one of the most modern and efficient buildings in the city.

C.C. Sawyer was the first president, I was vice president and treasurer, and A.W. Willis became the executive vice president and secretary. The directors of Mutual Federal were Sawyer, Willis, Hooks, T.H. Hayes (a prominent undertaker), George W. Lee (district manager for the Atlanta Life Insurance Co.), W.F. Nabors (public housing project manager), and George Stevens (president of Bondol, Inc., a major supplier of funeral home equipment). Willis and I became the legal counselors. So it happened that Mutual Federal Savings and Loan had its grand opening on Monday, September 17, 1956, at 9:00 A.M. Hundreds of people from across the city, black and white, attended the open house, including Mayor Edmund Orgill, Dr. J.E. Walker, Jesse and Allegra Turner, Arthur Bennett, Frank Kilpatrick, Maxine and Vasco Smith, key preachers, and businessmen. We opened hundreds of accounts from those attending the grand opening.

The black community was proud of the new business. I would often look out the window and watch as blacks would drive slowly down the street just to admire the building. The local black newspapers gave us extensive coverage. So did the black radio personalities. Mutual Federal became an important fixture in the Memphis community. Many blacks who had been turned down by majority lending institutions for mortgages found a receptive ear at Mutual. We were training blacks for careers in the banking industry.

I was the vice president of Mutual Federal Savings and Loan Corporation. At the time there were three other savings and loan associations in town, operated of course by white people. An association of these four institutions was formed and I represented my company. One afternoon, I attended a meeting of the group. I was sitting at the window facing west, the gorgeous sunset coming across the Mississippi River over my shoulder and somewhat obscuring my face. One of the other members came in late, dropped his briefcase on the desk, and cried out in exasperation, "I have just left a meeting with the national association for the advancement of nigger people!" The other representatives sat there, looking at me in dismay. Something about their body language made the speaker look around more closely and he realized that Ben Hooks, a black man, was present.

I thought—"What do I do? What do I say? Do I walk out? Do I engage in a verbal tirade? Do I demand an explanation?" Under God, I am convinced that this kind of statement has been made for years with no recourse, no shame, no regret, but today a black is present.

The point I am making is that my presence made all of the difference. What would have been routine and perhaps unnoticed became a burning issue. My point is that it is important that blacks become a part of the totality of American life. Their very presence makes a difference, creates a sense of awareness, and sets the stage for progress.

The fact is, I decided not to say anything to this man because I thought the look on his face spoke volumes. I am convinced that I was correct in remaining silent. For years afterward, until his death, I never met this man without either an apology from him or actions taken by him to refute that kind of racist statement. My presence at that meeting made a difference for him, and the presence of blacks in positions of authority, power, and responsibility will continue to make a difference.

As late as the early 1960s, Memphis was still rigorously segregated. There were black neighborhoods and white neighborhoods. White-owned banks engaged in red-lining and would not make loans to blacks who wanted to move into white communities. These same lending institutions also discriminated in the requirements they set for blacks who were looking to purchase housing in the traditional black community, or who wanted to purchase a car or invest in a business.

There was a particular all-white subdivision in Memphis made up of hundreds of well-constructed homes built in the late '20s. They were situated on large lots (comparatively speaking) on tree-lined streets. The subdivision was called Glenview. Someone made a conscious effort to make sure that the Glenview community remained all white. Realtors would not show houses to black homebuyers. The white-owned banks would not lend to prospective black buyers, and most homeowners would not allow their homes to be shown to blacks.

On Sunday afternoons after church services, African-American families would ride through the Glenview development looking at houses and dreaming of what it would be like to live there. They would drive by slowly, with the fathers and mothers pointing at one well-appointed house and then another. Many blacks were now earning incomes that allowed them, financially, to buy houses in any neighborhood in Memphis.

The blacks who cruised the Glenview area on Sundays were met by beautiful signs that were professionally printed and placed on the lawns of every homeowner. The signs said simply, "White Community, not for sale to Negroes." The signs really said it all. Blacks were not welcome. The three black financial institutions in Memphis, Tri-State Bank, Universal Life Insurance Company, and Mutual Federal, got together and agreed that they would each make a loan to one family who wanted to buy a home in Glenview, provided three whites could be convinced to sell to them.

Not long after, three sellers agreed to sell to blacks. As promised, the financial institutions financed the sales and made the loan. The first black to move in was Reverend R.W. Norsworthy, the pastor of Mt. Moriah Baptist Church in Orange Mound. Reverend Norsworthy was perhaps six feet tall, noted for his dynamic pulpit oratory, a great fisherman, and a consummate hunter. On the day that Reverend Norsworthy moved in, he very openly and ostentatiously moved his rifle and shotgun from the moving van into the house. Shortly after, he brought the guns out again to make sure that the neighbors knew that he was armed and intended to protect his house and his family. Reverend Norsworthy said jokingly afterward that he wanted to let his neighbors know that he was not non-violent when it came to his house and his family. Therefore, it would not be wise for anyone to mistake his smile and meekness for weakness.

The second black to move into Glenview was Bob Mason, the son of the founder of the Church of God in Christ, Bishop Charles Harrison Mason. Soon after these blacks moved in, the white lending agencies began to make loans fast and furiously. Before long, hundreds of blacks had moved into Glenview. Mutual Federal continued to, innovatively and creatively, force the majority institutions to respond to the needs of the black community. When I was appointed to the bench in 1965, I had to discontinue my active involvement with Mutual Federal. The institution continued as an invaluable asset to the community until 1972, when it, like so many other financial institutions, was forced to merge with other banks out of economic necessity.

My next significant venture into the business community came when A.W. Willis, my close friend and law partner, and I took a close look at possible business ventures. We had handled a number of civil rights cases together, supported progressive candidates for public office, and were among the principal black movers and shakers of the city. John Hooker was a successful politician with whom we had worked over the years. Unlike some people, Hooker believed in helping his friends, both black and white, if he could. He was not one who forgot easily those individuals who stood by him or helped him open the door. Hooker was now running, along with his brother, a franchise business that was the envy of the industry. They were making so much money and growing so fast, it was unfathomable. This was at the beginning of the franchise explosion. The company was Minnie Pearl Fried Chicken.

Hooker offered to help Willis and me acquire 20 Minnie Pearl stores. Also included in this partnership was Russell B. Sugarmon, Jr., a brilliant, progressive young black lawyer and politician. We had given serious thought to going into business with Hooker. Minnie Pearl was a fast-growing and prosperous business. It was doing well all over the country, but particularly in the South. The food was good, and the public relations campaign had proven to be very effective. We decided to make Hooker a counteroffer.

We wanted him to help us with another chain, a black chain. It would be called Mahalia Jackson Fried Chicken. Mahalia Jackson was a national icon with cross-appeal. She was known for her ability to cook and for her love of good food. Why not, we reasoned, spin off another company that would be majority owned by blacks, that would operate in the black community, and that would train and employ hundreds of our own people? It was not all altruism. We wanted to make money from the venture. People do not go into business for purely altruistic purposes. People go into business for the profit motive. Helping people may be an important objective, but it is not the only objective.

After some discussion and negotiation, John Hooker agreed to finance and to give business advice and direction to our Mahalia Jackson venture. It would be a majority black-owned venture. Hooker would own 49 percent of the stock.

I remember going to Chicago to meet with Mahalia about the venture. I had known her for years in my capacity as both a preacher and a lawyer. She was always gracious to me. She had a beautiful spirit and an unassuming manner. After singing, Mahalia liked to entertain. She was a wonderful hostess who loved to cook for her guests. Nobody could make gumbo the way the Mahalia did. Her fried chicken, another of her specialties, was really finger-licking *good*.

I had been with Mahalia on a number of occasions when she was performing before a mixed audience. I watched the faces of white women whom Mahalia seemed to have touched in a peculiar way. She was one of the few black artists of her era who early on had crossover appeal.

When I went to Chicago to talk to Mahalia about the chicken business, she was in her huge apartment overlooking the lake. She had bought all of the apartments on the top floor and removed the walls, making them into one large apartment. A focal point of the apartment was her well-equipped kitchen. She had every type of pot and saucepan imaginable. She called me Judge Hooks. She was so proud that I had broken the barrier in becoming a judge in the South that she refused to call me anything but Judge.

Mahalia was excited by the idea of having a business named for her. She agreed to come out for a number of store openings and special events at stores in or near cities she was visiting. Whenever she came to one of these events, the crowds would mob her. They would knock each other down just to touch her. Mahalia had legitimate star quality.

As I moved forward with this venture, I realized that I should give up my seat on the bench as a judge. The new venture would require my being on the road to organize and build new stores. I was serving as the pastor of Middle Baptist Church and Mt. Moriah in Detroit. I also had major responsibility for the Knights of Pythias and the Courts of Calenthe, an old-line national fraternal organization. Additionally, I was state secretary for the Prince Hall Masonic Grand Lodge of Tennessee, the black Masonic organization for our state. All of these duties weighed heavily on me.

If I left the bench, it was important that another black be appointed. I had just won reelection to an eight-year term. I desperately wanted at least one black on the bench. I had seen how my mere presence there had made a difference in both the tenor and the tone of the practice and the discussions of the other judges. My replacement would have to be appointed by the governor. He would have to be convinced, and I would have to have a commitment from him that another black would fill my spot on the bench if I resigned. Once I had Governor Buford Ellington's assurance, I resigned. A black lawyer, Odell Horton, was appointed and later became the second black to become a criminal court judge in Memphis. He was tremendously successful and later became an outstanding federal district judge.

With this matter now behind me, I plunged into the chicken franchise business. The Mahalia Jackson Chicken business took off like a rocket. With breathtaking speed we went into an intensive learning period. Hooker made sure that we learned the business from the bottom up and from the inside out. We learned how to set up a store, how to get a demographic survey done to determine if the market could sustain a store, how to set up a working franchise kitchen, how to prepare meals, how and where to order supplies (cups, napkins, bags, etc.), how to negotiate with bankers and vendors, how to hire and train staff, and how to do so many little things that made the difference between failure and success. We found ourselves in Nashville so often that we almost needed a second residence there.

We also began dealings with Gulf Oil. Gulf was going to build or remodel 100 stations for us and give us $20,000 apiece to convert them, in exchange for 7 percent of the gross receipts. Some would sell both Mahalia Jackson chicken and gasoline. This was the forerunner to the current convenience food "to go" concept that you see all over the country, with service stations and McDonald's, Wendy's, Burger King, or other food outlets at one location. We had a few tables at which people could eat, but this Gulf Oil concept was tailored for the to-go customers.

In a short period of time we had 27 stores in seven states, each employing nine to 30 people. They all came from the community. With a few exceptions, they were all black. The manager of each store had to come to Memphis for training before the store was opened. He or she learned how to hire and supervise a staff, how to prepare the chicken, how to market their store, and how to keep their books. This training department was run by my nephew, Robert Hooks III. His father, my brother Robert, resigned from the post office, where he was superintendent of the George Lee Station, to work for the Mahalia system. We had stores in Memphis, Nashville, Charlotte, Jacksonville, Milwaukee, Chicago, Houston, Cleveland, Detroit, and in the Bahamas. Our best store, in Detroit, took in over $10,000 per week. That was unheard of in 1969.

We developed, based upon the Minnie Pearl model, a formula for cooking the chicken. The breading was made of flour, meal, a variety of seasonings, and spices. We had barrels of the breading prepared and shipped to each of our stores. Since most blacks liked their fried chicken crisp, we cooked ours in pressure cookers at a consistent temperature. After we introduced our crispy chicken, Colonel Sanders came out with its own version.

The Mahalia Jackson Chicken System was doing quite well, but not well enough to sustain the business. It was necessary to raise additional capital. We had gotten $5 million from Hooker's companies to open the business. Now we needed an additional $10 million to grow the company. The only way we could raise the money we needed was by selling stock publicly. The Hooker companies owned 49 percent of the stock. Willis, Sugarmon, and I owned 41 percent, with 10 percent owned by a few friends, family, and Mahalia Jackson.

During the same time that we had the Mahalia Jackson Chicken business, we set up another company that was called Mahalia Jackson Products. This company was a distributor of prepared items for retail sale. We had 27 products that we sold to grocery stores, such as black-eye peas, greens, beans, spinach, corn, and the like. They were sold under the Mahalia Jackson label.

The production of these products was really simple. I worked out a deal with a major grocery chain, which at that time was one of the largest, if not the largest, retailer in the country. The chain had its own store brand. They owned a large plant in upstate New York. The plant had much more capacity than it needed. Our arrangement was to have products produced under our label by the store's plant. We worked out a deal with a frozen food company in Memphis to produce our frozen line.

With these two arrangements in place, Mahalia Jackson Food Products was able to supply, under its label, the foodstuffs that blacks were accustomed to. We had an ideal arrangement for manufacturing our canned goods. For instance, after the machines had produced, say, one million cans of greens, the labels would be changed to Mahalia Jackson, and another 10,000 would be run using that label. The products would be shipped to our warehouse for distribution to supermarkets and stores. Simply put, the store brand was the manufacturer, we were the wholesaler, and the supermarket or grocery store was the retailer. It was a win-win situation for everybody.

Once the product was produced, there was the challenge of getting it on the shelves of the stores so that customers could see it and hopefully buy it. If we could not get shelf space to display the goods, it would not be possible for potential customers to buy the items. If you managed to get the goods on the shelf but did not sell, the product would be taken off the shelf by the store management. Since no supermarket had shelf space for all of the brands produced, the competition for the available shelf space was fierce. It was necessary that a national, regional or local buyer be persuaded to carry our goods. Existing products that were selling well would not be pulled to display an unknown brand with no track record.

Despite the odds, we managed to get our products on the shelves, mostly in black neighborhoods. We put on a full-court press in advertising the products in Tennessee, Michigan, Illinois, New York, and Florida. We needed a lot of money to buy radio and TV advertisements. We had life-sized cutouts of Mahalia that were used in stores during that period. Former Florida Governor Leroy Collins and his son-in-law, along with another food company out of Miami, saw the potential of this venture—and encouraged us and partnered with us. They were just marvelous.

The Mahalia Jackson Food Products line did well, but again, not well enough for the business to grow in its early stages without outside help. Every aspect of wholesaling is plagued with pitfalls and roadblocks. You need a lot of money to begin a product line. You need money to buy advertisements to break into each new market. There was a need to convince local grocery store owners that Mahalia products would fly off their shelves. The manufacturers had to be convinced to stay with you long enough for the business to succeed. Finally, customers had to be convinced to purchase your products and to tell their friends and family about it. Ultimately, repeat business is essential in any sales operation. Without repeat business, you are dead in the water.

Some blacks had a tremendous amount of racial pride and would buy the products because they knew that blacks were involved. However, they were the exception. This experience was an eye-opener. I learned how to negotiate with manufacturers, distributors, suppliers, and local store managers. It did not sour me on blacks going into nontraditional businesses; it merely taught me that blacks have the right to fail at entrepreneurial ventures as well as whites if we are able to learn from those experiences. This experience merely strengthened my resolve to help others to find a way to make the system work for them. This is precisely what I did when I set up the NAACP's Fair Share Program, which opened doors and expanded opportunities for blacks to succeed.

We were optimistic in late 1968. It appeared as if things could not get any better. There was a lot of excitement. Crowds of customers were waiting in lines at Mahalia Jackson Chicken restaurants. Suppliers were delivering fresh chicken, paper supplies, cooking oil, and sundry other items. We trained hundreds of neighborhood residents in the art of food preparation and service. Our franchise was on a path of rapid growth. We were building additional stores and a headquarters building. We were building test kitchens and purchasing equipment and machinery. Stores were opening almost on a weekly basis.

If we were to continue along this track of expansion and repay some of the outstanding loans, we had to get an infusion of new capital. The tried-and-true way for a franchise to do this was through what is called an IPO, or initial public offering.

We got in touch with Kemmons Wilson and Wallace Johnson, who were the principals in the Memphis-based Holiday Inn hotel chain. They gave us invaluable advice on how to raise money for our franchise. They were very gracious to us, being of whatever assistance they could. We retained the services of a broker. We were in his office so often that some people thought we were employees of the firm. We had determined that we needed about $10 million to handle the debt and to deal with our immediate growth needs. We decided to go to the market with one million shares of Mahalia Jackson stock at $10 per share. This would yield $10 million before expenses were calculated.

This was the same path that Minnie Pearl and a number of other franchises had followed. There was no question in the minds of any of the financiers with whom we talked that selling one million shares of Mahalia Jackson Chicken System stock at $10 per share was feasible. At that point, our broker told us that he had a date set to go public. He warned us, however, that if the stock market, the Dow Jones average, fell below 700, it would not be a good time to go public. The stock market had to remain at 700 or above. Today, 700 looks so quaint, so minuscule.

I have no doubt in my mind that had we been successful with the stock market offering of $10 million and received the additional money to move forward, Mahalia would have been one of the biggest business success stories of the century. When the stock market fell below 700 and our public offering was postponed, then came the grueling, harrowing, excruciating, painful experience with the Hooker brothers and the Securities and Exchange Commission (SEC).

The Hooker brothers came under the scrutiny of the SEC because of the manner in which they handled the accounting for their franchise sales. The SEC began to question the accounting rules that allowed proceeds of sales of franchises to go directly to the bottom line and not be amortized over a period of years. Even though this was the rule, the SEC changed it. This change in the way money was allocated and accounted for caused many companies' income to drop precipitously. This was precisely what happened to Minnie Pearl. The stock market reacted violently. Eventually, shares of Minnie Pearl stock dropped from $66 to almost nothing. The stock certificates were only good for use as wallpaper.

The rise and the fall of Minnie Pearl, which by now was known as Performance System, was really more of a Wall Street phenomenon than a marketplace phenomenon. As far as most could detect, Minnie Pearl stores were still doing a booming business. Minnie Pearl Roast Beef restaurants had been opened, and the parent company had purchased the Orange Julius Company in Florida. The company had awesome plans for expansion. The reaction of the stock market caused creditors to become nervous. Lines of credit dried up. Vendors put the company on a cash basis. Supplies had to be paid for in advance of receipt. No company can withstand the loss of its creditworthy status and survive.

Prior to the Minnie Pearl difficulties, there was wide-scale speculation in the industry about which of the two major chicken giants would be the most successful, Colonel Sanders Chicken System, under the legendary direction of John Y. Brown, soon to be governor of Kentucky, or

Minnie Pearl Chicken System, under the direction of John Hooker, who wanted to be governor of Tennessee.

The SEC investigation could not have come at a more inopportune time. When the investigators came in, they demanded to see documents and wanted to interview John Hooker, and also Henry Hooker. From what I understand, it was a lot like an IRS audit. Meanwhile, with all that taking place on the business side of the Minnie Pearl system, the loss of expertise and undivided attention of its management was critical. The Hookers had to spend morning, noon, and night at the behest of the SEC investigators. The net result was that without the captain, the ship floundered. When Minnie Pearl went into bankruptcy, it was only a matter of time before Mahalia Jackson would follow. Minnie Pearl owned 49 percent of Mahalia Jackson.

Outwardly, the problems that Minnie Pearl faced had little effect on our business. Our stores were crowded, sales were increasing, we introduced new menus, and investors were expressing an interest in buying Minnie Pearl's interests in Mahalia Jackson. These potential investors were willing to pay a fair price. However, counsel advised the management of the Minnie Pearl team that its interest in Mahalia Jackson had to be sold at a hefty price to protect them from shareholders' lawsuits.

The fear was that if Mahalia was sold too cheaply and became a smashing success, stockholders would be in a good position to successfully pursue their claim of ineffective protection of the stockholders' interests. We were caught on the horns of a dilemma. The price tag for Mahalia stock set by Minnie Pearl was higher than prospective purchasers were willing to pay, even though a number of would-be purchasers were willing to pay a substantial price for the business. The same thing was true for the Mahalia Jackson Food Products venture. Again, although this business was doing well, because Minnie Pearl held a large percentage of shares in the company, the same obstacles had to be overcome.

Mahalia had the grave misfortune of operating two successful businesses that could not be sold. Neither the product nor the management was the problem. Had we been able to get an infusion of new capital, and if the stock market had remained above 700 for just a little while longer, Mahalia Jackson had the potential of being a phenomenal business success. But that was not to be.

Ultimately, the chicken system had to file for bankruptcy and the food product division ceased operation. This was a bitter pill for me to swallow. I saw the potential and knew that with a little luck we could have pulled it out. However, through the dark and difficult days, I never lost my courage, never gave up hope, and maintained my honesty and integrity. I am proud of the fact that through all of this, I was never accused of any act of dishonesty, deception, or abuse of any trust. I am a living witness that it is possible to walk through the valley of temporary defeat and still emerge as a victor. I had some sleepless nights and restless days. Some so-called friends whispered, "I told you so," and detractors jeered and laughed at my perceived failure.

The lesson that I learned from this experience was never to lose faith and never lose hope. Everybody wants victory, but there is a more important question that we must ask ourselves: Can you live with defeat? I am not suggesting that defeat should be a goal and should not be avoided where possible. I've been up and I've been down, but I can tell you that up is better. You live honorable and serenely through all that life has to offer if you maintain your integrity.

Many people we trained went on to become successful entrepreneurs in the fast-food industry. Some have even become millionaires. I run into some of the Mahalia Jackson workers from time to time. Almost without exception, they thank us for getting them started and for the training that made their success possible.

The Mahalia Jackson Chicken System came to an end. The signs came down, the stores closed, and the lights were extinguished. I have fond memories of this noble business effort. From time to time I run across some promotional paraphernalia or past one of the many beautiful buildings that we built. I do not spend time worrying about the "what ifs." Rather, I thank God for the privilege of helping hundreds of young men and women in getting their first job, and new hope.

Chapter 9

THE FEDERAL COMMUNICATIONS COMMISSION

Early one morning in 1972, Senator Howard Baker (R-TN) was on the phone saying, "It's an opportunity for you to become the first black commissioner of the Federal Communications Commission. I have been given the authority by President Nixon to select someone, a black, and I thought of you as the ideal person to fill it."

"Uh, no," I countered. "Thanks for thinking of me, but I don't think that's for me, not at this time."

"Well, it's an important appointment," Baker persisted, reluctant to give up on his pre-ordained choice, "and I think you should take some time and seriously think about it."

"Not now," I answered slowly, not wanting to tell him that, among other things, President Nixon just wasn't my cup of tea. "Not at this time, but thanks, anyway!" I hung up.

My wife, Frances, was curled up beside me. I thought she was sound asleep, one reason why I didn't want to prolong the conversation, not wanting to awaken her. But she stirred and asked, "Benny, who was that?" "Senator Baker," I replied, and told her what he had proposed. She sat straight up in the bed. Her movement was so abrupt, it startled me for a moment. "You get back on that phone right now, Ben Hooks! Call Senator Baker back and say yes!" Meekly, I picked up the phone and said, "Yes," a move that would bring radical changes in our lives for the next 25 years.

Recently, Senator Baker, in his plush suite of law offices on Pennsylvania Avenue in Washington, D.C., told a reporter he met me through George W. Lee, who was a lieutenant in World War I and who worked for Atlanta Life Insurance Company, one of America's premiere pioneering African-American firms. Baker said that it was not unusual for him, a white man, to meet and become friends with a black man in the rigidly segregated South. Said he: "I chose Ben because I knew him, thought highly of him, and felt he was the best man for the job. He would be one of the first blacks ever selected to any of the nine [at that time] powerful federal regulatory commissions that collectively had much to say about almost every phase of U.S. life."

The telephone conversation was the result of a particularly incendiary scene that took place earlier at the Senate Oversight Subcommittee hearing. Three white nominees to the Federal Communications Commission were being considered. William D. (Bill) Wright, president of Black Efforts for Soul in Television (BEST), interrupted the calm, orderly proceedings and demanded to know why no blacks were being considered for the post.

In the ensuing exchange, Pastore shouted that the committee does not nominate, but only holds hearings on nominees. Wright called him "a racist." Deeply hurt, Pastore, a white liberal, flashed his NAACP membership card, and, muttering, pointed to his other progressive bona fides. But Wright would not be consoled. He persisted, brashly declaring "you are not doing anything now" to promote equality, and vowed to hold the three white nominees hostage until the President nominated a black.

Hurriedly, Pastore, joined by Senator Baker, a ranking committee member, and Senator Percy, called on President Nixon concerning the problem. At any rate, Nixon gave Baker the go-ahead to rustle up a black for nomination consideration, and the rest is history. But Wright was the trigger. His stubborn refusal to back off the racist charge he hurled at the chairman and his adamant vow to hold the white nominees hostage until the committee received a black nominee resulted in my being selected by President Nixon, through Senator Baker. The fact is that even though Richard Wiley was nominated before me, he and I were recommended for confirmation on the same day by Senator Pastore's Committee.

The nomination sailed through without a ripple. I am glad I had the opportunity to thank Wright and the few other aggressive pioneer blacks, including Jim McCullough, the founding chairman of the National Black Media Coalition. Both men died prematurely. I often wonder today if the stress of their work, seeking to bring equality and justice in a stubbornly racist America, was not the causal factor. Pluria Marshall later became chairman of the coalition. He was extraordinarily successful in advancing the cause of minority ownership and participation. Throughout these years, a brilliant young lawyer, David Honig, has been at the forefront of change in the advancement of minority participation.

I repeat, without men like Howard Baker, the Civil Rights Movement would have been set back years, if indeed it could have remained viable at all. The pioneering, independent spirit of fair play and the old-fashioned Christian ethic of *do unto others as you would have them do unto you* were the life-giving mix in air and soil that nurtured these hardy men—transforming them into a different breed of white southerner who helped pave the way to a more civilized and humane South. Frances continues to be his highly articulate vocal supporter.

When I arrived on the scene in August 1972, so much needed to be done to bring a semblance of justice and racial equity to the powerful Commission and the vast industry it regulates by the authority of Congress in the interest, convenience, and necessity of the American public. The average American, if he or she thinks about it at all, probably assumes the priceless telecommunications spectra are owned by the giants, AT&T, MCI, Sprint, Bell Atlantic, and other spinoffs of Ma Bell, which was broken up over my and several other commissioners' strong objections in the 1970s, and by the individual owners of cable TV stations and satellite and wireless entities. This unsuspecting public will click on their TV or radio sets or pick up their cellular phones, perhaps in the mindless belief that the corporate and independent networks, and individual radio and TV station and cell phone owners, have carved out a huge chunk of the spectra, and now it is theirs to keep without accountability or public sass forever and ever, Amen.

Nonsense. Although it seems to work out that way in day-to-day and year-to-year practice, these priceless spectra are actually leased by our government to these entities for specific periods of time and under strict congressional regulation. Congress assigned the Federal Communications Commission as the watchdog regulating oversight, granting operating licenses to corporate groups and individuals to operate in the aforesaid interest, convenience, and necessity of the general public for specified periods of time—now eight or nine years, but only three to five years when I was on the Commission.

Radio, TV, and cable owners do not like license renewal time. The Commission has the power to probe into their behavior—personal, broadcast, fiduciary, employment, the works—checking their responsibility and accountability quotient. This the Commission can do anytime. But at license renewal time the licensee feels especially vulnerable. For even the FCC's perfunctory questions bearing on the licensee's past behavior can make the nervous licensee squirm. Licensees know that these can lead to questions serious enough to invoke suspension or revocation of the license.

Actually, the FCC seldom goes that far. Most licenses are renewed pro forma. It becomes an issue only when a public act captures the attention of the FCC or when someone brings a serious allegation in the licensing process. Then the licensee is subject to close questioning and a possible hearing on whether the license should be renewed, suspended, or canceled, or whether some lesser summary judgment such as a fine should be levied.

Common carriers, telephone and cable, are under the same regulations. I remember how swamped that understaffed FCC division was when AT&T, the telephone mega-giant at that time, had to come in for a hearing. AT&T would back up trailer-trucks loaded with records, purposely inundating the thin little crew of a score of lawyers in the Common Carrier Bureau. "Now sweat over this," they malevolently hissed at the beleaguered crew. It was payback time for the giant phone company against the bureau that had harassed them for months for relevant contested records. Overkill? Blatantly so. But what could the understaffed Fed do against this 900-pound gorilla? Gamesmanship—life was ever thus at the Commission.

Over-the-air broadcast communications has roughly followed the path of Hollywood filmmaking. That is, both media have been fueled by abject and cultural racism. Hollywood was founded with the infamous 1915 D. W. Griffith paean to the Knights of the Ku Klux Klan, *Birth of a Nation*, a masterpiece in technical filmmaking but a vile, malicious story that grossly maligned black people and glorified that murderous, terrorist, white supremacist organization, the KKK.

Hollywood continued from that odious point for more than 50 years, depicting blacks largely as mammies, maids, buffoons, Toms, clowns, morons—foot-shuffling, head-scratching, "yassuh boss!" menials, or maniacal lawbreakers. A visitor from Mars, viewing those early Hollywood films, would conclude that a black person was not of much human worth.

News and cultural broadcasting were designed to continue this badly skewed and highly biased hegemony. Nationally, blacks owned only 13 of the thousands of AM radio stations in the U.S. and not a single highly desirable FM station. The same was true for VHF (Very High Frequency) TV stations, the lucrative broadcast property that, if you owned one, was a literal money-making machine. UHF (Ultra High Frequency), higher on the broadcast band, was on the scene but not used much at that time except for education or public broadcast.

Blacks owned not a single TV broadcast license, VHF and UHF when I started with the Commission. While I was there, the FCC succeeded in allocating two UHF television stations to blacks, the Howard University station in Washington, D.C., and Channel 50 in Detroit, Michigan. But for the most part, black thinking on that radar screen was not developed enough at that time to comprehend the beneficial ramifications of vying for such TV ownerships.

A few blacks—Skip Finley, Ragan Henry, Percy Sutton, Eugene Jackson, Dorothy Brunson, Kathy Hughes, Dr. Bell, Art Gilliam, A.G. Gaston, John Johnson, and a few others—managed to acquire properties and enter this lucrative field. Of course, they were unable to secure the highest prize, a VHF TV station—not at the outset, certainly. A few years later, when the Commission voted to permit a VHF TV franchisee to gain a substantial tax break if the station were sold under distress conditions to a minority, some blacks were able to quickly acquire these coveted franchises. Robert Johnson was able to enter the lucrative field of cable TV programming.

The priceless telecommunications spectrum had been gobbled up by astute white concerns—first under the pioneering old Radio Communications Act of 1927, and later under the greatly amended 1934 Federal Communications Act that established the FCC by an Act of Congress and charged it with regulating interstate and international communications by radio, television, wire, satellite, and cable.

I mentioned earlier that when I arrived at the FCC in August 1972, the racial landscape was pretty bleak. This was not a casual observation. In preparing to take my seat on the Commission, I had read and absorbed mountains of communications and FCC material. I was determined not to be the dullest knife in the drawer. Indeed, I wanted to be well informed on issues confronting the Commission and ready to jump in and help resolve some of them in a timely and equitable fashion.

However, after a few days on the job, I began to open my eyes. I was already beginning to see that my task on the Commission, like it or not, was going to be confronting and trying to right some of the historic wrongs involving race and gender that the Commission and the industry it regulates had perpetuated for so very, very long. A monumental task, indeed! And one that I would not wish on my worst enemy.

These were nice people, my fellow commissioners. They were cordial and friendly to me in every way. They were easy to talk with, as easy as with, say, black folks—sometimes easier than with some black people. My skin color did not seem to matter at all. But injustice was here, no matter how smoothly, cordially, or gently it was covered up. And I had to confront it, no matter how distasteful. That was my mission. That was why I was there.

As a minister and a lawyer, I felt I would be able to bring to the Commission not only legal skills in problem solving, but also the overarching transcendental dimension that makes for spiritual unity and healing. As the first black member of one of our powerful federal regulatory commissions, I represented, like it or not, a strong cultural and racial shift in policy positions, if not fundamental racial attitudes in this country. I was representing these shifts, yes, but that did not mean actual change would be taking place soon. That would have to be fought and bled for.

The FCC was, after all, just a small chunk of vast continental America. It faithfully reflected its racism and virtues. Not only were there few black radio station owners, and no black ownership of TV, VHF and UHF or cable licenses, but the personnel policy of this Commission was embarrassingly racist. Of the more than 2,200 FCC employees (300 lawyers and 200 engineers), only three lawyers and two engineers were black, and the rest were mired in the lowest of job ratings. This meant that few if any were in supervisory or management positions.

With the concurrence of my fellow commissioners and before I left, we employed 70 black lawyers and several black engineers. It is one of the joys in my life now to meet Patricia Russell McLeod, J. Clay Smith, Clarence McKee, Tom Johnson, and other black lawyers and engineers hired during my tenure. It is also no accident that one of the most outstanding black business people, the first black billionaire, should come out of the ranks of telecommunications. Bob Johnson, owner of Black Entertainment Television, was an enterprising, dedicated, hardworking, successful staffer at the National Cable Association when I came to the Commission. In our respective capacities, we met quite often, and I found him to be sincere and well informed. Having watched him in those days, I am not surprised that he has become one of the most successful business persons we have produced.

The bad part of this equation was that I was entering a situation that was just as racist as any other in the United States. The good part was that I was selected to enter it at all, and thus there might be reason to hope for change, however forlorn that hope might be. So when I arrived, my thoughts were a mixed blend of hope and despair. Hope that, because I was selected to be there as the Commission deliberated timely issues, I might be able to correct some wrongs, but despair at finding barefaced racism staring me in the face.

As a Christian minister of the Gospel, I felt certain that I was bringing to the Commission an added dimension: a moral imperative to do the right thing. As a black man, I had the additional motivation—no, the mandated mission and determination—to seek to change historic racial policies and, hopefully, the attitudes from which these policies spring. My arrival was quiet, almost circumspect, even though I was armed with the determination to do justice and, in so doing, serve the best interests of mankind and the highest demands of my Lord.

What I hoped to bring to the FCC, then, was the quiet moral authority of the Christian, the urgent focus of the black man, and the persuasive articulation of a seasoned lawyer who had received more than his share of hugs and hisses in our turbulent, often treacherous society.

Because I was the newest commissioner, Chairman Dean Burch, with the concurrence of my fellow commissioners, designated me as the "back-logs" commissioner. Simultaneously, he targeted me as the internal and external EEO commissioner. The late Dean Burch, a lean, gently intro-spective man from the Midwest, often with a bemused twinkle of eye, was not acting in a Simon Legree fashion. He simply felt, I do believe, that the opportunity and the man, in my person, ideally converged. Anyway, some-body had to do the dirty work, so . . . !

In the backlogs mandate, I was given the onerous task of digging back into all the old unresolved cases, tangled legal disputes, and unanswered queries, which were voluminous, to say the least, and try to bring some order—indeed, some resolution—to it all. When you consider that the FCC in a "normal" year receives hundreds of thousands of inquiries regard-ing a new telephone regulation alone, you begin to get some notion of what I was confronted with. Then there were the hundreds of license re-newals; myriad questions regarding cable acquisitions; and issues regarding the fairness doctrine, which mandated that a station, having broadcast an issue of compelling public importance, must then provide ample time for the presentation of a contrasting view. It was also an issue that was a pain in the backsides of a number of licensees, who felt and loudly expressed that they could do without it very well, thank you!

This issue is distinctly different from the Equal-Time Provision, which is an act of Congress and deals with allowing qualified presidential candi-dates opportunities to debate. Some presidential hopefuls, especially those in the forefront, also think this ruling is a pain in the you-know-where and wished we would abolish it.

When I arrived at the FCC in 1972, microwave appliances were begin-ning to appear on the scene in mounting numbers, in some quarters raising public fears of emission safety. Microwave, of course, is part of that grand, sweeping, largely invisible electro-magnetic spectrum that provides radio and TV frequencies—Ultra Hi Fi, AM and FM, Marine, cellular, and microwave bands. The FCC, as spectra regulator, came immediately under scrutiny, and we were assailed with concerned queries over whether these wonderful new appliances that made food warming and cooking so easy were indeed safe to use or a distinct threat to the nation's health.

Cable, too, was beginning to come into its own. The core issues were anti-siphoning—stealing broadcast programming without compensation and determining the adverse impact, if any, of cable intrusion into established broadcast market areas of traditional TV. Cable screamed that FCC regulations were biased. It said cable always had to prove upon entering broadcast markets that it did not adversely affect that market, while no such up-front demands were made of new TV entering cable broadcast markets.

Much of the accumulated backlog, of course, had to do with numbers, cascading incoming inquiries, filings, etc., that just overwhelmed the understaffed agency. For example, minority queries beginning in the turbulent civil rights 1960s and escalating in the 1970s sought to increase or enhance broadcast programming that, for the most part, had all but ignored them.

Minorities and Public Television: An Appraisal, by a Ford Foundation-funded Advisory Panel on Minorities and Public TV, found that *Soul!* and *Black Journal* were the only two televised programs on public television that provided a forum solely for blacks to display their talent and their expertise on matters of interest to the black community. The two programs together totaled only an hour and a half a week. The panel added, "The merits of the two programs aside, *Soul!* and *Black Journal* cannot realistically be expected to do the entire job of presenting the black perspective. Attempting to make them the sole voice of the black minority distorts the real world." The report praised public television for its emphasis on local issues "that has resulted in an increased appetite on the part of these viewers . . . whetted by public television policies. . . . " "Nevertheless," it added, "the present form and content of non-commercial television must be reevaluated and restructured if it is to realize its potential. Public television is a public service institution supported principally by government funds; therefore, its obligations are similar to those of such other public institutions as universities and public schools. The obligation of public television is to help extend equal educational opportunities to all segments of the public. Indeed, the profound impact of television gives this medium a greater opportunity to bring education and intellectual stimulation to segments of the population that have long suffered from educational neglect. . . . Insensitive programming has the potential of subtly reinforcing negative attitudes that are all too frequently found in this society."

The report concluded that "public television fails to provide adolescents with the sort of information that is most important to their immediate concerns" and emphasized that public television must also beef up its programming to other minorities—to Hispanics, Asians, Native Americans, the elderly and infirm, and, yes, to women.

I quoted this October 1973 report compiled by a group headed by the late Robert C. Maynard, a black *Washington Post* associate editor and ombudsman, at length because it seems to me that 30 years later so much of it is still relevant and applicable to television broadcasting in general, and public broadcasting in particular. There is still much to do to make this medium live up to its promise of presenting meaningful program diversity.

My mind wanders back to my early years in Memphis. Folks of my generation, born before and growing up in the Great Depression years, did not enjoy the luxury of TV. Back in those days, talk of coming TV, in which pictures taken in London, Shanghai, and Nairobi could be shown simultaneously on a box screen in your living room, was so much "superman" talk.

We were brought up on radio: *Gangbusters, The Shadow, Amos n' Andy,* and *Beulah.* The last two were just about the only programming, until Jack Benny and Rochester came along, presented with the black listening public in mind. Humiliating fare? Yes! And yes again! But we laughed at it and with it, sometimes in loud guffaws to keep from crying. We were so completely stripped of human worth, so used to doors of opportunity of all kinds leading to lives of substance and dignity being rudely slammed daily in our faces, as Dr. W.E.B. DuBois so graphically described in his searing *Souls of Black Folks,* "So pummeled by hate and raw segregation were we, that we became numb, almost impervious to insidious insult, loud curses and abuse!"

As I stood observing my fellow commissioners, for some reason, Dr. Martin Luther King, Jr.'s famous Letter from the Birmingham Jail surfaced in my mind. This assembly of commissioners was, in so many ways, composed of fine people individually. They were folks you wouldn't be ashamed to call friend or have live next door in your neighborhood. There was no demonstrable meanness or racial hate manifested in any of them. They all appeared to be, indeed, God-fearing, hardworking, honest Americans sincerely believing they were daily doing the right thing.

A passionately caring man and a devout Christian, King had time to ponder and reply at length to the charges in his famous letter "To My Dear Fellow Clergymen" who had questioned King's civil rights crusade in the city of Birmingham, calling it "unwise and untimely." King said he was in Birmingham because "injustice is here." He said, "I must make two honest confessions to you, my Christian and Jewish brothers. First, I must confess that over the years I have been gravely disappointed with the white moderate. Shallow understanding from people of good will is more frustrating than absolute misunderstanding from people of ill will. Lukewarm acceptance is much more bewildering than outright rejection. The Negro's great stumbling block in his stride to freedom is not the White Citizens Council or the Ku Klux Klansmen, but the white moderate who is more devoted to order than to justice; who prefers a negative peace, which is the absence of tension, to a positive peace, which is the presence of justice; who constantly says, I agree with you in the goal you seek, but I cannot agree with your methods of direct action."

Actually, he declared, "time itself is neutral; it can be used either destructively or constructively. More and more I feel that the people of ill will have used time more effectively than have people of good will." For years, he continued, "I have heard the word 'wait.' This 'wait' has almost always meant 'never'! We must come to see, with one of our distinguished jurists, that 'justice delayed is justice denied'!"

King said his second major disappointment was, with some notable exceptions, the white church and its leadership. "When I was suddenly catapulted into the leadership of the bus boycott in Montgomery, Alabama, a few years ago, I felt the white ministers, priests, and rabbis would be among our strongest allies. Instead, some have been outright opponents, refusing to understand the freedom movement and misrepresenting its leaders; all too many others have been more cautious than courageous and have remained silent behind the anesthetizing security of stained glass windows! Perhaps I must turn my faith to the inner spiritual church, the church within the church . . . !"

In one of his most moving passages, Dr. King continued: "I have traveled the length and breadth of Alabama, Mississippi, and all the other southern states. On sweltering summer days and crisp autumn mornings, I have looked at the South's beautiful churches with their lofty spires pointing heavenward. I have beheld the impressive outlines of her religious education buildings. Over and over I have found myself asking: 'What kind of people worship here? Who is their God?' Where were their voices when the lips of Governor Barnett dripped with the words of interposition and nullification? Where were they when Governor Wallace gave a clarion call for defiance and hatred?' In deep disappointment I have wept over the laxity of the church. But be assured that my tears have been tears of love. There can be no deep disappointment where there is not deep love." Finally, among Dr. King's more trenchant observations, he noted, "Lamentably, it is an historical fact that privileged groups seldom give up their privileges voluntarily. Individuals may see the moral light and voluntarily give up their unjust posture, but as Reinhold Niebuhr has reminded us, groups tend to be more immoral than individuals."

I gasped when I opened my eyes and looked again at my fellow commissioners. They are simply human, like me. Like all of us—part saint, part sinner, sometimes separate, sometimes all at once. This is America—the home of the free and the brave, where all men are created equal (except to the founding fathers, who ruled black people as "three fifths of a human being"). America's faults are our faults. Its virtues are also ours.

Being the first black person selected to sit on the Federal Communications Commission, while a signal honor, was simply among a number of firsts for my family and me. After all, my forebears were the first blacks in the post-Reconstruction era to establish a going business in the state of Tennessee. I had already been honored with several "firsts" in Memphis. In 1961, I was appointed the first black assistant public defender in Shelby County, Tennessee. This was followed by another first, my appointment in 1964 to a judgeship in the county's Criminal Court. So with all this, I wear being "first" like the purple raiment of an ancient Egyptian monarch, proudly, comfortably, without swagger or braggadocio.

Equal Employment Opportunity Commissioner at the FCC

In 1975, I wrote an extensive piece for *Television Age* magazine. Because so much of it seems relevant to today's problems in the broadcast/communications arena, I want to quote from it:

> Employment of minorities, a large percentage of whom are black, increased substantially in 1974, from 11 percent to 12 percent of the full-time work force (according to a December 1974 report by the United Church of Christ's Office of Communications).

The United Church of Christ, Office of Communication, under the then-director Dr. Everett C. Parker, was an unquestioned authority in the field, and this was its third annual study of employment in television. This study, conducted by Dr. Ralph M. Jennings, associate director of the Office of Communications, was eagerly anticipated. The study was based on 1974 employment reports (form 395) filed with the FCC by 613 television stations then employing 41,087 persons full-time and 4,028 part-time, a total of 45,115, up from 44,692 in 1973.

Well, I mused, so far so good! As the Equal Employment Opportunity commissioner of the FCC, I was heartened by such gains. This marked progress. But why cite a United Church of Christ report? Where were the FCC's figures? That was the crucial point. Up until that point, FCC employment figures were a sometime thing. They represented the rather casual indifference the FCC displayed at license renewal times in demanding an exact accounting of the licensee's personnel with respect to determining whether equal employment opportunities were present or lacking in its workplace.

But the FCC shouldn't take all the blame. The responsibility goes higher—to the congressional oversight committees that didn't give a fiddler's fig for equal employment or any kind of justice and equity in the workplace, save for the protection of the feudal domination by white American males. The oversight committees were and are dominated by white American males, ergo the need to go outside to a responsible civil rights organization for an honest accounting of FCC licensees' employment figures.

Even today, federal agencies are indifferent to conditions of inequity and unfairness in the workplace almost to the point of criminality. Recently I was told that a number of black employees of several federal agencies, including the Department of Agriculture, the Social Security Administration, and the Internal Revenue Service, to name a few, showed up at a Capital Press Club (the oldest black press club in America) meeting and complained about conditions of inequality that stubbornly persist in their workplaces. But if Congress is indifferent and makes no demands in this area, it is understandable why the federal agencies are indifferent as well.

Said one particular spokesman from IRS: "The senior officials (all of whom are white) turn a deaf ear. They don't give a damn about our complaints. This is not like in the private corporate sector, where the bosses, with their eyes on the financial bottom line, have to respond to public concerns. The Feds don't particularly care about the public. They have no bottom line to worry about, like the corporate officials do."

The FCC heard no complaint from Capitol Hill urging acquisition of exact (or, for that matter, any kind of) broadcast licensee employment figures at renewal time, so it was business as it has been since the old 1927 Radio Commission was formed. This sluggish indifference bordering on hostility to equal rights permeates the broad body politic of America.

Absent a directive from congressional oversight committees, the FCC continued on its blissfully indifferent ways in dealing with the licensees they have a mandate to regulate fully in the public interest. So to me, the United Church of Christ report was a godsend. It stated: "The most encouraging fact about employment trends in television is the fact that between 1973 and 1974 the number of minority employees added was greater than the total of new employees, and the number of women added was also greater than the total." The report added, optimistically, "It seems that commercial television stations are replacing whites and men who leave employment with women and minority people!"

Ah, but there is a catch—as there always is in matters dealing with race. I asked, in what positions are these new employees placed? Although the report declared "startling increase(s) in upper-level jobs for minorities and women and the decline in clerical and service positions," this very fact raised the red flag of caution in the eyes of investigators. "Do more executives need fewer clerks to serve them? Do larger staffs need less janitorial service? It would be irresponsible not to raise the question: Are some broadcasters reclassifying low-level workers into upper job categories while keeping them in the same old jobs at the same low salaries?," the report asked.

As the FCC's EEO Commissioner and simply as a human being, as one of God's creatures and as an American citizen, such questions disturb me, for suggestions of similar designs from various quarters have reached my ears in recent months. I have suggested that improved employment reporting forms would enable the Commission to secure a clearer picture of a station's hiring and upgrading practices. The Church of Christ study also pointed out that despite improvements in overall employment, many broadcast stations still discriminate or fail to comply with broad standards of fair employment.

In 1974, for example, 674 commercial stations "filed employment reports." Of these, 131 stations (20 percent) reported no minority group members on their full-time staffs and 175 (27 percent) had none in the upper four categories. There were six stations with no women employees in the upper four job categories. Fifty-one stations (8 percent) had no women and no minority group members in the upper four job categories: officials and managers, professional technicians, and sales workers.

Conditions were as bad or worse at noncommercial stations: "In 1974, 36 (27 percent) had no women and no minority group members on their full-time staffs. Forty-nine (37 percent) had no minority group members in the upper three categories. Eight stations (6 percent) had no women on their full-time staffs and 21 (16 percent) reported none in the upper three categories. Eighteen stations (14 percent) reported no women and no minorities in the upper three job categories." (Noncommercial stations do not employ in sales.)

The principle of equal opportunity had been with us at this time for 32 years! Almost a quarter of a century before the enactment of the Civil Rights Act of 1964, with its Title VII (prohibiting racial discrimination in employment), the principle became public policy of the United States when President Franklin Delano Roosevelt in 1940, responding to a threatened march by blacks on Washington for wartime jobs, issued Executive Order 8802 establishing the first Federal Fair Employment Practice Commission. When Congress got around to establishing the EEO in the mid-late Sixties, a distinguished African American, Clifford L. Alexander, Jr., was appointed by President Lyndon Baines Johnson to be its first executive director. Alexander, by the way, was appointed America's first black secretary of the army by President Jimmy Carter in 1977, and Alexander was instrumental in pushing the promotions of a number of black officers to the rank of general, including then-Lieutenant Colonel Colin Powell, a bright young black official working at that time at the White House. In both positions, Alexander expanded opportunities for women and minorities and added luster to his own political and professional persona.

Prior to the issuing of Executive Order 8802 and Title VII through court decrees and judicial opinions based on various amendments to the Constitution prohibiting racial discrimination by agencies of the government, the earliest civil rights law (of 1869) had been studiously ignored by our government and its agencies, including the FCC.

Herbert Hill, former national labor director for the National Association for the Advancement of Colored People, who also taught at the New School for Social Research in New York until his retirement, pointed out: "When the Civil Rights Act of 1964 was enacted by Congress, more than 20 million employees already had the theoretical protection of a federal prohibition against job discrimination based on nondiscrimination clauses in all U.S. government contracts. These contractual provisions established that those seeking to do business with the federal government must not engage in job discrimination because of race, creed or national origin. Since 1941, the basis for enforcement of these provisions has been contract cancellation, but in the entire 33-year period this sanction has very rarely been imposed."

Just the mention of the phrases "equal employment opportunity" and "affirmative action plan" could and did (at that time) cause consternation among many licensees (as it does among so many white Americans today). How, they ask, can we implement this plan? Will it cause dislocation in our shop? Where do you find qualified blacks, American Indians, Asian

Americans, Spanish-speaking people, even women to do the job you want done? This is just adding to the burden of paperwork and disturbing our status quo, while the Commission is not really serious about implementing the plan, so who needs it? The questions seemed to project an intractability on the part of the licensees—a stubborn refusal to tackle a problem that admittedly, on its face, is tough and not prone to easy solutions. However, the questions often are honest: Where in the world would the licensees, who have no dealings with these people, go to find them? Certainly no blacks, Asians, American Indians, or even women served as equals in their shops; hence, they were not to be found on their radar screens. The FCC, like other federal agencies, indeed, like the rest of white America, besides mouthing a few general platitudes on the subject, had not demonstrated evidence of being very serious about extending equal employment opportunity to this broad affected class.

But there I was, the embodiment of FCC and its new stance on EEO. I strongly felt that the Commission was definitely interested in seeing that its EEO Affirmative Action program was carried out fully. We had no choice, I reasoned, for equal opportunities for all are part and parcel of our Constitution, and this includes job opportunities. My face flushed, my heart beat faster, my spine tingled. I was proud to be an American and felt that its undergirding constitutional guarantees were worthy and exalting. There is no problem of a human nature that we cannot overcome, if we so will it.

The complaints of job discrimination are not expressions of an aberration but manifestations of widespread, general, and institutional racism that prevents blacks, other minorities, and women from acquiring jobs or, once having acquired them, from upward mobility. It seems to me that much of the failure of equal employment efforts of the past has been due, unfortunately, to the fact they have been confined to "voluntarism." In our free society, "voluntarism" is a heady thing when considered abstractly. Specifically, especially as it applies to equal employment opportunities, it has been a disaster. Since many proclaim that "voluntarism" is the best way, and few in a position to make affirmative action really work seem to have employed it, EEO agencies to a large extent had deteriorated into passive, complaint-taking entities that do little more than pay lip service to the principle, until Title VII of the Civil Rights Act was enacted and became effective on July 2, 1965. It is doing more than all before it to combat bias.

In the Fifth Circuit Court of Appeals, in *Culpepper v. Reynolds Metal,* the court affirmed: "Title VII . . . provides us with a clear mandate from Congress that no longer will the United States tolerate this form of discrimination. It is, therefore, the duty of the courts to make sure the act works. . ." (421 F.2d 888-89). Voluntarism was out the window; legally enforced sanctions were in!

Herbert Hill, however, felt that "inexperienced . . . timid bureaucrats appointed for short terms and subject to political and budget pressures from . . . congressional committees and private interest groups have left the making of basic Title VII law to the federal judges who are appointed for life."

In some respects, I felt he was right. But it is a fact that until the Equal Employment Opportunity Commission was given the mandate to initiate court action in job discrimination cases, most corrective action was left to frustrating and ineffective "voluntarism." Implementing the Commission's EEO Affirmative Action plans should not be troublesome to the broadcasters, I reasoned. Soon the FCC will approve EEO guidelines that will instruct our licensees generally. Blacks and other minorities and women must be hired and upgraded on a basis of equality, no ifs, ands, or buts! Finding members of such minority and women groups should pose no insurmountable problems for the licensees. The FCC does not insist, as the pious foes of "quotas" say, that the broadcaster hire, say, 51 percent blacks, if that is their percentage ratio in the community of license. It only says the broadcaster should initiate Affirmative Action plans that lead to fair hiring of all, regardless of race, creed, gender, or color. Finding qualified blacks, Spanish-speaking people, Indian Americans, Asian Americans, and women will be hard, of course. But it is also hard to find qualified white people. So your hunting ground is expanded. Minorities and women are trainable, just as whites, and should be considered in this context.

The hypocrisy of those who cry "reverse discrimination"—the foes of so-called quotas—was pointed out succinctly during that time by two national columnists, one white, one black. Said black columnist Carl Rowan: "Qualifications always have been subjective, with whites making all the rules and all the decisions. In any event, when race has been the dominant factor in handing out good jobs in Alabama for two centuries, how is it that some people start preaching about 'merit' only after the judge decides that extraordinary measures are needed to give blacks a decent break? Even a philosopher ought to be enough in touch with reality to know that 'merits' of women or blacks or Chicanos or Puerto Ricans are not the basic issue. It is the pragmatic reality that what white males have, white males are not going to surrender except under extraordinary pressures!"

Rowan insisted that "I will not defend a rigid quota system" in the area of jobs or academic (school) selection. "Common sense," he says, "should be the watchword." White New York columnist Tom Wicker said: "White males once shut out women and minorities . . . in a deliberate, systematic, discriminatory manner. It cannot be said that white males now are being shut out in anything remotely resembling the same manner or approaching the same numbers. That they must share the opportunity of access to these institutions (education, in this case) and compete fairly for that access is not 'racism in reverse,' or sexism in reverse, but simple justice long overdue."

As a black who has had personal experiences with joblessness and underemployment, I feel most strongly about affirmative action. I know that loss of a job, no matter how lowly the employment, can be a devastating blow to the have-nots. Living with the fear of unemployment and struggling along on jobs where you are underemployed can be like a gnawing tapeworm in the gut. The sense of hopelessness, of worthlessness, is shattering, and when this turns inward, two things can happen: A person settles into a torpor from which he or she may never arouse, or that person experiences rage so intense that only violent acts—mugging, assaulting, breaking and entering, and maybe killing—can damp down the fury.

That year (1974), we adopted an EEO Program and Affirmative Action Plan for fiscal year 1975 for our internal agency. Both Chairman (Richard E.) Wiley and I attached covering memoranda urging full support and implementation of the plan. It was hoped that our EEO Plan for the industries we regulated would be issued soon. Because regulatory agencies such as ours are empowered to confer a privilege (the awarding of a contract—in our case, license), we are in violation of our mandate if we allow discrimination to occur. In other words, if we do not enforce anti–job discriminatory laws, we can be prosecuted ourselves!

This is a terrible thought. It is unthinkable that any agency, when its duty is clear, would fail to enforce the laws of the land. U.S. prosecution of such an agency would be exposure of its egregious failure to live up to the highest principle of its mandate. But that would never happen to us! We felt a glowing pride. We at the FCC were unanimously of one mind in terms of EEO and Affirmative Action. The U.S. Supreme Court, the President, and the Congress had all decreed that equal employment opportunity is the law and goal of our land. The U.S. Civil Service had certified it, and it had the backing of federal enforcement agencies like the Equal Employment Opportunity Commission and the Department of Justice.

In addition, we believed that this country could not remain a great nation if it denies job opportunities to minorities, to blacks, to women—or, once hired, if it denies them the freedom of upward mobility. We did not believe this country could be one thing for one group or race and an entirely different thing for others if it were to remain powerful and free. It must be for all or for none. As a man stated with disarming candor on TV recently, "If you have a cat, you don't clean out the litter box halfway. If you do, you still have a stink!"

With the set eyes of true believers, we seven commissioners thus turned to the future and confidently asked the general public to "Join us at the FCC and make the American dream a living reality for all Americans. It's good business, too," we proudly added!

Working with Commissioner Wiley was an interesting experience. He was a hard-working, hard-driving chairman. He gave his best and sought the best from his commissioners. I enjoyed working with him and all the other commissioners during my tenure. I got a particular kick out of working with Commissioner Lee and Commissioner Quello. I learned much from both of them. During my tenure, the commissioners and spouses got to-gether on a regular social basis after hours. Frances got along extremely well with the group and they enjoyed very much coming to our house. Even now, I delight in chatting with Quello and Wiley and their wives. Since the Commission, Wiley has built the most successful telecommunications law firm in the country.

During my service, I had an excellent staff—Doris Coles, Bessie Canty, Chester Higgins, Al Baxter, Norman Blumenthal, and, later, Clarence McKee. Norman, a brilliant lawyer, and I spent countless hours together arguing and discussing the work at the Commission. His wife, Sally, and Frances became good friends and often had to intercede in our verbal discussions, which tended to become quite vociferous. We are the god-parents of their daughter, Jeri. The first six commissioners with whom I served were Robert Lee, Rex Lee, Nicholas Johnson, Charlotte Reid, Richard Wiley, and Dean Burch. On every major issue involving minori-ties during our tenure, the vote was 7-0. This was a remarkable time for progress of minorities at the FCC. In many, many ways, that trend has continued.

I am grateful that since I left the FCC, there has been a continuous black presence on the Commission, including Tyrone Brown, Andrew Barrett, William Kennard—the first black chair—and current chairman Michael Powell.

Chapter 10
THE DECISION

I was serving as a member of the Federal Communications Commission and living in Washington, D.C., in 1973. My days were loaded with a myriad of activities: attending a variety of briefings, reading briefs and petitions, meeting with representatives of varied interest groups, and going to a never-ending series of luncheons and receptions on Capitol Hill.

As the only black on the Federal Communications Commission (FCC), it was important to me that I attend to every detail, regardless of how minor it might have appeared. I made a point of dotting every "i" and crossing every "t." The other commissioners were also focused on their responsibilities, but I could remember the stern admonishment of my parents: "You must be twice as good as any white person to have the same opportunity." In a real sense, sometimes it felt like I was carrying the entire burden of the race on my shoulders. Any perceived shortcoming would reflect not just on my fitness to serve, but on the entire race. Being the first has many advantages, but it is also weighted with unseen burdens.

I was serving as pastor-on-leave of Middle Baptist Church in Memphis and Mt. Moriah Baptist Church in Detroit. Every weekend I would leave Washington National Airport and commute to one of the two cities. I tried to be at each church twice a month, leaving an able assistant in charge on the Sundays that I would not be present. It was through these weekend visits that I kept my civil rights iron in the fire. When I arrived in Memphis, I would get in touch with Jesse Turner and Maxine Smith. Jesse was treasurer of the National NAACP. He was a breathing

NAACP legend in Memphis. He was also president of the Tri-State Bank, the only black bank in the city.

Maxine Smith was the executive secretary of the Memphis branch. She was a dynamic, uncompromising, and multi-talented leader. Maxine had been an educator who took over the day-to-day activities of the Memphis branch of the NAACP in the 1960s. My conversations with them would go on well into the night. Jesse was a Joe Friday, a "just the facts" person. He would give me an update in a staccato, machine gun-like fashion. Maxine, on the other hand, would fill in all of the details, the color—who was at the meeting, what each had to say—and the reactions of the powers that be to what had been said or done.

While in Detroit, I would talk to a number of activists and NAACP local and national leaders. The Memphis branch was the second largest in the nation. There were four national branch members from Detroit. The Detroit branch was also the largest NAACP unit in the country. Both branches had an enormous pool of talented and well-connected individuals. There were many judges, lawyers, union leaders, local politicians, corporate executives, physicians, educators, ministers, and others who were engaged in civil rights and the NAACP.

I would offer advice and participate in strategy sessions in both cities. This was an important personal oasis for me. It kept me in touch with the civil rights community in an ongoing way. Therefore, the invitation to speak on Youth Night at the 1973 Annual Convention of the NAACP may have come from any number of individuals.

In the 1970s, the NAACP National Convention was the most important meeting held in the black community. It might have been that my name surfaced at a convention planning meeting or at a senior staff meeting because of my position on the FCC. In any event, the letter of invitation was sent, signed by Roy Wilkins. Doris Coles, who served as my personal assistant, filed the invitation along with many others, to be dealt with later. I was receiving no fewer than 35 speaking invitations a week from a variety of organizations; I could not honor them all. Doris and I would go over the invitations once or twice a week, and I would decide which I wanted to accept.

When I read the invitation to speak on a Wednesday night, my first reaction was to turn it down. First, the convention was being held in Indianapolis, which is not the easiest place to get to. Next, the engagement was in the middle of the week. This would mean that I would have to lose almost two full days from the office. I was very careful not to give anyone at the FCC grounds to criticize my commitment to my Commission responsibilities.

Nonetheless, when I thought of my NAACP friends and my commitment to the organization and the struggle for civil rights, I decided to accept the invitation. After all, if it had not been for the work of the NAACP, there would have been no blacks on the Commission. What better forum to address than those young people who were being molded and shaped by veterans of the NAACP like Jesse Turner, Tom Turner, Bill Lucy, Clarence Mitchell, Enolia McMillan, Hazel Dukes, Maxine Smith, and others?

Doris called the National Office and accepted the invitation for me. She then sent a letter setting forth my travel schedule. During the time between agreeing to speak and the event, I talked to many NAACP people, including Tom Turner, a national board member who often attended my church in Detroit; Herbert Henderson, a lawyer from West Virginia; and, of course, Maxine and Jesse. I did not decide what I was to talk about until I had boarded the plane. I must admit I did not expect a large crowd. This was Youth Night. I had been young once. I was aware of the fact that when young people get together, the major agenda item is having fun. In a word, they would party.

When I arrived at the convention center, I was shocked. There was a huge crowd of more than 8,000 people, half of them under 24. The other half consisted of veterans of the fight. As I looked out over this sea of humanity, I was struck with the abiding faith that the old-timers had in our system. The reality for African Americans was that America had never lived up to its promise. I was deeply moved by the program, which had been organized by articulate, intelligent, and well-prepared black young people. I thought, what a shame there is so much talk in the media about the shortcomings of young black people. Why don't these white men with their press pads in hand tell this story?

Suddenly it was time for me to speak. I was already lifted up in the emotions of the moment. The choirs had lifted everyone's spirits. The pathos of the dream of freedom permeated every inch of that vast auditorium. The gray hair of those who had come from the dark valleys of Mississippi, where every step forward was preceded by the shedding of blood, was in evidence, as were those who came from Harlem, where the aspirations of many had been dimmed by the hard realities of white racism.

My mind flashed back to my personal struggle—the triumph just to be where I was, professionally. I thought of my grandmother, who had worked so fervently to end racism in Memphis. I thought about my mother and my father, who had worked so hard to raise a loving family.

I thought of many of the men and women I had known who, like Martin King and Medgar Evers, had given their very life. Medgar Evers was one of the greatest and most effective leaders of the civil rights movement. I was with him often in Jackson, Mississippi, and saw him organize that state for the NAACP. I was present at his funeral; what an awesome march we had after the funeral. Medgar's name deserves to be remembered forever when the roll of civil rights visionaries is called. His wife, Myrlie, also has served well.

For the next 25 minutes, I put aside my notes and spoke from the heart. Never before, not from any pulpit, not from any podium, and not from any other platform, had I had such an electrifying experience. The applause was deafening. The convention center was transformed into a revival. People were standing waving handkerchiefs. This was an exalting and frightening experience! This was to be eerily duplicated at the NAACP Annual Convention in St. Louis, Missouri, in 1977, when I gave my acceptance speech as executive director of the NAACP.

When I finished the Indianapolis speech, the platform was rushed by hundreds of people. I did not know what to do. I just stood there transfixed. The NAACP had its own security, and there were local police present. They were prepared to deal with disruptions from hostile sources. But how do you deal with the adulation of a friendly audience? Suddenly men began to lift me up and carry me out of the auditorium on their shoulders. To this day I can still hear and feel the love and affection of that summer's eve. It is a memory that has never faded with the passing of time.

This introduction to the national NAACP family, I am certain, had a lot to do with the search committee's decision to contact me less than four years later when the search for a successor for the legendary Roy Wilkins culminated in my selection. What an introduction! What a way to enter the NAACP national family! I believe that divine intervention had a lot to do with my message and the way it was received by these civil rights warriors in Indianapolis.

It was early in 1976 when I was first approached about the NAACP's executive director post by my good friend Jesse Turner. The organization had established a search committee and was serious about finding a replacement for Roy Wilkins, who had already announced his retirement. I had worked with Jesse for years and knew him to be a dedicated, straight-laced, no-nonsense civil rights activist, and a successful banker. He was an outstanding branch president.

Jesse had served as vice chairman of the national board and was at that time serving as the national treasurer. For some reason known only to himself, Jesse felt that I needed to succeed Roy Wilkins. He would say to me, "Hooks, you have been talking about what the organization should be doing. Here's your chance!" Maxine Smith, the local executive secretary of the branch, would add her two cents worth. "Benny," she would say, "the NAACP needs fresh blood. We need a young man full of vigor and vinegar, with new ideas. If the choice is between your comfortable job at the FCC or being in the trenches with us, you better get your boots on and come on in!"

I felt like any black American would—just the thought of being considered was mind-boggling! At that time, many viewed the executive director as the president of black America. Roy Wilkins was a living icon and the personification of civil rights achievement. It was the most prestigious and important job that any black could have. Without question, your every word, or maybe your every thought, was recorded and discussed.

Frankly, the thought, the dream, of becoming executive director had crossed my mind. However, I never thought that I would ever be considered. When the offer came, I was honored—and torn. I had lots of other great job offers. One prominent law firm offered $175,000 per year plus a share of the profits if I wanted to work hard. And if I wanted to work lightly, the firm offered $150,000 per year. And these were 1977 dollars. And, of course, there would have been numerous opportunities to serve on boards of directors, which pay well, by the way. I've already indicated that if I had remained at the Commission, there was a great possibility I would have been appointed chairman.

I had seen the organization close up on the local level. I was aware of the fact that the NAACP had a plethora of internal divisions and an unwieldy board of 64 individuals with 64 different agendas. I was aware of the fact that the leadership of a national organization required an enormous amount of work. I had served on the Southern Christian Leadership Conference Board and saw how difficult it was for Dr. King to reach a consensus with a much smaller and less diverse group of people. Why in God's name would I want to leave Washington to go to New York?

I had settled into my regular work routine at the FCC and was honestly enjoying my work. Every day was a new challenge and a new experience. I had come to know and like many of the people with whom I worked. I could travel and speak to audiences all over the country without having to worry about clearing my speeches or remarks with any supervisor or board. Then there was Frances, my wife. Frances had been phenomenally successful in her career while we lived in Memphis. She had started a special program which by then had sent hundreds of young black students to some of the most exclusive colleges and universities in the nation. Many of these youngsters came from families in which no family member had even finished high school. Others came from disadvantaged single-parent homes. She had a way with young people and a unique ability to convince the power brokers to buy into what was now a citywide effort. After spending years in the classroom, she had finally found her niche.

Like so many other spouses, she had put her ambitions on partial hold and concentrated much of her mental energy into furthering my career. Now she was traveling back and forth to Washington. She had turned the house that we bought into a very comfortable home. My nephew, Robert, was living with me. This was an excellent arrangement, for it gave me company when Frances was not there. My brother's son and I were very close. He had come to live with my mother when he was about three years old and I was 15. He had joined me as vice president of Mahalia Jackson's Chicken system and was now living with me in Washington, D.C.

Frances had found pieces to fill every nook and cranny. By now she had made friends. When she was in town, she enjoyed the cultural events that Washington was famous for. Frances took a leave of absence from the school system for one year to live with me in Washington. During the year she spent in Washington, we alternated weekends in Detroit and Memphis, where I served as pastor on leave of Middle Baptist and Mt. Moriah Baptist churches. These trips allowed us to keep in touch with our families and with old friends.

In addition, Mrs. Dancy, Frances's mother, suffered a debilitating stroke in 1975, and from then until her death in 1992, she was unable to speak or walk. Frances and her sister Anita, who lived in Beaumont, Texas, took excellent care of their mother. They were assisted by their brother, Buddy, and her father, Andrew, until he died in 1985. This was a loving family, and Frances and I took Mrs. Dancy all over this country. You name the city and she had been there—Philadelphia, New York, Los Angeles, Miami, Houston. Not only was she there but she enjoyed it. And I am convinced that her later years were some of the happiest that anyone could have because of her family's loving care.

There was still another factor militating against my going to the NAACP. The commission chairman, Richard Wiley, was a Republican. With the new Democratic administration having taken control on January 20, it was understood that President Carter would probably name a new chairman. I was one of seven commissioners, and it was rumored that the President was thinking about appointing a black to the chairmanship. Although I was appointed by President Nixon (I was an active Democrat at the time of my appointment), I had a good relationship with both Carter and some of the key appointees of his administration. This included Andrew Young, who was at that time the U.S. ambassador to the United Nations. I had known Andy since my SCLC days. In fact, Andy had spoken to President Carter directly after his election, and I felt strongly that I had a good chance to be named chair of the FCC.

Although we all worked hard, I set my own schedule while at the FCC. My free time was my own to do with as I pleased. In addition, I wanted to put in at least five years of service, and I only had four years in at that point. At that time, I was unaware of the full breadth and scope of the schedule of the NAACP's director, but I knew I was not interested. The compensation for the position was low, only $35,000 per year. The director's salary had been increased for Mr. Wilkins a year earlier from only $27,000.

Although I was making more than that, the money was never really an issue. There are a number of factors that come into play when a person makes a life-altering decision. One such factor was a conversation I had with my father-in-law, Andrew Dancy, one evening after he returned from a day at the 1976 NAACP Annual Convention, held in Memphis.

You would have to know the man in order to put his comments into their proper perspective. I shall never forget Mr. Dancy, who was a quiet, well-spoken, affable southern gentleman, not given to rash or intemperate speech or exaggeration, coming that day to the house with a bag of goodies that he had been given by the exhibitors at the NAACP's Commerce and Industry Show. He had on one of his best suits with a tie that looked like it was made just for his outfit. His shoes were dazzling and everything had the look of freshness after a long day at the convention center.

I shall never forget the look on his face, elated yet bemused. Mr. Dancy went into the den, kissed his wife, and took his seat in his familiar easy chair. He began to recall some of his experiences of the day with characteristic positive observations. He talked profusely about the thousands of black people he saw in the hotels, the speeches of the speakers, and the other side aspects of the convention. But I detected that he was omitting something. I asked, "Mr. Dancy, how did you like the convention?" He gave me a somewhat puzzled look and said, "It was all right."

When you have known someone well for a long time—if you have lived in the same house, as Frances and I had done for years—you can tell, almost instinctively, whether you are being told the whole story. I just laughed and asked again, "What did you think of the convention?" He smiled and said, "Well, Ben, I have never in my whole life seen so many intelligent colored people fussing and fighting among themselves! How in the name of God can they ever get anywhere when our leaders spend all of their time forming firing squads in a circle and commencing firing?" It was ironic that Mr. Dancy made this observation. That was the year when there was an awful fight between Mr. Wilkins and some of the members of the National Board of Directors.

I did not give the inquiry regarding my availability much thought for a good while. Of course, I was honored by being considered—and who would not want to have been considered among the civil rights giants that had led the NAACP: W.E.B. DuBois, Mary White Ovington, James Shilliday, James Weldon Johnson, Walter White, Roy Wilkins, and others? I decided that I would raise the issue with Frances. Frances was always practical. She would certainly put the brakes on any lingering thoughts I might have had about leaving the FCC and Washington for New York and the NAACP.

I should have known better. Frances had always been supportive of whatever I wanted to do. I was, however, hoping that this time she would tell me to go fly a kite. Instead, she was her customary self. She said, "If you want to do it, you ought to do what you think is best." Now, I thought, I cannot possibly use Frances's opposition as the reason for not taking the position. You know, sometimes one wishes that one's spouse would just say, "No way." That way you don't have to consider an unpopular course or have to make a decision loaded with ambivalence. For me there was no such luck.

After talking it over with Frances, I decided to discuss the matter with my family. We had always been very close, and I knew that I would have the benefit of their best advice and counsel. I talked to my sisters, Bessie, Mildred, and Julia, individually. I got mixed reactions from them, starting with "Why in the name of God would you ever think of doing that?" to "Well, it's an opportunity for you to do something for our people." Mildred told me that this was probably something that deep down I always wanted to do.

One by one I talked it over with my brothers, Robert, Charlie, and Raymond. They were intrigued with the possibility of my making a significant contribution in the nation's socio-political landscape. Robert, my second-oldest brother, warned me that the NAACP was like a huge ship—it would require a lot of work to change its course and bring it into port. Charlie suggested that I would have to put in long and hard hours, but he too felt that it was a challenge that might be worth the effort. Some nights, when I was at the office until 2:00 or 3:00 A.M. or on the road, I would remember his words. Raymond, my youngest brother, always thoughtful and perceptive, told me that I needed to look at every aspect of leaving a job that I liked and weigh that against being on the front line of a struggle that our family had always thought to be important.

By this time, both my parents were dead. I had always valued their advice and counsel and wished that they were here to advise me now. I talked it over with my daughter, Pat, and she was very ambivalent. I also discussed it with my brother-in-law, Buddy, my good friends Donald Jackson, H.C. Nabrit, Leonard Mitchell, Charlie Turner, Eurline Couch, my nephew Robert Hooks III, Raymond, Freddie, Ronald, Michael, and many others. The advice was all over the place and no consensus emerged.

I found myself being pulled inch by inch, centimeter by centimeter, to the decision to at least take a close look at the NAACP. I turned a receptive ear to news broadcasts that were related to the NAACP or civil rights in general. I would wake up some mornings and say to myself, "Darn it, I think I will do it." At other times I would say the opposite.

It seemed that I was constantly running into people who were active in the NAACP. They all seemed to want a candidate who did not need an introduction to either the black or the white community. The name of Walter Leonard, the former president of Fisk University and a Harvard law graduate, was mentioned often. Max Robinson, the first African-American network anchor, was another. The name of former U.S. Senator Edward Brooke, Congressman Louis Stokes, Vernon Jordan, Jesse Jackson, Gloster Current, Nate Jones, and Washington Bureau Director Clarence Mitchell were mentioned often in connection with the post. I have no way of knowing if any of these outstanding candidates had any real interest in the position.

I was contacted formally by the search committee chairman, Dr. Montague Cobb, who lived in Washington, D.C. Dr. Cobb was Professor Emeritus of the Howard University School of Medicine. He was also a former president of the National Medical Association (NMA). The NMA was founded in 1895 as a protest to the exclusion of black physicians from the American Medical Association. Dr. Cobb was a widely respected and well-known activist who had been a fixture in both the local branch and the national NAACP.

Cobb was a friendly, sophisticated renaissance man. He was from the old school of well-trained, well-bred intellectuals. I sat down with Dr. Cobb, who was pulling on his ever-present pipe. He would work into a conversation by discussing the philosophical insights of Plato, the wisdom of Socrates, and the convictions of James Weldon Johnson. You could count on him to discuss complicated social issues in anatomical terms. It was an interesting and arresting conversation, and as always, I learned from this intellectual giant.

When we got down to discussing the NAACP directorship, Dr. Cobb made it clear that the organization was looking for a person of vision, a person who was multi-talented and committed to the struggle. The NAACP needed someone with the vision of Isaiah and the tenacity of Moses. I told him that I did not know if I had the fire in my belly to take on such a weighty challenge.

After lunch we parted. I still did not know what I was going to do. I was contacted informally by other members of the search committee and by a variety of board members. When word got out that I was a serious candidate, I began to be cornered by NAACP officials, or by members who had heard me speak at the Indianapolis meeting in 1973 or at some other function.

It should be noted that at this time the NAACP was in a difficult period. The renowned Roy Wilkins was leaving after 21 years. The Board did not see a suitable successor on the staff. There was conflict between the Board and Mr. Wilkins, which had extended in many ways to the staff. The association was facing financial bankruptcy because of a $1.5 million judgment rendered against it in the Port Gibson, Mississippi, boycott case. (During my term, the Supreme Court later voided the Port Gibson case.) It required a $3 million cash appeal bond that we did not have. The climate for civil rights was not as favorable, the support was wavering, attention was dissipating, CORE was on the ropes, SCLC was in financial trouble. SNCC was no longer operating.

These were the conditions under which I had to go to the NAACP—leaving the FCC, where I had a chance of becoming chairman after the election of Jimmy Carter as President. A great work was in progress there. Nevertheless, the NAACP at that time continued to be and is now the most important, powerful, and prestigious secular organization in black America.

Little by little, I was being drawn into the orbit of agreeing with those who wanted me to take the helm of the NAACP. I prayed for guidance. I have discovered that somehow, if you follow the will of God, things have a way of working themselves out. I decided that I would wait to hear from the search committee. If it was offered, I would accept the challenge and do my best. If the torch was passed to another, I would do all I could to help him or her succeed.

The deliberations of the search committee were completely secret. I am told that they talked with a number of nationally known candidates and decided to submit only my name to the Board of Directors for its consideration. At its January 6, 1977 meeting, the board voted unanimously for me. I was advised by Jesse Turner of the board's decision. I cannot say that I was surprised; I can say that I was humbled by their confidence in me, and anxious to accept the challenge.

By the time the board's decision was announced, I was psychologically ready for what was to become the challenge of my life. I realized that there were others who could lead the NAACP, and lead it well. But both fate and destiny conspired to give me both the privilege and the burden of leading the nation's oldest and largest civil rights organization.

That day I prayed for guidance, strength, and courage to carry the fight for equality forward. I wanted to do it not for myself, but for the many nameless and faceless people who lived and died in our nation's South, men and women who gave all they had to our struggle, but never lived to see America rid itself of discrimination and racism. I thought of my grandmother, my father, my mother, and my sisters and brothers, all of whose shoulders I was now figuratively standing on. I promised that I would do my best. Each day when I got out of bed, I dedicated my talents and whatever strengths I had to their memory. The call to leadership is not one that can ever be earned. It is thrust upon us by a power external to us.

My work on behalf of civil rights in this country would sometimes put me at odds with another venerable movement run by the Nation of Islam. I had become acquainted firsthand with the Nation of Islam, or the Black Muslim Movement, in the 1960s when I was an assistant public defender. All of my clients were in jail and I spent hours there interviewing them, many of whom had embraced the Muslim movement. It appeared that this provided great protection against assault, sexual attacks, and other mistreatment behind bars.

Minister Louis Farrakhan was a great spokesman for the Nation of Islam by the time I arrived on the national scene. We met on one occasion in my Brooklyn NAACP office. Our conversation lasted a little more than two hours and we discussed many things. The gist of the meeting was that when it came to building black bakeries, operating black banks, and building black hospitals—that is to say, building economic enterprises—he and I were in agreement. I wanted to see the black community develop a strong economic base. A.G. Gaston, famous black millionaire of Birmingham, pointed out that it was right, just, and altogether important that we have a right to check into the Holiday Inn. It was also important that we had the economic wherewithal to check out decently.

So I made it clear to Farrakhan in our meeting that I would never em-
brace any racial divisiveness or racial hostility or look with disdain upon
any group of people simply because of their race, creed, color, or religious
beliefs, and that was the position also of the NAACP. The meeting was
pleasant and we left, I suppose, with each of us having our own separate
agenda.

Chapter 11

NAACP: RELATIONSHIP WITH THE BOARD 1977-1984

My discussions with the search committee and with key members of the NAACP Board of Directors did not prepare me for what I was to face in the ensuing months and years. During the negotiations with the personnel committee, there seemed to have been an inordinate amount of time spent and emphasis placed on restrictions. The board felt it was necessary to ensure that the new director was given the time and effort necessary for the proper management of the organization. On the surface, that appeared to be a laudable objective. In reality, it had more to do with a segment of the board that wanted to make sure that no other chief executive would have the autonomy and power that Roy Wilkins once wielded. There was also a perception—a mistaken one, I might add—that Roy was making a lot of money from private speaking engagements and from his columns in a number of national newspapers.

Among the concerns was that I could not pastor at any church full-time. Well, I had been pastor on leave all the time that I served on the Federal Communications Commission. Federal commissioners were prohibited by statute from holding outside employment. So, while I was on leave of absence from my church, I was unpaid. I was required by the NAACP contract to report all of my outside paid public speaking engagements, and all income beyond a prescribed amount would have to be shared with the Association. I had no problem with this stipulation. After all, I was prohibited from receiving any compensation for speeches while at the FCC. The final stipulation was that I had to live in New York City. This, in theory, was to facilitate my being easily available and accessible to the National Office, which was located at Columbus Circle in Midtown Manhattan.

Once the terms of my employment were worked out, I began the transition from the FCC to the NAACP. Although I was not to assume office until August 1977, I took advantage of this time to meet with key staff members in both New York and Washington. I had a number of extensive discussions with a cross-section of board members, branch presidents, and leaders of other civic and civil rights groups.

During this period I relied upon my friends on the board to fill me in on the essentials. Jesse Turner fed me volumes of financial data, board and annual reports, and other information that was exceptionally helpful in my ability to understand the inner workings of the vast organization that was the NAACP. I read every piece of paper I could get my hands on. I got copies of the minutes of some of the board meetings, which gave me a flavor of what I had gotten myself into. I would take this material with me and read into the early hours of the morning. I made notes and asked questions of persons who I thought had the facts.

I found out after my selection, in a conversation with Clarence Mitchell, that there was an agreement among the "Big Three," Clarence Mitchell, Gloster Current, and Nathaniel Jones, that they would support and work for whomever among them was selected to succeed Roy. The rumor mill reported they would not work for anyone selected from outside the group.

Clarence Mitchell was a longtime chief of the Washington Bureau and had gained such status that he was affectionately known as the 101st senator. Much of the credit for the passage of all of the civil rights bills belongs to Clarence Mitchell. Gloster Current had for more than 30 years been director of branches and had built them to the strength of 2,000 or more. Next to Roy Wilkins, he was the most widely known and respected among the NAACP hierarchy. Nate Jones was a general counsel and filled with dignity and ability the job once held by the late Thurgood Marshall. He is an outstanding lawyer and went on to become a tremendously able federal appellate judge.

I met with each of them individually. Each, I might add, went out of his way to pledge his support and was as helpful as I could ever have hoped for the entire period that all of them remained employed by the NAACP. Gloster, who had a better understanding of the vicissitudes of the inner workings of the board and the way that the convention policy-making process operated, was exceptionally helpful. Clarence gave me a global view of the personalities and peculiarities of the sister organizations with which the Association coalesced, and of the member organizations of the Leadership Conference on Civil Rights, which historically had been headed by the NAACP executive director.

Nate provided me with helpful information on pending and active litigation. The NAACP never got the credit it deserved for the variety and diversity of lawsuits that it handled with a limited legal staff. This was a source of personal frustration to me during my tenure as executive director and long after I retired.

At the time I became executive director, the NAACP had in place an unwieldy operational structure requiring board approval to hire or fire top association staff. This policy, which denied the director the authority to run his own office and choose his staff, made no business sense. Previously, directors consulted with boards and boards routinely approved the director's decisions.

From the first day of my tenure, my relationship with most of the board members was good. There was a desire to move forward with programs and to put behind us the divisions that had been so painful and public. Even the caucus made an attempt to be cooperative and helpful. I was invited constantly to speak at events at the branches and state conferences where board members lived or served.

I recognized from earlier experiences in dealing with organizational dynamics that people have to be convinced of your judgment. This means that what might be impossible today to get people to understand becomes self-evident and possible tomorrow. In any event, I was able to get most of my initiatives implemented.

Vernon Jarrett, a columnist with *The Chicago Tribune*, brought me a program that he had started in Chicago to encourage academic excellence. We established a new youth program based on the Jarrett model that caught on in communities around the country. It was called ACT-SO. This program was designed to reach talented youth who would not ordinarily become involved in civil rights activities and to showcase on a national level their skills and talents. The ACT-SO acronym stands for African American Academic, Cultural, Technological, Scientific Olympics.

The beauty of this program was that it also brought to the fore an armada of adult advisors who worked locally to put on the competitions. The winners came to the national conventions, where they competed for national prizes in their respective areas. More than 25,000 young people participated in local, state, regional, and national competitions every year.

Another outstanding and highly successful program that we instituted was the Our Fair Share Program. This program was designed to get more blacks into entry-level and managerial positions of major corporations; to secure vendor opportunities for entrepreneurs who were, by and large, locked out of opportunities to bid competitively on contracts for goods and services; to get more blacks and other minorities appointed to corporate boards where they could help change the adverse policies that restricted the economic development of the black community; to have corporations take advantage of professional services that blacks could provide but had been locked out of historically (accounting, legal, banking, and advertising services); and to encourage the corporate community to contribute to minority charities as they had become accustomed to doing for majority charities.

By the time I retired in 1993, we could document billions of dollars in benefits to the black community resulting from the 70 agreements that we negotiated with the private and public sectors.

The board strongly supported our efforts to strengthen our youth department. When I became executive director, I recognized that if the organization and our people were to have sustained progress, it was necessary to have a strong youth component actively involved in altering the political and social landscape. After all, many of the initiatives of the '50s and '60s were student-led. Fortunately, young people are not wedded to past disappointments or current fears.

There were only four regional youth directors in August of 1977 when I arrived. In most instances they did not even have secretaries, but shared a secretary with the adult regional directors. We hired a college director to work exclusively with college students, which added significantly to the Association's always-strained financial condition.

During the same period, there were signs of serious conflict and division on the horizon. The chair became increasingly involved in the administrative affairs of the organization. The NAACP board had always been led from the top, and board members did not frequently challenge the chair. By the time I came on board, the caucus was setting the agenda, projecting the budget, and selecting the organization's goals. The problem for any new director was how to assume the managerial duties of the Association and present plans to the board for approval.

I have used the word caucus. The caucus was an informal, loosely organized but tightly disciplined group that met before each session and made irrevocable decisions on what would happen at the official meeting. If the board meeting was held on Sunday, the informal caucus meeting would gather the day before, set the agenda, discuss and vote on every item, and decide on new board members, new officers, and the budgets. All I can say is it was a board within a board. Whoever controlled the caucus controlled the organization.

I am told the caucus was originally set to protect the interest of Mr. Wilkins and his agenda. The way the board was constituted contributed to control by a small group of activist members. There were 64 members of the NAACP's board, 21 elected each year for three-year terms; seven were elected by the youth units; 24 were elected at-large; and 12 were elected directly by the board of directors. The caucus also wielded significant influence in regional elections in which 21 board members were elected in staggered terms of three years. The seven youth members were elected by the regions that were influenced heavily by the caucus.

Committee assignments were a prerogative of the chair. Most board members of any entity relish the opportunity to serve on key committees or to be named chair of a powerful committee. The same is true in the House and the U.S. Senate. The Speaker of the U.S. House of Representatives and the Majority Leader of the Senate exercise an inordinate amount of power and influence in this way.

With control of the apparatus of the election, many of the 64-member board owed their seats and thus their loyalty to the ruling caucus. Those who challenged the ruling order were challenged when their terms expired by handpicked candidates of the caucus or never again received desirable committee assignments.

In the meantime, it was apparent that the chair, Margaret Wilson, and I were having difficulty seeing eye-to-eye on how the NAACP should be run. A source of irritation to me was her insistence that more and more written information be supplied at executive committee meetings, which she called monthly. It was already my standard operational procedure to make sure the board received timely and comprehensive reports. The board met quarterly. I presented my reports at each of the four annual constitutionally mandated meetings. Each report was more than 70 written pages long. There was always a financial report, detailed rationales for each new initiative, membership reports, and a public relations update at each meeting, delineating the media coverage that our units and staff had received for their activities during the period. In addition, we prepared comprehensive reports for each of the Executive Committee meetings called at the discretion of the chair. We had a very small staff, and the demand for an ever-increasing number of reports was an enormous hardship. Remember, this was at a time when we, like most small, cash-starved nonprofits, were not computerized. If this trend had not been challenged, the NAACP would have been mired in a mountain of paperwork.

Our work and mission were important to me, and I discussed how the reporting demands made it difficult for me to lead the organization with the leaders of the caucus: James Kemp, William Oliver, Vice Chairman Kelly Alexander, Sr., Treasurer Jesse Turner, Edward Hailes, Silas Craft, Montague Cobb, Thomas Turner, Sarah Green, Aaron Henry, Charles Cherry, William Pollard, and a number of noncaucus members: Hazel Dukes, Arrell White, Evelyn Roberts, Charles Johnson, Louisa Fletcher, Nathaniel Colley, Herbert Henderson, and Julian Bond. I was assured that they would make efforts to get the chair and me together, to resolve what they thought to be merely a difference in styles and management philosophies.

Meanwhile, Mrs. Wilson appointed Dr. Edward Hailes, an Opportunity Industrial Center executive and member of the board, to conduct an on-site evaluation and assessment of the operational procedures and capabilities of the national office. Hailes spent days at our New York offices meeting with all key staff members. Special attention was given to our finance operations, internal controls, the budgeting process, fund-raising, the executive director's office, and field operations.

In his report, Dr. Hailes pointed out that the national office was adhering to all of the necessary management and financial procedures. The report was highly complimentary of our ability to do so much with so few staff persons to carry out a multiplicity of responsibilities. Dr. Hailes indicated the existing staff was doing an excellent job in managing the internal systems. He indicated that the staff was greatly overworked and underpaid.

What I did not know was that at the same time, my deputy director, Charles Smith, was working privately and independently on a report the chair knew about, which would later be submitted to the board. Reverend Smith was a talented and seasoned NAACP staffer whom I had selected in April of 1981 to serve as deputy director. He had been a member of the board with extensive civil rights experience. Smith was a member of the search committee and later became a candidate himself for the executive directorship in 1977. I never viewed his ambitions as a threat, however. To the contrary, I believed he could do an excellent job for me.

It became obvious to me by late 1982 that Smith could not adjust to being number two in the organization. This is not uncommon among people who are accustomed to being the leader and who called the shots in the positions from which they came, and Smith had been the pastor of one of the leading churches in West Virginia and the director of the Huntington, West Virginia, OIC. I met with Smith in early 1983 to discuss the problem. At that meeting I told him that our working relationship had not worked out. He did not disagree and gave no indication that he was bitter in any way. We shook hands and he left the office. That was the end of it, I thought.

In February of 1983, Mrs. Wilson advised me of the schedule of Executive Committee meetings. The first of five scheduled meetings was to take place on March 12 in Chicago. Through the grapevine at the national office I had heard that Charles Smith had been asked by the chair to disclose to the committee his appraisal of the status of the national office and its management operations.

On the same day and time as the NAACP's Executive Committee meeting, the presiding bishop of the Fourth Episcopal District of the African Methodist Church, Bishop Hubert Robinson, had asked me to come to his district meeting so that he could present me with a check for the NAACP in the amount of $10,000. Because the bishop wanted to present the check to me personally, I asked Charles Smith to represent me at the Executive Committee meeting, which was to take place at the same time. As I was preparing to leave for my visit with the bishop, Smith was digging into a box of papers. The chair, who obviously knew about the report and the contents therein, said, "The deputy has some information that he wants to share with the board."

When I returned from the bishop's meeting, I learned what had been passed around by my deputy in my absence. The report turned out to be critical of all of our office operations with the exception of the efforts of Smith himself. I was not angry, but deeply, deeply disappointed by this turn of events.

Meanwhile, during the same period, the chair had set up a committee to evaluate my effectiveness as director. This process was stressful. Every decision I had made was being second-guessed, and I was being blamed for not doing things that I had been prohibited by the board from doing. Naturally, I defended my stewardship and cooperated with the evaluation.

My working relationship with the chair deteriorated to the point where I would come to a meeting and she would call for a report from a committee that I didn't even know existed. Finally, after the receipt of the letter in which the chair unilaterally discharged me, I left the organization. When all is said and done, my record reveals explicitly that I did a good job in handling the affairs of the NAACP. Whether it was the membership programs, financial stewardship and integrity, or public relations, we were doing well.

Later it was found that Mrs. Wilson had discussed the matter of my dismissal with no one on the Executive Committee, although she did call a member of the board to tell him about it. That member immediately got in touch with other board members, and none of them knew anything about it either.

After I received the letter, Howard Henderson, vice president of Operations; Hazel Dukes, a tremendously effective and concerned board member; and Jerry Guess, my very fine and loyal personal assistant, spent the next few days trying to set this situation on the right course. They were joined by Vice Chair of the Board Kelly Alexander, Sr., Board Treasurer Jesse Turner, and many other board members who were trying to set the record straight. They held that if I were not doing my job, the board should say so and either direct me in better ways, reprimand me, punish me, or fire me, but whatever was to be done, it should be done through normal protocol and not by the unilateral action of the chair.

Two board meetings were subsequently held, one without the chair and another that she called. In the first board meeting, 48 members were present and 47 voted to reinstate me and to relieve the chair of her duties. In the second board meeting, 62 attended the meeting and voted 57-4 to reinstate me and to relieve the chair of her duties.

An even stronger voice spoke later. It so happens that Mrs. Wilson was running for reelection to the board that year. The above incident occurred in March, and the election was to be held that December. There were seven positions open. Nine people ran and Mrs. Wilson came in eighth. Ironically, one of the seven people who won had died, and Mrs. Wilson filed a lawsuit alleging that she should be seated, since the seventh person had died. The court did not agree with her.

Obviously, this whole episode was unfortunate because it delayed the progress of the NAACP for a number of weeks, but I hold no grudge or animosity in my heart against anyone involved. I am a preacher of the gospel, a born-again Christian, and I do recognize that we have to love everyone if we wish to see God.

Chapter 12

THE NEW DAY BEGUN: 1977-78 AND SOUTH AFRICAN INVOLVEMENT

After I was installed as executive director of the NAACP, the weight of the awesome responsibility hit me. The feeling was similar to the time when I was sworn in as a judge in Memphis in 1965 and as a member of the FCC in 1972. There is a difference between being nominated, appointed, or elected and the point in time when the responsibility is yours. I found myself praying for guidance, strength, and the wisdom to do the right thing. Frances was extremely supportive, although deep down I knew that she had reservations about my taking on the physically taxing obligation that goes with leading this vast, far-flung, lumbering, 68-year-old institution.

My family and friends, who had traveled to New York for the occasion, also shared Frances's reservations, although none verbalized them. They were happy for me. They wanted what I wanted. They would do anything that they felt would further my career. There is nothing more important to a person taking on the challenge of a lifetime than having the unreserved and boundless support of one's spouse, family, and friends. In this sense I was blessed.

Because of my busy schedule and the problems of leaving one position and going directly to another, I did not have an opportunity to find a place to live. Our furniture and other personal possessions were in Memphis and Washington. We stayed in a hotel, which I will not name. It had a large ad in the Red Book, which was used by travel agents and large companies to make reservations for their traveling executives. To put it mildly, the hotel did not live up to its billing. The service was poor, the rooms were in need of modernization, and there were tiny little brown guests. In Memphis, we called these uninvited guests roaches. In addition, the hotel had mice. One was exceptionally bold. One night it sat on the dresser looking as if it were a full paying guest entitled to all of the rights and privileges. You can imagine how happy we were when we finally found an apartment on Central Park South, two blocks away from the national office.

From the day I was elected, branch members, state conference presidents, board members, and staff were unrelenting in their requests for me to come to their area for a rally, mass meeting, banquet, breakfast, luncheon, or just for a meeting. Even though I wanted to accept every invitation received, it is not humanly possible to be three or four places at the same time. Additionally, some rudimentary housekeeping chores had to be attended to. I had to meet with the staff, make some basic budgetary decisions, make an assessment of where we were as an organization, and attend to the all-important matter of fund-raising.

I had at that time an aggressive West Coast regional director, Virna Canson. She had been a lobbyist before assuming her position after the death of her predecessor, Leonard Carter. Actually, the West Coast was the first region to have a full-time regional director, Franklin Williams, who later became head of the Phelps-Stokes Fund. Our West Coast branches felt that they were the stepchildren of the national office. This was due in part to the distance and the expense involved in travel. As a result, fewer national officers visited the area. Virna was a master politician—she knew how to exploit this disadvantage to her advantage. On top of this, she was persistent. She never learned how to take no for an answer. She convinced me that I should come to the West Coast early in August. She would arrange for a "welcome tour" for me to speak at a series of branch and community functions.

As the day for my departure neared, I wondered how in God's name I allowed myself to be talked into giving so much time to one region. We had seven regions in the NAACP, each wanting their new director to visit. In any event, Frances and I headed westward. From the moment our plane landed, a series of planned events began. It started with an airport press conference, followed by meetings with ministers, community leaders, politicians, black businessmen and businesswomen, and corporate executives, in addition to branch meetings and rallies. I must give them credit—day after day they had mass meetings and rallies scheduled, with upwards of 10,000 people present at some of these events. We went to Oakland, where the turnout was phenomenal. The same was true in Los Angeles and San Francisco—packed churches, stadiums, and auditoriums. We motorcaded from place to place, all scripted by Virna. By all measures, the welcome tour was extremely successful.

Leaving Los Angeles and returning to New York, I realized that there was really no other organization with the power, influence, and local presence of the NAACP. Others may have had the rhetoric and received a lot of publicity, but we had the troops. During the first 27 days of my tenure in office, I made 72 speeches to or for NAACP units.

On days that I had evening engagements, I would come back to the office and work until early in the mornings. I met with senior members of the staff, made calls to board members and fund-raising sources, and tried to return as many calls as possible. The schedule that I had set for myself was a killer. I would never have allowed someone else to set the schedule for me that I set for myself. To this day I do not know how I kept up with this pace during the 16 years that I served the NAACP.

The executive directorship of the NAACP is a unique office. Nothing is comparable to it. The complexities of the NAACP and the myriad problems it addresses made it different from other secular groups. When the position was initially discussed with me, I was given a general description of the duties. Among them were chief fund-raiser, chief spokesman, principal public relations officer, and chief executive and administrative officer.

I later discovered that this was merely the tip of the iceberg. Besides the duties outlined above, there were many others. The executive director was also responsible for convening meetings, writing policy positions on controversial issues, leading the demonstrations and marches, and serving as the chief program officer for the Association. The director was expected to respond to crises, testify before the Congress and state legislative committees, and serve as the chief liaison to Hispanic, Jewish, and women's organizations. The director is also the chief letter writer and letter answerer. He is the principal lobbyist and the preparer of reports for three board meetings and for the annual corporate meeting of the Association. He serves as the preparer of reports and publications, the convener of national conferences and meetings chairman of the Leadership Conference on Civil Rights (an organization of leading civil rights organizations and activists such as Urban League, SCLC, NOW, League of Women Voters, La Raza, UAW, AFL-CIO, and NEA.

It is the most potent lobbying organization, and during my tenure we passed more than 27 civil rights bills, such as the Americans with Disabilities Act, Martin Luther King, Jr. Holiday bill, and the Civil Rights Act of 1992. I also served as chairman of the Black Leadership Forum (which was organized by Vernon Jordan and me and consisted of major black civil rights organizations), and I was the chief financial solicitor for the black fraternal and religious groups and black national organizations. As if that were not enough, they expected me to be talk show host and talk show and news magazine guest. The director was also an op-ed columnist, chief administrative officer for the NAACP Special Contribution Fund, and publisher of *The Crisis* magazine, the oldest continuously published black publication in the world. I also had a national TV show called *Go Tell It* running monthly.

To understand the dilemma that anyone faces in running the NAACP, one would first have to understand its nature. The NAACP is a massive entity unlike any other secular organization in the nation. One's perception of what it is and what it is capable of doing is based upon one's point of view.

I heard a story that I think sums it up. A number of blind men were holding on to various parts of an elephant. The one holding on to the elephant's trunk was asked, what is it? He responded, "It's a huge drain pipe." The one holding on to a leg was asked the same question. He responded, "It's a tree trunk. I'm sure of it." Another holding on to the tail said, "I know what it is. It's a long, tightly knitted fireman's rope." The one holding on to the elephant's ear said, "It's a large blanket." And the one holding on to the elephant's lip said, "It's an inner tube of a tire." Like that elephant, the NAACP is different things to different people. It all depends on what part you have been exposed to.

Some see the NAACP as a legal aid organization that answers the distress cries of those blacks who are in desperate need of legal assistance. If you ask the seven Scottsboro boys who were accused of raping two young white women in Alabama in the early 1930s, or Lenell Geter, who in 1982 was sentenced to life in prison for a robbery he did not commit (see chapter 26), or Corporal Bracy, whose conviction for being a Russian Spy we also had overturned, or the thousands of others whose rights we have defended in the courts, they will tell you that you are correct. The NAACP is a legal aid organization.

If you ask Nelson Mandela or Jean Bertrand Aristide what the NAACP is, they will tell you that it is the first organization that fought for an end to apartheid and dictatorship in their countries when no one else was interested in their plight. They will tell you that the NAACP is the model upon which they patterned their struggle for liberation.

If you ask members of Congress, both present and past, they will tell you it is the one black institution that has been on Capitol Hill in season and out. It is the organization that is unafraid of championing unpopular causes. It has troops in every congressional district raising unrelenting hell about matters of racial, social, and political inequities. And to some congressional members, it is a royal pain in the rear!

When I arrived at the Association, there were fewer than 60 full-time executive staff members. This included staff outside the national office in our regions, Washington Bureau and Voter Registration and Education office. We were spending $746,165 on our legal services, $76,895 on voter registration, and a mere $208,213 on our education programs. This gives you a feel for how limited the resources were. Thus, it is easy to see why the volunteer efforts of the leadership of our branches were indispensable. With a budget of less than three quarters of a million dollars, the NAACP's legal department was challenging the federal government, a number of states for their school desegregation practices, and the giants of the corporate world. What is not factored into the legal department's budget is the fact that we had more than 800 active legal redress committees. Many of these committees had some of the best legal minds in the nation serving as volunteers and filing cases for the NAACP pro bono. The billable hours that these lawyers could have charged if they were not serving as volunteers would be valued in the tens of millions of dollars.

To look at the NAACP in terms of its annual budget and the dollar amount that is spent in a given programmatic area is therefore very misleading. The last full year that I served as executive director, 1992, a group of black certified public accountants and urban bankers who had given the Association invaluable volunteer assistance over the years estimated that if we had to pay for the volunteer time of the lawyers who worked in our branches and for the volunteers who worked with our many programs it would cost us conservatively between $500 million and $600 million. We had, in our more than 2,200 units, more than 50,000 full- and part-time volunteers working in our branch and youth units' offices. Additionally, the popular ACT-SO program, led by chief volunteer Vernon Jarrett, had more than 5,000 volunteers who worked with our 600 participating units in competitions held in 450 communities. The total actual budget of the NAACP in 1992, my last full year, was $19,900,000.

The ACT-SO volunteers were housewives and college professors, teachers and physicians, scientists and accountants, lawyers and salespeople, zoologists and repairmen, stenographers and psychologists. Many of these dedicated persons donated hundreds of hours annually working with youngsters at the local, state, regional, and national levels. It angers me when I hear people talk as if blacks who have made it are not giving anything back to the community. Not only is this simply not true, but it belittles the efforts of so many who reach back and help those who might otherwise be left behind.

During the remaining five months of 1977, significant developments occurred at a fast and furious pace. On November 18-19, the Association held a National Invitational Conference on Energy at the Mayflower Hotel in Washington. The conference was set up to analyze the effects of the Carter Administration's energy policy on minorities and the poor. We were particularly concerned with job creation and the availability of energy supplies in the future. The shortage of energy had a devastating impact on the poor. Jobs that depended on low energy cost were being lost. The impact of the downturn in the economy was hardest on those at the bottom rung of the economic ladder.

The principal speaker for the conference was Secretary of Energy James R. Schlesinger. I also spoke, along with Congressman Charles Rangel of New York and the noted economist and NAACP national economic consultant, Dr. Andrew Brimmer. The conference received significant national media coverage, not all of it favorable. There were some in the media and other groups who felt that we had gotten into bed with the energy lobby. Of course, that was not at all the case. Our concern was with looking at alternative forms of energy to ensure that the American economy was not crippled by future Middle-East oil-producing nations' boycotts. We recognized that in any major economic downturn, African Americans would be hit first and hardest.

Any objective observer who looks back at that period would conclude that the actions taken by the NAACP were prudent not just for blacks, but for the nation in general.

On October 12, the U.S. Supreme Court heard oral arguments on *Regents of the University of California v. Bakke,* which involved Allan Bakke, a white student denied admission to the University of California at Davis Medical School. The University of California at Davis had designed a special admissions program to overcome the discriminatory history of the school, which had admitted only one African American since it opened its doors in 1966. With the Minority Student Program that set aside 16 seats for racial minorities, only four blacks were admitted in 1971, five in 1972, six in 1973, and six in 1974. No black students were admitted through regular admission during these years.

Bakke alleged that the special admissions program, one for which he was not eligible to apply, constituted reverse discrimination. The NAACP held that race could be used as a factor in the admissions policies of the medical school. The Supreme Court had stunned the civil rights community by agreeing earlier that year to grant certiorari and entertain oral and written arguments on the question of whether race may be considered by a state agency in fashioning a special admissions program.

The NAACP filed an amicus curiae (friend of the court) brief in support of the affirmative action concept with the U.S. Supreme Court. As I and others in the civil rights community saw it, the issue in the *Bakke* case was whether the University of California at Davis could constitutionally reserve for admission up to 16 places for economically disadvantaged students and consider race in the process. It was our contention that should the U.S. Supreme Court hold that the Fourteenth Amendment's equal protection clause absolutely prohibits the use of race as a criterion, for all practical purposes, the amendment would have been effectively repealed!

The following year the Court handed down its decision in the *Bakke* case. Our hopes were realized when Justice Lewis F. Powell, a southerner from Richmond, Virginia, appointed by President Richard Nixon, agreed with our position. By a 5-4 vote, the Court allowed race to continue to be used as a factor in admissions and hiring.

I had countless discussions with some of the best lawyers in the country, many with decades of experience in constitutional law. I cannot begin to tell you how I agonized over the impact of an adverse decision. As I traveled across the country and appeared on a variety of TV and radio talk shows, I made a point of trying to educate the public on the issue. Neither I nor anyone else in the civil rights community had argued that race alone should determine admission to any medical school. Our argument was simple. If you could reserve seats for the sons and daughters of alumni, for in-state residents, for veterans and others, why not consider race as one of many factors? There is a little-known fact of which the public is not aware. Most colleges have special admissions programs that have nothing to do with grade-point average or SAT scores.

To say that only race cannot be considered as a factor—one of many—is both hypocritical and specious. The argument of reverse discrimination is a canard bantered about by those who want to maintain the status quo or those who seek to disguise their basic disdain for the hopes and futures of those who have been the victims of years of government-sponsored and -condoned negative action.

We got some good news in November, when the Mississippi Supreme Court unanimously reversed and dismissed a libel-slander judgment against the NAACP. In this instance, a Mississippi jury had issued a judgment against the Association in a lawsuit filed by a white state patrolman charged by the NAACP with beating a black motorist in connection with a traffic arrest. We had been forced to post a $262,000 bond in order to appeal the case.

The NAACP holds its state conferences in the fall months. All of the meetings are held on weekends to accommodate the schedules of the participants, who, by and large, hold full-time jobs. This was a very important season for our volunteer leadership. Elections were conducted and new strategies for the coming year were decided. Resolutions were adopted and new branch leaders were trained. One of the most important functions these events served was to facilitate camaraderie among the delegates. It gave them an opportunity to deal with a number of state and regional concerns.

There were 36 state conferences. Most of these conferences had more delegates in attendance than many national groups had in total membership. And yes, each regional director or chairman expected me to make at least one event. This was my first year, and I did not know any better. I was constantly on and off planes, going from one meeting to another. I did not make the entire circuit that year, and I never tried again. It was simply too much for any human being. I did make it a point to visit at least 10 state conferences each year. I also attended as many regional conferences as I could, within reason.

By the beginning of the new year, 1978, I had basically settled into the post. My office was on the tenth floor of the Westside Federal Saving Bank building at 1790 Broadway in Manhattan. It was a modest office, tastefully appointed but not elaborate. It was the office out of which Roy Wilkins had worked since 1967, when the national office moved from Freedom House at 20 West 40th Street. I had a good view of Columbus Circle. I convinced Gloster Current to stay on and serve as my deputy. He was a tremendous help. His knowledge of the intricacies of the Association was indispensable. Michael Myers, who had been an assistant to Mr. Wilkins, was helping me on policy questions and with research. Mildred Bond Roxborough, who had been Mr. Wilkins' assistant, was working closely with me in fund-raising, special events, and a number of other areas.

Chapter 13

THE DAWNING OF A NEW YEAR/ PROTESTS AGAINST APARTHEID

I had a feeling that 1978 was going to be an exceptional year. The annual corporate meeting was scheduled for the weekend of January 6-9. We had moved the pre-banquet activities to the Harlem State Office Building on 125th Street in Harlem. This symbolic gesture was designed to tell the people of the nation's inner cities that the NAACP intended to focus increased attention on the problem they had to deal with every day. It was also intended to take our leadership to a part of New York that very few of them had ever seen before. I must admit that there were a number of New Yorkers and others who did not find the move from the splendor of a downtown New York hotel to Harlem appealing. However, the majority of the weekend's participants understood what we were trying to do.

We had a number of workshops and, as I had promised in my St. Louis address, we expanded the annual meeting to include branch officers and committee workers who had not normally attended previous meetings. I emphasized the need to develop a better system for dealing with our finances, increasing our membership base, and getting more blacks to vote.

At the annual banquet that was held on Sunday, January 8, I was very proud. I had convinced the board to create a national award in Walter White's honor. Walter White had served as executive secretary of the NAACP from 1931 until his death in 1955. For whatever reason, there had been nothing done to perpetuate and exalt his memory and his contributions. White had almost singlehandedly led the fight against lynching for years. He had strongly supported W.E.B. DuBois in his effort to end colonialism and imperialism by European powers. He had been a

true visionary. Walter White had been a hero to the people of my generation. In simple terms, he deserved some type of formal recognition.

There might be those who will disagree with the criteria we decided to
use for the recipient of the award. The Walter White Award was to be
given annually to a non-African American who had made an outstanding
and selfless commitment to the cause of civil rights and human dignity.
Why a non-African American? We already have a Spingarn Medal that is
given annually for outstanding achievement of an African American. There
were a number of non-black Americans whose sacrifice and dedication to
our fight for freedom deserved recognition. Walter White prided himself
on his ability to reach out across racial lines to people of all races and
creeds to support the movement. He felt, as I do, that in the struggle for
human rights, no group of persons should be denied the opportunity to
participate because they are not black.

With that in mind, we selected as the first recipient of the Walter
White Award one of the best friends that the civil rights struggle has ever
had. He had stood his ground and challenged the racists in his party in
1948 at the Democratic National Convention. He was booed by most of
the southern delegations because of his insistence on the inclusion of a
civil rights plank in the party's platform. He had fought for national laws
to protect the rights of African Americans. He was the "Happy Warrior"
from Minnesota, Senator Hubert Horatio Humphrey.

As fate would have it, Senator Humphrey was critically ill and could
not attend the January 8 dinner personally. His sister, Frances Howard,
accepted the award in his absence. Five days later, January 13, 1978, Senator
Humphrey died. I was told that this award was the last that he received in
life. He was pleased to have been recognized in this way by an organization that he both admired and respected, the NAACP.

I also introduced at the annual meeting the ACT-SO program, conceived by Vernon Jarrett. Again, ACT-SO is the acronym for the Afro-
Academic Cultural Technological Scientific Olympics. The program was
positive and sought to reward students for outstanding scholastic achievement. It had begun as a pilot program in September of 1977 and would
be showcased at the 69th Annual Convention, which was to be held in
Portland, Oregon. It was designed for students in grades 9 through 12
and was created to promote excellence and academic achievement among
black high school students.

Black students were encouraged to compete nationally for prizes and
scholarships in three areas: the arts and humanities, the natural sciences,
and the social sciences. I made it clear that I did not believe this program
could solve all of our problems. It was intended to show that our young

people could and did excel academically as well as in sports and entertainment. The program was also designed to encourage parents to become partners in the quest for scholastic achievement. At the Portland convention, we had 57 participants from 13 cities in the seven regions. We awarded a total of $15,000 in prizes and gifts to the winners.

I also called for a meeting of distinguished African Americans in my St. Louis convention speech in July of 1976. At the meeting of the board in January, the board endorsed the concept and formally issued a call for black leaders and organizations to join the NAACP at a conference on May 6-8 to be held in Chicago. The objective of the meeting was to map a coherent national strategy for the next 10 years. The focus of the conference was to establish priorities and direction for the next phase of the struggle for equality. I might add, much has been said about bringing black groups together. The NAACP had convened meetings of national black organizations for years.

On May 6, more than 300 civil rights leaders, educators, lawyers, urban planners, elected officials, appointed officials, economists, ministers and other religious leaders, physicians, psychologists, labor leaders, sociologists, journalists, social workers, and representatives of the poor assembled at Chicago's Conrad Hilton Hotel. We adopted an agenda for the next decade and agreed to guidelines for a more effective working relationship. Principal speakers included Ronald Brown of the National Urban League; Dr. Joseph Lowery, president of the Southern Christian Leadership Conference; Dr. Carlton Goodlet, of the National Newspaper Publishers Association; William Coleman, former U.S. Secretary of Transportation; Clarence Mitchell, director of the NAACP Washington Bureau; William Brock, the chairman of the Republican National Committee; and John White, chairman of the Democratic National Committee.

The conference succeeded in bringing together the organizations and individuals who were working, each in their own way, in communities around the country dealing with the plight of the poor, the disadvantaged, and minorities. This, we believed, would minimize the duplication of effort that was so prevalent. That coalition is still held together by common interests and the mutual recognition of the others.

South Africa: Protesting Apartheid

Growing up in the South in a period when segregation and racial discrimination were in full bloom, I found South Africa's immoral system of apartheid to be an anathema. The systematic oppression of 34 million native black Africans by five million whites of European descent was repugnant and intolerable.

In the 1950s, Dr. King, Walter White, and Roy Wilkins made reference to the immoral treatment of blacks in that land. They saw, as I did, a direct parallel in the morality of our struggle here in America and that of our brothers and sisters in South Africa. I realized early that one major difference in our respective plights was that at least here in this nation, we had a Constitution that gave us a mechanism through which black America could seek redress. In South Africa, blacks were excluded by the guiding legal instruments from any such redress.

I had followed the NAACP's involvement in the affairs of Africa since my childhood. I had read the writings and speeches of W.E.B. DuBois and Walter White, Roy Wilkins, Thurgood Marshall, and others in *The Crisis* magazine. They railed against the conditions blacks faced in South Africa. I remember Dr. King visibly showing emotion whenever he talked about apartheid. Andy Young, the Reverend Billie Kyle of Memphis, and countless other preachers who were active in the movement were also deeply committed to seeing the system completely dismantled.

Today it is fashionable for some to attempt to rewrite history. There are some who say that the Civil Rights Movement began in 1954 with the *Brown v. Board of Education* decision. Some say that the civil rights movement began in 1955 in Montgomery with Rosa Parks and Dr. Martin Luther King and the bus boycott. That is not true. To many, the fight against imperialism, colonialism, and apartheid had its beginnings in the 1950s and in the 1980s with TransAfrica. That also is not true.

Further, it is psychologically damaging for young people, particularly black youngsters, to be led to believe that blacks in this country were for decades oblivious or indifferent to the struggles of our brothers and sisters in Africa or even in Haiti, for that matter. This is not to take away from the role a number of individuals and other groups played during the final phase of the fight for freedom. I hold that the revolution started in 1619 when many in America—both blacks and whites—were agitating for citizenship, inclusion, and equitable treatment of blacks. We must not forget Harriet Tubman, Sojourner Truth, Elijah Lovejoy, Wendell Garrison, Dred Scott, Julia Ward Howe, Frederick Douglass, Nat Turner, and John Brown.

I salute particularly the contributions of TransAfrica and others. I laud the help that we got from members of the Congressional Black Caucus, especially from Congressman Charles Diggs of Michigan, in the early days of the struggle. I pay tribute to Reverend Leon Sullivan, president and founder of Opportunity Industrial Center, who worked tirelessly to bring down the immoral system of apartheid in South Africa. It was Dr. Sullivan who called, early on, for the divestment in South Africa by U.S. firms and institutions. It was Dr. Sullivan who crafted the Sullivan Principles, which called for equal pay for equal work, for the end to the pass system, and all other vestiges of apartheid. I also pay tribute to non-African Americans in the House and the Senate who supported us in the long and arduous fight, which culminated in majority rule.

Consequently, it is instructive to give some background on the NAACP's involvement in the South African fight. All who witnessed the historic elevation of Nelson Mandela from the status of political prisoner to his election as president of South Africa can be proud. The NAACP's involvement with Africa is a long-standing one. Among the individuals who were responsible for the organization of the NAACP was Dr. William Edward Burghardt DuBois, a leader of the movement known as Pan-Africanism.

In 1900, Dr. DuBois headed an American delegation to the first Pan-African Congress in London. (Other delegates included attorney Sylvester Williams, of Trinidad, and Bautista Sylvan, of Haiti.) In 1905, Dr. DuBois helped found the Niagara Movement, a precursor of the NAACP. Meetings of the Niagara Movement included references to African independence. Since 1910, the Association has been actively involved in international affairs. Four NAACP delegates attended the first Universal Race Congress in London. The second Universal Race Conference, scheduled to meet in Paris in 1915, was canceled because of World War I.

In 1909, the NAACP was founded, and Dr. DuBois accepted the position of director of research and public relations. In 1910, Dr. DuBois went to Paris with the specific purpose of regenerating and reorganizing the dormant Pan-Africa movement. The most significant product of Dr. DuBois' work in Paris was his assistance in the founding of the African National Congress, which was organized in 1912. The ANC adopted the practices and legal strategies of the NAACP as a model until the legal strategy and nonviolent protest efforts were rendered ineffective because of repressive practices of the white minority South African apartheid regime. In the 1950s and 1960s the organization's leaders were imprisoned, and the ANC eventually was banned by the government, a prohibition finally lifted by State President F.W. De Klerk in February 1990.

In 1918, the NAACP sent Dr. DuBois, then editor of *The Crisis*, to report on the Versailles Peace Conference as historian, to collect material for a history of the Negro's part in the just-ended World War, and "as representative of the NAACP to summon a Pan-African Congress." Despite great difficulties, permission was finally secured from the French government to hold the Congress, but the United States and the colonial powers refused to issue passports to those who wished to attend. Most of the delegates who attended were already in France because of the war. It was finally an NAACP-financed Congress that opened in Paris in February 1919. Of the 15 countries represented, nine were African, accounting for 12 delegates out of 57. Twenty-one representatives came from the West Indies and 16 from the United States.

Throughout the years, the NAACP continued its efforts on behalf of emerging Third World countries, with specific emphasis on Africa. In 1919, its executive secretary, John Shillady, developed the theme "Africa in the world Democracy" for the NAACP Annual Meeting. In 1927, the fourth Pan-African Congress was held in New York City on August 21-24. This conference was called by Mrs. Addie W. Hunton, former field secretary of the NAACP. There were 58 delegates from 28 states and 11 foreign countries. A committee was formed to call a conference in 1928, at which time plans were made to develop a structure for a permanent organization.

Subsequently, NAACP staff, including James Weldon Johnson, Walter White, Thurgood Marshall, and Roy Wilkins, were sent on fact-finding tours to Africa and other countries, from which the NAACP's policy evolved. Roy Wilkins also participated in the drafting of the United Nations Charter at Dumbarton Oaks in 1944-45. In 1972, Roy visited South Africa. Subsequently, in 1977, an NAACP task force was sent on a fact-finding mission to South Africa and issued a voluminous report.

W.E.B. DuBois returned to the association at the invitation of the Board as Director of Special Research. His duties included preparing the case of Africans and persons of Negro descent for the peace conferences and postwar planning authorities; clarifying and unifying their ideas, plans, and demands; facilitating the collection of facts concerning colored people, in war and peace; and relating these facts to democracy and peace in the future. In 1947, DuBois issued "An Appeal to the World" for the NAACP and presented the document to the United Nations. The appeal aptly represented the apogee of the NAACP's long struggle to draw international attention to the inhuman exploitation of colonial territories by the imperial powers as well as to the rampant manifestations of racism in America. This was the NAACP's mission.

The NAACP moved aggressively and quickly to bring the issue of the subjugated peoples in Africa and other colonies to the attention of the world. With the adoption of the United Nations Charter, the NAACP maintained its pressure on the international community for a satisfactory resolution of the colonialism question. A resolution adopted at the NAACP's Annual Convention in 1946 urged the U.N. to "appeal to the conscience of mankind and to proceed with all speed toward the implementation of the trusteeship and non-self-governing territories provisions of the Charter, not only for the former mandates, but for all colonies and possessions of all nations."

The NAACP welcomed the independence of the Philippines. And, in unusually harsh language, the Association "vehemently" protested "the imprudent demand of the Union of South Africa for annexation of Southwest Africa." This demand, the NAACP noted, was being made by a ". . . country which, of all nations in the world, has proven itself shamelessly incompetent to treat darker peoples decently or with elementary justice."

The NAACP's support of the U.N. as an indispensable peace-keeping institution has never waned. No human rights issue has drawn more sustained denunciation from the NAACP than the South African government's system of subjugation. Here are a few highlights of that effort.

- Pressing the fight, the NAACP convention in 1951 denounced the granting of a World Bank loan to South Africa. In repeated resolutions and demands to the State Department, the NAACP called attention to South Africa's annexation of Southwest Africa as well as to "its brutal disregard for the human and political rights of its native and Indian population." The following year, the NAACP Convention declared that the U.S. government "should be especially quick to support nationalist movements among colonial peoples because independence is the best answer to Communist intrigue." Americans reaffirmed the policy in 1960, when the NAACP called for a boycott of South African goods.
- That year, the NAACP also demanded that the U.S. "press for prompt action by the U.N. on the complaints which have been brought against the Union of South Africa on behalf of both Africans and Asians, including, if necessary, military intervention by the U.N."
- 1965—The boycott call was widened and extended to the international community. That year, the NAACP convention recommended ". . . that the U.S. government, in accordance with requests by the U.N. Special Committee on Apartheid, take steps to encourage Presidential and Congressional action to discourage, if not prohibit, further U.S. investments and loans to South Africa."
- 1968—NAACP repeated its call for the prohibition on U.S. in-

vestments and loans to South Africa, and in addition, urged the
U.S. "to sever all economic, diplomatic, military, and cultural relationships with the racist regimes of Portugal, Rhodesia, and South
Africa, and to extend recognition and aid to the currently existing
liberation movements of these areas."

- 1971—NAACP calls for a boycott of U.S. companies that did not
  use their influence to change the system of apartheid. This demand
  was repeated and expanded the following year, when the NAACP
  Convention urged American companies to make "a fresh review"
  of their employment practices so as to improve the conditions of
  their black workers in South Africa. All of this occurred long before
  the South African issue became popular.
- 1972—Roy Wilkins visited South Africa on a fact-finding mission.
- 1976—The NAACP National Board of Directors adopted a resolution, which, among other things, directed its chairman to establish a task force on Africa. This group was charged with studying
  and developing "a meaningful and lasting policy on Africa for the
  guidance of its members and the nation."
- The NAACP Task Force, chaired by Dr. Broadus N. Butler, then
  chairman of the International Affairs Committee of the NAACP
  National Board, was sent on a fact-finding mission to South Africa.
- October 20, 1976 through June 5, 1977—The task force conducts
  its deliberations in nine meetings and one month of African visits.
- 1977-1985—Clarence Mitchell and Althea Simmons lobbied aggressively for the U.S. to pressure South Africa to end its policy of
  apartheid. Executive Director Benjamin L. Hooks made a series of
  speeches and called on corporate executives and business and foundation leaders to support efforts to force the Pretoria government
  to end apartheid in South Africa.
- 1978—March 18: Led by Executive Director Hooks, the NAACP
  mounted a huge demonstration against participation of a South
  African team at the Davis Cup tennis matches in Nashville, Tennessee. The march against apartheid, termed by the media as "the
  biggest demonstration since the '60s," brought together nearly
  20,000 persons from all over the country and from the universities
  in Nashville—Fisk, Tennessee State, Meharry, and Vanderbilt—
  swelled by other student groups from the South. Vanderbilt University refused to withdraw sponsorship on the grounds of
  "adherence to an open forum" policy under which Vanderbilt permits free speech for all ideological spectrums. The NAACP demonstration was in line with the recommendations of the NAACP

Task Force on Africa, a group headed by Dr. Butler, chairman of the NAACP National Board Committee on International Affairs, which visited several African countries in 1977.

In addition to Opportunity Industrial Center, the NAACP was one of the first groups to arouse public opinion against the atrocities in South Africa through this march. The NAACP, which has been fighting against colonialism since its inception, by the rally in Nashville March 18 once again demonstrated that through various pressures the country can be forced to take another look at a racist ally whose repressive tactics against the black majority are abhorrent to many in the United States of America and elsewhere throughout the world.

The report and the recommendations of the Task Force on Africa were endorsed and adopted during the 69th Annual NAACP Convention. As set forth in the resolution, the NAACP recognized from its inception that the freedom of black people in the United States is linked to the freedom of black people everywhere, and especially in Africa, when it helped finance the Pan-African Congress held in Europe in 1919, 1921, and 1923. One of its founders, Dr. W.E.B. DuBois, made this point 10 years before when he participated in the organization of the NAACP. The NAACP from its beginning dedicated itself to Pan-Africanism and the liberation of all black people. Specific reference is made to Resolutions on South Africa passed by the NAACP National Convention in 1966, 1971, and 1972. These resolutions called for the elimination of apartheid, divestment, and the adoption of the Sullivan Principles.

Donald Woods, former editor of *The Daily Dispatch* in East London and author of the most widely syndicated column in South Africa, made his daring escape from South Africa. The story made headlines in the world press. Since his escape, Wood has continued his indictment of the Vorster regime and its policy of apartheid before an international forum. Woods also met with President Carter, Vice President Mondale, Secretary Vance, and a number of State Department officials. He testified before the Senate Committee on Foreign Relations and the House Committee on International Relations. He talked to the Executive Council of the AFL-CIO and was invited to give a major address at the NAACP's National Convention in Portland, Oregon. These speeches were, in part, responsible for the sanctions being levied against South Africa.

- 1981—At its regular quarterly meeting in New York City, the NAACP National Board of Directors adopted a resolution that strongly criticized the Reagan Administration for blocking U.N.

Security Council resolutions condemning South Africa's invasion of Angola, which "violated our own pledge of unity with our Western allies."

- 1984—NAACP National Board of Directors adopted a statement attacking South African policies along with the Reagan Administration's continuing tolerance of the minority-ruled country. The board's criticism followed a series of uprisings that resulted in the deaths of scores of blacks and helped create what the statement described as a "volcanic situation."

- 1985— *The Crisis* magazine featured an in-depth interview with the wife of imprisoned ANC leader Nelson Mandela, "A CRISIS Special Report from South Africa: The Soul of Nonzamo Winnie Mandela." *The Crisis* magazine featured an eyewitness account article commenting firsthand on South Africa by investment banker Nadine B. Hack.

Call to Action Produces Results: 1985

I called upon branches of the NAACP to intensify demonstrations against apartheid actions. Branches demonstrated against the South African Embassy and consulates in Washington, D.C., New York City, Los Angeles, Chicago, Houston, Boston, Portland (Oregon), Seattle, and Mobile (Alabama). Regional Directors Dockery, Shinhoster, Canson, Brown, Anderson, and Burns coordinated these efforts.

- Led by Midwest Regional Director Charles Anderson, 160 NAACP members met with the vice counsul of the South African Consulate in Chicago to discuss the Association's concerns over the treatment of blacks by his white-dominated government.

- Earl Shinhoster, Southeast Regional Director, coordinated an NAACP "teach-in" at St. Louis Street Missionary Baptist Church, Mobile, Alabama, where Mr. Kelly M. Alexander, Jr., president of NAACP North Carolina Conference of Branches, led discussions on South African issues.

- Richard L. Dockery, Southwest Regional Director, led a huge delegation of NAACP members in Houston, Texas, in meeting with South African Consulate officials.

- Irvington, New Jersey Branch President William Rutherford led protests against South Africa's apartheid policies and U.S. trade policies with that country. The branch president, along with other community leaders, was arrested.

- Albany, New York Branch members were arrested in the lobby of the Leo W. O'Brien Federal Building in a sit-down protest against South Africa's policy of racial segregation.
- Regional Director Dr. Emmett C. Burns coordinated protest rallies sponsored by the Prince Georges County, Baltimore, Howard County, Montgomery County (Maryland), Alexandria, Arlington (Virginia), and the Washington, D.C. branches.
- The Detroit (Central), Michigan Branch sponsored a series of demonstrations denouncing apartheid in South Africa.
- The NAACP sent a telegram to President Reagan, commending the Administration's public denunciation of the "official violence" being carried on in South Africa.
- New York City: 300 NAACP members led by Michael A. Lawrence, special assistant to Benjamin L. Hooks; Paula Brown, Northeast Regional Director; and Leroy Mobley, director of the NAACP Prison Program, demonstrated against apartheid with a labor coalition at the South African Consulate.
- NAACP Convention passed resolutions in support of H.R. 1460, the Anti-Apartheid Act. Branches of the NAACP followed with messages to congressmen urging passage.
- Executive Director Hooks, Mrs. Enolia McMillan, OIC President Reverend Edward Hailes, and other NAACP officials participated in three marches.
- The Norwalk, Connecticut Branch held a demonstration and candle-lighting service protesting apartheid in South Africa.
- The Atlanta, Georgia Branch sponsored a march to dramatize the NAACP's opposition to the violence in South Africa and that country's apartheid government.
- Alabama NAACP branches sponsored a march protesting apartheid in South Africa. The march ended at Kelly Ingham Park. Speakers included Regional Director Shinhoster and representatives from the Urban League, SCLC, and other organizations.
- 1986—Led by Executive Director Benjamin Hooks, the NAACP took its plea for economic sanctions against the apartheid regime in South Africa to President Reagan's doorstep on September 15. On that day, more than 1,000 NAACP demonstrators marched before the White House to urge the President to sign the sanctions legislation. Presidential aides had expressed opposition to the bill, saying it was counter to the Administration's policy of "constructive engagement."

- The NAACP sponsored demonstrations in New York against apartheid and racial violence in South Africa. The initial series of demonstrations were held on Wednesday, Thursday, and Friday (August 28-30) in front of the South African Mission and Consulate at the United Nations, located at 326 East 40th Street between First and Second Avenue in Manhattan.
- The NAACP called for a National Day of Mourning on October 5, 1984. All NAACP branches were requested to participate.
- The NAACP conducted a National Day of Mourning ceremony at St. Patrick's Cathedral, led by Executive Director Hooks, Cardinal O'Connor, and New York City Mayor Koch. Thousands attended the service—and more than 10,000 joined in the march down Fifth Avenue.
- Park East Synagogue held a continuation of the ceremony in the evening with New York Conference Branch President Hazel Dukes. More than 200 branches across the nation conducted services on this historic day.
- 1986—The NAACP presented its William Edward Burghardt DuBois International Medal to Nelson Mandela, the leader of the African National Congress, who was then imprisoned in South Africa, requiring a presentation in absentia. *The Crisis* magazine featured "A CRISIS Report on the NAACP and South Africa," which chronicled the history of this important relationship. In an address to the Union Mutual Benefit Association Allied Educational Foundation on September 23, Benjamin L. Hooks, executive director of the NAACP, stated: "Race is a central element of the struggle in South Africa; yet at bottom, the struggle in South Africa is not just a matter of race, it is a matter of humanity; in the last and final analysis, the struggle there is but another example, another battleground, of the struggle between good and evil." For years the NAACP has worked vigorously to bring an end to apartheid in South Africa.
- In June 1986, the NAACP sponsored the "March for Human Dignity in South Africa and at Home." The march began on June 1 in Los Angeles, California, and culminated at the NAACP's 77th Annual Convention in Baltimore, Maryland, on June 30. This march was led by Joe Madison.

The purpose of the 3,000-mile trek (the first cross-country civil rights march in history) was to seek worldwide support of a one-person, one-vote policy in South Africa and advocate a peaceful political change from the government's denial of basic political and economic rights to the country's 72 percent black majority population. Some white South Africans vowed they would never allow one person, one vote in South Africa, which has a white population of only five million. One person, one vote would mean the transition from apartheid to self-determination. In addition, the NAACP launched a national voter-participation program that linked domestic and international issues.

Local NAACP chapters and marchers along the route collected signatures for petitions and conducted rallies and symposiums demanding the rights for South African blacks. The petitions were presented to the U.S. Congress, the South African Embassy in Washington, D.C., and the United Nations. Senator Charles Mathias (R-MD) received the petitions at a plenary session of the 77th NAACP Convention.

Also in June, the U.S. House of Representatives overwhelmingly approved the Dellums Amendment, which called for the cutoff of all trade between the United States and South Africa. The measure also imposed strict penalties against corporate violations of these sanctions. The NAACP made passage of the Dellums Amendment by the U.S. Senate a high priority simply because this legislation would accomplish what otherwise would require years of piecemeal effort.

All NAACP branches across the country were moved into high gear. I requested that they contact the senators from their states and ask them to support the Dellums legislation (S.2570) when it was considered in the Senate. I reminded branches, "There is no more urgent task before us than passage of this vital legislation." The branches were instructed to "let their senators know the strength and passion of the NAACP's determination to secure passage of the Dellums Amendment."

S.2570 called upon U.S. firms to make a complete economic withdrawal from South Africa and would prohibit direct or indirect investment by U.S. firms in South Africa. In addition, the legislation would ban the importation of any South African products, except for materials that were certified by the President as essential for the defense of the United States. The NAACP's nationwide lobbying effort for the enactment of South African sanctions moved into high gear in July, when a special task force met on Capitol Hill to plot strategy to secure passage of S.2570.

1987—The first meeting of the South African Task Force was held on August 22, 1987, in New York City. Task force members developed the following goals:

- Get American companies out of South Africa.
- Have Congress pass measure to reach congressional intent regarding South African sanctions.
- Establish closer liaison with international free trade unions.
- Encourage all leading industrial nations to stop doing business with South Africa.
- Communicate with people in South Africa to assure NAACP support for people of South Africa.

The second meeting of the South African Task Force was held on October 22, 1987, in Little Rock, Arkansas. At this meeting, the task force made a preliminary report to the National Executive Board on the previously reported goals and recommended the following actions:

- Explain findings from USIA for furthering South African programs.
- Continue the NAACP's support of the Shell Oil boycott.
- Publish an article in *The Crisis* relating to the NAACP's actions on South Africa.

The third meeting of the South African Task Force was held in New York City on February 19, 1988. The following activities were endorsed:

- A South African roundtable was held on the legislative mobilization on Tuesday, March 8, 1988.
- A South African Day was designated during the National Convention.
- Active support was provided to encourage passage of national legislation that addresses the South African concern.

The fourth meeting of the South African Task Force was held in Atlanta, Georgia, on June 18, 1988. The task force reviewed plans for the South African Day scheduled for the National Convention on July 14, 1988, in Washington, D.C. The task force recommended that the NAACP adopt the following position statements:

- The NAACP vociferously opposes the continuation and escalation of repressive actions in South Africa.
- The NAACP objects to further bans on the press in South Africa.
- The NAACP deplores the restrictions placed on the rights of assembly for groups opposing apartheid.

For the first time in the history of the NAACP, on July 14, 1988, at the Washington, D.C., convention, the entire convention left the site of its meeting to engage in a protest against apartheid. The more than 8,000 delegates, alternates, and guests, joined by thousands of anti-apartheid opponents, conducted peaceful protests.

- 1990—Nelson Mandela is released from prison on February 11. In anticipation of his official visit to the United States, the NAACP distributed tens of thousands of posters to NAACP members in cities to be visited by Mandela. The posters captioned the NAACP's support of sanctions, one man/one vote, and self-determination, and welcomed Mandela to the United States.
- In New York, NAACP National President Hazel Dukes worked diligently to ensure a huge turnout for the ticker-tape parade honoring Nelson Mandela.
- In Detroit, NAACP Board Chairman William F. Gibson worked with board member Tom Turner, visit coordinator, to welcome Mandela to that city.
- Southeast Regional Coordinator Earl Shinhoster coordinated activities in Atlanta for the Mandela visit. Board Chairman Gibson was among the many civil rights activists who greeted Mandela.
- In Miami, Johnnie McMillian, local president of the NAACP, labored in her area to ensure a warm welcome for the Mandela party.
- I joined Mandela in Washington and Boston as an official delegate to welcome him to this country.
- September 21, 1990—I issued this statement on the White House visit by South African President F.W. DeKlerk: "The NAACP endorses the demonstration organized by TransAfrica to protest the visit of President F.W. DeKlerk of the Union of South Africa to the White House."

The controversy over Vanderbilt University's role as host to the Davis Cup tennis matches escalated as the NAACP, religious and civic organizations, and students and faculty members in Nashville and throughout the nation protested the university's implied support for a racist regime whose team was playing on campus. Dr. Emmett D. Fields, the president of Vanderbilt, and the chancellor, Dr. Alexander Heard, continued to assert that although they were opposed to apartheid, the university would not be pressured into canceling the matches.

I was working with the Coalition for Human Rights in South Africa. This was an ad hoc group consisting of a number of groups headed by Franklin H. Williams. Williams was a friend of the Association. He had served as our West Coast regional director at one time. He was one of the first persons to offer his assistance when I was elected to the directorship of the NAACP. Franklin was now president of the Phelps-Stokes Fund.

After a series of meetings with representatives of Vanderbilt University and the U.S. Tennis Association failed to resolve the chasm between the principles, we called for a boycott of the matches and for a massive demonstration to draw attention to the rogue nation of South Africa's participation in the event. This was the first mass demonstration that I was to call after coming to the NAACP.

Demonstrations are the court of last resort. They are complicated to organize and carry out. They are also extremely costly. We had to arrange for transporting marchers; provide for restroom and first aid stations; print signs and handbills; obtain permits and permissions; make security arrangements with local law enforcement and public safety personnel; invite and confirm speakers; and build a platform.

I considered the expense in time, staff, and funds in making the decision to go forward. There was also the element of turnout. If, for any reason, including weather, there was not a crowd, the media would have a field day. "The NAACP Can Only Attract 500 People for a National Demonstration" would be the headline in the major newspapers. The television networks would show wide-angle shots of a sparse crowd.

In short order I decided to move ahead. This demonstration was about principle. It was about an American institution of higher learning granting refuge to the most racist nation on the planet. We would make it work. I called in Gloster Current, who was serving as my deputy, and Althea Simmons, then director of branches, and told them that we had to pull out all the stops. We would have to send staff out immediately to handle the logistics of the march. We did not have much time. We had to mobilize our branches. The participating groups were not grassroots organizations, nor did they have a membership base. The burden of producing demonstrators would have to be ours.

We sent Janice Washington, regional youth director, and James Brown, Jr., national youth director, to Nashville. We set up telephone banks and produced reams of flyers and thousands of signs. Staff worked evenings and weekends making calls. Our public relations department swung into action. The effort paid off; we began to get calls from those who shared our disdain for the South African government and who wanted to join the march. There was a feeling of excitement in the air.

Apparently in an effort to allay some of the international pressure that was mounting, the South African Tennis Union selected Peter Lamb, a "colored" 18-year-old sophomore at Vanderbilt, and appointed him to the South African team. The ploy did not work. I pointed out in a statement released by the national office that "The designation by the South

African Tennis Union of Peter Lamb to South Africa's Davis Cup appears to be tokenism, 'too little and too late,' and fails to meet the NAACP's objections to the participation by the United States in the Davis Cup tennis tournament in Nashville, March 17-19."

The statement continued, "It appears that Mr. Lamb, who is 'colored' in the South African sense, will not be playing, but is merely selected as an added member of the South African team. Based on our knowledge, we cannot buy this arrangement." With those words the die was cast.

The momentum continued to build. As the days leading up to the March 18 demonstration approached, groups, faculty members, local civil right organizations, and our Nashville branch sponsored "speak-outs" on or near Vanderbilt's campus. Julian Bond, then a Georgia state senator and president of our Atlanta branch, addressed overflow crowds at Fisk and Tennessee State universities on March 16.

Bond reminded the young people that it was difficult to discuss South Africa with Americans who are used to living in a country where civil rights are more or less guaranteed. Bond challenged the students to become an "informed, articulate, and aggressive force for change in South Africa, for the dismantling of racism, for the beginning of a better day."

When the marchers assembled on the morning of Saturday, March 18, there were hundreds of buses. Most were charters, but there were also some church and organizational buses. The enthusiastic crowd was in good spirits. It was estimated that around 20,000 protestors attended the demonstration. Many newspapers across the country termed the turnout as "the biggest demonstration since the '60s."

Ossie Davis, the famous actor, director and producer, presided. Among the day's speakers were Bayard Rustin, president, A. Philip Randolph Institute, and famous civil rights leader William H. Booth, New York State Supreme Court judge, and civil rights activists Dick Gregory; Dr. Joseph Lowery, president, Southern Christian Leadership Conference; Clarence Coleman, deputy executive director, National Urban League; and Margaret Bush Wilson, chairman of the NAACP Board of Directors. I was the final speaker.

I wanted to say something that would lay out clearly the case for our nation to take seriously the problems that blacks faced in South Africa. Most white Americans had a problem understanding the problems we faced at home as African Americans. To get them to focus on problems thousands of miles away would require a clear message. The networks were covering the rally. We had only one chance to get our message across.

This is how *The Crisis* reported excerpts from the speech:

In a rousing address, frequently interrupted by cheers and applause, Executive Director Hooks closed the rally with one of his greatest speeches: "We have come today to say by our presence, to our brothers and sisters in South Africa—we do care; we are concerned. We have come to protest the brutal death of Steve Biko; to protest the investigation into his death which absolved the authorities; to applaud the courageous, massive protest by thousands of black students in Soweto Township; to protest the more than 3,000 South Africans detained without trial; to protest a vicious pass system which restricts free movement; to protest a tennis match, but that is incidental; to protest those who host it, those who participate in it, those who come to watch it. We have come to protest against those who would use the tennis matches as proof that the world is really not concerned about what South Africa does; to score points for humanity and humane treatment everywhere; to raise the consciousness level of Americans everywhere so that they can no longer claim to be innocent as it relates to South Africa; because our own memories are not short, and we remember only too well how just a few short years ago we had to protest, march, demonstrate, boycott, roll in to change things here in Nashville, and in America; to say thanks Mr. Ali, thanks Mr. Spinks, for not going to South Africa with your title match. We support economic sanctions against the racist South African government. We urge stockholders of those industries doing business in South Africa to call upon their companies to withdraw. We urge bank depositors to withdraw their accounts from banks making loans to South Africa. We urge the exclusion of racist South Africa from all athletic and cultural competition until all South Africans, regardless of race or color, are able to compete freely. We come here today to volley against injustice in tennis, to volley against injustice in sports, and to volley against the total injustice in South Africa. We come because we know we have been effective in the past."

He ended his speech by calling on his hearers to fight in until victory is won over apartheid.

The NAACP rally drew national attention to the growing disenchantment of many Americans with South Africa's apartheid policy. *The New York Times* declared in an editorial on Sunday, April 2, 1978, that the issue of South Africa had stirred the campuses again and that:

protest flows from the base proposition that Americans should not profit from a political system and economy that are rooted in racist doctrine and envision the permanent exploitation of South Africa's black majority. Some of the protestors believe that American pressure sure could significantly improve the conditions of blacks. All of them want, in any case, to cleanse the American conscience by moving toward an end of all collaboration with apartheid.

The objective of the protest is clear and admirable. We support it. South Africa is not the only racist nation on earth, certainly not the only oppressive one. But no other contemporary government—and certainly none that stands for the culture of the West—has dared to define itself as the embodiment of white supremacy. To Americans now, such doctrine is simply unacceptable.

Chapter 14

THE BUMP IN THE ROAD

During the spring of 1978, I visited more than 50 NAACP branches, state conferences, and youth units. Spring for the NAACP was the season for regional conferences. There are seven regions in the Association. All hold conferences annually between January and May. It was here that our volunteer leaders were trained in new strategies and informed on matters of mutual concern to their respective states' conferences, branches, and youth units. These meetings are important opportunities for NAACP representatives at the local and state levels to renew old acquaintances.

I made a point during my first year of going to each of the regional conferences. I believe that my attendance was as beneficial to me as it was to the participants. Just observing the vitality and excitement of the volunteers had a way of reinvigorating me. The outpouring of love and support was also heartening.

My first annual convention as executive director was held in Portland, Oregon, in June. I was somewhat nervous because I did not know all of the intricacies and subtle nuances of such a large and complicated convention. I had experience in putting on national meetings for fraternal and other related organizations. However, an NAACP convention was quite different. The sheer size of these meetings, the number of delegates, the alternates, observers, visitors, exhibitors, and local citizens attending the public sessions is staggering.

There were speakers to be invited and resolutions to be prepared. We had to plan for a separate youth convention that was being held simultaneously with the adult convention. The youth had their own workshops, speakers, luncheons, and awards banquets. Then there was the new program that I had introduced along with the volunteer national ACT-SO chairman, Vernon Jarrett, the previous year. We had to make special logistical arrangements to accommodate the ACT-SO competition. Special stages, lighting, and props were necessary. All of these diverse activities had to be brought together harmoniously.

An NAACP convention is unlike any other national meeting in the nation. We had more than 3,000 voting delegates, up to 3,000 alternates, 2,000 observers, and 2,000 invited guests attending. We also had more than a dozen workshops, inspirational speakers, and addresses from the leaders of both political parties. Often, the President of the United States addressed the convention. Starting in the early 1970s, we began to have a national exposition where exhibitors from a variety of companies displayed their products and services. Some exhibitors recruited employees on the spot. Resolutions on every conceivable subject were introduced and voted upon by delegates. There were luncheons and banquets held throughout the week. We had religious services and gospel concerts. There were receptions for adults and dances for our youth.

Then there was the press and its demands that had to be considered. The media coverage was of paramount importance. We might have 10,000 people attending a convention, but the impression of what took place was dependent upon what the average American saw on the evening news or read in the morning newspapers. Arrangements had to be made for a working pressroom, press tables for the business and mass meetings, and press conferences for invited speakers.

We were all excited about the upcoming Portland meeting. Then came the bump in the road. On the eve of the annual convention, June 28, the U.S. Supreme Court ruling in the *Bakke* case was announced. I got word within minutes of the announcement. However, I did not have a copy of the actual written opinion. We had anxiously awaited the Court's opinion. We knew that if the Court threw out race as a valid and constitutionally permissible factor that could be considered in college admissions, affirmative action was a dead issue. This would be a lethal blow to the civil rights movement.

The phones began to ring. I spoke with Nathaniel R. Jones, who was our general counsel. Jones, a brilliant constitutional lawyer, suggested that although he did not have a copy of the opinion, he had it on good authority that all was not lost. It was a mixed opinion, he said. By now the news media was calling to get my reaction to the Court's decision. If I learned one thing early as a young lawyer in Memphis, it was this: Never speak on a matter until you have all of the facts in hand. It is always better to wait until you have a copy of a court's decision before commenting publicly.

For the next 45 minutes I fended off calls from reporters. It should be remembered that very few offices had fax machines in those days. If you needed something from Washington, you had to have it sent by train or plane if it was to be delivered that same day. Clarence Mitchell, our Washington Bureau director, told me that he had sent someone from his office to the Court to pick up a copy.

The reporters were getting impatient. Some had already arrived at our office for an official response. Then I received the call that I was waiting for from Clarence. He had a hard copy of the opinion in hand. Clarence and his Bureau counsel, Frank Polhaus, had read it. The Court had agreed with Allan Bakke. He should have been admitted to Davis. That was the bad news. The good news was that race could be a factor in admissions considerations. Affirmative action was still alive!

I met with the members of the press and pointed out the key legal issues set forth by the decision. I made the point of emphasizing that it was a mixed decision. The Court had not abandoned affirmative action. All three networks led off the evening news broadcasts with the U.S. Supreme Court's *Bakke* decision. Their coverage, upon close examination, told the story accurately. However, the next morning most of the major newspapers had headlines suggesting that *Bakke* had won. Affirmative action was a dead issue, according to them. It took some time before most Americans realized that while upholding Bakke, the Court had also left in place the foundations of affirmative action.

Meanwhile, it was important that we communicate to our friends and allies in the civil rights community what the opinion actually meant. When I got to Portland, many of the delegates were confused and apprehensive. Some were even crestfallen. They knew the importance of affirmative action. Many came from the Deep South, where they had experienced public-supported, all-white universities where blacks could not be admitted regardless of how high their test scores were. Some, like me, had to leave their native home states and go north or west in order to get into professional schools— law, medical, and dental. The news of *Bakke,* as reported through the prisms of many of their local newspapers, was devastating!

In order to address the growing apprehension and confusion over what the ruling meant and the implications of the pronouncement, I conferred with Nate Jones. We agreed to arrange for a special plenary session for Wednesday, July 5, to give the delegates an informed assessment of the *Bakke* case. The National Board considered the *Bakke* issue at a special meeting, and so did the lawyers at their annual breakfast meeting. They also analyzed the case in depth.

At my and the general counsel's suggestion, the convention approved a resolution calling for a post-*Bakke* strategy to deal with the implications of the decision. This three-day symposium was held on July 20 in Detroit with 300 legal, government, education, civil rights, and labor representatives present. At the conclusion of the symposium, we adopted the *Bakke* Manifesto, outlining a strategy for dealing with the challenges posed by the Supreme Court's handling of the affirmative issue.

Despite the pall that hung over the convention in the wake of the *Bakke* decision, the 69th Annual Convention met all of my expectations. We had a number of outstanding speakers to address the convention including, Patricia Harris, Secretary, U.S. Department of Housing and Urban Development; Eleanor Holmes Norton, chairwoman of the EEOC; Nathaniel R. Jones, NAACP general counsel; Nathaniel Colley, West Coast NAACP counsel; Julian Bond, Georgia state senator and president of the Atlanta branch; Ernest Green, Assistant Secretary of Labor; Douglas Frazier, president of the United Automobile Workers; Dr. Andrew Brimmer, noted economist; Alexis Herman; and Dr. Kenneth Tollett. I spoke on Tuesday morning.

When the time came for me to speak, I was mindful of the thoughts and emotions of our delegates. They had seen so much progress made as a result of their efforts and those of others like themselves. I desperately wanted to speak to their hopes and not to their fears. I wanted to give them reasons for believing that our fight was still winnable. Honesty also compelled me to realize that I could not just sugarcoat the dilemma we faced. I had to tell them that we were facing—as a people and as a movement— some very dichotomous circumstances. Despite the acrimonious protestations of our adversaries, however, acquiescence was not an option available to us. When I came into the convention center, the portion of the auditorium that we were using was packed. We had to open up another section to accommodate the overflow.

I compared life in America today, good and ill, alternating between a nation that permits free expression to one in which equality is a will-o'-the-wisp; with one million blacks enrolled in colleges, yet thousands finishing high school functionally illiterate; with more than 100 million people at work in America and 10 million blacks employed, yet six million jobless, with black unemployment double that of whites, and among black teenagers, as high as 70 percent; with 25 percent of black families in the middle class, yet 30 percent below the poverty level; with inflation and taxation eating away wages, destroying lifetime savings; with legislation and Supreme Court decisions threatening to wipe out meager gains; with hiring practices improving, but fiscal belt-tightening; with Proposition 13 and other tax revolts around the nation knocking out the last hired, and reducing the delivery of essential human services to minority and poor people.

Proposition 13 is "a bull in a china shop," I said, "threatening to wreck local governments' very source of financing and its ability to match federal initiatives." In this assessment, I intentionally offered a more critical view of this new taxpayer revolt than did the keynoter on the previous evening.

I pointed out that while President Carter was concerned with the poor and outcast, having made good appointments, including Pat Harris, Andy Young, and Cliff Alexander, and issued executive orders sympathetic to civil rights, housing, education, and federal contracts, the President had moved neither fast nor far enough, nor had he been able to win cooperation and muster the votes in support of much-needed programs from a lethargic Congress.

I then gave a laundry list of objectionable items, including: a heavily Democratic Congress passing laws restricting the power of HEW to desegregate school systems; delay in the passage of the Humphrey-Hawkins full-employment bill; denying equal rights to poor women and filibustering labor reform; national health insurance languishing into oblivion; urban crisis exacerbated by massive unemployment; Africa's natural resources becoming the center of competition of many new colonialists and grounds of a new Cold War; South Africa apartheid continuing to defy all rules of decency and humanity; the United States still refusing to impose effective economic sanctions or to regulate the investments of its multinational corporations doing business in South Africa; 80 percent of the white people in America feeling that enough has been done for black people—that it is no longer necessary to give any special attention to racial problems; and 80 percent of the black people believing exactly the opposite.

In my comments to the convention of the *Bakke* decision I was careful to term the *Bakke* decision as both "a victory and a defeat," a victory "for affirmative action because a majority of the Supreme Court had approved the consideration of race in the selection of students to fill highly competitive seats in professional schools." Further, I explained that the Bakke decision upholds affirmative action in concept and practice as a constitutionally appropriate voluntary tool for breaking up patterns of racial exclusion and discrimination. Further, I stated that the Court's decision suggests that where the congress, the president, administrative agencies, and the courts have made findings or reached conclusions about racial discrimination, effective remedies to such practices and patterns of discrimination are in order. These remedies can include goals, timetables, and quotas to bring minorities in where they have been purposefully shut out.

I also explained that "black people suffered a defeat when the Supreme Court ruled that the Davis Medical School Affirmative Action Plan was unconstitutional."

Then I praised Justice Thurgood Marshall. I pointed out that Justice Marshall's opinion reminded us that for many decades the denial of black talent and the frustration of black achievement was a national, public policy, and that this nation has not yet taken enough or sufficient actions necessary to correct these injustices. I agreed with Marshall that 350 years is long enough to wait for our constitutional rights: "It doesn't help for the highest court of the land to say that Allan Bakke was a victim of racial discrimination."—Allan Bakke, who was turned down by eleven medical schools thirteen different times; Allan Bakke, who was rejected by his own alma mater; and rejected by a medical school that did not even admit one black— This is the Bakke who wrote to the dean of Davis Medical School asking for a suggestion as to a way "any way at all" that he could overcome the factor of his age, and be allowed to study medicine. Mr. Bakke chose to challenge the special admissions program that sought to accelerate the admission of qualified blacks. He did not challenge the unofficial, unseen quota system that specially-admitted the sons of politicians, or the dean's special friends and donors of the school.

Citing these rejections of Bakke by other schools, I declared: "The Supreme Court decision must be viewed as a cynical affirmation that all too often "white makes right" in America. A nation that allegedly believes in the rule of law is more concerned with the soothing of white egos than it is with the protection and enforcement of equality for black people, long denied their rights as human beings and as citizens.

Nearly 3,000 delegates and several hundred visitors leaped to their feet as I recited a litany of blacks being tired: We're tired of being used. We're tired of being tricked. We're tired of being patient with such commitments to hypocrisy.

Arguing that there is nothing in the history of Title VI of the Civil Rights Act of 1964 to suggest that it must be strictly construed as requiring color-blindness, I pointed out that the Act was enacted in recognition of the history of this nation's racial prejudice—its national and legal policy of subjugating the black race. It is too late to act like you're color-blind when the majority of whites have benefited from these policies, and the majority of blacks have been kept down by them. To say that any part of the Civil Rights Act of 1964 requires absolute color-blindness, in the context of these realities, is to ignore the truth of history and to subvert the English language. It is an attempt to frustrate, if not deny, the essential means of moving black people into the mainstream of full citizenship except in token numbers.

Taking a militant stance on the decision, I reminded the delegates that the "power arrangements" in America and "the slow progress that black people have been making in overcoming institutional barriers and race prejudice make it crystal-clear that we have got to talk about setting aside a critical mass of spaces in the professional schools to ensure the acceleration of black advancement."

I also served notice on universities, industry, and every institution in America "that if they misread the clear teachings of America's racial history, they are inviting confrontation."

I made clear my belief that the media should cease misrepresenting the *Bakke* decision; the Supreme Court did not outlaw quotas. Then, throwing down the gauntlet to those who oppose meaningful implementation of affirmative action, I said, "Whether it comes in the form of hostile litigation or legislation, wanton and reckless opinion and speculation, foot-dragging by the private sector, or apology and double-talk by government bureaucrats, we will be there to oppose any form of hostility toward the meaningful inclusion of blacks into the American mainstream."

I then announced a follow-up strategy conference in Detroit to be held July 20-22. It would be a meeting of lawyers, social scientists, and keen thinkers to counsel together with us on the meaning, significance, and implications of both the *Bakke* decision and the reactions to it. The purpose of this meeting would be to do the analysis, to lay the plans, and to devise the strategies for measuring and testing this nation's commitment to affirmative action. We would no longer accept pronouncements of public policy that say blacks should be equal when private policy dictates our continued inequality. We could not, should not, and indeed would not let this very narrow personal victory for Allan Bakke obscure the larger verdict of the Court.

In my address on Tuesday morning, I called for the strengthening of black institutions, churches, and business; better financing of organizations; including youth in our programs; and increasing registration and voting, saying to Democrats: "Don't take us for granted, and Republicans, don't ignore us."

I took advantage of the opportunity to praise the NAACP's new youth program of ACT-SO (Afro-Academic Cultural Technological Scientific Olympics), saying that ACT-SO pointed up the great yearning in the hearts of blacks for educational opportunity and the achievement of educational excellence. I promised that the NAACP would press to see that every church basement and every lodge hall becomes an educational sandlot or a mental gymnasium.

Returning to Proposition 13, I sternly warned the delegates that we couldn't allow another "message" like Proposition 13 to pass in another state. Those who have been hurt the most by this reckless and unthinking act must now join together in a common coalition to ensure that their best interest is hereafter protected.

In closing, I paid tribute to the retired and soon-to-be retired senior NAACP executives: "To Roy Wilkins for invaluable counsel, advice, and support, and to Gloster Current for incredible devotion to the cause of duty." I also said thanks a million to Clarence Mitchell, who was retiring soon, but who, like Gloster and Roy, would not by any means be leaving the fight for freedom, justice, and equality.

As what had now become a sermon on civil rights ended, delegates were standing in the aisles waving placards and signposts, as I called the NAACP "the only ship of the past . . . the ship of the present and . . . the ship of the future."

Using that old Negro spiritual "Go Tell It on the Mountain," I summed up my address with these words: "So, go tell it—tell it on the mountains; go tell it on the plains; go tell it in the cities; go tell it in every village, every hamlet; go tell it in every City Council chamber; go tell it in every state house; go tell it in every congress; go tell it in the White House; tell it over the hills, everywhere—Go tell it, that the NAACP is here!"

During the remainder of the convention, wherever delegates saw me or heard me speak at one of the many luncheons or convention sessions, they would shout back at me, "Go tell it!" "Tell it" became the rallying cry of the convention. "Go tell it" became a rallying cry across the nation.

What had started out as a somewhat downcast convention ended on a high note with the NAACP troops marching off to engage the enemies of racial equality in city after city, town after town, and hamlet after hamlet. When we left the convention in Portland, we went right back to work dealing with the myriad of problems confronting our constituents around the country.

We had many stunning victories during the remainder of the year. Undaunted by the damage wrought by the Court's decision, our staff and the volunteers forged ahead. By a vote of 289 to 127 the House approved H.R. Res. 554, although the U.S. Senate failed to approve a companion bill. This action would have amended the Constitution to treat the District of Columbia as a state and permit residents, most of whom were black, to have congressional and Electoral College representation and participation in presidential elections and the ratification of proposed amendments to the Constitution.

We succeeded in getting Congress to approve the extension of the life of the Civil Rights Commission (after a series of maneuvers that seemed to threaten this important agency), which would have ended on September

30, 1978. The NAACP had successfully fought for passage of the 1957 Civil Rights Act that brought the Commission into being.

We won a major case in Alabama. Charles Smith, a black merchant seaman and a part-time security guard, was charged with murder in connection with the killing of a 20-year-old white man. Smith was protecting his home and his family when a group of young white "toughs" sought to drive his family from their newly purchased home in Mobile, Alabama. The NAACP handled the case. Smith was found not guilty.

The Charles Smith case, reminiscent of the Ossian H. Sweet case in Detroit in 1925, undergirded the right of a black man to defend his family, using deadly force if necessary.

Although economics is a subject that some would regard as alien to civil rights, looking back at the history of the NAACP since its inception, I was cognizant of the fact that the NAACP, since the time of DuBois, Ida B. Wells, Mary Church Terrell, and Mary White Ovington (to mention just a few), had been concerned with the economic well-being of black Americans, be they sharecroppers, public school teachers, engineers, physicians, or lawyers. The thrust of the Association's concerns had been concentrated in well-defined civil rights areas.

I, along with the chair, Mrs. Wilson, and other members of the board, felt that the changing times necessitated a significant change in our traditional approach. It was for this reason that we decided to create an Economic Policy Advisory Council. While at the convention in Portland, Dr. Andrew Brimmer, former member of the Federal Reserve Board was appointed to head this unit.

Although the Council's primary focus was on national economic issues, it was also charged with dealing with the impact of regional and local issues, such as taxpayer revolts. Californians had voted on Proposition 13 in June. There were tremendous anxieties and concerns regarding the impact that the massive tax cuts would have on the elderly and the poor. The Council was also charged with detecting and forecasting economic trends, both long-term and short-term, and with reviewing legislative and administrative decisions that might have a significant impact on our constituency.

Also named to the Council was Robert S. Browne, president of the Black Economic Research Center; Dr. Herrington J. Bryce, vice-president of the Academy for Contemporary Problems; Dr. Paul W. McCracken, formerly chairman of the President's Council of Economic Advisors; Dr. Phillis A. Wallace, professor, Alfred P. Sloan School of Management; Dr. Bernard Anderson, associate professor, Wharton School of Business; Dr. Raphael Thelwell, director of the NAACP's Economic Analysis Unit; Dr.

Andrew Brimmer, chairman of the NAACP Economic Advisory Council; Dr. Bernard Gifford; Dr. Barbara Bergman; Dr. Karl Dwight Gregory, management and economic consultant; and economist Sir W. Arthur Lewis. I was also able to keep another one of the promises that I had made the previous year at the St. Louis convention. We established a Department of Communications. I appointed Angela Shaw, a lawyer and former intern at the FCC, to direct the program.

The charge to the newly created department was to provide technical assistance to our branches in identifying local communications problems and concerns; provide training and educational materials; conduct surveys, seminars, and workshops; monitor rating services, advertising agency practices, and television and radio; and organize communications committees within our branches and local communities.

The department moved quickly and effectively, meeting with TV outlets regarding hiring practices and programming, reviewing FCC license renewal applications, and organizing communications committees within our branches. A series of workshops was held in October in Atlanta. The NAACP finally had an arm to watch and to hold the electronic media accountable.

Looking back over my first full year at the helm of the NAACP, at the year's end I was proud of our accomplishments. It was a roller-coaster ride with a few downs, but infinitely more ups. I also learned an invaluable lesson that year: The NAACP was an organization not just steeped in tradition, but deep in both staff and volunteer leadership. The public expected much from us. What they expected was impossible, but somehow, with the hard work that often meant 18-hour workdays for many of our staff members, and volunteers who never received a paycheck, we managed to get things done. Observing the tireless efforts of our volunteers gave me greater appreciation of my grandmother's and my sister Julia's earlier sacrifices.

Early New Year's Day of 1979, after returning home from church dead tired at three o'clock in the morning, as I prepared to go to bed, I asked myself, "What would my mother, what would my father, think of me now?" Musing over that thought and knowing the type of people they were, the answer came quickly to me: "Benny, you are merely doing your duty—paying your dues. Never mind the hard work and criticisms. Just do that duty of the hour." From that point on, I never concerned myself with the physically and mentally punishing rigors of the jobs, nor with what other people thought. The next 15 years, although grueling, were much easier to endure. I just did what I thought was right.

Chapter 15

THE YEAR OF ANDREW YOUNG

If 1978 was a year dominated by the *Bakke* case, 1979 was the year dominated by U.N. Ambassador Andrew Young. Young was a product of the civil rights movement. He had served as top aide to Dr. Martin Luther King, Jr., president and founder of the Southern Christian Leadership Conference. He was with Dr. King from the birth of SCLC until Dr. King's tragic assassination in 1968, and then went on to win a seat in the U.S. Congress.

Young was an early supporter of Jimmy Carter in his successful bid for the presidency in 1976. His support, along with that of Dr. King's widow, Coretta Scott King, was crucial to Carter's winning black support in his race against President Gerald R. Ford. After his election, President Carter appointed Andrew Young as ambassador to the United Nations. This was a very prestigious position. Young was the first African American to be so honored.

The Spingarn Committee selected Ambassador Young to be the 63rd recipient of the coveted Spingarn Medal, awarded each year by the NAACP "for the highest or noblest achievement by an African American." Its purpose is twofold—"first to call attention of the American people to the existence of distinguished merit and achievement among Negroes, and secondly to serve as a reward for such achievement, and as a stimulus to the ambition of colored youth." The award was instituted in 1914 through a fund established by the late J.E. Spingarn.

Famed West Coast lawyer Nathaniel S. Colley presented the medal at the Annual Dinner of the Association in New York City. This was a stellar event attended by the high and mighty as well as NAACP leaders from across the country. Among the distinguished guests were seven previous Spingarn recipients: Roy Wilkins, Gordon Parks, Robert C. Weaver, Daisy Bates, Kenneth Clark, Damon Keith, and Clarence Mitchell.

I had known Andy Young for years. He was and is a man of unusual compassion, talent, and skills. I could not have been more pleased with the committee's selection. I have always believed that we become richer when we recognize and show appreciation to persons who have made outstanding contributions. Little did I realize that the man we honored at this star-studded event would become the center of a storm in August, a storm that would have reverberations that continue to this day.

At the Annual Meeting, I gave my first full report as the new director. In that report, I cited our successes on Capitol Hill and in a number of court cases, addressed the chilling impact of the *Bakke* case, called attention to the *Weber* case (the Court agreed to review Brian F. Weber's challenge to Kaiser Aluminum's special hiring and promotion program, opening up new dangers to affirmative action), announced that William M. Ellinghaus, president-elect of American Telephone & Telegraph Corporation, had agreed to head a three-year drive to raise $3 million for the NAACP among major businesses, and reported an increase in our youth and adult membership.

After the Annual Meeting was over, I began to make plans for the 25th anniversary celebration of the *Brown v. Board* decision, which was on May 17. The board had voted to go to South Carolina for the occasion. Clarendon County, South Carolina, was the site of the *Briggs* case, one of a number of cases consolidated in what became known as *Brown v. Board*.

We arrived in Columbia, South Carolina, on May 15, 1979. After making several appeals to the county school board for better facilities for their children, the parents had filed a petition in November 1949 seeking the equalization of educational opportunities. When the parents got no relief, they sought the assistance of the NAACP. On May 16, 1950, lawyers for the NAACP filed the original suit in the Federal District Court in Charleston. At a pretrial hearing in November 1950, it became obvious that the petitioners' goal was to abolish segregation.

Arguments were presented in the case on May 28-29, 1951, before a three-judge court comprised of Senior Circuit Judge John J. Parker, of Charlotte, North Carolina; Federal District Judge J. Waites Waring, of Charleston, South Carolina; and George Bell Timmerman of Batesburg, South Carolina. On June 21, 1951, the three-judge court handed down a 2-1 opinion upholding segregation, but ordering the school board to provide Negroes with equal educational opportunities. The case was appealed to the U.S. Supreme Court on July 20, 1951. The NAACP lawyers were Thurgood Marshall, Robert L. Carter, and Harold Boulware of South Carolina.

It is difficult for some white Americans to understand the impatience and sometimes the indignation expressed by African Americans regarding justice in this nation. If we just look at this one case, in November of 1949, a group of black taxpayers brought to the attention of elected public officials a problem of disparate treatment of their children. Four years and six months later, May 17, 1954, the U.S. Supreme Court said that they were right. They would get justice "with all deliberate speed."

Let's just examine that "all deliberate speed." Were the schools integrated, as the Court ordered, as soon as possible? No! What did the white power structure do? They engaged in massive resistance. Were any of them jailed for contempt of the highest court in the land? No! When they finally had to integrate the schools in the early '60s, did they comply? No! According to a personal observation and a segment of *60 Minutes*, the white parents withdrew their children from the schools and placed them in private all-white academies, and refused to approve school bond issues to improve the public schools.

Have the black children suffered because of the official actions and inactions of the white power structure? Yes! According to *The State* newspaper, which published a survey from the South Carolina Department of Education, National Center for Education Statistics, of the 77 school districts in the state of South Carolina, Clarendon School District ranked 71st in SAT scores.

I cite this case merely as one of many that demonstrate that black Americans are the only group of people who are expected to wait patiently for years for simple justice. If we cite racism, we are called hysterical. If we are angered by these gross miscarriages of justice, it is thought that we are not being reasonable.

In 1979, we were returning to Clarendon County, South Carolina, to call to the attention of the people of that state and the nation the fact that after 25 years, South Carolina had not fully complied with the 1954 Court decision. We planned a series of activities as a part of the anniversary celebration. Beyond the board meeting, we had scheduled workshops, a trip, a demonstration in Clarendon County, and a public meeting.

We had a march from Zion Baptist Church to the State Capitol. A delegation of board members and staff was welcomed by the then-

Governor Richard W. Riley, later to become Secretary of Education under President Clinton, and then taken to the governor's mansion.

On May 17, 1979, while we were in Columbia, we received the news that our general counsel, Nathaniel R. Jones, was appointed to the U.S. Court of Appeals for the Sixth Circuit. President Carter used the occasion of a special White House commemoration of the *Brown* decision to make the announcement.

Nate had been the NAACP's general counsel since 1969. He had now been appointed to the federal bench, like his predecessors, Thurgood Marshall and Robert L. Carter. This said a lot about the quality of men who had served as our chief legal officers. We were justly proud of Nate. Nate had been instrumental in charting the Association's strategy of northern school desegregation. He had conducted investigations into discrimination on military bases in Europe and rebuilt our legal department after the resignation of Robert Carter in 1968. Carter resigned in protest over the board's firing of Lewis Steele, one of Carter's assistant counsels. Nate came in at a critical period and rebuilt the legal staff. I knew that finding a new general counsel would not be easy, but I was glad to see another one of our number appointed to one of the most important circuits in the federal judiciary.

I had been in the Deep South during the dark days of segregation. I had seen, firsthand, the disrespect accorded to blacks. Now, in 1979, to see young black men and women working at the Capitol, or elected black officials going about the business of making laws; to see black and white people working together and walking the streets a few blocks from where the architects of the Confederacy met to secede from the union— demonstrated to me that we had indeed made significant progress.

Senator Ernest F. Hollings, the junior U.S. senator from South Carolina, said that the NAACP not only freed black people, but also freed white people to be themselves. Here was a privileged, aristocratic white man thanking the NAACP for breaking the chains of tradition and ending the cycles of racial hatred. This was one of the greatest tributes that I have heard attesting to the effectiveness of the NAACP by any non-African American politician.

While *Brown v. Board of Education* had not accomplished all of the objectives that had been envisioned when it was handed down 25 years earlier, it had transformed the landscape of the nation nonetheless. It became the wedge by which doors were at least partially opened in employment, housing, public accommodations, and a host of other areas.

The Unwanted Family Dispute:
NAACP v. NAACP Legal Defense Fund

Long before I joined the NAACP's staff, there was a major conflict loom-
ing. This controversy was to have no winners. The NAACP and the
NAACP Legal Defense Fund had been quietly embroiled in a family
dispute that had been simmering under the surface for years, but had not
yet broken out in public conflict. We shared a name but had become two
separate and distinct entities.

In the late 1930s, another weapon was discovered to cripple the NAACP,
which had become increasingly aggressive and successful. That weapon was
the U.S. Tax Code. The Internal Revenue Service had concluded that the
Association had violated the existing tax code. Therefore, if the Association
insisted on lobbying efforts and other forms of direct action, it would lose
its tax-exempt status. A tax-exempt status is critical to any nonprofit, and
the NAACP was no exception. Ever resourceful, the legal staff, headed by
the legendary Charles Hamilton Houston, came up with the idea of creating a special legal arm for receiving tax-deductible contributions. That legal arm was the NAACP Legal Defense Fund.

Until 1957, the two organizations had interlocking boards of directors
and functioned as one. After the *Brown v. Board of Education* Supreme
Court decision in 1954, many southern members of Congress and the
U.S. Treasury Department began to threaten the tax status of the NAACP
Legal Defense Fund. They argued that the two organizations not only had
a symbiotic relationship, but that the fund was actually directed and controlled by the parent body, the NAACP. This, in fact, was true. At the
suggestion of the director/counsel of the NAACP Legal Defense Fund,
Thurgood Marshall, and the recommendation of the NAACP Legal Committee, the board voted in 1957 to end the interlocking boards in an effort
to protect the Legal Defense Fund's tax status.

Despite the severing of legal ties, there was a cooperative relationship
and a close alliance between the organizations until Thurgood Marshall
left the fund in 1961. After Marshall's departure, the cooperative spirit
progressively deteriorated. The Legal Defense Fund began to pursue independent courses of action, sometimes in competition rather than in
cooperation with the NAACP. The fund also sought financial support
from the public using the initials NAACP, but did not follow basic
NAACP policy and procedures.

There had been quiet negotiations over the years in an effort to get the
Legal Defense Fund to stop using our initials if they wanted to pursue an
independent course. Those efforts at negotiations were unsuccessful. Suits

were being filed in areas where our branches had no knowledge of action. The public could not make a distinction between the NAACP and the Legal Defense Fund. Many individuals, groups, associations, corporate givers, and charities sent contributions to the NAACP Legal Defense Fund thinking that they were giving to the NAACP.

After an impasse was reached, the board voted to challenge the use of our initials by the Legal Defense Fund in court, if need be. At the opening session of the Annual Convention held in Louisville, Kentucky, on June 25, 1979, the delegates overwhelmingly passed a resolution "calling upon and directing the board to withdraw and revoke the permission previously granted (in 1939) to the NAACP Legal Defense Fund, Inc., to use the initials 'NAACP' in its name, publications, publicity, activities, and solicitations."

The Board of Directors retained the services of the law firm of former Senator Edward Brooke to pursue the matter. Ultimately, the Legal Defense Fund prevailed. We won the judgment in the trial court. The judgment was appealed to the Appellate Court by the Legal Defense Fund. The Appellate Court overturned the judgment of the trial court. The appellate court based its verdict on the fact that the NAACP had allowed the fund to use its name for 40 years. Accordingly, the legal doctrine of *laches* applied. This doctrine in American law is similar to the law of adverse possession. Depending on a given state statute, if one allows a person to occupy or keep and to use as his own a parcel of property or something else of value for a period of five to seven years, the property belongs to the party who possesses it.

The public dispute with the Legal Defense Fund that I had desperately hoped to avoid created a public relations problem for the administration. There were some who questioned the efficacy of two sister organizations fighting in the courts when there were so many other external problems to deal with. The NAACP is a democratically controlled organization with a constituency of volunteer leaders, members, and staff. Once the delegates voted to withdraw the use of the NAACP's initials, the Board of Directors and the staff were obligated to carry out their will.

The special committee appointed to negotiate with the Legal Defense Fund had exhausted its options. Leadership requires hard and sometimes controversial decisions, and that certainly was the case in this instance. Even while the litigation was taking place, we managed to cooperate on matters of mutual concern to our respective constituencies. Today that cooperation continues. During the latter years of my tenure—after the litigation was over—we forged a close and productive working relationship.

FAMILY LIFE

Benjamin Hooks's grandmother, Julia A.B. Hooks, "The Angel of Beale Street"

left: Bessie White Hooks, Mama, (holding sister Mildred) cousin Ethel, sister Julia, brother Robert, brother Raymond, and, in front, Benjamin Hooks

above: Benjamin Hooks in 1945 at age 20, a photo given to his mother

Benjamin Hooks's parents, Robert Britton Hooks, Sr. and Bessie White Hooks

Benjamin Hooks's sisters, Mildred, Bessie, and Julia

The Hooks brothers, Raymond, Robert, Benjamin, and Charles

The wedding of Benjamin Hooks and Frances Dancy, March 24, 1951.
Front row, left to right: Mildred Hooks (Benjamin Hooks's sister), Delores Frazier, Benjamin Hooks, Frances Hooks, Thelma Whittaker, and Janet A. Seymour (Frances Hooks's cousin)
Back row, left to right: Charles Hooks (Benjamin Hooks's brother), Andrew Dancy (Frances Hooks's brother), Donald Jackson, and Herman Sweet

seated: Frances and Benjamin Hooks and grandson, Carlton
standing: daughter, Pat and grandson, Carlos, Jr.

standing, left to right: Benjamin Hooks, Michael, Sr., Michael Jr., Marcus, and Kristin
seated, left to right: Janet, Frances, Julia, and Mildred

left to right: Benjamin and Frances Hooks, Carlos Jr., Fred, Pat, John, Amberly, Shyanne, Angie, Cherie, Bryanna, and Carlos III

Benjamin Hooks with Sierra

left to right: grandson Carlos, Jr., daughter, Pat, and grandson Carlton

left: Frances Hooks

above: Frances and Benjamin Hooks

PROFESSIONAL LIFE

Benjamin Hooks as a young lawyer

Benjamin Hooks, appointed as the first black criminal court judge in Shelby County Tennessee in 1965, W. Preston Battle, Arthur Faquin, and Perry Sellers, seated.

Mahalia Jackson's Chicken restaurants, a black-owned business franchise co-founded in the 1960s by Benjamin Hooks

As NAACP Executive Director, addressing the press at a Sickle Cell Council fundraising conference

Benjamin Hooks at the pulpit

Benjamin Hooks, a frequent speaker on civil rights issues

David Dinkins and Benjamin Hooks

Benjamin Hooks, Edward Brooke, and Colin Powell,
who was receiving the Spingarn Award in 1991

Andrew Young, left, and Benjamin Hooks, speaking before a SCLC event in Washington, D.C.

left to right: John Jacob, Andrew Young, Hank Aaron, Benjamin Hooks, and Joe Lowery

Benjamin Hooks receiving an award from Edward Brooke

Benjamin Hooks, holding a leadership
award presented to him by the Memphis
State University Black Student Association

Benjamin Hooks, Jesse Jackson, and Frances Hooks

Coretta Scott King and Jesse Jackson before a SCLC event

NAACP March on Sacramento in 1992

NAACP voter registration drive

Joseph Lowery, President of the SCLC and Benjamin Hooks,
Executive Director of the NAACP at a 1981 Atlanta news
conference, held during a meeting of black organizations to
discuss the killings of 20 black children and the disappearance
of two others, which Dr. Hooks described as "a tragedy in the midst
of troubled times."

Benjamin Hooks, John Kluge, Enola McMillan, Kelly Alexander,
Patricia Kluge, and Frances Hooks at a NAACP convention

Benjamin Hooks and President George H. W. Bush, February 19, 1992

President Bill Clinton and Benjamin Hooks, May 22, 2000

Certainly, the Legal Defense Fund continues to be one of the most powerful organizations in America striving for constructive change. Its chairman, William T. Coleman, is surely one of the most perceptive, brilliant, and successful lawyers in this nation. In civil rights history from the early 1950s to the present, his name appears on the roster of great civil rights lawyers over and again. As I have already stated, Julius Chambers and Elaine Jones have done outstanding jobs as executive leaders of the organization. Ed Brooke, the first black senator of the 20th Century, served ably and well. We often had to call on him for help in passing difficult bills, and he always responded to us positively. His voice was one of the great voices for the Civil Rights Movement.

70th Annual Convention: July 25-29, 1979, Louisville, Kentucky

Among the highlights of the convention was the presentation of the coveted Spingarn Medal to the legendary Rosa Parks. The medal was presented by Judge Damon J. Keith, of the U.S. Court of Appeals for the Sixth Circuit. Vice President Walter Mondale was the guest speaker for the Tuesday evening mass meeting.

We had a large contingent of youth in Louisville. More than 500 official youth delegates had registered. Our ACT-SO program had also grown. There were over 200 contestants representing 36 cities in the second annual competition. That year we gave out prizes totaling $35,000.

Both New Orleans' Mayor, Ernest N. Morial, and I addressed the closing Freedom Fund Banquet. Morial spoke on "Economic Equality—The Great Unfinished Agenda." In my speech, which was short, I told the audience that while we could celebrate the Supreme Court's actions in the *Weber* case, we must now gear up to oppose the Mottl (D-OH) Amendment. This amendment, if passed into law, would eliminate pupil transportation for desegregating our nation's public schools.

Toward the end of the speech, I reminded the convention that we must do something to counteract the growing negative spirit that abounds in black America. "We have come a long way as a people," I said. "Let us never forget we have not gotten where we were all by ourselves. We are standing on the shoulders of those who made the sacrifice so that we might move forward." I then called upon black America to celebrate the first day of January, the anniversary of the Emancipation Proclamation. I told them that I would like for the NAACP family to call this day Jubilee Day. "We must rebuild our family altars," I continued. "On that day we ought to call our children in from their play or work. We ought to eat some bread and water, symbolizing the diet of our slave forefathers and mothers on the slave ships. We ought to eat some rice, corn, peas, and greens symbolizing what we had in slavery. Then we ought to have some vinegar and oil, symbolizing our new day begun." I wanted them to know it was important that our children knew where they came from so they might appreciate where they will be able to go. We need to teach our children their history.

More than 480 NAACP units reported Jubilee Day celebrations the next New Year's Day. In addition, many church and fraternal groups adopted Jubilee Day as their own. Over the years, the effort evolved into public services held at churches, community centers, and town halls. In Memphis, I involved the Masons in the celebration. They came, by the hundreds, dressed in their regalia. Their uniforms added flair and visual images that the media loved. I urged other branches to follow the Memphis format. Many did so, with great success.

Unfortunately, in the NAACP it was not always possible for us to set the agenda. No sooner had the convention ended than we found ourselves having to fight the anti-busing bill. The proposed amendment to the U.S. Constitution was sponsored by Ohio Representative Ronald Mottl. Our Washington Bureau had advised me that the Mottl bill's momentum had to be stopped. I was told that many of our friends in Congress would be tempted to vote for the legislation if they felt that no one was watching. Although tired from an exhausting convention and a schedule that should have driven me to bedrest, I decided that we could not let this happen. This end-run effort had to be stopped or we would have to fight the battle all over again in the Senate, the state legislatures, or some other venue.

Immediately after the convention, we began planning for a highly visible show of opposition in Washington. I decided that we would invite a few thousand people to come to Washington for the protest. Rather than having an ordinary march, I decided that we would have a prayer vigil the night before and a rally and a lobbying effort on the following day. Despite the very short time we had available to us, we managed to have a turnout for the events of more than 3,000 people. We received splendid support from our allies in the civil rights and labor communities. The Mottl anti-busing bill was defeated.

The Thunder of August

Ambassador Andrew Young became embroiled in a controversy that would exacerbate already strained relationships that existed in the late 1970s between certain segments of the black and Jewish communities. For years the stability of this historic alliance was taken for granted. Both groups faced discrimination and hostility in America from racists and anti-Semites. Both had been persecuted. Both groups were once enslaved—although our enslavement was recent and in this land.

We had worked together during the early days of the movement. Many of the founders of the NAACP and the Congress of Racial Equality were Jewish. Jewish youngsters had died in Philadelphia, Mississippi, in 1963 while helping blacks win the right to vote. Jewish philanthropists had supported scores of black colleges and universities and human rights causes, including the Southern Christian Leadership Conference (SCLC), the Student Nonviolent Coordinating Committee (SNCC), the Lawyers Committee for Civil Rights (LCCR), and the National Urban League.

Incendiary rhetoric used by both sides exacerbated an already fragile alliance. Irresponsible Jewish and black self-appointed leaders brought the situation to a boiling point. There was and still remains in the two communities a difference in the way each group views affirmative action. Blacks, who have been systematically excluded from opportunity, see affirmative action programs as a temporary measure designed to include those who were excluded. Therefore, goals and timetables are seen as a desirable yardstick to measure progress. On the other hand, Jews have been limited in their ability to be admitted to colleges, professional schools, law firms, and the professions by quotas that said, in effect, "You can have two Jews admitted to medical school, but no more." They see anything that creates goals and timetables as quotas.

It must be said that some Jewish groups did, and continue to, support affirmative action. The truth is that one's views are influenced by personal experience and the perspective from which one sees life. It can be argued that most problems in marriages are caused by missed communications.

The *Defunis* and *Bakke* cases (both involved admission to professional schools) merely added more fuel to the fire. Blacks and Jews, as a rule, had different views on the efficacy of the arguments of the plaintiffs, both of whom were Jewish. It is against this backdrop that the Andrew Young incident took on special significance.

In 1979, U.S. officials were forbidden from meeting with any representative of the Palestine Liberation Organization (PLO) as long as that organization refused to recognize the right of Israel to exist as a state. Young had met with representatives of the PLO to discuss pending business at the United Nations. Young's meeting was to be secret, but news of it leaked out and produced a formal protest from Israel and cries of outrage from many in the American Jewish community. So strident were the protests that days later Young submitted his resignation, which was promptly accepted by President Carter.

The black community in general was incensed by what had happened to Ambassador Young. Some blamed the President for not sticking with the man who arguably made his election possible. They reasoned that Carter could not have won the 1976 election without overwhelming support from the black community. A far greater number blamed what they termed "the powerful Jewish lobby" for Andrew Young's forced resignation. The airwaves and black news outlets were filled with virulent and anti-Semitic comments.

I must confess that when the news first broke about Young's meeting with representatives of the PLO, I did not see what all the fuss was about. Was he not our U.N. ambassador? Don't diplomats meet privately with our most bitter national enemies? Did not the U.S. Secretary of State meet with the "Red Chinese," although our official policy was total non-recognition of "Red China"? We have since learned that other American diplomats (whites) had met with the PLO both before and shortly after Ambassador Young's resignation.

Andy Young was a hero in the black community. He was not a publicity seeker. This trait of personal modesty had endeared him to many in the civil rights movement who resented those who merely sought attention and adulation. To the man on the street, Andy was a fighter who had fought for him. The Andrew Young matter became one around which blacks from every social and economic strata could rally.

I had discussions with dozens of leaders of major black organizations, groups, and associations. I spoke to a number of black elected officials. The common thread that ran through all of these conversations was that something had to be done. If Andrew Young could be treated in such a shabby way, what hope was there for black leaders who did not hold cabinet-level positions?

I called Joseph Lowery, Vernon Jordan, Coretta Scott King, Dorothy Height, Bayard Rustin, Jesse Jackson, and Carl Holman, all members of the Black Leadership Forum. I suggested that we call for an emergency national black leadership meeting to address the Andrew Young issue. We agreed on August 22, 1979, as the date for the meeting.

Since it was my idea, they left the logistics of notifying the invitees to me and my overworked staff at the NAACP. The staff made hundreds of calls over the next two days. With few exceptions, most of the leaders of national organizations agreed to attend the meeting. Very few who received the invitation said they could not adjust their calendars to attend. It was also agreed that only black leaders or the deputies of those leaders would be permitted to attend. On a highly sensitive and important issue such as this, we needed to have persons with authority to make decisions for their organizations.

We held the meeting in the conference room of the National NAACP at 1790 Broadway in Manhattan. I had hoped for a turnout of maybe 50 to 75 people. The notice was short and air fare was high without the advance purchase of tickets.

Our conference room could comfortably hold 125 to 150 people. When the meeting began, there were no more seats. We sent for folding chairs and put them in the hallways and in every nook and cranny that was available to us. Soon there were more than 230 people present. Some participants had to stand.

I had the responsibility of presiding. That day it was not a difficult task, despite the fact that we had the bulk of the black leadership of the nation under one roof at one time. I often think, looking back, of what would have happened if some sick and determined racist had planted a bomb while the meeting was being held. The experienced leadership of black America would have been decimated.

I then read a prepared statement to open the meeting and to set the parameters.

Statement by Benjamin L. Hooks, NAACP Executive Director, at Black Leadership Meeting on Implications of Ambassador Andrew Young's Resignation as U.S. Permanent Representative to the United Nations, August 22, 1979, NAACP National Office, New York, New York:

This meeting was called for the purpose of dealing with the fallout surrounding the circumstances of the resignation of Ambassador Andrew Young as Permanent Representative of the United States to the United Nations.

Over the past week, events have been moving so fast that it has been difficult to consider the whole issue in a comprehensive manner. Many of the issues that we have planned to discuss have been dealt with in other forums. But, there are still many questions unanswered by Mr. Young's resignation. The issues demand that we express our concerns and attempt to give some direction to the search for an ultimate resolution of this crisis.

I strongly believe that in the national interest, the U.S. Government has a responsibility to provide its citizens with the truth while taking every precaution against besmirching or destroying the credibility of so worthy a diplomat and statesman as Mr. Young.

In our meeting today we plan to do three things:

1. Issue a statement holding up to the light the double standards by which Mr. Young has been judged.

2. Call upon this nation to live up to the ideals of decency and candor that Mr. Young established as ambassador.

3. Call for continuing dialogue with the Jewish community in an effort to lessen the deep polarization which has been worsening between them and black Americans. Underscore the historical involvement of blacks in developing U.S. foreign policy.

We at the NAACP have already expressed our dismay at the resignation of Ambassador Young. We have made known our views that he has contributed immeasurably to elevating U.S. relations with Third World countries, and, with regard to the incidents leading to his resignation, we are convinced that he acted in the best interest of this nation. It seems necessary and appropriate now that we comment further on the situation that precipitated the Young controversy.

Because of our background, heritage and tradition, there is a natural tendency for many black Americans, historically, to have tremendous sympathy with people who are deprived wherever they are. This is true of the Jewish people, the Arab people, the Palestinian people, Native Americans, Vietnamese boat people, Haitian refugees, European peoples who have come to this country in search of a better life, as well as many others.

In the difficult problems of intercultural relations, we must take into consideration, forthrightly, the human component. There is no way that there can be sides where simple humanity is concerned. Moreover, the key to a peaceful world is a resolution of the profound differences that separate and divide peoples for whatever reason.

In our view, this is what the enlightened foreign policy of the United States under this Administration is all about. It equates the Israeli child, the Palestinian child, the Egyptian child, the Vietnamese child, the Nicaraguan child with our own children, particularly in the International Year of the Child.

We therefore applaud all efforts to have people talking, conferring, and understanding one another, and it ought to be the function of our government as a leader of the free world to bring people together for this purpose.

We believe that what Ambassador Young did was aimed at this objective. We further believe that this search for ways to be even-handed and fair-minded must be pursued, because by doing what is best for everybody, we do what is best for America.

What we hope to do here today is to achieve a broad consensus. Obviously we do not intend to circumscribe the ability of any group to pursue these objectives in its own way at its own pace.

This is not the time for arrogance or intransigence, but a time for a mutuality and tempered dialogue. We believe that all thoughtful Americans of all faiths and persuasions concur in these views.

The decorum and respect for the opinions of others exhibited that day were phenomenal. That is not to say that there were no disagreements. To the contrary, there were sharp philosophical differences of opinions. But those disagreements were expressed in a spirit of love and brother- and sisterhood.

Once we got a consensus of the group, I appointed committees to write position statements for consideration by the entire body. We were to receive reports and act upon them. One statement was designed to laud Andrew Young and to express our collective consternation with his forced resignation. Another was to address the delicate issue of black-Jewish relations.

We had agreed before the meeting that the press would not be permitted to attend. What we had to say we wanted in writing to avoid the media reporting only the most irresponsible comments. Additionally, we knew that some of the participants would play to the cameras, thereby taking away from the dignity and solemnity of the occasion.

As you can imagine, the media showed in record numbers. New York was and remains the media capital of the world. There were more than 50 TV camera crews from across the nation and, indeed, the world, and maybe 100 or more print reporters. The lobby of the building was not that large. Others who had business in the building were having difficulty getting to the bank of elevators. The management called repeatedly asking my office to do something about the situation. Finally, I sent a staff member downstairs to advise the media that all statements would be issued at a press conference that was going to be held at the Sheraton Hotel.

The writing committees did a splendid job. Within an hour, all of the statements were completed and voted upon. There were no dissents. We made sufficient copies of the statements for all of the participants and members of the media.

We went to the hotel, where the throng of media representatives waited anxiously for the statements to be distributed. The statements would speak for themselves. No one was to make any comment beyond what the written documents actually said. Once again, amazingly, everyone cooperated. This was one meeting of hundreds of black leaders where the members of the press would not be able to pit one leader's statement against another's.

Our message was unambiguous, civil, thoughtful, and coherent. Following are Statements unanimously adopted by the Black Leadership Meeting, August 22, 1979.

Freedom of Expression

In support of the Southern Christian Leadership Conference, we affirm the right of black citizens and organizations engaged in dialogue with individuals and groups whose actions have serious consequences for them. We applaud the initiative of those individuals and organizations that have come to the defense of Ambassador Andrew Young, our colleague and brother.

We respect and affirm the right of the Southern Christian Leadership Conference and any other individual or organization to express their views on international and domestic issues.

We join with Ambassador Andrew Young in rejecting the notion that any foreign nation should dictate the foreign policies of the United States. We summarily reject the implication that anyone other than blacks themselves can determine their proper role in helping to shape and mold American foreign policies, which directly affect their lives.

—Statement Unanimously Adopted by
Black Leadership Meeting, August 22, 1979,
NAACP Office, New York, New York

Blacks and U.S. Foreign Policy

Given the history of racial discrimination in the United States, it should hardly be surprising that the forthright conduct and candor of Ambassador Andrew Young would be the cause for so much consternation throughout our government and the nation. Readily acknowledged by friend and foe alike, Mr. Young's historical contributions in advancing United States foreign policy in areas of the world that are crucial to us are in the country's interests.

Ambassador Young was a spearhead in opening doors that were previously closed to the United States. He was immensely successful in a role in which so many others were or are dismal failures. As a black person in an establishment controlled by whites and which historically has functioned for the advancement of whites-only interests, he is color-blind. He pursued his mission as an American representing all people, not as a black American.

Ambassador Young conducted his office knowing full well the interests that are at stake in the pursuit of peace around the world, especially, in this instance, in the Middle East. In every war since the founding of this nation, black citizens have borne arms and died for their country. Their blood was spilled from Bunker Hill to Vietnam. It is to be expected that should the United States become drawn into war in the Middle East, black Americans will once more sacrifice their lives.

Nevertheless, the involvement of blacks and their concerns in foreign policy questions is repeatedly questioned. Black American citizens deplore the arrogance that is implicit in this attitude. As a result, the treatment that was accorded Mr. Young by the U.S. Government, especially by the State Department, was totally abhorrent. Black Americans strongly protest the callous, ruthless behavior of the United States State Department toward Mr. Young.

We deplore the history of racism and the bureaucratic recalcitrance that is so endemic to that agency. Black Americans protest the history of employment discrimination at the State Department and call upon the President and Secretary of State to exert their full authority in pressing for the desegregation of that institution. Every effort must be made to place and advance blacks in positions of authority there.

We hold the State Department fully accountable to the American people for events surrounding Mr. Young's resignation and call upon President Carter and Cyrus Vance to make public the complete details surrounding the Ambassador's meeting with the P.L.O. and the circumstances pertaining to the public disclosure of that encounter.

We demand once more to know why the American Ambassador to Austria was given a mere reminder about the U.S. policy prohibiting meetings with the P.L.O. while Mr. Young was harshly reprimanded. We call upon the Carter administration to account for this gross double standard.

Clearly, the stakes for minorities in the conduct of American foreign policy continue to be high. In energy, the Middle East represents one of the primary areas of supply. As we have seen in recent years, any disruption or uncertainty of supply can have a disastrous impact upon the U.S. economy and that of its principal trading partners as well as throughout other areas of the world.

Africa, likewise, provides the United States with the bulk of many scarce minerals that industry needs. Black people, furthermore, have historical and cultural roots in that continent. The moral aspects of the gross violations of human and political rights by the white minorities in southern Africa constitute a direct affront to black Americans. So, it is imperative that we who have so much to contribute to the further improvement of relations with countries on that continent continue to be even more involved in developing U.S. policy on Africa as well as the rest of the world.

Finally, as Americans, black people very strongly resent having the right of their involvement in the development and conduct of U.S. foreign policy questioned.

Neither Jews, Italians, Germans, Irish, Chinese, British, French or whatever other ethnically or nationally identifiable group have any more rights to be involved in the development and conduct of United States foreign policy than Americans of African descent. If there is any single area where the melting pot concept applies, it is with foreign affairs. For we either all pursue the common interests of this nation together or help it sink separately.

—Statement Unanimously Adopted by
Black Leadership Meeting, August 22, 1979,
NAACP Office, New York, New York

Andrew Young—We Are Proud of You

It is an accepted fact of American mentality that for any black person to attempt to speak for this country on international matters invites the wrath of those who have assigned unto themselves the role of world leaders. Naturally, this attitude is directly tied to the 400 years of Western colonialism which saw whites as the subjugators of the darker race.

Within the context of this master-servant relationship, Europeans extended their dominance thousands of miles away from their home bases to lands as distant as the Far East. They had near-total control of the principal sea lanes around the world as well as of much of the underdeveloped territories and countries in Africa, the Caribbean and Asia.

With powerful navies, their new technologies and the resultant need to find an abundant supply of cheap raw materials as well as markets for their expanding industries and commerce, they fashioned ways to control the minds and bodies of those over whom they had assumed control.

Given this history—and nostalgia—it should therefore come as no surprise that so many white Americans would regard with great alarm the initiatives of such a superb diplomat as United Nations Ambassador Andrew Young, first black to hold that post. The old colonial empires are dead. But that mentality, undergirded by racism, still lingers on in the minds of too many whites.

It follows, therefore, that the singular contributions of Ralph Bunche, another great diplomat who also was black, have been all but written out of American history. He was, among other things, Undersecretary for Special Political Affairs at the United Nations shortly after World War II. It was he who fashioned the details for Middle East peace in 1949 which resulted in the creation and recognition of Israel as a nation. For these efforts, we are sure the world is grateful, although so little recognition is given to the man who fashioned the settlement of war-torn Palestine.

Against this background, it is somewhat ironic 30 years later that we find the Middle East question now bringing an end to the brilliant tenure of Andrew Young as the American Ambassador to the United Nations. Ambassador Young has been mercilessly assailed for having met with representatives of the P.L.O. He has been made a sacrificial lamb for circumstances beyond his control. Pointedly overlooked, however, is that he was exercising his best judgment, first in carrying out the wishes of his government in getting a postponement of an issue coming up before the Security Council that could have forced the United States into an embarrassing stance.

Second, as president of the Security Council, it is his duty to meet with all parties involved in questions scheduled to be considered by that body. And the P.L.O.was at the center of the question.

Ambassador Young, in the manner which he met with the P.L.O. on a procedural issue, demonstrated great maturity and skill. The overreaction by the national news media, some of the Jewish community, the Carter Administration and some congressional leaders was a regrettable consequence of the double standard by which this nation judges its black leaders. Pointedly and tragically overlooked in the hysterical reaction to Ambassador Young's meeting with the P.L.O. is that the encounter did not change—neither was it intended to alter—U.S. policy regarding United States dealings with that group. Furthermore, Ambassador Young did succeed in his mission. He won an agreement on postponing the upcoming debate on Resolution 242 and the Palestinian homeland issue.

The question of black-Jewish relations being worsened by Ambassador Young's resignation, not surprisingly, has flared into the open even more heatedly than in the past. It must be emphasized that for blacks, the issue is not one of anti-Semitism or irrational hatred of Jews. Historically the object of bigotry, Jews easily empathized with the traditional victims of racial hatred in this country.

Blacks, however, were deeply affronted by the inherent arrogance of the attacks upon Ambassador Young by certain Jewish groups and the news media for his having dared to place the interests of the United States above all other considerations.

To his inestimable credit, Ambassador Young has warned about inciting black-Jewish tensions in his support. That certainly was appropriate. The Ambassador's gentlemanly response to the circumstances leading up to the premature curtailment of his United Nations tenure cannot mask the double standard by which he has been judged. He has been excoriated and pilloried by the nation's media, sundry people and organizations. Yet rare is such a giant of a man who has served his country with such outstanding success.

Because of this double standard, we find that the American Ambassador to Austria met with the P.L.O. in that country three times, yet he was only "reminded" of his government's policy. No public explanations, however, have been given about the full nature of Mr. Wolf's meetings. We fear, however, that at this stage, not much more will be revealed about those encounters. It really matters little. For the whole history of the treatment that was meted out to Ambassador Young demonstrates that it will be a long time

before this double standard of judging black people will be brought
to an end.

—Statement Unanimously Adopted
by Black Leadership Meeting, August 22, 1979,
NAACP Office, New York, New York

Black-Jewish Relations

Since the beginning of this century, some American Jews and Jewish
organizations have openly joined with black Americans in the struggle
against religious bigotry and racial hatred. They saw in the treatment that
was accorded blacks a reflection of their own suffering extended back
over thousands of years. The interests of blacks and Jews in seeking an
end to the destructive and irrational hatred were mutual.

However, the key question before us as representatives of the black
community in America is the more immediate problem of the extent to
which the successful demand for the resignation of Ambassador Young
has in fact further damaged an already unhappy relationship between the
American Jewish organizational spokesmen and the rank-and-file and
the leadership of American blacks.

Since it is clear that the resignation of Ambassador Young has seriously intensified tensions in black-Jewish relations, then any attempts to
seek to relieve these tensions must be based upon contemporary realities.
At this time, attempts to deal with this problem by emotional rhetoric,
past defenses, and denials can only exacerbate the problem.

There is no question that individual Jews and Jewish organizations
and their leaders have worked as part of a liberal coalition with blacks
and organized labor to form a powerful political force for social and
economic reform in the United States. It is also clear that Jewish organizations and leadership have done so when it is in their perceived interests
to do so, as we do. It is reasonable to believe that they will continue to
work with blacks when they believe that it is in their interest to be allied
with us and our aspirations.

However, it is a fact that within the past 10 years some organizations
and intellectuals who were previously identified with the aspirations of
black Americans for unqualified educational, political, and economic
equality with all other Americans abruptly became apologists for the
racial status quo. They asserted that further attempts to remedy the present
forms of discrimination were in violation of the civil rights laws.

Beyond, organizations within the Jewish community opposed the interests of the black community in the *DeFunis*, *Bakke* and *Weber* cases, which went to the United States Supreme Court.

Beyond that, some Jewish intellectuals gave credence and policy substance to such concepts as "reverse discrimination" and "quotas" as reasons for restricting further attempts to continue to seek remedies for present discrimination against blacks. The term "quota," which traditionally meant the exclusion of Jews, was now being used by Jews to warn against attempts to include blacks in aspects of our society and economy from which we were previously excluded. To many blacks, this seems to be a most perplexing Orwellian perversion of language.

Black America is also deeply concerned with the trade and military alliance that exists between Israel and the illegitimate and oppressive racist regime in South Africa and Southern Rhodesia. That relationship, in our view, imposes upon Jewish organizations in this country an obligation to insist that the state of Israel discontinue its support of those repressive and racist regimes.

These causes of black-Jewish tension could only give aid and comfort to those who previously were as anti-Semitic as they were anti-black. It is also possible that it completed the circle of black separatism and bitterness.

Realism demands that the burden of resolving the black-Jewish tension which has been brewing for years cannot be placed disproportionately on the backs of already overburdened blacks; Jews must show more sensitivity and be prepared for more consultation before taking positions contrary to the best interests of the black community.

Realism demands also that all discussions seeking to ameliorate or resolve fundamental differences between American blacks and Jews be conducted in terms of specific issues and problems rather than in terms of emotions, supplication, subtle or flagrant threats, and coercion or arrogance.

Whenever the legitimate concerns of blacks are or are perceived to be in conflict with the interests and policies of Jewish organizations and leaders, then those differences must be made clear and, if possible, resolved. If those concerns cannot be resolved by rational discussions and in an atmosphere of mutual respect, then realism demands that blacks will differ with Jews even as Jews will differ with blacks. Each group will then use whatever power and influence it has to pursue its own goals.

With the statements released, members of the media sought desperately to have the participants expand upon them. After repeated attempts without success, we left and returned to the difficult task of trying to repair the bridges that were damaged during the Young affair.

Meanwhile, President Carter appointed Donald F. McHenry, who had served previously as the deputy U.S. representative to the U.N. Security Council, as the permanent representative to the United Nations. Ambassador McHenry was also an African American.

Some blacks never forgave President Carter for bowing to pressure in the Young affair. That bitterness carried over to 1980, an election year. The rift between the African-American and Jewish communities took much longer to heal. Many Jewish leaders reached out to us as we reached out to them. Unfortunately, the media—to this day—chooses to report the racist and anti-Semitic comments of the most vile and bizarre self-appointed leaders of both communities. This single factor has been more responsible than any other for keeping the old wounds open.

In my capacity as executive director of the NAACP and chairman of the Leadership Conference on Civil Rights, I made it a policy to build bridges among all groups—Jewish, Hispanic, women's organizations, etc. It is essential that those of us who are involved in the fight for human rights recognize, in the words of Dr. King, "We are all inextricably tied together, caught up in a single garment of mutuality."

I believe that if we are to ever become one nation, we must not only learn this lesson, but make it a part of our daily thinking, lives, and actions.

As the head of the NAACP, I became increasingly aware of the contributions and service, and may I add, the much-needed services and contributions of other ethnic groups. The Jewish community has, from the very beginning, been associated in positive ways with the NAACP. Among our early supporters were the Spingarn brothers, Joel and Arthur, who served as officers, heavy financial contributors, and workers.

Their genius was their willingness to cooperate and work with the black community in arriving at solutions and in setting out paths and programs. David Stern, commissioner of the National Basketball Association, was another hard-working member of our National Board who gave special leadership to our "Black to School" program. And Rabbi David Saperstein continues to be a valuable member of our National Board. The future continues to look positive.

Not to be forgotten is the last non-black NAACP president, Kivie Kaplan, who worked tirelessly to help build and strengthen the organization. One of the enduring problems of the NAACP and other black organizations was to obtain help from other ethnic groups without those

groups seeking to dictate the outcome of events. From the very beginning, as one reads the record, Jewish supporters of the NAACP worked
diligently to overcome this problem. That has not always been easy, but
thank God the cooperation continued, the partnership endured, the coalition stayed together, and fruitful ideas continue to grow into positive
programs.

Chapter 16

1981: THE REAGAN VICTORY AND ITS IMPACT

On November 4, 1980, the American people went to the polls, and, for the first time since 1888, turned an incumbent Democratic President out of office. Ronald Wilson Reagan was America's new leader. Reagan carried 43 states; Carter carried six. The magnitude of the Reagan victory could best be seen in the Electoral College vote margin and in the senatorial elections.

Reagan received 483 electoral votes to Carter's 49. The Republicans also took control of the U.S. Senate, winning 11 seats formerly held by the Democrats. This established Republican control of the U.S. Senate by a margin of 51-47. At the same time, the Reagan juggernaut won 33 additional seats in the U.S. House of Representatives.

Many of the allies of civil rights causes in Congress were swept under by the Reagan tide. The prospects for civil and human rights causes looked bleak, and not simply because Republicans had won the White House and the U.S. Senate. Rather, the situation appeared ominous because of the announced intentions of Reagan and his people to roll back much of the progress that had been made in recent years and because of his longstanding promise to turn over to the states many functions that we felt belonged with the federal government. There was, in my opinion, a good possibility that there would be an attempt to dismantle the entire infrastructure of President Lyndon Johnson's War on Poverty and the Great Society programs.

Many in the civil rights community saw disaster lingering around the corner. I did not; I believed we could find allies to fight the good fight. I knew we could convince people of good will, Republicans and

Democrats, white and black, to join us in blocking the deleterious conservative efforts that were sure to come. I knew, however, that the fight would be difficult.

There was one bright spot. We now had 18 members in the Congressional Black Caucus, more than at any time in our history. These men and women were dedicated to fighting the same battle. I also got assurances from members of the Leadership Conference on Civil Rights that they would join us in turning back any effort to undo the progress of the '60s and the '70s.

My personal philosophy, learned from my father, is to persevere—to go on despite the obstacles one faces. One should never give up or give in to wrong. Our challenge, as I saw it, was to develop a strategy to succeed even amid adverse circumstances. I realized that would be a daunting challenge.

It soon became apparent that the new Administration planned to use a circuitous approach in its attempt to dismantle social programs. Using the economic difficulties as a cover, Reagan's people set out to remove the safety nets from the poor. The changes were to be implemented under the guise of stimulating economic growth and curbing inflation.

The NAACP, often accused by its critics of being reactive, had beaten others to the punch. Back on September 22, 1980, the NAACP had issued, under my direction, *A Policy Statement of the NAACP on the Economic Well-Being of Blacks*. (Those who authored the report have been named previously.)

This document and another major policy statement we were developing would serve as our talking points in dealing with the presidential transition team and the media in addressing the concerns of the African American community. The President's team was preparing a series of economic policies that would adversely impact the black community.

We requested a meeting with the President-elect to discuss with him our concerns and to seek an understanding of what his Administration's priorities were. Much to my surprise, Reagan got back rather quickly and agreed to meet with members of the Black Leadership Forum, of which I was president at the time. Among those members were Carl Holman, Jesse Jackson, Coretta Scott King, Joseph Lowery, Bayard Rustin, Ramona Edlin, Julius Chambers, John Jacob, Eddie Williams, and Parren Mitchell.

The day of the meeting, our delegation assembled early to discuss the strategy we planned to use with President-elect Reagan. We decided who would ask which question. We planned to have follow-up questions if we received evasive answers. We also decided we would insist that Reagan, and not his aides, answer the questions posed. Since Ronald

Reagan was famous for his use of index cards during the election campaign, most Americans thought that if he did not have a prepared script, he would be in serious trouble.

We were ushered in to see the president-elect. He was smiling, wearing his usual dark blue suit, white shirt, and red tie. When meeting with a president or president-elect, you have to be very conscious of the time. Normally, groups or individuals are limited to 30 minutes to an hour at most. If you are not careful, it is possible to use most of that time engaging in small talk and pleasantries.

Personally, President Reagan was a very engaging person. There was both a charm and a warmth about him. He was personally as warm as his policies toward the poor and the disadvantaged were cold. We began to ask him one question after the other. "Mr. President, what is your position on affirmative action? What is your position on busing? Will you enforce previous executive orders of previous presidents on minority set-asides? Will you appoint African Americans to the federal courts and to your cabinet?"

To our surprise, Reagan did not ask a single assistant to respond to a question. He answered every question put to him without referring to a card or a note pad. He would occasionally, in the process of answering a question, reach into his pocket and pull out a letter to make a point. If you asked him about pupil transportation for the purpose of fostering desegregation, he would say, "I'm glad you asked me that question. Just last month, I received a letter from a black lady in Michigan. She has a daughter who is being bused across town. She asked to do something to end this practice. Her poor little girl has to leave home at 6:00 A.M. to catch a bus, and she wants this stopped."

For more than an hour, the President-elect responded in this manner to every challenge put to him. President Reagan saw the world and the problems that we faced in simple, anecdotal terms. He honestly did not believe that discrimination really existed in America in 1980. He seemed to feel that his homespun stories adequately addressed complicated problems.

During his eight-year tenure in the White House, I saw how effectively he used the tactic of personalizing the most complicated situation with a parable-like story. It often did not make sense to me, but it did to some people.

When the meeting was over, we had a chance to assess the man who was to lead the nation for at least the next four years. He was not a great intellectual. He was often simplistic, but he was a formidable adversary.

After the meeting with our president-elect, I met with our Washington Bureau director, Althea Simmons, and other members of the senior staff. I advised them that we were in for a very difficult period. The Voting Rights Extension Bill, the Martin Luther King, Jr. Holiday Bill, anti-apartheid legislation, and a plethora of other legislation that we deemed vital were in trouble. Nevertheless, during the 16 years I served, including 12 years of the Reagan/Bush administration, the NAACP, LCCR, and the civil rights community succeeded in having 27 civil rights bills passed by Congress.

Among the most pressing challenges facing us were the proposed budget changes that the Reagan people were planning to implement. It would, in my opinion, have a devastating effect on the poor. Blacks, as a group, were disproportionately poor in 1980, as they are today. I knew that it would not be enough to hurl hot and fiery rhetoric. Calling news conferences after a budget had been adopted was a non-starter. Reagan had won a landslide victory a few months before. If we were to have an impact, it would have to come through the power of competing ideas. We would develop an alternative budget that both protected the poor and encouraged economic growth. We would then go to the Congress and the public with our alternative policies in the public interest for economic growth.

Our Economic Analysis Unit, assisted by the NAACP's Economic Advisory Council and our Washington Bureau, swung into action. We received help from individual members of the Black Congressional Caucus and from our friends in Congress. Academics and members of the civil rights community offered their help, which was quickly accepted. I found myself spending more time than I would have liked dealing with obscure and obtuse economic theory.

We had endless meetings and heated discussions as we hammered out the document. By the early part of April, it was largely complete. All that remained was to work out some of the detailed language. Once the document was finished, we circulated it to members of the House and Senate for comment. Finally, the NAACP's Policy Recommendations for Economic Growth and Combating Inflation was ready to be delivered to the President.

In late April, the chairman of the board and I went to the White House to formally present the NAACP's alternate budget plan. David Stockman, director of the Office of Management and Budget and the author of the Administration's rigidly astringent budget proposals, had laid down the gauntlet: "If you don't like ours, present one of your own." We had done just that. Now we were at the White House with an alternative budget that we knew was workable.

We expected only a brief visit from Vice President George Bush. The vice president was standing in for the recuperating President Reagan, who was recovering from an assassination attempt earlier that month. Instead, we spent nearly an hour with Mr. Bush and with chief White House economic advisor Murray Weidenbaum, who spent most of his time thumbing through the 130-page NAACP document.

The document addressed the specifics of the Reagan budget proposals that so alarmingly and adversely affect the bread-and-butter needs of the poor and the working poor, of which blacks were a disproportionate number. These included chronic joblessness, deterioration of the inner cities, federal funds to education, Medicare, food stamps, and the centerpiece of the NAACP proposals: instituting a zero tax bracket for a family of four earning $12,600 a year, instead of the President's $7,400.

To the Administration's credit, Vice President Bush proved to be a good and careful listener as I outlined in a cordial but firm fashion the chief points of the plan and the dire necessity for the Administration to address them realistically if the country were to avoid suffering and chaos.

After tea and soft drinks were served in the quiet elegance of the West Wing office (a room of period furniture, gold-framed oil paintings, and a handsome fireplace), we got down to serious business. Mr. Bush interrupted occasionally to ask a question, to mildly dispute a point, or to ask his chief economic advisor to look up information on a point at a later time.

At the end of the meeting, no one was lulled into believing the other side was ready to capitulate. Indeed, as later events proved, the Administration, riding the crest of the President's almost unprecedented popularity following the assassination attempt, swayed Congress to pass, initially, some of the more flagrantly odious (to the poor) portions of his budget initiatives.

The NAACP meeting at the White House was important in two respects: (1) For the first time in its history, the NAACP was able to present a carefully crafted alternate budget plan for consideration at the highest levels of government. The plan was also sent to the 535 members of Congress (previous White House-NAACP meetings almost always dealt with basic and general civil rights problems without presentation of detailed economic initiatives designed to help in their correction); and (2) by presenting our bold new alternative budgetary plan, we signaled that we were prepared to play a far larger role in helping to lead the fight to determine the kind of tax program the Administration would ultimately have to settle for.

The NAACP's meeting at the White House made yet another salient point. As the representatives of a grassroots, morally motivated constituency, the Association had the mandate of its membership to oppose Administration programs that appeared to be reckless, wrong, and disastrous for the nation.

I made the point that the Administration's supply-side economics was so heavily weighted on the side of the nonproductive military and the rich, against the poor and the working poor, that our choice of sides was clear and unmistakable. "Reaganomics" would ultimately self-destruct. An enormous deficit would be created that would take years to eradicate.

My satisfaction (if you can call it that) came from the certain knowledge that we did not choose to shrug our shoulders indifferently when dangerous policies were being loosed on the land, but that we tried to act responsibly in defense of the poor and downtrodden and oppose the questionable "new beginning" with what we believed to be something better.

The following is a summary of the recommendations we shared with the Administration, the Congress, and the American people.

* * *

Sustained real economic growth is in the public interest and is essential to improve the economic condition of the United States, black Americans and other minorities. However, economic growth alone is not sufficient, and provisions must be made for unemployment resulting from government policies, from recessions which are a part of the business cycle and, as a matter of right, for the care of those unable to find jobs even when the economy is at full employment. The government has an obligation to promote employment and productivity.

The Administration's proposed budget implements an intentionally restrictive fiscal policy and supports a restrictive monetary policy, a combination that permits high rates of unemployment in 1981 and 1982. The President's proposal for a $345 billion deficit tacitly accepts the proposition that deficits are not inflationary. The Administration's proposal relies on the effects of a tax cut which favors those with higher incomes and on doubtful supply-side theories which promise that such cuts are a necessary condition to large defense investments and to a significant redistribution of income from the poor and working poor to those with higher incomes.

The proposed budget cuts will have an immediate disparate impact on low-income citizens (a disproportionate number are minorities) that will be exacerbated by a policy of intentional high unemployment. Such policy ignores the long-term costs of reducing productive people to dependency. The anticipated benefits of the President's proposal will not accrue until the future and rest on a doubtful chain of supply-side economic assumptions that cuts in personal income taxes will stimulate productive investment and lead to new jobs. Conversely, the budget proposal immediately rewards those with higher incomes who run no present or future costs or risks whether the supply-side theories succeed or fail.

The Administration's proposal, while seeming to recognize the need to increase productivity as a means of simultaneously simulating economic growth and fighting inflation, nonetheless seems unrealistic to minorities who find that the social investment necessary to assure their productivity is being curtailed. It is unrealistic because the Administration, while fostering high unemployment through its restrictive fiscal and monetary policies is also reducing support for the unemployed and thereby reinforcing the effects of a dual and unequal economy. In addition, those comprehensive managerial reforms which would improve delivery systems were not proposed, and no attempt has been made to eradicate fraud, waste and mismanagement. Instead, while the need for programs and services still exists, the programs themselves are being severely curtailed or eliminated. This situation cannot be tolerated by black Americans in the 1980s.

The proposal is also suspect because many of these needed services and human resource investments are being repackaged as block grants to be returned to state and local governments. There is no apparent recognition on the part of the Administration that these programs were created to correct the failure of state and local governments, in the past, to provide these services on an equal basis to the poor and the working poor. The NAACP, therefore, is firmly opposed to such block grants.

Finally, minorities find it disturbing that a full discussion of alternatives to the objectives and methods of the Administration's proposal has been discouraged, with adamant insistence on acceptance of all the proposals without change.

After carefully reviewing the economy's performance and the record of economic growth on the well-being of blacks, the report concludes that despite the United States' relative good economic record, the growth

which has been experienced over the last 25 years has not been sufficient
to permit minorities an equal share of its benefits. The record also reveals
that past fiscal and monetary policies, as applied, often conflicted with
each other. However, the review does not lead to the conclusion that past
monetary and fiscal policies were inappropriate to today's dilemma of
sustaining growth while combating inflation.

It is clearly in the interests of the country and its minority citizens that
the Administration immediately provides the environment which is essential for growth and productivity by making the necessary investments
in human resources while encouraging growth, especially in urban centers.

The NAACP believes that there are alternate approaches; it therefore
makes the following recommendations for national policy:

- Adopt stimulative fiscal and monetary policies which reduce unemployment and enhance productivity without resort to the unrealistic and untested assumptions of supply-side theories. A monetary
  policy which maintains current growth rates of the money supply
  would not unduly restrict future growth. A complementary fiscal
  policy would stimulate the economy with a non-inflationary deficit of $55 billion and would finance $10 billion which could finance needed government investments. Such policies, which would
  immediately reduce unemployment, are the most important part
  of what the Administration has called the "safety net."
- Follow a more prudent transition to an economy in which the
  government plays a smaller role. This prudent transition is accomplished by limiting receipts to the 1981 share of gross national
  product. Such a limit will provide receipts of $672 billion and can
  be achieved by implementing the following changes to a more equitable tax system:
  a) Eliminating all federal taxes for taxpayers with incomes be-
      low the threshold, which the Bureau of Labor Statistics de-
      fines as raising social concerns of malnutrition and deprivation;
  b) Indexing individual income taxes for inflation to remove the
      inflation-induced incentives for government growth;
  c) Eliminating special tax provisions (tax loopholes) which no
      longer serve their intended purposes.
- These two recommendations will provide $32 billion to implement
  programs associated with the following policies combating inflation, increasing employment and providing for the economic development of our cities.

Stimulate business investments by:
- Targeting government incentives to productivity-related investment;
- Providing special tax concessions for small businesses;
- Providing a tax exemption for interest on savings accounts.

Increase productivity by:
- Using general tax revenues to meet the deficiency in the Social Security retirement fund;
- Fostering cooperative labor-management relations to devise incentives for rewarding increased output with increased earnings, to the benefit of both sides, their customers, and the economy;
- Deregulating and encouraging competition in those industries and markets where regulation primarily stifles competition and is not necessary to safeguard the health, safety and welfare of citizens or to enforce affirmative action/civil rights regulations and objectives.

Make "the market" work by:
- Enforcing the antitrust laws aggressively and repealing the antitrust exemptions in regulated industries to bring their anticompetitive activities (other than the conduct of legally recognized utilities) under the jurisdiction of the Department of Justice;
- Stimulating economic activity by assisting small businesses to ensure that they have the opportunity to develop and expand without being stifled by anticompetitive practices of large businesses, and assisting minority-owned business to compete on fair terms and with access to markets, through aggressive affirmative action and contract set-aside provisions under federal guidelines;
- Combating inflation by pursuing common-sense approaches to trade agreements with other countries, seeking fairness for industry, labor, and the consumer with respect to pricing and supply and demand of imports.

Promote investments in human resources by:
- Providing incentives to private employers to invest in human resources as a condition for receiving tax benefits on investment in capital equipment;
- Helping private industry in providing support services such as flextime, day care centers, etc.

Improve labor force participation by:

- Enhancing the role of government by better targeting of existing job opportunities to stimulate and encourage meaningful participation of blacks;
- Improving the United States Employment Service as a national information network and placement service that can match people and jobs, thus facilitating geographic and occupational mobility of disadvantaged workers and the unemployed.

Enhance federal support for education by:
- Channeling all federal funds for elementary and secondary education directly to the public school systems to ensure quality desegregated public education for children throughout the United States. The NAACP opposes voucher systems, tax credits, and block grants.
- Establishing a much closer relationship between future job opportunities, placement, and training by developing cooperative efforts with private enterprise.
- Providing public sector training or employment to assist the long-term unemployed and to increase youth employment.

Combat unemployment by:
- Enforcing sanctions on employers who hire illegal aliens, and imposing stiffer and certain civil penalties on employers who hire workers at wages below the federal minimum wage;
- Continuing to support those CETA programs and job-training programs that have effective and efficient abilities in providing necessary services and helping the disadvantaged to obtain employment;
- Strengthening and enforcing civil rights and affirmative action programs.

Revitalize the central city by:
- Targeting available funds to high-need areas of cities;
- Encouraging and rewarding suburban metropolitan resource sharing efforts;
- Encouraging and promoting public/private cooperative efforts. In particular, concepts such as the Enterprise Zone should be explored.

Increase the effectiveness of government by:
- Improving the management of federal programs to eliminate abuses, poor service, and fraud;

- Rejecting block grants because they do not contain necessary safe-guards to ensure that recipients achieve the valid objectives of the categorical programs which they are replacing.

These policy recommendations do not contain all of the changes necessary to assure equal opportunity in a prosperous future for all Americans. Nor can these recommendations immediately end inflation and unemployment. Instead, these recommendations constitute a reasonable approach which avoids the major pitfalls of the Administration's proposal. It contains recommendations that offer a realistic chance for growth and provide for the prudent and necessary investment in unused human resources while shielding the poorest from abject poverty and deprivation occasioned by the uncertainties of the economic system.

* * *

Among the cuts proposed by the Reagan Administration was a reduction in federal grants to states for Medicare. The program was to be cut $100 million in 1981 and $1 billion in 1982. The President proposed to abolish the minimum Social Security benefits and reduce or eliminate student benefits under the program. The Administration proposed to reduce basic eligibility for food stamps and to eliminate a job training program. Unemployment insurance was to be cut by $1.2 billion in 1982. The Arts and Humanities Endowments were to be cut by 25 percent. Social services were to be cut by 25 percent. Educational spending was cut by $1.25 *billion*. Mass transit funds were to be gradually eliminated.

These draconian cuts threatened not just black Americans, but the elderly, the poor, the young in public schools, workers who use public transportation, and all who depended on any form of government assistance. The battle to preserve these vital programs was to continue for most of the President's time in office.

Chapter 17
1981-1992—FAIR SHARE: AN ECONOMIC ROAD MAP

There is no problem facing black America that is more pernicious and all-consuming than the lack of economic parity between African Americans and whites. The statistics bear out the fact that blacks have less wealth than whites, earn less in wages, have proportionately fewer businesses, have less disposable income, and, for those and other reasons, have not enjoyed the fruits that other groups take for granted.

I grew up around men who owned their own businesses. My father and my uncle ran the Hooks Brothers' Photography Studio. My first job was selling hot dogs and Cokes for my brother Robert, and my second job was selling a black newspaper. When I went into the practice of law, I chose to enter private practice as opposed to working for a governmental agency in Chicago where I would have a guaranteed salary. I helped to organize one of the first black franchises in the nation, the Mahalia Jackson Chicken corporate chain. Before coming to the NAACP, I had helped to organize a black savings and loan association. The entrepreneurial spirit was in my blood.

I realized, as did Dr. King and many others who had been involved in the Civil Rights Movement, that winning the right to use public accommodations was just the beginning of the long and arduous trek to independence and full equality. Joe Lowery, who headed the Southern Christian Leadership Conference for more than 20 years, used to say often that it's not enough to have the right to check into a hotel, you have to have the money to check out. In a country like ours, most of what we can do is based on economics. What good does it do a man who lives in the ghetto, trying to rear his children and be a good husband to his wife, to know there is a law that says he can move to any neighborhood he can afford if the only neighborhood he can afford is the house he lives in or one just like it? It is of little consequence to say to people they can fly first class on an airline if they do not have the money to get to the airport or to buy a first-class ticket when they get there. The civil rights struggle without an attendant economic component is anemic and hollow.

Getting a good education and getting a good job moves a person from the abstract notion of equality closer to the reality of equality in a capitalist society. The NAACP had a labor department for years. When I came to New York in 1977, Herbert Hill was the department's director. The department did a fine job of working with employers and labor unions. In communities around the country, it had persuaded corporate leaders to end discriminatory practices that had effectively locked many blacks out of good-paying jobs.

In the early 1970s, Robert Easley and Grover Smith were hired, under a special grant, to assist the National Office in identifying cases of discrimination. In 1969, the NAACP received a grant from the U.S. Department of Housing and Urban Development to identify and catalogue minority contractors who could bid on federal work. Increased numbers of lawsuits were filed using the information that the labor department's assistants unearthed. We had over 500 active labor committees in our branches. Some, like the Pittsburgh, Pennsylvania, and Buffalo, New York labor committees, were exceptionally successful.

In 1978, the NAACP established an Economic Policy Advisory Committee in a major effort to develop a cohesive economic strategy for African Americans. We took a very unpopular position, at that time, to support a national energy plan. The plan would promote the creation of jobs for African Americans by fostering vigorous economic growth. Our position was that unless there was a healthy economy, blacks who were disproportionately at the bottom of the economic ladder would continue to suffer adversely from high rates of unemployment. Unemployment among blacks was more than twice as high as it was for whites. Additionally, a staggering 33 percent of African-American families were living below the poverty line.

In July of 1978, we appointed an NAACP Economic Advisory Council. These noted economists and experts on monetary policy developed a comprehensive 170-page document entitled *Alternative Policies in the Interest of Economic Growth*. This report was a road map, as we saw it then. With hindsight, I believe our approach, if adopted as national policy, would have ended earlier the economic downward spiral that conspired to keep so many Americans, black and white, out of the economic mainstream. Meanwhile, I kept the drumbeat going in speeches, news conferences, pronouncements, and TV appearances that a good job was the best anti-poverty prescription for the national economy. In 1979 we made jobs and job creation a national priority of the Association.

Our Fair Share Program was a logical and evolutionary outgrowth from those efforts. We recognized that economic development was more than merely getting jobs and ending discrimination among wage and salaried employees. What was desperately needed was to find a way to create employment opportunities through black economic development. This was not new to America. As Oscar Handlin pointed out in his book, *The Newcomers,* written in the early '60s, all immigrant groups that came to New York started off by creating businesses as soon as possible.

Initially the Italians, the Irish, the Germans, and others worked for wages—exploitive wages, I might add. Soon they began to develop small businesses, like the ones that blacks had on Beale Street when I was a child. Those black businesses and others around the city provided many of the goods and services for our people. Later, many of these businesses grew and became an integral part of the economic mainstream of Memphis.

I hired a younger lawyer, Curtis Rogers, who did a marvelous job in laying the groundwork for what was to become our Fair Share program. When establishing a new department in an organization, it is important that the parameters as well as goals and outcomes be established clearly. The primary objective of the department would be to negotiate agreements with corporations that would ensure the widest possible participation at the entry levels; increase the number of blacks in managerial positions; expand minority vendor opportunities; place blacks on the boards of directors of major corporations; and increase the philanthropic giving to black charities.

Waymon Dunn, a very resourceful and community-minded executive at Con Edison, was at the time serving as my special assistant. He was the organizer of our newly created Community Outreach Program. The goal of this program was to develop at the grassroots level, in places where we had NAACP branches, a mechanism by which local residents could receive information and direction on governmental services that were available to them.

Waymon worked with Curtis during the initial stage in arranging meetings with corporate executives in New York to discuss the Fair Share idea. The first company we met with was Con Edison, the electric utility of New York City. In 1982, we signed our first Fair Share agreement with the Edison Electric Institute and the American Gas Association. The agreement called for the trade organizations to have their member affiliates agree to implement the Fair Share principles.

When we first announced the Fair Share initiative, we received inquiries from blacks who were working in the movie industry. They complained about the flagrant exclusion of black tradesmen and professionals, producers, directors, writers, and others in the industry. Another sore spot was the lack of work that was available for black actors. Michael Lawrence took over the direction of the public sectors of our Fair Share agreements.

We had a very active branch in Hollywood. The leadership included Maggie Hathaway, Geraldine Green, and Willis Edwards. They were clamoring for the National Office to take on the major studios in Hollywood. I can't tell you how many meetings we had during the first year of the program. Collecting data was a tedious and time-consuming process. The studios claimed that the information being sought was not kept by racial designations. It was strange that blacks who worked in the industry could get their hands on the numbers of black directors, producers, and actors under contract and other data that the studios swore did not exist. Our efforts were met with sustained resistance. The movie industry erected roadblocks at every turn. The delay and stall tactics that I had seen used in the South during the '50s and the '60s had been refined in the '80s and used to great effect by the movie moguls and industry titans.

We did manage to make progress with MGM, United Artists, and Disney Studios. We applied pressure on the entire industry during my tenure as executive director. Gradually—too gradually—doors began to open to blacks in Hollywood. However, like many other industries in America, racism and discrimination are still deeply rooted in the body politic of the industry.

It appears that many movers and shakers in Hollywood are satisfied as long as blacks go to the theaters and spend their money. They will pay large salaries to megastars like Eddie Murphy or Denzel Washington, because they know that they will bring in huge audiences. But there are roles that will not be offered to black actors. Spike Lee, John Singleton, and others have ventured to produce and seek independent financing for their films. With limited budgets, they have proven that audiences, white and black, will go to see a good movie with no regard for the color of those who are in front of or behind the cameras.

In 1981, Curtis Rogers asked to be transferred to the legal department. His departure left a vacancy that was filled by Fred Rasheed. Fred had extensive experience in business. Additionally, he was both effective and aggressive. Under his leadership, our Fair Share program blossomed. Soon we had a private-sector component, a pilot incubator program in Hartford, Connecticut, and a regional office in Little Rock, Arkansas. Much of the success for the program was due, in large measure, to the unique skills and the creativity of Fred Rasheed.

The NAACP's Fair Share program was by far the most effective national program in securing economic opportunities for African Americans. In the decade between 1982 and January 1992, 58 agreements were signed with private-sector corporations and associations. We established a public-sector program in 1985. Between 1985 and January of 1992, 19 agreements were signed with public colleges, city agencies, electric utilities, and a host of other public agencies. It is conservatively estimated that the dollar value of these 77 agreements was over $10 billion. More than 15,000 blacks were employed at the professional level, and more than 25,000 additional blacks were employed by minority vendors who were beneficiaries of our efforts. Michael Lawrence took over the direction of the public sectors of our Fair Share Agreements.

Reporters and those who merely wished to criticize the program asked me repeatedly, "How do you know if the signatories to the agreements lived up to their written comments?" On the surface, that appeared to be a logical if not an innocuous question. But it was based in the fertile soils of doubt and suspicion. No one bothered to ask others who negotiated with companies to prove the facts contained in the statements made in their press releases or at their press conferences. Therefore, I insisted that there be a mechanism for monitoring negotiated agreements. An integral part of our agreements was the provision that the signatory agreed to cooperate and participate in a comprehensive review of the progress or lack of progress that had been made.

Fred Rasheed was extremely effective and efficient in monitoring each agreement. After this process was completed, a report card was issued rating companies on their diligence in reaching their goals. We did not have quotas, but we had goals and timetables. Without them, the agreements were of little value. The old excuse that they could not find qualified blacks in entry-level positions had no validity. If a company was serious about finding blacks to serve on its board of directors, it could find them. If the company wanted to advance and promote blacks already employed, it could do that too.

In 1991 we held 38 monitoring meetings. Let me give you an idea of the breadth and scope of the kinds of industries we dealt with in that year alone: American Gas Association, Arkansas/Louisiana Gas Company, Atlanta Gas & Light Company; Atlantic Electric Company; Bi-Lo Foods, Inc.; Brown & Williamson Tobacco Company; Commonwealth Edison; Coors Brewing Company; Dillard's Department Stores, Inc.; Edison Electric Institute; Energy Operations, Inc.; Kmart Corporation; Louisiana Power & Light Company; New Orleans Public Service; McDonald's Corporation; Mississippi Power & Light Co.; Myrtle Beach Hotel & Motel Association; New Jersey Sports & Exposition Authority; Nations Bank; Pacific Bell; Philadelphia Gas Works; The Quaker Oats Company; Safeway, Inc.; Sony Music Entertainment Inc.; South Jersey Gas Company; Southern National Banks; the *Sun* newspaper; Supermarkets General Corp.; Toys 'R' Us; United Airlines; Virginia Power Company; Walt Disney Productions; Washington Gas & Light Company; Wendy's International; and the William Wrigley Company.

Astonishingly, our entire Economic Development staff consisted of just six people. Fred Rasheed not only led the all-important monitoring effort that year but negotiated eight additional agreements, and prepared and released a comprehensive report on allegations of economic exclusion and discrimination against blacks in the television and film industry. After a year of intensive investigation, the report of the task force, *Out of Focus—Out of Sync*, was released in September 1991.

I am also extremely proud that during that same year we were able to conclude a historic agreement with Nations Bank, the fourth largest financial institution in the country. As a part of our agreement, I insisted that the newly merged bank make every effort to provide better banking service to the economically disadvantaged to the tune of $10 billion dollars over a period of 10 years.

The bank agreed to commit $1.1 million per year to fund five NAACP Community Development Resource Centers in key cities in the South where it operated. These pilot centers were to be evaluated after two years. If they proved successful in helping Nations Bank in achieving its community investment goals, we would expand the program to include other cities within the Nations Bank market. Nations Bank had 1,900 banking offices in the South.

Following the signing of the agreement, I said to Bennett Brown, chairman, and Hugh McColl, CEO of Nations Bank, "The concept of Community Development Resource Centers was both an exciting and bold new direction for the NAACP. The involvement of our organization will foster a strong identification at the community level and ease any fears that African Americans might have of that which is new and unfamiliar to them. We will provide badly needed consumer loan counseling, loan packaging, and education programs for high school students; we will analyze their corporate credit policy and minority business development."

No other group, white or black, civil rights-related or unrelated, can lay claim to the type of success that we had in this arena. I take my hat off to the fine staff we assembled, not just in this area, but in practically every area in which we operated. It is ironic that those who choose to criticize us for not doing more in the area of self-help and economic development are completely ignorant of our enormous accomplishment in this area.

On April 26, 1991, we held the first meeting of our newly organized Fair Share Commerce and Trade Council. The Council was a group of diversified companies consisting of eight manufacturing firms, two publishers, and 11 service companies. Several of America's largest black-owned businesses were represented, and five members were listed on the *Black Enterprise* magazine 100 list. The purpose of organizing the Council was to gain contract opportunities for Council members who had been the victims of a recessionary environment in which many Fair Share signatory companies were downsizing their supplier base.

There were critics, some in the black community, who felt that we should not help the few blacks who were in business become millionaires. This was a myopic and narrow view. In 1991, and I would venture to say it is true today (according to a U.S. Department of Labor study), more than 80 percent of all jobs created in the nation were created by small businesses. Businesspeople tend to hire people they know and people who look like them. It is therefore logical to extrapolate that if we build our economic base of black businesses, we will increase black employment and, ultimately, enhance the wealth of the entire community.

I am also extremely proud of what we were able to do in challenging the record and music industry. I am proud of the pioneering agreements we were able to negotiate with both the private and the public sector. Today, hundreds of thousands of African Americans are gainfully employed because of our efforts. There are scores of blacks sitting on boards of directors that are making a significant impact on the policies of those entities.

Chapter 18
THE *LENELL GETER* CASE

It is a gloomy, humid, hot, and overcast day. A young man languishes in a Texas jail cell. He has been convicted of a crime that he did not commit. He is a college graduate and an engineer. He has overcome many obstacles that were designed to confine him to blasted dreams and postponed hopes. He left his native home state of South Carolina to pursue his dream, a job as an engineer. He is a devoted churchgoer. He does not drink or smoke. He has never been in trouble with the law before. Suddenly he is a number, confined to a jail cell and outfitted in a prison jumpsuit.

He had grown up believing that the guilty are punished and the innocent are set free. A jury has convicted him, and a judge has sentenced him to life in prison. The famous American justice system has failed him. He does not have money for private investigators, expert witnesses, or a famous lawyer who specializes in his type of case. Suddenly, a thought comes to him: I will contact the NAACP. Maybe they can help me.

The young engineer sits in his stark prison cell. He takes a piece of paper and begins to write. He does not have a name to target. He merely addresses his letter to the NAACP legal department. The letter arrives in the mailroom of the National Office in Brooklyn a few days later. It is processed by the mail clerk and taken to the legal department with many others. Some are from people whose names are well known—lawyers, judges, politicians, or branch officers. Others are from individuals who are seeking help in education or employment discrimination cases. A few are from people who feel they were denied a house or an apartment because of racial discrimination.

The day's mail is logged in by the department's secretary. Lenell Geter's letter is referred to George Harrison, associate counsel. George handles criminal cases for the NAACP. Upon reading the letter, Harrison is convinced that this is a case that deserves intervention. There has been a flagrant miscarriage of justice, Harrison concludes.

As a general rule, the NAACP does not handle individual cases. The reason for this policy is obvious. The NAACP is not a legal services agency with vast resources for the defense of those charged with criminal offenses. Rather, the NAACP intervenes in criminal cases to set important legal precedents, and to selectively take on cases that are so egregious that by winning them, a larger fundamental principle can be established. One of many such cases during my tenure was the *Lenell Geter* case.

Lenell Geter was a 26 year-old engineer, a graduate of South Carolina State University, a black state-supported college. Geter, along with his roommate, Anthony Williams, moved to Dallas, Texas, after graduating in 1981. They were employed as mechanical engineers with E-Systems, Inc., in Greenville, Texas. The two soon established themselves at the company and were well thought of by their co-workers and the management.

On August 23, 1982, a Kentucky Fried Chicken restaurant was robbed in a Dallas suburb, Balch Springs. The day before, a Taco Bell restaurant had been robbed in Lewisville, Texas, another small town outside of Dallas, and a 7-Eleven convenience store had also been robbed. What happened after this was an innocent man's nightmare. Geter was arrested and charged with the Balch Springs robbery and Williams was arrested and charged with robbing the 7-Eleven convenience store.

Law enforcement officials had concluded that the robberies, all committed by a young black man, were the work of some organized gang, not an individual acting on his own. There were six young black engineers working at E-Systems, Inc., from out of state. They had to be the perpetrators, the police reasoned.

According to court documents, Greenville Police Lieutenant James Fortenberry launched an investigation of Geter earlier in the summer of 1982 after receiving a tip from a citizen who was suspicious of Geter because of his frequent visits to a municipal park. Fortenberry's informant was later identified as Jewell Peavey, a 68-year-old white woman from Greenville, who testified that "colored people" scared her. He was carrying a black athletic bag, not uncommon, I might add, for a person exercising in a public park. Nonetheless, she gave the police Geter's description and the license plate number of his car.

It is interesting to note that the sight of a young black man sitting in a public park financed by taxpayers' dollars, his and others, reading a book or a newspaper, or carrying an athletic bag, was sufficient grounds for a full-fledged investigation by the Greenville police. Geter's crime was sitting on a park bench and reading while black. This experience by blacks is more common than many whites would like to admit or that some blacks want to reminded of. This accounts in large measure for why blacks and whites view law enforcement and our legal system quite differently.

Fortenberry gave Geter's name to the Plano police, who obtained his photograph from driver's license records and passed it to Garland police, who gave it to Balch Springs police. After the Balch Springs robbery, Geter's photo was shown repeatedly to the victims and to eyewitnesses in a photo lineup. He was being targeted as an armed robbery suspect solely because of his race and foreign resident status.

What should be remembered was that Geter did not have a police record. He was a young black professional working for a well-known company. He shared an apartment with a male co-worker in a nice section of Greenville where a number of other young people beginning their careers lived. None of this mattered to the police. He was a young black man. He was merely targeted and arrested. After Geter was arrested, Fortenberry went to the E-Systems security officer and obtained identification card pictures of all six of the black engineers who had been recruited in 1981 and 1982 from South Carolina State College.

Dallas County at that time had a district attorney, Henry Wade, who, according to published news accounts of that period, prided himself on having a 99 percent conviction rate in robbery cases. He had earned a reputation for being one of the most tenacious prosecutors in the state. His tactics were highly suspect by civil libertarians, and he was viewed by many in the black community as being racist in his motivation and conduct.

At the first trial, Geter was defended by a lawyer whose ability to try a criminal case was questionable. This often happens in criminal cases. One's ability to retain good counsel can mean the difference between conviction and acquittal. The first trial received very little publicity. Geter was convicted and given a life sentence. Ordinarily, this would have been the end of the story. At this juncture, Geter wrote the NAACP.

Shortly after I arrived at the NAACP, I had the general counsel assign each of our staff lawyers to his or her specialty. For instance, a lawyer who had expertise and the requisite experience handling labor cases was assigned to employment cases received by the National Office for review and recommendation. This way, I believed, we could best decide what cases deserved additional consideration and could, if we took them on, serve a significant national good. The amount of correspondence received by the National Office was mind-boggling. Our legal department received hundreds of letters from people who felt they were being discriminated against in the workplace, and hundreds from inmates claiming to have been convicted of a crime they had not committed.

I kept a mail log in my office during my entire tenure. There was scarcely a year that I worked at the Association that I did not receive over 20,000 pieces of correspondence on all kinds of issues. I had a very small personal office staff, but I insisted that all be responded to. We had well-tailored form letters that addressed precisely the issues raised in the correspondence. The letters were personalized, with copies going to the appropriate office. All requests for legal assistance went to the general counsel's office.

I remembered the day that Geter's request was brought to my attention along with a number of others requesting help with their appeals. What the public may not understand is that our legal system is very expensive. Justice does not come cheap. The NAACP, unlike your typical law firm, does not receive retainers from the petitioner seeking help. We do not charge fees. Our decision to take a case or not, therefore, had nothing to do with the petitioner's ability to pay for our services. The decision on whether to take a case depended solely on the merits of the case. I originally told the general counsel I did not think the budget would allow us to take on any additional criminal cases. Most criminal cases involved hiring investigators and retaining local counsel. The cost of transcripts of the original proceedings alone could be staggering.

A few days later, as I boarded the elevator to go to my office, George Harrison, the lawyer who handled our criminal cases, got on. George was a young African-American lawyer who was excited about his work and was convinced that he could singlehandedly turn the legal world upside down if need be. This is an admirable trait. All people, regardless of their profession, should never lose that burning desire to do what they do well. George focused on the *Geter* appeal like a laser beam. I got off on my floor and he followed me down the hall trying to present his whole case in rapid-fire fashion. I asked him to send me some additional information on the case. That afternoon there was a memorandum from George with some of the highlights of a possible appeal in the *Geter* case.

Persistence paid off. Every time I saw George, and that was often, he would bring up the Geter matter. If he had that much faith in the case, I reasoned, we would move forward. I let him know that we had a very tight budget, but we would go forward with this one. "There is not an endless pot of money for this case. We will have to make every dollar spent go as far as possible," I told him.

With George's persistence—and my approval—we were on our way. If all of the information we had on the case were accurate, Geter would one day be a free man. In the ensuing months, George made countless trips to Dallas. He would return both fired up and angry. He was enraged by the obvious injustices that he saw surrounding the case. This was obviously a case where the police had identified Geter as a target to be charged with a convenient crime. Any crime would do. Nine of his co-workers had testified at the trial that Geter was at work the day the crime was committed. The fast-food restaurant that he allegedly robbed was some 50 miles away. It would not have been possible for him to drive a total of 100 miles to and from the robbery and not be missed by his co-workers and his supervisor.

At his first trial, seven witnesses identified Geter as being the robber. Anyone familiar with criminal proceeding and witness identification can tell you that, despite the credence that juries put on eyewitness testimony, eyewitness testimony is highly unreliable. A witness's testimony can be easily influenced by the witness being shown the same picture of the suspect over and over again, even after the eyewitness had failed to identify the suspect in an earlier police photo lineup. Interracial identifications are the most unreliable of all, according to studies that were readily available at that time.

After months of hard and unheralded work by George Harrison, we decided to involve the news media in the case. CBS decided to look into the matter. The case stank on its face. Anyone who took a close look at the *Geter* case immediately recognized that there was something terribly wrong. Here you had a young, educated black man charged with committing a crime in a small, conservative community outside of Dallas. He had a full-time job some 50 miles away from where the robbery occurred. He was respected and, according to his supervisors and co-workers, was doing an excellent job at E-Systems, Inc. He had a flawless record, never having been arrested in his life. Why would he risk all for a mere $600 that he could get by robbing a fast-food restaurant? The case just did not make sense. Then there was the matter of Geter being in two places at once. He was at work shortly before and shortly after the robbery occurred some 50 miles away. His co-workers testified that he was at work that day.

The CBS producers were also suspicious of the case against Geter. Why should a call from a scared 68-year-old white woman about a man sitting in a public park spark a full-fledged investigation? Don't many white people living in a town sit in parks every day? Why would a police officer testify that he spoke to a sheriff in South Carolina who informed him that Geter was a "bad character" when it was not so? The sheriff flew to Dallas and testified, under oath, that he never said such a thing.

CBS reached the same conclusion that we had reached earlier: Lenell Geter was innocent. Geter had been given a life sentence for an armed robbery that he had not committed. On Sunday, December 4, 1983, CBS's *60 Minutes*, the most popular show of its kind on TV, presented a segment that dealt with the Lenell Geter story. Anyone watching that show had to be appalled as the facts were laid out before the American public in a very vivid and graphic way.

That night the *Geter* case became a *cause célèbre*. The pressure on the city of Dallas and the Dallas district attorney's office increased. Seven days later, the district attorney, Henry Wade, agreed to ask the judge to grant a new trial. On the 17th of December, Geter, who had by now served 14 months of his life sentence, walked out of prison without handcuffs, but not yet free. He was freed on a $10,000 bond.

The district attorney made an offer to drop the charges if Geter agreed to take and pass a lie detector test administered by a Dallas police officer, William Parker. To the general public, this might sound like a reasonable request. Unfortunately, it was not. Polygraph tests are very unreliable. They are only as good as the person who administers them. There was no reason for Geter and his lawyers to believe he could trust the Dallas Police Department and the district attorney's office to administer a test that would be used to exonerate him when these same persons were responsible for his wrongful conviction in the first instance.

We decided instead to bring Geter to New York, where we had a noted former FBI polygraph examiner conduct the test. Geter passed with flying colors. He later took a second test in South Carolina that he also passed. The Dallas district attorney, of course, would not accept the results of those examinations. It really did not matter. We had both the facts and public opinion on our side. If he wanted to have another trial, we were ready, willing, and able.

Geter's roommate, Anthony Williams, who had been charged with the armed robbery of a 7-Eleven convenience store, had been acquitted by an all-white jury in only two hours and 17 minutes of deliberations. We were optimistic that another trial for Geter would produce the same results.

On January 30, 1984, there was a pretrial hearing in Dallas on the *Lenell Geter* case. Upon my arrival, I was taken immediately to the Dallas County Courthouse. George Harrison and local counsel were already there. So was Geter, dressed in a three-piece pin-striped suit. I had seen Lenell in New York when he came by the office, but seeing him in Dallas, standing ramrod straight with his dignity intact, was worth all of our efforts and expenses.

I sat at the defense table looking at State District Judge John Ovard, who was presiding. My mind went back to my early days as a lawyer, a public defender, and a judge in Memphis, to a point in time when you instinctively knew that the odds were stacked against any black man who sought justice in the courts. The state flags were different, but the lawyers sitting at the prosecutor's table were all white and so was the judge. The defendant was black. There was a big difference in 1984. Because of people like Charles Houston, Thurgood Marshall, Bob Carter, and Constance Baker Motley, Jim Nabrit, George E.C. Hayes, Spottswood Robinson, Nathaniel Colley, Herbert Henderson, Oliver Hill, Sam Tucker, A.C. Walden, Z.A. Looby, and a host of others, we could and would ultimately secure justice under the law.

Judge Ovard set a trial date for April 9, 1984, but on March 31, 1984, all charges against Lenell Geter were dismissed. The district attorney determined that a convict being held in Houston was responsible for the robbery spree of 1982. His name was Curtis Eugene Mason. Wade acknowledged that Geter's 1982 conviction was a mistake. He blamed erroneous eyewitness testimony and incomplete policework for his office's prosecution of the case.

Later that day at a press conference in Dallas, I said, "What happened to Geter could have happened anywhere in America because our criminal justice system is flawed, and, particularly in the South, it is flawed against black people." I went on to point out that the mission of the NAACP and other similar organizations is to reshape and mold the American system of justice. We would not rest until we made our criminal justice system fair for all of our citizens, despite race, creed, or national origin.

Finally, it was over for Lenell Geter. He could now get on with his life. Today, he is married and lives with his wife and children in Columbia, South Carolina. He is a motivational speaker and very active with his church. He is not bitter, but he is determined to make sure that others will not have to endure the pain and suffering that he was forced to endure. I look back at the vindication of this young man as a major triumph for the NAACP during my administration.

One reason I support the NAACP's position against the death penalty is because of the inequalities in our criminal justice system and the role that racial and cultural bias play in the handing out of sentences. If I had no moral abhorrence to the death penalty, which I do, I would still have difficulty accepting its use in an imperfect world. I realize there are many who say that with all the checks and balances we have in our legal system, the chances of a miscarriage happening are minimal. The question we need to ask ourselves is, "Would I want to entrust the life of my son or daughter to an imperfect system?"

The NAACP never received a dime for the tens of thousands of dollars that we spent in the appeal of Lenell Geter. Very little money was raised to assist that effort. What we did manage to do was notify prosecutors across the country that there was a powerful force looking over their shoulders. How many lives were saved by our actions? No one knows. How many other innocent blacks were not prosecuted on flimsy evidence because of our success in the *Geter* case? Only God knows. We educated the public in a dramatic way to the fact that racism is a factor that must be considered while we, as a society, continue to boast of having the best system of justice in the world. For me, that was enough.

Chapter 19

NAACP: AN AGENT FOR CHANGE

When I became executive director of the NAACP in 1977, the Beverly Hills/Hollywood, California, branch had been sponsoring an annual event known as the Image Awards. The branch was originally organized in 1962 to motivate and encourage the Hollywood establishment to give African Americans opportunities in the industry. The first Image Award was given in 1967.

By the time I arrived, the program was 10 years old. The event itself was held in December of each year. Geraldine Green, a lawyer, was president of the branch when I came. She was assisted by a young man who was well connected in Hollywood, Willis Edwards. Willis later became president of the branch.

I will never forget the first Image Awards I attended. It was held at the beautiful Wilshire Theater and was modeled after the Academy Awards. It was a star-studded event, featuring the "Who's Who" of black Hollywood. The glitter and glitz were impressive. After the event itself, the participants and hundreds of others who attended the event went to a dinner fit for royalty and several receptions that followed. It was an unbelievable affair that rivaled anything given by any group. Today there are many black awards programs, but when the Image Awards began there were no others.

The theater was always packed for the event. It received wide-scale attention from *Variety* and other similar publications. John H. Johnson, the publisher of *Ebony* and *Jet*, made a point of covering the stellar affair in his publications. John Johnson was one of the most unusual business-men and journalists we have ever produced. *Jet* magazine is the weekly vehicle that reaches out and connects the total black community of America. If an event did not appear in *Jet*, it is almost as if it did not really happen. From humble beginnings he put together a media empire and raised the hopes and aspirations of millions. The NAACP honored Mr. Johnson by awarding him the Spingarn Medal. At my invitation he spoke before the NAACP on numerous occasions. He is a strong supporter of the Chicago branch of the NAACP. As busy as he was, he always kept the door open for me and the NAACP, and I could reach him at any time.

Of course, we also covered the awards program in our *Crisis* magazine. The majority media gave the event scant coverage. This meant that the majority of white Americans were not aware of the Image Awards. Scores of Hollywood actors and stars worked with us and were proud to be NAACP supporters and members. To name but a few, Harry Belafonte, Brock Peters, Bill Cosby, Oprah Winfrey, Lena Horne, Bryant Gumbel, Denzel Washington, Michael Jackson and the Jackson family, Diana Ross, Stevie Wonder, Sammy Davis, Jr., Ray Charles, Jayne Kennedy, Spike Lee, Count Basie, Cab Calloway, Duke Ellington, Ella Fitzgerald, Ossie Davis and Ruby Dee, and many other outstanding singers, writers, directors, and gospel luminaries, including Mahalia Jackson and Ethel Waters—you name them, and they worked hard with me during my tenure. When I needed help, not once did they turn me down. This was true of Mr. Wilkins and Mr. White and our Mr. Mfume today.

Stevie Wonder is one of the nation's great stars. He came to the NAACP convention on several occasions. We will always be grateful to Stevie for the work he has done for our association. He was instrumental in helping to persuade the nation we needed a Martin Luther King, Jr., holiday. I have also known Aretha Franklin since her childhood. She is always cooperative and supportive and willing to do anything possible for the NAACP.

I met with Michael Jackson one day at his palatial home in Los Angeles. This meeting was prompted by criticism of black performers and their failure to support black causes relating to insufficient hiring of black performers and associates. The Jackson Five was one of the groups criticized. Prior to the meeting, I had a cordial preliminary discussion with his sister, Janet, and his mother and father. They mentioned their knowledge of and support of the NAACP from their Gary, Indiana, days.

Michael talked freely and made several promises—to hire more people from the black community and to be more responsive to the black community. He kept those promises. After attending a huge banquet at his home that night, I felt encouraged as I left. I think Michael is aware of the conditions that afflict our people. I believe that if people would talk to him about being more responsive to the black community, he would do so.

The Gordy family of Motown fame was very supportive. Esther Gordy, Berry's sister, arranged an unforgettable evening in Detroit with my father and mother and her parents. They truly enjoyed the fellowship in that fine mansion. Often I met with Berry, and on one occasion Frances and I enjoyed viewing the movie *Lady Sings the Blues* at his home in Los Angeles. The evening was even more memorable because Billy Dee Williams and Diana Ross were there. Billy Dee was kind and affable and after dinner expressed his support for the NAACP. Diana Ross was always friendly and enjoyable to be around.

On several occasions, the stars organized small benefit and fund-raising efforts and informational meetings in their homes. Bill Cosby is truly an outstanding example of a supporter. For many years he gave a day's activity to the NAACP, the Urban League, the Southern Christian Leadership Conference, or the National Council of Negro Women. That is, he would give a performance and turn over the proceeds to one of these groups.

I shall never cease to be grateful to Oprah Winfrey for her support. She is a child of the South and a pioneer of the early television days before "the breakthrough." On several occasions I was a guest on her show, and this opportunity gave me the greatest exposure I could ever hope for. In 1989, Oprah was a guest at our convention and made a generous contribution of $50,000. In 2000, the NAACP named her the Spingarn Award winner.

One of my first objectives as executive director was to have the event televised so that Americans could witness this unique program and appreciate the role the NAACP was playing in trying to change the images of blacks that Hollywood sends out around the world. Getting a program televised nationally is not an easy undertaking. The production costs run into the hundreds of thousands of dollars. Convincing a network to carry the event is a difficult task. Putting together an amalgamation of stations to constitute a national audience is difficult.

Willis Edwards, one-time president of the local branch and later a member of the National NAACP board, was extremely helpful in getting the Image Awards on national television. Without his persistent and sustained efforts, I doubt that we could have made it into the national scene. Commercial stations rely on advertising revenues. They are driven by the bottom line, not by philanthropy, benevolence, and charity. Unless they were convinced that it could be sold, they were not interested.

Our breakthrough came in 1982 for the 15th Annual Image Awards, held at the Hollywood Palladium. The program was produced by Paula Cook Milligan, president of Kashmir Productions, and directed by Arthur Forrest. The program was taped and later televised in January of 1983.

The event was one of the most impressive I have ever witnessed. Image Awards were given in the categories of theater, sports, television, motion pictures, and recordings. The previous year we were unable to have a "Best Actress" category because of the lack of actresses in meaningful roles. In 1982, Jayne Kennedy was voted best actress for her role in "Body and Soul." She was the only actress in her category for a major role. This was indicative of the problems blacks faced in the industry in that era.

The unfortunate lack of black actresses in leading roles in 1981 touched off a concentrated effort by the NAACP to gain greater employment opportunities for blacks in the industry both in front of and behind the cameras. The 1982 NAACP Convention, held in Boston, sanctioned a proposed box office boycott of a targeted studio to rectify the disproportionate employment practices and to improve the media image of blacks. To avert a possible boycott, studio executives met with NAACP representatives.

In my speech that night, I put Hollywood on notice that a boycott of a targeted studio might still be possible. I emphasized to the audience, which included representatives from most of the major studios and television networks, that the NAACP was thoroughly dissatisfied with the meager progress that had been made. We had recently entered into an agreement with Walt Disney Productions to include more blacks in all facets of its operations.

Through our negotiations with other studios, we ultimately succeeded in getting more major roles for blacks at all levels. During my remaining years at the NAACP, we were able to break down many barriers and impediments to blacks in the industry. By the time I left in 1993, the Image Awards were televised every year and were attracting a larger and larger audience. Rather than being a net loser, the National Office, for the first time, received a small but significant return on its investment.

Today there are many black awards shows. None, however, has been as effective at changing the image and practices of the film industry as our show. When I see the growing number of African-American producers, directors, and people working behind and in front of the camera, I am proud to say that I had a hand in that. When I see blacks portrayed in a positive light on one show after the other, I am proud to say that I had a hand in that, too.

I learned a very important lesson in life. It is not enough to complain about conditions; you must turn that negative energy into positive energy and act as an agent for change. I am sure that many of the blacks who hold important positions and draw unbelievable salaries in Hollywood today do not know the names Walter White, Maggie Hathaway, Geraldine Greene, Willis Edwards, or even Ben Hooks. That is sad. But we did not do what we did to have our names listed in some hall of fame. We did what we had to do because we knew that it was right. Our reward is having new opportunities available to a new generation.

20th Anniversary March on Washington

In 1983 we celebrated the 20th anniversary of the legendary 1963 March on Washington for freedom and justice. That march propelled Dr. King to international status as an orator and made Martin Luther King, Jr., a household name. Two years before the anniversary of that event, people started talking about having a commemorative march to put a spotlight on how far we had to go as a people to have unfettered freedom and equality. We decided that there should be a 20th Anniversary March to call the attention of the nation to the incomplete agenda for which the protestors marched in the historic 1963 event.

I was now serving as chairman of the Leadership Conference on Civil Rights, an umbrella group of over 160 civil rights and allied organizations. This great organization is now being led by Wade Henderson as its executive director and Dr. Dorothy Height as chair of the board. For many years it was led by Ralph Neas, who was executive director and did a simply outstanding job. Wade Henderson is a former NAACP lawyer and former head of the NAACP Washington Bureau. I marvel at his leadership. Ralph Neas now leads People for the American Way and is doing his usual stellar job.

Dorothy Height and John Lewis are the only two survivors of the Big Seven, the group that conceived and organized the 1963 March on Washington. The Big Seven included A. Philip Randolph, head of the Brotherhood of Sleeping Car Porters; Roy Wilkins, executive director of the NAACP; Jim Farmer, head of the Congress of Racial Equality; Whitney Young, Executive Director of the Urban League; Martin Luther King, Jr., head of the Southern Christian Leadership Conference; Dorothy

Height, President of the National Council of Negro Women; Bayard Rustin, Executive Assistant to Mr. Randolph; and John Lewis, head of the Student Nonviolent Coordinating Committee. These were the movers and shakers, the fabled, famous, and fabulous persons who conceived and directed the 1963 March on Washington, which forever changed the landscape of America. Jack Greenberg was Thurgood Marshall's hand-picked successor as director counsel of the NAACP Legal Defense Fund. Mr. Greenberg was, and continues to be, one of the most able and successful civil rights lawyers the nation has ever produced.

Dr. Dorothy Height was the only woman in the group. She continues to do a magnificent job as President Emeritus of the Council of Negro Women. And by the way, this organization was founded by one of the truly historic figures of black America—Mary McLeod Bethune, President and founder of Bethune-Cookman College in Florida and former director of the National Youth Administration. She was appointed by President Roosevelt in the 1930s and was a close confidant and friend of Mrs. Eleanor Roosevelt.

I knew from my experience in speaking on college campuses, meeting with our youth members around the country, and talking to the young people at my church that too many were unaware of why we marched. An anniversary march would be instructive to them. There were other Americans who were frustrated by what they saw as a national administration determined to turn back the clock on civil rights progress. For them, the march would be therapeutic and motivational. For the old-timers, and by now I was among them, it was an opportunity to reminisce and to be reinvigorated for the new fight we faced.

Coretta Scott King, Joe Lowery, head of the Southern Christian Leadership Conference (SCLC) (the organization that Dr. King founded and led until his death), and I all thought we would be remiss if we did not do something to commemorate the 20th anniversary of the march. Leadership in the black civil rights movement in America is difficult. One is called on to lead a specific organization and then is expected to be responsive to amalgamated groups of other persons involved in the civil rights model. Joe Lowery served not only as the head of the SCLC very effectively but also served as president of the Black Leadership Forum, where he very effectively harnessed the joint efforts of many other groups. It was a joy working with him when I headed the NAACP. Joe succeeded me as president of the Black Leadership forum. He has done an excellent job there. Jesse Jackson and I also worked closely together in all the years that I headed the NAACP, and I am grateful for the many outstanding contributions he has made.

There were a number of problems trying to put together a national march. The first—and the easiest to solve—was deciding on a date. All of us wanted the march to be held on a Saturday to eliminate the need for people to have to take off from work. The economy was still in the doldrums in mid-1982, when we began planning in earnest. Many of our people could not afford to miss a day's work. They could, however, leave on Friday evening and come from as far as Chicago in time for the march.

The second problem was getting a crowd. We knew that if we had 50,000-75,000 people, our detractors would say that it was a failure. The media gave a count of 250,000 people at the original March on Washington. The numbers game has become increasingly important for civil and human rights causes when it comes to protests. A small crowd is interpreted as a lack of interest on the part of the people you claim to represent, or a lack of credibility on the part of the leadership of the event.

Once we decided on the date and time for the march, the next challenge was getting word out and getting people to Washington in August. There was also the question of who would speak at the march. At the 1963 March on Washington, there were only eight national civil rights organizations. In 1983 we had scores of such organizations, and an even larger number of people who wanted to speak at any event where there was a large audience. I went back to my office and assigned a special task force to organize the effort.

The day of the March for Jobs, Peace and Freedom arrived. There was a sense of electricity and anticipation in the air. I was expecting 200-300 buses from NAACP units to arrive in Washington that morning. I wanted to stop by and just say hello to the NAACP demonstrators and to make sure we had our banners, signs, and other paraphernalia available for them. Much to my surprise, there were more than 560 NAACP buses—most chartered, but a lot of church and other private buses.

When the march began, there was a vast sea of humanity. The crowd was so thick that people were literally carried along by those surrounding them. The stifling humidity made it seem like 110 degrees. As we approached the ellipse on the Mall between the Washington Monument and the brooding, multi-pillared Lincoln Monument, I began to reflect on how far we had come as a people since that August day 20 years ago. In 1963, I was a practicing lawyer in Memphis. Since that march I had become a judge, an FCC commissioner, and now executive director of the NAACP. I looked around and saw the faces of a large number of members of Congress, mayors, and network reporters, and realized that African Americans had indeed made significant progress. I also began to contemplate the tremendous challenges that were before us as a people.

When we got to the platform where the program participants and honored guests were assembled, I saw so many faces from the past. Men and women who had been on the firing lines for years were still optimistic that we would ultimately overcome. For many, time had turned their hair white. Deep furrows were now etched in their brows. Some of the older participants now needed aid mounting the platform. A few who made that long march on that historic day in 1963 were now in wheelchairs. Yet, their eyes still held the sparkle of hope, and a vision of a new day dawning for the birth of freedom.

There was Rev. Ralph David Abernathy, Dr. King's closest friend and successor as president of the SCLC; Coretta Scott King, Dr. King's widow, and their daughter Yolanda, who was now a young adult; and Sammy Davis, Jr. and Harry Belafonte, two world-renowned entertainers and veterans in civil rights causes. Andy Young, Dr. King's executive director and now mayor of Atlanta, was trying to see to it that everyone got a seat. Clarence Mitchell, the old warrior, was there talking with Senator Charles Mathias of Maryland. The congressman from the District of Columbia, the man who worked with Dr. King in writing his famous *I Have a Dream* speech, Walter Fauntroy, was there. Dorothy Height, C. Delores Tucker, Congressman William Gray, Jesse Jackson, Washington's Mayor Marion Barry, Julius Chambers, Elaine Jones, Norman Hill, Parren Mitchell, John Jacob, Charles Adams, and a host of other old-timers were all present to be a part of history once more.

I was happy to see the huge crowd present that day. I believe that each person in the crowd was, by his or her presence, saying to the forces that wanted to stop and reverse the progress made since 1963, "We shall not go back."

There were more than 20 people who spoke on that day. I was introduced midway through the program. In my address, I tried to give a historical perspective on the significance of the March and challenge the more than 250,000 witnesses there to struggle on. Following is the text of my remarks.

* * *

Twenty years ago Martin Luther King, Jr. stood here transfixed between a weeping heaven and a wicked earth and declared, "I Have a Dream." We have returned not simply to reaffirm that dream, but to renew that hope, recharge that faith, rekindle that courage, reassert that demand.

We are not destroyed, we are not defeated. We are not discouraged. We still have a dream . . . A dream that every human being will enjoy not only freedom from slavery, but deliverance from servitude; not only freedom from ignorance, but deliverance from indigence; not only the right to vote, but the money to pay the note. This is the dream that has propelled black Americans since their arrival here on these alien shores. It was a dream of A. Philip Randolph, noble originator of the 1963 March. It was the dream of W.E.B. DuBois, a founder of the NAACP, whose death in Ghana was announced by Roy Wilkins from this very podium on this date twenty years ago. Out of respect for the legendary W.E.B. DuBois, and Whitney Young, A. Philip Randolph, Roy Wilkins, Walter Reuther, and Martin Luther King, let us bow our heads now in a moment of silent prayer and remembrance.

We break that silence to make the announcement that even in our quest for world peace we have come to declare war—political war, if you please—on the present policies of the Reagan Administration—policies that punish the poor and reward the rich; policies that talk about the trickle-down theory but somehow the trickle never gets down; policies that provide a safety net for the truly greedy, but nothing for the truly needy.

We serve notice on President Reagan that we are not here to live in the past and leave here simply singing "We Shall Overcome." We are here because we are committed to the elimination of Reaganism in 1984. We've had enough of Reaganism. Reaganism no more in '84! Say it loud, say it proud, Reaganism no more in '84!

We have come to declare war on unemployment. Unemployment is not just a word, it is a condition. It is a family that has lost its home. It is students forced to leave college because they cannot get a student loan. Unemployment is a family standing in line in the supermarket having to choose between ground beef or dog food.

It is a father forced to leave his family in order that they may qualify for welfare.

It is a mother holding in her arms a sick child, with no money to pay for the doctor or medicine.

It is the indignity of standing in cheese lines.

It is seeing bills not being paid and utilities cut off.

It is filing for bankruptcy and having your credit stopped.

Unemployment is more than a word; it is a killer of the dream.

It is the robber of aspirations, the breeder of despair.

It is the cancer that eats away at the heart and soul of otherwise healthy people.

There is a sickness sweeping across this nation. It is a virus of elitism cloaked in garments of fiscal austerity and wrapped in the trappings of patriotism. This virus has spread across the land from the Atlantic to the Pacific. It has created massive unemployment—20 percent in the black community and 50 percent among black youth. It has created doubt, dismay, and despair among the poor and increased the number of people living in poverty. No Centers for Disease Control will be able to identify it, but I can tell you that this infection is REAGANITIS!

America, our schools are failing, while thousands of teachers are thrown out of work. Provide jobs and we can once again take our place as a nation that believes that our greatest resources are not MX missiles and B-1 bombers, not Trident submarines and tiger tanks, but our children, black and white, brown and yellow. Provide jobs, and teachers who have been fired and laid off can march back into the classrooms and teach those young people, black and white, who hunger and thirst for knowledge.

America, the hour is late, the clocks of destiny are ticking, the time is now to restore hope to the more than eleven million of your citizens who walk the streets of our cities, towns, villages, and hamlets, day after day, yet can't find employment in the land of plenty. The time is now to bring to an end the sad saga of young men and women who have moved into their mid-twenties and early thirties yet have never had a job experience.

America, provide jobs and we shall help those whose aspirations have been mugged, those whose hopes have been lynched, those whose dreams have been blasted by the bombs of double-digit unemployment.

Provide jobs, and we shall rebuild our crumbling cities.

Provide jobs, and we shall put dedication and determination in education.

Provide jobs, and we will build houses where there are now slums, decay, and rubble.

Provide jobs, and we shall rebuild our family structure and halt the deterioration of the black family, over 40 percent headed by women who are the victims of the dual-edged sword of racism and sexism, and whose children are destined to a life of poverty and degradation.

America, we are marching today—20 years later— for much more than we marched for in 1963. The dream is bigger because the problems are more complex. The enemy is more subtle, racism is more sinister.

Twenty years ago we were marching for political freedom. Today we march for economic equality and total parity.

Twenty years ago we were marching for a seat on the bus. Now we are marching to drive the bus, to run the bus line, to own the bus company.

Twenty years ago we were marching to eat in front of the counter; now we are marching to manage the counter.

Twenty years ago we marched for the right to vote. Today we are marching for the right to be elected and to serve.

Twenty years ago we were marching to participate in the political process. Today we are marching to change, to reform, and to redeem the entire society.

Black people have already begun this modern-day crusade.

One aspect has been the NAACP's Black Dollar Days Demonstration where black Americans across this country will make their purchases during the Labor Day weekend by using either Susan B. Anthony silver dollars or two-dollar bills.

This will demonstrate the power of the black spending in this country and help us bring more jobs and business opportunities in the black community.

This is our dream and more.

Not only do we have a dream, but we have:

A plan to register and vote like never before;

A plan to redirect our resources in the interest of our freedom and power;

A plan to spend our money and bank with those who spend their money with us;

A plan not to bank or buy where we cannot get work, promotions, procurement contracts, or management positions.

Yes, we have:

A plan to form and reform the disinherited and dispossessed and discontented of this earth into an effective and meaningful coalition.

A determination not to stop, a determination not to quit, a determination not to relent, a determination not to turn around until the dream comes true.

More than a plan
More than a determination
More than a faith
More than a hope
More than a prayer
More than a memory
More than a dream

We have a God who fights on the side of the dispossessed, despised, and disinherited. We have a God who doesn't like evil, hatred, war, and injustice. We have a God who commissioned Moses to liberate Israel, who spoke through the prophets that they should cry for justice and peace, who visited this earth in Jesus Christ, who spread His fruits through the church, who called and consecrated Martin Luther King—a God who has directed and inspired every stride toward freedom, every step toward justice. We have a God who can turn Red Seas into freedom highways. We have a God who will not allow the Herods, the Pharaohs, and the Hitlers to rule forever. We have a God who will not let wrong prevail and injustice reign or trouble last always. There is a God who will march with us—a God who brings down the walls of interposition and nullification. A God who rules above with a hand of power and a heart of love, and if we are right, He'll fight our battle and we shall have peace someday. We shall have jobs some-day. We shall have equality someday. We shall overcome this day:

So lift every head and shout
Lift every heart and hope
Lift every hand and vote
Lift every foot and march
Lift every voice and sing

Let us dream—but also let us work on, let us plan, let us march on:

March on March on
March on 'til victory is won!
Yes, there is a balm in Gilead. There is a moral force in America.

* * *

At the conclusion of the day's events, the tens of thousands of marchers boarded their buses, their trains, planes, and cars and headed back to the cities, towns, villages, and rural communities from which they had come. As I headed back to my hotel, I once again began to reflect. Yes, we had problems. Yes, it is true that unfettered freedom had not yet dawned. There were still high hurdles that had to be leaped and barriers to be overcome. But who among us, just 20 short years ago, could have envisioned the changes that had taken place? Who among us could have foreseen rights that we now took for granted?

I was mindful that many had given their lives. Some slept in unmarked graves in the rivers, the swamps, and the bayous of the South. Some, like Martin King and Fannie Lou Hamer, had been martyred. Others, like Whitney Young, had met death by accident, and still others, like Roy Wilkins, had slipped away in quiet sleep. These, all having "received a good report," now were relying on us, the living, to carry on their unfinished work.

The anniversary march was good for me, and for all the others who dipped their fingers in the fountains of renewed hope, trusting that, in the final analysis, the dream of the dreamer would become a reality in our troubled land.

October 1987 was a milestone in the Association's history. It marked the 30th anniversary of the integration of Central High School in Little Rock, Arkansas. For some time now, we had held national board meetings in locations that were not large enough to accommodate a national convention. When I came to the Association, the board met every quarter. It was later changed to three meetings annually. The January meeting, later changed to February, was always held in New York City. The NAACP is a New York state–based membership corporation. Therefore, the annual meetings are held in New York pursuant to statute. It was my desire to have at least the April or fall meetings of the board at a location of historical significance to the NAACP. The chairman of the board, a number of key board members, and I decided to hold the October 1987 meeting in Little Rock.

On September 23, 1957, nine young black students enrolled in Central High School in Little Rock. The effort was coordinated by Daisy Bates, who was the president of the Little Rock branch of the NAACP. Central High School was the premier high school in Little Rock. It was all white, built for whites by the white power structure. The school building was an imposing stone gothic structure, sitting on a hill. It resembled a college more than a regular southern city's high school.

Within hours after they enrolled, the black children were driven away by a mob of angry whites. The mob was motivated by then-Arkansas Governor Orval Faubus, who went on television to announce that he would oppose the integration efforts by using the state police. The speech catapulted the segregationists into action. There are many who believe that if the governor had not stirred the cinders of racism, the school would have been peacefully integrated.

Governor Faubus ordered the Arkansas National Guard out on September 25, 1957, to prevent Central High from being integrated. Two days after the mob action and the failure of the governor to comply with the U.S. Supreme Court's *Brown v. Board of Education* decision, President Eisenhower ordered the U.S. Army's 101st Airborne Division into Little Rock. Checkmating the governor, he federalized the Arkansas National Guard. There were 1,100 paratroopers standing guard when the nine young black children, led by Daisy Bates, returned to school.

President Eisenhower was a West Pointer. He had spent most of his adult life obeying orders from his constitutional superiors. He had led the nation to victory in Europe. Commenting later on the Little Rock crisis, he said, "I had no alternative but to enforce the rule of law. We cannot pick and choose the laws we want to obey. The absence of law and order is anarchy." Some modern historical revisionists point to comments like these to downplay the role played by President Eisenhower. He deserves credit for being the first president since Reconstruction to order American troops into a violent situation in the South—to protect the rights of black citizens against white mob violence. It is, therefore, only just and fair that we give him credit for the decisive action he took during the Little Rock crisis.

It was, for those of us who were on the front lines, a refreshing experience to see U.S. troops with fixed bayonets standing tall, protecting the Little Rock Nine. This action sent a chilling message to other segregationists who were contemplating similar opposition to integration orders in the South. It would not be tolerated. Now, 30 years later, the NAACP was returning to Little Rock, a changed city, to hold its national board meeting.

We invited the Little Rock Nine to return to the city. We wanted to honor them, and to commemorate their courageous actions of 30 years ago. The group had not been together since they graduated. With the exception of one, they had all moved away. I was elated to learn that they had all made arrangements to join us for this historic celebration. This was to be a special treat for the NAACP and the city of Little Rock.

I will always remember that Friday morning, with TV cameras rolling and a crowd of reporters standing in front of the doors, as, one-by-one, they assembled at the base of the stairs of Central High School. They hugged each other. There were squeals of excitement from seeing one another for the first time in decades. As the first drops of a light rain fell early Friday, the nine black adults, some now graying, slowly mounted the steps of Little Rock Central High School.

Thirty years ago on those steps, the nine were young black students forced to endure threats and curses as they walked into the school. This time, when they reached the top of the stairs, they got a different reception. Central High cheerleaders and other students, black and white, broke into applause. With a herd of photographers and reporters following, the Little Rock Nine signed autographs and visited old, familiar classrooms. They talked with students and teachers. At a moving reception in the school library, I said, "We don't come to open old wounds, but rather to celebrate and commemorate the great moment in history that changed the course of this nation and changed it for the better."

Lottie Shackelford, Little Rock's second black mayor, tearfully welcomed the former students and Mrs. Daisy Bates, the black newspaper publisher who counseled the nine during the crisis. "Today we start another 30 years of Little Rock moving forward. Little Rock Nine, for all that we have become, for all of what we dare to be, we owe it to all of you."

Then the governor, Bill Clinton, said that the crisis in 1957 "cut our state in two and threatened our very soul and spirit. Now the shining success of public education in these halls has brought the state and the school a new reputation." Governor Clinton hosted a reception for the NAACP and the Little Rock Nine at the Governor's Mansion on Thursday night, October 23. He went out of his way to make the NAACP and its guests feel welcome. We could not have asked for better hospitality.

I do not lay claim to any prophetic claims, but that night, in introducing Governor Clinton, I jokingly said that he was a probable future occupant of the White House. Little did I know then, and few would have believed, that those comments made in jest would be fulfilled on January 20, 1993.

On Friday night we held a banquet at the Statehouse Convention Center. More than 1,500 people from all walks of life joined us in saluting the Little Rock Nine and Daisy Bates, who, although ill, attended the event. A 30-minute documentary was presented. Ernest Green, Melba Patillo, Terrence Roberts, Herbert Wright, Carlotta Walls, Thelma Mothershed, Minnijean Brown, Elizabeth Eckford, Gloria Ray—all of the Little Rock

Nine reunited for the first time, and their advisor, Daisy Bates, watched with well-deserved pride. Ernest Green was now serving as a valued member of the NAACP board.

We ended our national board meeting with a challenge to President Reagan. The President had been reluctant to impose punitive sanctions against South Africa. I announced that the board had adopted the recommendations of its task force on South Africa, which called for a grassroots lobbying effort to raise the nation's awareness of the evils of apartheid. The NAACP's efforts were focused in the 135 congressional districts where there were significant numbers of blacks. We also approved a measure that was designed to persuade shareholders of multinational corporations to divest in South Africa until it changed its apartheid practices. I pointed out that although Little Rock, Arkansas, had not overcome all of its racial problems, we were encouraged by the progress that was being made and would press to eliminate every vestige of racial discrimination.

The Little Rock visit underscored the importance of having an organization or an institution that is in the fight for the long haul. Without a local organization in Little Rock augmented by a national organization with clout and staying power, Little Rock could have never made the progress that it made in just three short decades.

NAACP Wrap-Up

The NAACP is without question the nation's premier civil rights organization. Let me take this moment to congratulate Kweisi Mfume on his leadership. As CEO of the NAACP, I know of his struggle to continue the leadership position of the NAACP. Let me also congratulate Julian Bond for his outstanding work as chairman of the board of the NAACP. These two dedicated and courageous young men are moving forward in a marvelous way to continue to tackle the unfinished business of America, and to create a nation where every citizen can be free. I also congratulate Roslyn Brock, a young lady who started as a youth Board member, became an employee, and is now vice chair of the Board. She continues to be extraordinarily effective. As I look back at my work in the NAACP, I am happy about some of the things I was able to accomplish and saddened that other things never came to fruition.

Litigation
First, litigation has always been one of the most powerful tools of the NAACP. The work of legendary lawyers such as Charles Houston, Thurgood Marshall, Robert Carter, Constance Baker Motley, George

E.C. Hayes, James Nabrit, Spotswood Robinson, Oliver Hill, Richard Marsh, A.T. Walden, Z. Alexander Looby, Ernest Morial, Elaine Jones, Julius Chambers, and Herbert Henderson should never be forgotten. Jack Greenberg was the handpicked successor of Thurgood Marshall and he did an outstanding job as the director counsel of the Legal Defense Fund. Someday I hope the story of his accomplishments can be pulled together for future generations to see.

I am grateful for the work of Nathaniel Jones, who became general counsel of the NAACP and who served in my administration as general counsel. Nate had a finely-tuned office, a number of outstanding lawyers who worked with him, and I'm only sorry that I do not have the time or space to name those people who helped Nate to achieve such a marvelous record. In 1979 Nate went on to become a federal judge on the appellate bench in Cincinnati, Ohio, and he did a great job. During my tenure, Nate continued to handle and wind up many outstanding cases involving school desegregation and employment law, and gave advice and counsel on all types of legal matters to our far-flung network of branches.

The *Bracey* case was a case where a young black military man was accused of treason and releasing military secrets to Russia. I'm convinced that but for the intervention of the NAACP, Bracey would be in jail today.

The *Lenell Geter* case (see chapter 18) was a case again where our representation of Lenell made the difference between a man spending his life in jail and being free.

Legal Department

The Legal Department, in collaboration with the education department, pulled together a whole series of actions relating to the issue of school desegregation.

Nate Jones was succeeded by Tom Atkins and Grover Hankins. Later, Herbert Henderson of West Virginia (a National Board member) filled in and did extraordinarily well. Dennis Hayes now serves as distinguished legal counsel and is doing a fine job.

The department created a legal institute and the Clarence Mitchell Award. The legal institute was designed to give training and help to lawyers in the civil rights area and to publicly compliment them for their efforts. The President's Award, named in honor of Kelly Alexander, Sr., gives recognition to the best state conference president of the year. I could not close this without giving a word of absolute thanks to John Johnson, who I brought on staff. He had been Louisville branch president, Ken-

tucky State Conference president, and National Board member. He functioned as my administrative assistant and later my program director, and
is still carrying a remarkable load at the NAACP. John Johnson was raised
in the work of the NAACP. He was active as a young man in local branch
work. He was president of his local branch in Louisville, Kentucky, president of the Kentucky State Conference, Regional Chair of Region 3
(midwest states) and then as a member of the National Board of the
NAACP. He resigned his board positions and came on staff in 1984. He
was invaluable as Labor and Veterans Affairs Director, my administrative
assistant, and, finally, as program director. He labored mightily and still
carries on very well at the NAACP.

Lobbying Activities and Legislation

Clarence Mitchell was a brilliant Washington bureau director of NAACP
for more than 30 years. From that position, he so influenced Congress
that he was affectionately referred to as the 101st senator. Mr. Mitchell
retired shortly after I assumed the executive directorship of NAACP and
died a short time later. His successor was Althea Simmons, and she did a
remarkable job as well.

During my years, many of the great victories we won in the courts
and in Congress were being knocked down by the Supreme Court. It
was my lot both as head of the NAACP and as chairman of the Leadership Conference of Civil Rights to lead the fight to restore what we were
losing. We secured 27 major legislative victories, including passage of
civil rights laws, Americans with Disabilities Act, Martin Luther King,
Jr. Holiday bill, repassing the Voting Rights Act (there had been a sunset
provision in the original bill), passage of sanctions against South Africa
and the override of Reagan's veto, and our last major legislative victory,
the Civil Rights Act of 1991.

There are many who feel that the sanctions bill and the override of the
Reagan veto was the straw that finally broke the camel's back of apartheid
in South Africa. I am particularly proud of the passage of the sanctions bill
against South Africa. President Reagan vetoed this bill. It was primarily the
grassroots lobbying effort of the NAACP and the Leadership Conference
on Civil Rights that caused Congress to override this veto. Many distinguished observers feel that this sanctions bill and the override of the veto
was the decisive action in eliminating apartheid in South Africa.

Judicial Nominee Activities

We also took part in a number of confirmation hearings. We opposed
several nominees, won some, and lost some. We opposed with all of our

strength the nomination of Clarence Thomas to the Supreme Court (see chapter 25). One of my proudest accomplishments was that there was not a single major anti-civil rights bill passed during my 16-year tenure as head of the NAACP.

Research, Conferences, and Publications

For many years, the NAACP had to do most of its own research. We did it very well and during my tenure published a number of outstanding scholarly research papers. We also convened a number of conferences that were instrumental in helping effect the forward movement of civil rights.

For a conference on the black family, we called John Jacob, who had succeeded Vernon Jordan as CEO of the Urban League. John compiled an outstanding record in the 12 years he served in that position. I believed that one of the real problems was the deteriorating structure of the family in the black community. The question was, if we addressed that problem, would we be able to deal with it? We did pull together the conference. The Urban League and the NAACP convened it at historically black Fisk University, and over a three-day period we brought in some of the most outstanding minds and authorities to address this question.

I think we made tremendous progress, and I will always be grateful to John Jacob for his support and leadership on this issue as well as on all the issues that confronted black America during the time we served as heads of the NAACP and Urban League.

Demonstrations

The first demonstration I led after becoming head of the NAACP was held in Nashville. The concept of sports participation and leadership seems to have a great effect on the nations of the world. South Africa was proud and jealous of its reputation as a great sports nation. Upon my arrival at the NAACP, I found out that the Davis Cup matches were to be held at Vanderbilt University in Nashville and that the nation of South Africa had a strong presence in that competitive event.

The decision was made by the leadership of NAACP in 1977 to boycott that event, and we staged the most massive demonstration of a civil rights community since the heyday of the movement back in the sixties. There were more than 35,000 participants.

We were also in the leadership of all of the commemorative marches that dealt with the observance of the 1963 March on Washington. We led in the formation of a large rally and march in Forsythe County, Georgia, where for many years no blacks lived after having been run out in the early 1900s. We led or participated in many other marches.

At the last Washington march I led, the "silent" march, the Park Service estimated 95,000 people. We estimated 150,000.

The culminating march in my tenure was a march in Sacramento, California, protesting the Rodney King verdict. There were more than 20,000 participants.

Youth Programs

We introduced several programs during my tenure at the NAACP. Among them was Vernon Jarrett's ACT-SO. There was also the Back to School, Stay in School Program. This program was designed to deal with the mounting problem of absenteeism and dropouts in our school system. The board of the NAACP charged me with the responsibility of ascertaining what the real figures were. All kinds of figures were being batted about—that perhaps 40 percent of the children who started never finished public school, that on any given day 10 percent of the school population of New York City would be found lingering on the streets. So, we conceived the concept of giving attention, honor, and recognition to those students who attended school regularly.

We were not honoring them because they made all A's or because they were gifted in music or sports, but because they would go to school on a regular basis. We felt that it was important they be in school, and that no matter how deficient the school system, it was better for the student to be in school than to be out. The motto was "don't be a fool, stay in school." This movement swept across the nation. We were proud, and we received great support from the Readers' Digest Foundation, the Ford Foundation, and other philanthropic groups. David Stern, commissioner of the National Basketball Association, really picked up this program and helped us to achieve great success. This program is still being carried on.

We were able to do a great deal of work in our youth programs, and I'm proud of the many young people I brought into the association as workers or worked with as they served as members of our board of directors. Names that come to me easily are R.L. White, John Davis, Reverend Nelson, Randy Brock, and Roslyn Brock. The youth department of the NAACP continues to be the largest youth movement in the black community outside of the organized church. All hail to our present staff for keeping this moving.

The ACT-SO program has expanded from less than 50 to more than 2,000 national participants in the ACT-SO activities at our national convention and with ACT-SO activities in more than 300 cities.

Prisoners' Assistance

Mr. Wilkins started a program to place NAACP branches into prisons. We revitalized that program, and when I left the association, some 45 active NAACP prison branches were in operation. It is now being greatly revitalized. Leroy Mobley was a very fine director of this program.

Health Issues

At a board staff retreat, we decided to use our tremendous clout in other areas that may not be thought of as traditional civil rights activities. One of the things that evolved was the health bureau, headed by Roslyn Brock, under the able direction of Mildred Roxborough. We tackled issues of AIDS, lead poisoning, sickle cell anemia, and prostate cancer in black men. She did an outstanding job, and the program continues today. Ms. Brock now serves as vice-chair of the NAACP national board and is doing a tremendous job there.

Her husband, Randy, who unfortunately died at a very young age, was hired by us to work in our economic development programs. He dealt with an incubator project in the city of Hartford, Connecticut. This project was caught up in the economic downturn and had to be discontinued. Its focus was establishing an incubator, or a place for black businesses to move forward, in the city of Hartford as a pilot project for other cities. Randy was an especially gifted young man who brought much to the NAACP.

Corporate Giving

The NAACP had never conducted a financial campaign among corporate America. The board decided that it was fair and just that we should reach out to the corporate community for help. The NAACP receives very little from the governmental community, and I congratulate that stance. But we did decide to push the corporate community. It was my privilege to initiate the first nationwide corporate giving program.

Over a period of two weeks under the leadership of William Ellinghaus, president of AT&T, and Charles Luce, president of Consolidated Edison of New York, we met, over breakfast or lunch, 80 percent of the major business leaders of America who were headquartered in the New York City area. The purpose was to introduce them to the programs and policies of the NAACP and to make an appeal for financial aid. During that first financial campaign, we raised over $3 million dollars. Since that time the campaign has been kept alive. We employed a very gifted fund-raiser, Gill Jonas, as our outside consultant. He did a great job. Mildred Bond Roxborough was our in-house leader in this effort.

Since that time, the NAACP has conducted a yearly corporate campaign, and some outstanding people have led it, such as United Airlines chair Steve Wolf; chair of General Motors, Roger Smith; chairman of Metromedia, John Kluge; chairman of Federal Express, Fred Smith; and many others.

Over these years we have raised through that corporate campaign more than $100 million. Under the leadership of Julian Bond and Kweisi Mfume, it continues today. The foundation's support was in effect when I came to the NAACP. Franklin Thomas, who became head of the Ford Foundation, was interested and concerned about NAACP programs, and supported us greatly while he headed that foundation. One of his chief assistants was was Lynn Huntly and I shall always be grateful for her help. Bernard Charles and Jim Gibson were very helpful at the Carnegie and Rockefeller foundations.

When I came to the NAACP, it had never owned a corporate headquarters. The board had made a decision prior to my coming to the NAACP that they would move out of New York City. I was not aware of this at the time. There were many reasons advanced for this. Suffice it to say that it had to be done. Their first choice was Washington, D.C. There was no boundary placed on where we could move, and it was not specified whether we should buy or rent. Due to the efforts of Enolia McMillan, a great activist leader of the civil rights movement in Baltimore and national president of the NAACP (who when I came was about 75 or 80 years of age, but still full of fire), we settled on Baltimore.

Mrs. McMillan conceived a simple plan to sell NAACP pins/buttons to raise funds for the headquarters. This plan raised over $250,000, and she personally raised $75,000. I still feel proud and humble that we were successful under my leadership in purchasing, equipping, and owning, free of debt, a $6 million headquarters site located on a beautiful 5-acre plot of land.

The Honorable C. Delores Tucker pulled together a beautiful and meaningful dedication ceremony for our opening. We are proud of the Moon Library, the Frances D. Hooks Dining Hall, the Roy Wilkins Auditorium, the Clarence Mitchell Walkway, the W.E.B. DuBois Drive, and the Kelly Miller Alexander cul-de-sac.

Pat Kluge led a very successful fund-raising event at the Waldorf-Astoria.

Those assisting included Mr. and Mrs. John W. Kluge; chairs, Bernard B. Jacobs; Gerald Schoenfeld; Percy E. Sutton; and John F. (Jack) Welch, CEO of General Electric, as general co-chair. The ballroom was beautifully decorated and filled to capacity. This star-studded event raised over $1 million. Mildred Roxborough was our staff supervisor. President Bush was our principal speaker, although he had to speak by remote because his plane could not land in New York City. Dr. Julius Hope was hired as Director of Religious Affairs during my tenure. He also served as Director of Region 3. In both of these positions he did remarkably well. He was then, and still is, a ball of fire.

It was my privilege to lead the NAACP into purchasing its first and only corporate headquarters in Baltimore. It was a tremendously exciting and challenging time. The repairs to the building and relocation of the staff and furnishings exceeded $6 million. When I left, it was fully paid for.

NAACP Finances

Shortly before I left the NAACP, we were moving into a shortfall position. I advised the chairman of the board, Dr. Gibson, of that fact and suggested we should start retrenchment. He suggested that we should not move now, but wait a few months. Six months later we did start a short-range intensive fund-raising effort to retire all debt and produce a surplus for my successor. We succeeded beyond our wildest dreams and the board, staff, and far-flung volunteer army of the NAACP ought to be congratulated for the way we bit this bullet. We did not want to leave a Mother Hubbard's bare cupboard for our successor.

When we left May 1, 1992, all of our bills were paid to date and we left over $2 million in the treasury, with $1 million being earmarked for the specific use of the CEO, at his discretion. Unfortunately, when the new administration came in, they spent money freely and fast and collected slowly, if at all. The net result was that in just a few months, a budget surplus had been turned into a deficit—a real, huge, and overpowering deficit that threatened the very existence of the association. Fortunately for us, under the great and inspired leadership of Myrlie Evers, who became chairman of the board, and, later on, Kweisi Mfume, who became president and CEO, the debt was retired and a surplus was established.

Under the leadership of Kweisi Mfume and Julian Bond, who succeeded Myrlie, the NAACP now stands in perhaps its strongest-ever financial position. The Ford Foundation, in particular, reviewed our books and records, congratulated our financial stewardship and integrity, and made a marvelous gift of over $500,000 that we might have a treasury that could help the new director move forward. The fact that the NAACP went into financial panic so soon after I left obviously caused some to wonder why. I can only state that the audited record shows without a doubt the surplus that I have referred to, which speaks for itself. In any organization, if you slow down raising money and speed up spending money, you will soon be in trouble. This is one of the reasons I thank God that the NAACP has had an annual audit performed for more than 50 years. The audit of 1992 speaks for itself and leaves my financial stewardship and financial integrity at the highest level.

One of the interesting things about my stewardship was that when we were building and we were speaking at all of these meetings, I would ask the NAACP branch leadership whether I could raise a public offering for the building fund. It became a sort of a joke because they knew this was going to happen. They always agreed to it. During the period of our building program, I raised and brought back to the national office more than $1 million from these public offerings.

Membership

We put the NAACP membership at its highest number in history. Janice Washington and Izetta Spikes worked hard and were successful in Life Membership and other solicitations. Emmett Burns had also been a fine Life Membership chairperson. He succeeded Ed Muse. *The Crisis* magazine was also left in good shape, and our circulation by post office records reached a high of 423,000 mailings a month. And we were proud not only of that large circulation but of that tremendous clout. Ken Wilson, a former editor of *Dawn* magazine, was tremendously effective in helping to get *The Crisis* magazine strengthened financially. Hats off to Ken! *The Crisis* magazine will forever be in his debt. And, of course, thanks to Jerry Guess and Fred Buford and Harriet Dimes.

We had another unusually gifted person, J. Howard Henderson, who worked very hard with us in administration. Howard came on staff as director of programs about the third year of my tenure. I assigned him so many things to do that he soon became chief of staff, responsible for most of the day-to-day work of the association, personnel relations, office management, travel conferences, and operations. He saw to it that the building was clean and personnel records straight, spent money correctly, bought equipment in a timely manner, operated the convention precisely, and took care of all of the details for conventions and meetings. Howard, Ana Aponte, Barbara Brown, and other members of his staff did a great job.

When I think of outstanding volunteers, I think of Dr. John Arradondo, a medical doctor, who in these past 25 years has spent as much time and energy as anybody I know working with the association. Hazel Dukes has exhibited a loyalty and friendship, her love for the NAACP, and a devotion to me that are beyond compare.

Fred Rasheed, as before mentioned, was a superb leader of our Fair Share Department. Early in my tenure, I also worked with a brilliant young staffer, Michael Myers, who is still very much involved in the civil rights effort. Denton Watson, Paul Brock, and Jimmy Williams served us well as public relations directors, along with my old friend Chester Higgins, whom I was able to bring from *Jet* magazine with me to the FCC and to the NAACP. William "Bill" Pollard, after our move to Baltimore, resigned from the National Board and became deputy executive director. He was extremely helpful and indeed was a dedicated NAACPer.

Our national television show, *Go Tell It,* put us on the national TV map. We shall forever be grateful to the *Washington Post* television station for sponsoring this great show.

I cannot name them all, but I want to recognize Regional Directors Ina Boone, Julius Williams, Virna Canson, Richard Dockery, Paula Brown, Nelson Rivers, Ruby Hurley, Carolyn Coleman, Earl Shinhoster, Emmett Burns, Caesar A.W. Clark, Jr., and Shannon Reeves, along with my personal helpers Doris Coles, Bessie Canty, Vilma Jenkins, Karen Winn, and Murial Outlaw, and my friend and driver Frances Baker, along with Philip White. We will always be indebted to Earl Shinhoster, who took over as interim director when the association was at its lowest ebb. We are thankful for all he did with the help of Myrlie Evers.

In my administration, the NAACP reached unprecedented heights. Obviously, I inherited a good, strong, vibrant staff and a good name in the NAACP, respected by decent people everywhere, though violently disliked by those with a vicious right-wing mentality. To try to fill the shoes of a Roy Wilkins, Walter White, or James Weldon Johnson was awe-inspiring. To be in the leadership of an organization that represented overwhelmingly the ideas, hopes and aspirations of African Americans was both an honor and a challenge.

On a personal note, I shall always be grateful for having received the Spingarn Award, the highest honor any black in America can receive.

The NAACP went through some difficult times immediately after I left. Later, Mrs. Myrlie Evers was elected chair. Earl Shinhoster, who served as regional director of Region 5 during my tenure, was selected as interim executive director. Francisco Borges became treasurer. These three people,

with the help of the board and the staff, worked wonders in rehabilitat-
ing the work of the NAACP. Kweisi Mfume came on board and has
done a tremendous job in the completion of the task of clearing the
debt. Julian Bond is an outstanding chairman. They are to be congratulated for the work they are doing. Hazel Dukes, former president; Bishop
William Graves, former board vice chair; Rubert Richardson, former
board president; and Roslyn Brock, present vice chair, work well in moving the objectives of the NAACP into the front line of the American
scene. Unfortunately, after Earl left the directorship, he was killed in an
automobile accident.

Sail on, Ole NAACP, sail on, humanity with all its hopes and fears, to
paraphrase . . . is waiting to see you lead us on.

Chapter 20
WOMEN IN THE NAACP (WIN)

One night, Frances and I began to discuss ways of expanding the role and the opportunities for women in the NAACP. The Association historically depended heavily on women for leadership and as volunteers. Women were then, and remain today, the backbone of the national organization.

From its founding, the NAACP was a place where women were free to hold leadership positions. In fact, Mary White Ovington was the first executive secretary of the NAACP. The executive secretary at that time was, as is the case today, the chief executive officer of the organization. When I was appointed, the NAACP board chairman was a woman. Some of the key positions on the staff were held by women. Many, if not most, of our state conference presidents were women, and over half of our branches were headed by women. As is the case with most volunteer-based organizations, most of the workers in the NAACP were women.

Despite the fact that women were thoroughly interspersed throughout the NAACP, I got the feeling from my travels and my experience as a pastor of two churches in two different urban cities that, notwithstanding our already having women in key positions, they were still underutilized. The Urban League, our sister organization, had a very effective women's group called the Urban League Guild. This group was headed for a long time by Molly Moon, a pioneer in the league and the wife of legendary Henry Moon, editor of *The Crisis* and long-time public relations director for the NAACP.

Most national black, male, fraternal, and Masonic organizations had women's affiliates or ladies' auxiliaries. Every black, religious, and missionary society was made up almost entirely of women. Most of our churches relied heavily upon the women to raise money and to supply the pools of volunteers needed to carry out our programs. There is an expression, "If you take women out of the churches, most would have to close their doors."

The National Council of Negro Women, organized by Dr. Mary McLeod Bethune, was an excellent example of the effectiveness of organized women in action. The National Beauticians League did a marvelous job reaching out to those in the community who were in need. The Phyllis Wheatly Society and the Dunbar Society were famous for organizing culturally enriching events for the community.

In a number of cities, the NAACP organized groups of women called women's auxiliaries. Our Pittsburgh, Chicago, and Buffalo branches had very active auxiliaries. The auxiliaries worked in tandem with the branch in raising money to implement programs, register voters, work with NAACP youth groups, work with young women to prevent teenage pregnancy, and a variety of other needed and worthwhile programs.

Nationally, there were very few auxiliaries. When I first came on board, I was told that many of our branch leaders had difficulties with their units over the years. Some auxiliaries had separate bank accounts, and the branch president had no authority over how the funds were spent, even though technically he or she was responsible for all money raised in the community in the name of the NAACP. In other instances, the leadership of the women's auxiliaries made public statements on matters of policy. This created the problem of having more than one spokesperson speaking for the organization, sometimes with different voices. Sometimes there was just the normal clash of personalities and natural leadership jealousy. As a result, most branches disbanded their women's auxiliaries earlier. The rivalry was simply too much.

Frances and I went back and forth discussing the pros and cons of starting a separate women's group. Frances was my closest advisor. She was my chief critic and my chief supporter. I knew that I could count on her to be completely honest with me. If she did not think that an idea had validity, Frances was not reluctant to let me know. I did not have to ask her for her opinion. It came readily and boldly.

Before we could decide how or if we would move forward, there were some important questions that had to be answered. How would our branch leadership respond to having a separate NAACP group operating in their communities? What would the group be called? How would it be organized? Would the group have a structure similar to our existing branch structure? What was to be the mission of the newly formed organization? How can we avoid problems of separate treasuries? These were all questions that needed answers. There was another important question that needed answering: If we attempted to launch this as a national program, who would coordinate it?

The more we talked about the concept, the more plausible the idea became. Frances suggested that the new group should be called WIN, an acronym for Women in the NAACP. We agreed that the only way the idea would work was to have all funds raised turned over to the branch. There would be no separate accounts. The WIN leader (we had not yet decided if it would be a chair or a president) would have to approve the expenditures from funds raised by WIN.

Now, all we needed to get started was a director, someone to shepherd the project. I looked at Frances, and she looked at me. After two people have been together for a long time, they can often anticipate what the other person is thinking without a word being spoken. I was reluctant to ask Frances to take on another burden. She was already helping me as a personal advisor/assistant and as my appointment secretary. We were at the office from early in the morning until early the next morning. Frances had very little time for herself. On weekends, we usually went to either Detroit or Memphis for church.

I knew that we did not have the money to add new personnel. Additionally, if we had to recruit from the outside, we would have to do a lot of on-the-job training. This is not the way one wants to get a new program started. Very carefully, maybe even sheepishly, I asked Frances if she would volunteer to head up the WIN effort. I assured her that as soon as the program was launched and structured, we would hire someone full-time to direct the effort. Frances reminded me that she was already overloaded, but she agreed to handle WIN during its embryonic phase. Little did we know then that Frances would head the organization until after my retirement.

Having agreed on the initial leadership and some organizational matters, we moved ahead with the project. Frances bounced the idea off a number of activists she knew and worked with on one venture or another. She was as busy as a bee and really excited by the prospect of involving women who would otherwise merely give their money and their volunteer time to other groups they felt were addressing problems of interest to them.

One of the staff persons who took a particular interest in the new program was Earlene Bollin. Earlene, a longtime employee of the NAACP, joined Frances in crafting and organizing WIN. One would have to know Earlene to appreciate what an unusual person she was. Born in the South, Earlene moved north like so many blacks looking for more opportunity in the late '30s. When the war erupted, Earlene joined the U.S. Army as a WAC, serving with distinction. Shortly after being honorably discharged from the military, Earlene became a member of the NAACP staff. She began as a clerk, as did most of the clerical staff of that era, and worked her way up to become secretary to the executive director. She was Roy Wilkins's secretary, and for a while she served as my secretary. Later I promised her the directorship of the department of personnel. She was serving in this position when she began helping Frances with the WIN program.

Earlene had a magnetic personality that drew people to her. She was a tall, stately woman who carried herself with the regal dignity of an African queen. Very articulate and soft-spoken, Earlene was also a bundle of energy and a lot of fun. During my entire tenure, she was the life of every staff social function—always singing, reciting poetry, or playing one musical instrument or the other. Having been at the NAACP for more than 40 years by then, she worked for Walter White and knew W.E.B. DuBois, Thurgood Marshall, Robert Carter, and a host of other civil rights legends. There was very little about the organization that Earlene did not know. Frances and Earlene were joined in the work by Vilma Jenkins, also a longtime employee and former secretary to Mr. Wilkins, who knew the organization from top to bottom.

Before I knew it, Frances and her cadre of workers had come up with an official logo and stationery. They were holding meetings with large numbers of women. Some of the women from our office whom I had never seen active in any outside NAACP activity became immersed in the WIN program. Soon Frances was getting calls from people all over the country who were interested in the new program. Before I could get my breath, they had organized state and regional WIN groups. Frances hit the road, going to state meetings and annual conferences. There was something almost magical about the way WIN took off. I had expected to get some negative feedback from branch leaders and possibly some state conference presidents. None was forthcoming. There seemed to be universal acceptance of WIN. For the NAACP, a group made up of strong-willed people, this was nothing short of a miracle.

WIN undertook emergency relief as one of its major projects. Frances and her WIN organizers felt that this was an area that needed to be strengthened. We were excellent in dealing with pure civil rights matters organizationally. However, we were not strong dealing with natural disasters or man-made catastrophes. Hurricanes, floods, tornadoes, and urban riots occurred on a relatively frequent basis. Our units were not equipped to deal with these unfortunate developments.

We were in business to deal with securing civil rights, not to provide aid for disaster victims. Yet, there were times when it was absolutely necessary for the NAACP to reach out to help our people who were in need of direct assistance. People whose homes had been destroyed in South Carolina by hurricane Hugo or in Florida by hurricane Andrew needed help, such as clothing, food, and the basic necessities of life. We were not interested in taking the place of the Red Cross. We merely wanted to have the capacity to reach out and be one among many entities providing help to those who were at the greatest point of need. The public that we served expected no less from us. We knew and later were specifically able to point out racial segregation and discrimination even in passing out disaster relief. So many times after the flood, after the storm, after the tornado, black babies were the last to be fed, black children were the last to be clothed, black families were the last to be aided, and black communities were the last to be rehabilitated. So unfortunately, there were severe civil rights problems even in the distribution of relief supplies.

WIN became the NAACP's emergency relief arm. It was WIN that led the NAACP outreach to the Haitian refugees who were sent by our government to Guantanamo Base in Cuba in 1991. Thousands of Haitians were rescued or interdicted by the U.S. Coast Guard as they sought asylum in the U.S. Unlike Cubans seeking to escape oppression, the Haitians were denied entry to America. Instead, they were housed in camps on the U.S. military base on the island of Cuba. Thousands of tons of relief supplies were taken to Guantanamo. Frances and I had the privilege of heading a delegation that delivered the supplies. It was a humbling experience to see how grateful they were for little things: disposable diapers, shaving equipment, shoes, towels, soap, clothes, and food.

When riots broke out in Los Angeles in 1992 after the Rodney King verdicts, WIN was swift to act. Truckloads of food and clothing were sent to Los Angeles. In conjunction with the Los Angeles branch and with First AME Church and Second Baptist Church, WIN provided relief for thousands of Central Los Angeles residents whose homes and workplaces were destroyed by the devastation of the riot. Again, Frances led that relief effort, arriving in an 18-wheeler. It was rewarding to see the expressions on the faces of the children and parents who had nothing as they received help from an organization made up of people who looked like them.

Another role that WIN played was reaching out to young people. Seminars and workshops that addressed the growing problem of teenage pregnancy were held all over the country. Working with parents, educators, church counselors, and others, young girls were encouraged to abstain from having premarital sex. For those already active, or for whom abstinence was not a viable option, birth control was taught. Young boys were urged to postpone fatherhood until they were ready to assume those responsibilities. Those who were already fathers were taught how to become active in their children's lives.

WIN units set up counseling programs for persons who had become addicted to controlled substances. WIN's effort in this area was one of encouraging such persons to get treatment, facilitating their getting into a drug program, and working with the families of the addicts to encourage them to be or to remain supportive of the person in treatment.

In Los Angeles, New York, Detroit, and Baltimore, WIN sponsored tutorial programs that assisted high school students in the areas of science, mathematics, and English. These programs were phenomenally successful. Other WIN units organized volunteers to work in soup kitchens, preschools, nursing homes, and a variety of other outreach programs.

Many of WIN's activities centered around helping our local, state, and regional units raise money for special projects. At the national level, WIN units helped to furnish some offices at the National Office, purchased computers for students, and set up scholarships.

One of the highlights of each annual convention was the WIN Annual Fashion Show. Initiated just a year after WIN was organized, in 1989, the show was put on by Frances, Earlene Bollin, Carol Winn (Frances's assistant), Menola Upshaw (Region IV coordinator), Jonnie McMillian (Region V coordinator), Ophelia Averitt (Region III coordinator), Sylvia Williams (Region VII coordinator), Louise Samuels (Region II coordinator), and Joan Willis (Region I coordinator). Josephine Bridges of Memphis, longtime friend of Frances and a professional organizer of elegant fashion shows, pitched in with all of her strength to make the fair succesful. The beauty of this event was that the models in the show were ordinary people, women from size 2 petite to size 50. Some female models were 4'9" and others were 6'3". The male models were likewise of different sizes, shapes, and heights. Each model wore his or her own fashions. The variety of outfits worn in the fashion show spanned the spectrum. There were ultramodern outfits as well as conservative outfits.

After witnessing a WIN fashion show, it was impossible to see a traditional fashion show with only professional models who were over-rehearsed or over-stage-managed. Watching men and women who got a real kick out of "strutting their stuff" before an adoring crowd of people with whom they shared a common bond was enormously enjoyable and memorable.

WIN served so many purposes. It gave women in the NAACP another avenue for involvement. It enabled them to participate in a program that provided direct service to people in need. For the branches, WIN gave them an additional source of both volunteer service and fundraisers. For the general public, WIN gave the NAACP an emergency relief arm that could reach beyond the previous span of NAACP involvement and make sure that discriminatory practices were abated and supplies distributed equitably. For me, it was having an idea transform from a mere concept into an ongoing reality.

I cannot thank Frances and all of the women who worked with her enough for making WIN work. The program opened new vistas of service for women, who are, by their nature, creative, resourceful, compassionate, and efficient.

Chapter 21
SPORTS CAMPAIGN 1987

The importance of sports in the transformation of society cannot be overestimated. When Jackie Robinson broke into professional baseball with the Brooklyn Dodgers in 1947, his performance, both on the field and off, altered permanently the way many people perceived African Americans. The American and Chinese ping-pong teams, in the early 1970s, helped to lay the groundwork for the thaw between the United States and the People's Republic of China.

While blacks made astonishing progress on the field and on the basketball courts of professional sports, very few managed by 1987 to hold key positions in the executive suites or management levels of the industry. Baseball's Hall of Famer Henry Aaron was serving on the NAACP's National Board of Directors and brought the problem to my attention. Aaron was very vocal and persistent. He was a vice president of the Atlanta Braves organization, but unlike many similarly situated, he was not satisfied to make progress only for himself. To him, being the highest-ranking black in an industry was not a cause for celebration, it was a reason to fight to open the doors for others. He suggested that the NAACP become directly involved in working to eliminate discrimination in the sports arena.

I was in frequent contact with the baseball commissioner, Peter V. Ueberroth, the football commissioner, Pete Rozelle, and the basketball commissioner, David Stern, regarding the lack of blacks in key posts in their respective sports. We had discussed in general terms the need for a meaningful affirmative action program. We had made some progress, but not much, and I continued to focus much attention on the problem.

Social progress is normally ignited by a spark that focuses attention on a situation, making it impossible to be ignored. That spark came in April of 1987. In early April, Al Campanis, vice president of the Los Angeles Dodgers, suggested on ABC's *Nightline* that blacks lack the mental ability to hold thinking positions in professional sports. He suggested that while we were swift afoot, we were slow when it came to gray matter. Naturally, his comments infuriated the black community and thinking communities across the nation.

On April 10, 1987, I issued a stinging rebuke that said in part:

Al Campanis is an anachronism, a throwback to the days when the prevailing mentality in baseball was to bar the door against black players. It is really pathetic that as baseball marks the 40th anniversary of Jackie Robinson's debut into the major leagues, Campanis is spouting off that blacks are not capable of becoming baseball executives. The problem is not that blacks lack the capabilities. The problem is people like Campanis. It was a statement that probably has Branch Rickey twirling in his grave.

At that time, Dr. Anthony Brown was working with me as an executive on loan from the Wisconsin Power & Light Company. Anthony was helping us to establish a closer working relationship with the sports and entertainment communities. He had many excellent contacts with black athletes and entertainers. When the Campanis controversy broke, I put him in charge of helping pull together a meeting. He was also charged with helping me to develop a model fair share program for the sports industry.

On April 14, I issued another statement announcing a national campaign to promote affirmative action in professional sports. That statement follows:

NEW YORK – Dr. Benjamin L. Hooks, Executive Director of the NAACP, announced today that the nation's largest and oldest civil rights organization will mount a national campaign to increase the representation of blacks in managerial, executive, and other non-playing positions with major league professional teams in baseball, football, and basketball.

Dr. Hooks said that while improving the status of blacks in baseball will be the first objective, the other two sports, football and basketball, which he said have also failed to deal equitably with blacks once their playing days were over, will also be targeted.

The principal thrust of the NAACP's campaign will come through its local branches located in cities with major league franchises. Representatives of more than 20 of those branches met this morning in New York City to formulate strategies to be used at the local level.

Our local branches will immediately request an early meeting with the owners of the professional teams located in their city, beginning with baseball. The meeting will be to determine the status of black employment in field positions and in the front offices. Much of this information is, of course, already available, but we are concerned with the total range of employment, from the anonymous receptionist who greets visitors to the high-visibility positions as managers and general managers.

We will then enter into negotiations with the ownership to establish an affirmative action program that will actively recruit and train blacks for all the jobs available in organized baseball.

Once an affirmative action program has been agreed upon, we will closely monitor its progress and make periodic reports to the public.

We are prepared to mount massive demonstrations against the recalcitrant baseball clubs. Those who are familiar with the NAACP and its long history of demonstration against segregation, discrimination and racism know that is no idle threat—we will deliver.

We will apply pressure on the owners at every possible point, up to and including litigation.

On May 27, 1987, I gave the nation an update of our progress. In that statement I said, in part, that six weeks after the NAACP announced the opening of a national campaign to increase black representation in non-playing field positions and in the front offices of major league baseball, football, and basketball, contact had been established with 20 baseball clubs, 15 football clubs, and five basketball clubs.

We are very pleased with the progress we have made to date in such a short time, particularly since the problem we are addressing has been around for so many years. As can be easily understood, our concentration to date has been on baseball, since we are in the midst of its season. However, as the numbers grow, we have not neglected the other two major sports, and our tempo in these areas will pick up speed over the next several weeks.

The update on the progress of the NAACP's campaign followed the first meeting of the NAACP's Sports Advisory Committee, which was established to assist and advise the Association in the implementation of its plans to create more career opportunities for blacks in professional sports. The committee included some of the most illustrious and respected names in sports. Among the individuals who agreed to serve were Howard Cosell, noted sportscaster; Monte Irvin, formerly of the New York Giants and later on the staff of the baseball commissioner; Bob Lanier, basketball great with the Detroit Pistons and Milwaukee Bucks; Willie Davis, former standout with the Green Bay Packers and now a successful businessman; Wayne Embry, a star with the Boston Celtics and currently vice president and general manager of the Cleveland Cavaliers; and Larry Doby, first black player in the American League and former manager in the majors.

The meeting, held on May 26, opened up fresh insights into professional sports for us. I stated, "We have asked the committee to advise the NAACP on both the broad and specific goals it should seek in this undertaking, to evaluate and advise us on our plans for reaching our goals, provide appropriate information to us, and monitor our performance."

The NAACP's establishment of a Sports Advisory Council dealing with professional sports was announced at a press conference in New York City on April 15. At that time, I announced that our major thrust would come through the local branches in cities where there is a major league franchise or multiple franchises.

With NAACP representatives from over 20 cities present, I announced that our branches would first request a meeting with the franchise owners and executives to obtain information on the employment makeup of non-playing and front-office personnel. This would be followed by the development, in concert with management, of an affirmative action plan. I stated, "Once an affirmative action program has been agreed upon, we will closely monitor its progress and make periodic reports to the public. Should this fail to occur in any instance, we are prepared to mount massive demonstrations against the recalcitrant baseball clubs."

I reported that none of the teams that had been approached had refused to open up a dialogue. In those few instances in which a club had not been approached, it had generally been because our local branches, given the heavy demands already placed upon them, and limited personnel, had not been able to gear up for this activity or had to confine their activity to one sport. I advised the media that we were developing a plan to have our regional paid staff visit those cities to provide assistance.

We progressed to the point that negotiations had already been started with 27 baseball clubs, two football clubs, and three basketball teams. I was confident we would be entering this phase of operation with the other teams we had contacted very soon. We were very optimistic about the pace of the campaign. I followed our traditional policy of demonstrating good faith by not revealing the names of specific companies or institutions with whom we were engaged in negotiations.

In the week following the New York City press conference, 24 of the NAACP branches held similar press conferences in their own cities to announce the beginning of their campaigns. Among the cities were Baltimore, Buffalo, Chicago, Cincinnati, Detroit, Houston, Indianapolis, Kansas City, Philadelphia, Pittsburgh, Sacramento, San Antonio, San Francisco, Seattle, St. Louis, Salt Lake City, and Tampa.

At the 1987 Annual Convention, held in New York City, we were able to announce at a joint press conference an agreement with both the national baseball and national basketball commissioners to increase minority hiring in front office and management positions. Both David Stern and Peter Ueberroth agreed to use their offices to prod the team owners to comply with the agreements.

On July 9, 1987, I issued the following statement at a joint press conference with Commissioner Ueberroth:

> Baseball Commissioner Peter B. Ueberroth and I met earlier today. We had a good discussion of the need to open employment opportunities in the front office and other key jobs to blacks and other minorities. This meeting was one of a number between the Commissioner and myself and between key members of our staffs.
>
> The Commissioner and I agree that the NAACP's nationwide network of branches and state conferences has a major role in the achievement of our shared goal of expanded employment opportunities. The NAACP's local units have met with owners and top executives of more than 20 baseball franchises. When we return to our national office in Baltimore, we will continue our review of a number of proposed agreements that have been submitted by our branches and individual teams.
>
> The NAACP will continue to work with Commissioner Ueberroth; the firm of Alexander & Hill, which has been retained by major league baseball to develop and evaluate affirmative action plans; and Dr. Harry Edwards, the Commissioner's special assistant, as we pursue our mutual objectives. Let me pause here to

congratulate Clifford Alexander, who worked tirelessly to assist major league baseball in fulfilling this objective.

We of the NAACP will continue our local contacts and negotiations with individual clubs. The NAACP will work cooperatively with the Commissioner to mesh our efforts.

Let me say, Commissioner Ueberroth is to be commended for his initiative effort, and for his leadership in dedicating this baseball season as a memorial to the 40th anniversary of Jackie Robinson's major league debut.

I was honored to have been asked to throw out the first ball at the World Series in Detroit in 1984. When I looked up at the Detroit Tigers' electronic scoreboard that evening, I saw a salute to the NAACP. I said to myself, we have made some progress. We are not where we want to be, but thank God, we have come a long way.

Once again, we were able to use the clout of the NAACP to bring about, in short order, a commitment to bring blacks in doors that had previously been closed to them. Today, while things are not perfect, they are infinitely better than they were before 1987. There are very few teams, if any, that do not have blacks in management positions.

Chapter 22

MEMBERSHIP DRIVES AND RADIOTHON 1988-1989

One of the most difficult and challenging problems I experienced was trying to build the membership base of the Association and make our collective branch structure more visible. When I came to the NAACP, I announced a goal of one million members. I was laboring under two mistaken impressions. First, I accepted the commonly held belief that the NAACP had 400,000 members. Second, I honestly believed that it would not be difficult to dramatically increase our membership rolls.

One day early on, Gloster Current, the former longtime director of branches and probably the most knowledgeable person on the staff, came to me and said, "Ben, we won't be able to get a million members in a year. We only have around 200,000 members. That means that we will have to get 800,000 new members by the end of your first year." I was shocked. I had relied heavily on the figures that I had always seen and heard. It had become an article of faith that the NAACP had somewhere between 400,000 and 500,000 members. I was out on a limb. I knew that the media would constantly badger me about where we stood on our goal. If we could only manage to add 250,000 members to our rolls, the media would insist that we had failed.

It did not matter that there was no other similar organization whose membership came near our 200,000-member figure. We were expected to have the million that was announced. The closest thing to the NAACP in terms of structure, local units, and a membership base was the National Organization for Women. The fact that they had only 100,000 members with a 100 million-plus membership base was seen as unimportant.

The NAACP did not have a national renewal process. Our membership expired every year on the month that it was taken out. We had thousands of memberships expiring each month. Those whose membership expired, unless the local branch reminded them of that fact, would not be aware of it. For years, NAACP memberships for adults began at $2.00, $4.00, and then $6.00. After I became the director, we increased the membership dues to $5.00 and then to $10, including *The Crisis* magazine with membership. The branch did not have the resources, the staff, or the money to generate a renewal letter. Therefore, until computers came along much later, we did not have the ability to reach the vast number of expiring members each year. Ultimately, we reached an all-time high of 500,000 members and mailed out 423,000 magazines.

We initiated a program in which the National Office sent out renewals as they became due. The problem was that it caused confusion for members. It also gave some the excuse, when asked by their local solicitor to renew their membership, to say, "I have already sent my money to the National Office," which was not always the truth. Soon there was a revolt among our volunteer solicitors. Since we did not have enough workers in the field, nor could we afford to hire them, we discontinued the process that had only yielded limited results. In an organization like ours, the will of the volunteers, the people, had to be respected.

For every member who had paid their annual dues, there were four or five people who were walking around with expired membership cards honestly believing they were still bona fide members. I cannot tell you how many hundreds of people I ran into over the years who proudly pulled out their membership card to show me that they were active, paid-up members. Much to their surprise, they discovered their membership had expired. So while there were over a million persons who believed they were active members of the Association, we only counted those who had paid their dues during the past 12 months.

We had a real dilemma. We did not have the resources to deal with the renewal process, and unless we did something dramatic, our membership base would not increase significantly. Meanwhile, we had a public relations problem to deal with, and we needed the money from additional memberships to move the organization forward. All I knew was that we had to do something, and immediately.

I decided that we would implement a number of initiatives in an effort to increase our membership base. In 1978 we organized a special drive called "Operation Sweep." This effort involved concentrating our resources in seven cities, one in each of our geographical regions, for a week, to launch a successful membership campaign. We sent in a team of membership, public relations, and church work specialists, and generalists. Our team worked closely with the branch leadership in reaching out to all segments of the community. While the effort achieved success in each instance, we discovered that it was not cost-effective.

We had another outreach effort in an attempt to reach young, urban, professional blacks who benefited most from the movement. We used direct mail, receptions, and new marketing techniques. Again there was some success, but it was limited. This, too, was not cost-effective. Most young people were right out of college and had student loans to pay off, they were starting their families and had very little disposable income, or they had not yet reached the point in their lives where contributing to causes was a major priority. That lesson is one that all volunteer organizations have now learned. People normally become more active as they become older and more secure in their careers.

We hired membership workers based out of our regional offices. The objective was to have these individuals work with our regional directors in increasing the membership base. The special membership workers were assigned specific branches to work with on a sustained basis. This followed the format that had been used in earlier days of the NAACP, when field directors-at-large went to selected cities, spent time setting up, and then followed through on membership campaigns. The problem with reinstituting this approach was also cost. In the old days, the national campaign worker stayed in the homes of volunteers, was fed by the local branch, and was single. This meant that the national membership worker only cost the National Office a nominal amount of money for travel and a salary.

In the 1980s, the national culture and working expectations had changed. No one wanted to stay in homes and have no choice but to eat home-cooked meals. This meant that we had to pay hotel bills for lodging and for meals. We had to pay competitive salaries for workers who were willing to stay on the road away from home. Many of our membership workers had families. Therefore, we had to share in the expense of frequent trips back home for our national field directors-at-large. The combination of these factors made this approach less attractive than it used to be.

As early as early 1979, I came upon the idea of trying to get our branches to include a minimum membership in the cost of admission to their freedom fund banquets. Most branches had annual fund-raising banquets or luncheons. There were normally hundreds, if not thousands, of supporters of the branches in attendance. Most of those who attended were not dues-paying members. The idea was to add to the ticket the cost of a minimum membership. If we had 1,000 people attending a local banquet, we could add to the local membership roll 1,000 new members. Those who were already members had the option of donating the included membership to a non-member of their family or a friend. If they wanted to extend their membership for the following year, we would accommodate that also.

The resistance to this very simple approach was unexpectedly strong. Either a member of the staff or I would meet with the branch leadership and explain how the program would work. There would, in most instances, be an agreement to try the membership inclusion process. At some point between the initial agreement and the actual event, there was, in most cases, a change of heart. The branch would go on with business with usual. I want to point out that I never tried to have the program mandated by board or convention action. Volunteers must be allowed to make decisions like these voluntarily. When I would talk to the president of the branch and asked what happened, I was usually told that the executive committee or the branch membership had decided that those who wanted to become members should fill out a membership application and pay for their membership separately.

I later discovered that there were other reasons why the program never really took off. Some of our people felt that by including a minimum membership in each ticket, we would be "giving" membership. Some were fearful that the new people might become active in the election process and could jeopardize their reelection efforts. Our units had elections every two years. Every member, regardless of how they became a member or how much they paid for their membership, could vote in branch elections if they had been a member for 30 days.

There were a few cases in which branches adopted the minimum membership program, and at the next election, a number of new members either ran for office or participated in the election, and ousted the incumbents. Accounts of these occurrences had the effect of freezing the initiative in its tracks.

I also had a number of executives on loan who worked directly with me on these and other membership initiatives. Ted Childs, a bright young executive from IBM, did an excellent job of helping us modernize our literature and introduce a number of new marketing approaches. Later, Anthony Brown of Wisconsin Power & Light Company helped me to involve a number of celebrities, sports figures, and entertainers who helped in our membership and life membership campaigns. He later did a marvelous job of helping to set up a national sports program.

Building up our life membership base met with greater success. Most of our regular members had $10 memberships. Life members, on the other hand, paid a minimum of $50 per year. This provided both the local branch and the National Office with the lion's share of the money that we needed to run our programs. The National Office received 60 percent of these payments and the responsible branch received 40 percent. Many of our life members paid off their membership in five installments of $100 each or the entire $500.

By far the most successful life membership effort was the Detroit, Michigan, annual life membership banquet. It had become, over the years, a must-attend event for "anybody who was anybody" in Detroit. It was also a must-attend event for every politician from the governor to the candidate running for dog catcher. I had help from Jim Thrower, former professional athlete with the Detroit Lions football club. Jim was helping me organize Freedom Fund dinners across the country. The Detroit branch, our largest branch, had a membership of over 20,000. Each year they sponsored a Freedom Fund dinner, and the cost of the ticket included the $50 payment on a life membership to the NAACP.

Eventually, this dinner attracted more than 10,000 sit-down participants and brought in gross revenues of more than $1 million. *The Guinness Book of World Records* credited the affair as being the largest sit-down dinner in the world. During my tenure, it was held in Cobo Hall, 10 football fields long. It was necessary to have four head tables so that no one was seated too far away. I dispatched Jim Thrower in an effort to establish this concept across the nation. If we had been successful, this would have greatly satisfied our need for funds. Just think of 50 cities raising from $100,000 to $2 million, and how this would have helped us with fund-raising. Julian Bond, Kweisi Mfume, and Roslyn Brock are to be congratulated as they encourage local fund-raising.

Using the Detroit model, I convinced the Memphis branch to initiate a life membership dinner. By the time of my retirement in 1993, the branch had outgrown the facilities available in the city and had grossed over a half million dollars. Dr. Vasco Smith had long advocated that we adopt this approach. His wife, Maxine Smith, who was the executive secretary of the Memphis branch, worked long and hard to pull off one of the most successful fund-raisers in the Association's history.

As noted earlier, during my first nine years at the Association, we built the membership base to over 500,000, including life members, and we were mailing out over 400,000 copies of *The Crisis* magazine, the official publication of the organization. When we implemented our last minimum membership increase to $10 for adults, we included the magazine. We had over 35,000 churches, fraternities, sororities, Masonic groups, and other organizations that did not receive *The Crisis*. Additionally, we had almost 45,000 youth members, only 5,000 of whom paid the additional fee to receive the magazine.

William Penn, our director of branches and field administration, provided me with documentation, based upon extensive research from official National Office records. His exhaustive study confirmed the fact that during the 1980s, the Association had the highest membership in its history. To me, increasing the NAACP's membership and visibility became an obsession. I never stopped trying to find ways to accomplish this objective. One of the traditional strengths of the NAACP was replication of programs that had worked elsewhere.

In Atlanta we had a creative, seasoned, and hard-driving local executive secretary, Jondell Johnson. Jondell was one of a few paid full-time employees we had at that time. Over the years, she had become a legend in that city. Very little happened in the black community without Jondell's input. She had been a schoolteacher, a principal, a writer for the *Atlanta World* (a black publication owned by the Scott family in Atlanta), a hell-raiser, and a well-respected personality in the Atlanta political and civil rights community.

I have not met many people like Jondell. She was a person who appeared to know everybody, where they were, what they were doing, and how they fit into the mosaic of Atlanta life. She was folksy in both speech and demeanor. Her heavy, low-country South Carolina accent dripped like syrup. If she was at the other end of the phone, you immediately knew that it was Jondell on the line. She was as comfortable with Ted Turner, Major Jackson, Congressman John Lewis, and the governor as she was with the shoeshine man at the airport, children in the street, or the drug addict on the corner.

Jondell had an excellent working relationship with Julian Bond, who was the president of the Atlanta branch at that time. She set up a successful annual Radiothon in Atlanta that was second to none. The Radiothon raised both membership and money for the local branch. More important, the Radiothon had a public relations and public education value that transcended the event, the thousands of members it drew, or the money that was contributed as a result of it.

I had a chance to see the Atlanta effort personally and saw great potential for it as a national effort. I knew that we did not have anyone on staff who had the connections and the complex experience to implement the program on a national basis. How could I get Jondell to come to the National Office? She was both successful and comfortable in Atlanta. All of her friends and family were there. Then, even if I could convince her to come to Baltimore, where we were now headquartered, I did not want to be accused by the branch of raiding their staff and taking away their anchor.

When I finally talked to Jondell about helping us set up a national Radiothon, she was excited. We talked about her taking a leave of absence. However, to do it right, we both agreed that it would require a long-term commitment. After some discussion, the Atlanta branch, which then had a staff of approximately eight people, was well structured and capable of functioning with Jondell's advice from a distance. So Jondell came to Baltimore and we began to plan our first Radiothon. After the general structure and a date were decided, our campaign swung into action. I decided that we would need to bring in our field staff and key volunteers from all seven of our geographical regions for training.

A national Radiothon is both complicated and labor-intensive. The training session was held at our Baltimore headquarters. Jondell decided that it should be set up as a sort of college extension program. It was called "Membership University." Public relations and fund-raising professionals conducted the courses. The sessions began at 8 A.M. and went on until after dinner. The courses provided detailed information regarding the upcoming Radiothon. At the conclusion of the three-day training session, the participants received certificates of completion.

In addition to the Radiothon, Jondell and Ozell Sutton, a long-time supporter of my administration from Atlanta, who was employed by the U.S. Department of Justice, agreed to head a special fund-raising effort to get 1,000 friends and supporters to give at least $1,000 over a period of eight years. During the first year, we succeeded in getting over 100 people to sign up and pay their first installment on the pledge. The program was called the Thousandaire Club. We planned to provide funds for an endowment program for the Association over the long haul. The first year, 1988, we put the mechanism in place for our national effort and worked out the inherent bugs. We managed to get over 200 NAACP units involved in our test effort.

By 1989, the campaign was in full swing. More than 600 branches held a local membership Radiothon on September 24, 1989. Working together to build a stronger civil rights organization, they demonstrated cohesive strength in preparation for the 1990s. Dr. William Gibson, our board chairman, was an enthusiastic supporter of the Radiothon concept. The South Carolina State Conference of Branches, of which he was also state president, had conducted successful Radiothons in the past.

During the Radiothon, branches were supported by youth councils and colleges in their respective areas. Percy Sutton of New York City most effectively served as chairman of this event.

Our more than 20 prison branches were very supportive in the Radiothon effort. Although they worked under restrictions, they were able to report memberships in numbers similar to other units of the Association. Among the prison branches participating in the national effort were the Missouri Training Center for Men, Maryland State Penitentiary, Iowa State Penitentiary, Jefferson City Prison Branch, Leesburg Prison, and Lewisburg Prison.

We received assistance from over 500 radio stations across the nation. Many of these stations agreed to donate free radio time following a request from the National Office and our local branch leadership. Some branches wrote their own local programming and gained the support of local celebrities as well as community leaders who served on their planning committees. Where there was more than one branch in an area covered by the same radio stations, they formed coalitions. They worked together on programming and in securing participants. Our branches used NAACP offices, shopping centers, lodge halls, churches, school buildings, union halls, bank offices, insurance buildings, nightclubs, and other areas for their membership reporting centers and remote broadcasting locations on Radiothon Day.

The local programming supplied community residents with a wealth of historic and current facts about NAACP activity. For many community residents, the Radiothon was the first opportunity they had to have their questions answered about what the NAACP was doing locally and nationally. After the local programming ended, they held social affairs where new members could pay their pledges, take out memberships, and get to know those who were active in the local civil rights community.

The National Radiothon segment originated from ABC Radio Network in New York City and Tom Snyder's television studio (ABC affiliate) in Los Angeles. The second annual three-hour national broadcast reached stations in the NAACP Radio Network by satellite. That segment was aired between 4 P.M. and 7 P.M. Eastern Time and between 1 P.M. and 4 P.M. Pacific Time. Cooperating radio networks included the National Black Network, United Press International, Sheridan Broadcasting Network, and Gannett Broadcasting Company.

The Sheridan Broadcasting Radio Network (a black-owned network) produced the entire program. Chuck Woodson of Sheridan produced a fast-moving, entertaining, and informative program. I served as one of the commentators. Board Chairman Vince Sanders, president of the National Black Network, and veteran broadcaster Hal Jackson served as the anchors.

We had a vast array of celebrities who donated their services to the effort. Our East Coast host was Lawrence Gregory Jones. Hosting in the Los Angeles studio were comedian Sinbad and Frankie Crockett, a well-known radio personality. The program featured interviews, music, appeals for memberships, and testimonies. Celebrity guests included heavyweight fighter Evander Holyfield, James Nabbie, The Ink Spots, Coretta Scott King, singer Cheryl Lynn, talk show host Phil Donahue, Cameo recording group, Manhattan Borough president of New York City David Dinkins, Barry White, Melba Moore, Lisa Lisa, Vesta Williams, Jerry Butler, Keith Butler, Regina Bell, The Clarke Sisters, Lynette Hawkins, Bee Bee and Cee Cee Winans, Peabo Bryson, Mica Paris, Isaac Hayes, Stacey Lattisaw, Terry Tate, Heavy D, Sybil, Omar Hawkins, Blue Magic, Kashif, SOS Band, Michael Cooper, Hank Aaron, Roberta Flack, and many others.

The work of the NAACP was highlighted by the New York state conference president and NAACP vice president, Hazel Dukes, and Frances Hooks, national chair of Women in the NAACP (WIN). I do not believe any other group or organization had the clout and reverence that the NAACP brought to bear to assemble the variety of groups and individuals we assembled that day. This helped to give us the opportunity, for the first time in modern history, to tell our story to a vast audience of Americans.

Our command center was at the National Headquarters in Baltimore. Scores of volunteers staffed the 800 telephone lines. Listeners of the national segment called in and made memberships and pledges. Our staff and volunteers reported receiving more than 5,000 calls during the Radiothon alone. We received hundreds of others days after the Radiothon was over. Many people called seeking information regarding how they could get in touch with their local branch, or to find out what the Association was doing about one situation or another.

An integral component of the success of the program was celebrity public service announcements (PSAs). PSAs were taped for radio and television weeks before the September 24 Radiothon. Among those who helped us by agreeing to tape public service announcements were Hank Aaron, Jean Carne, Sister Shirley Caesar, Phil Donahue, Irene Cara, Isaac Hayes, Maya Angelou, John "Spider" Salley, Sweet Honey and the Rock, Bernice Johnson, Butch Lewis, Evander Holyfield, Jeffery Osborne,

Michael Spinks, Leontyne Price, Nancy Wilson, Melba Moore, James Nabbie, The Ink Spots, and Jeff Gripper. We also managed to get over 100 heads of national organizations around the country to give support to the Radiothon. The heads of these organizations served as honorary chairpersons for the Radiothon. This, again, was another first. Never before had any organization managed to get so many organizational leaders to agree to join in getting its message out.

Another major source of publicity garnered by this special effort was our success in getting our message up on billboards across the nation. If you drove down a major highway, chances are you saw a billboard letting you know that the NAACP was alive and well. In many downtown areas, there were also billboards letting one know the NAACP was having a Radiothon on September 24. Members of the Outdoor Advertising Association, 3M-National Advertising Company, Neagle Advertising Company, and 8 Sheet Outdoor Advertising Association contributed 4,000 billboards in 55 cities across the nation. Many branches kicked off their Radiothons by holding press conferences with company officials in front of billboards in their community. This visible image was powerful and effective.

We managed to get a number of national companies to underwrite the tremendous cost of getting the artwork done, reproduced, and mounted. Among the principal sponsors of the Radiothon were Inner City Broadcasting, John Deere Company, R.J. Reynolds Nabisco, Kraft Inc., Fruit of the Loom, Federated Department Stores, ABC Radio Network, Sheridan Radio Network, National Black Network, Gannett Radio Broadcasting Co., UPI, A&M Records, CBS Records, Clark College, WXIA-TV, Polygram Records, Arista Records, Capitol Records, New Plateau Records, Kmart Inc., Atlanta Gas & Light, and Coca-Cola USA.

The Radiothon met my two primary objectives. First, we were able to trace the increase in our adult membership base by over 30,000. These were people we could not have reached through traditional NAACP approaches. Next, we received millions of dollars' worth of publicity and were able to tell what our local branches and national organization were doing.

Until I retired, and even now, the national Radiothon is a vital link in our membership recruitment efforts and our ongoing ability to get our message out to millions of people. No, the membership Radiothon was not a panacea. We never reached the one million membership mark. We did, however, significantly increase our membership base and add new life and vitality to the NAACP.

In addition to initiating the corporate drive within the white corporate community, instituting a membership drive among white professionals, beefing up income from the branches, and securing advertising for *The Crisis* magazine, I also had the job of raising money from the black community. I found the best way to do this was to speak to groups. We, as black people, are well organized, and there must be 75 national organizations that contributed to us. If I add the state and regional levels of some of these organizations, the number would shoot up to over 300. I made it a point to get to most of the national organizations on some systematic basis. So I visited and spoke to perhaps 30 national groups a year.

I must say that the hosts were inevitably gracious and kind. Many times I went to groups where I had no prior invitation. The presiding officer would say, "Here's Hooks, Mr. NAACP. Let's hear from him." I raised millions of dollars over my 16 years from these meetings.

Because of our rural background, many of our groups met in summer months. It was not unusual for me to make three appearances in one day, quite often 10 in one week. I might mention one other feature, my constant appearances on television. I appeared rather frequently on the three network morning news broadcasts and sometimes on evening broadcasts. I appeared on CNN and "Crossfire" quite often. I was a guest on the shows hosted by Larry King, Oprah Winfrey, Tony Brown, Phil Donahue, and others. I suppose I participated in more than 2,500 press conferences during my tenure.

Chapter 23
THE SILENT MARCH

Faced with an increasingly conservative Congress, a recalcitrant Supreme Court, and a vacillating President, 1989 appeared to be the precursor to the beginning of a second Reconstruction. As a race, we stood on the precipice of losing many of the hard-won gains of the '50s, '60s, and '70s. The hands on the clock of time were being pulled back.

In 1989, the Burger Court issued a number of stinging decisions that reversed or severely altered earlier rulings of the United States Supreme Court on affirmative action. The *Richmond v. Crosen* decision was the most visible and potentially psychologically devastating. The issue in the *Crosen* case was the ability of a local government entity to address past discrimination in the city's construction industry by using affirmative action as a tool to remedy the inability of minorities to enter the construction industry and participate in government vendor opportunities.

The city of Richmond, Virginia, passed legislation that set aside 30 percent of all city work for minority-owned businesses. This provision included not only blacks, but white women, who had been historically excluded based upon gender. This is what affirmative action is at its best—allowing those who have been locked out now to be included. Under the Richmond Plan, the successful minority or woman would have to be competitive and have proven capabilities of getting the job done.

The Burger Court's ruling was on a very narrow issue—the matter of proper hearings not being held by the city prior to the enactment of the ordinance, and the matter of those who were to participate not having a proven record of having been discriminated against personally. The matter of intent to discriminate also resurfaced.

The fight for civil rights and justice in the 1980s became more and more a matter of winning, not just in the courts, but in the court of public opinion. The media was quick to react. Both the press and the electronic media immediately proclaimed, through incendiary rhetoric, that the cause of civil rights had suffered a fatal blow by the series of cases in which the Court had issued adverse rulings on the issue of affirmative action. The only alternative left to those of us who were fighting this battle was to have Congress enact, and the President sign, legislation that would correct the defects cited by the Court in its series of rulings. This we managed to do in 1991 with the enactment of the Civil Rights Restoration Act.

We were at our Annual Convention in Detroit. A pall of pessimism hung over much of the civil rights camp. I knew that we needed to do something to dislodge the notion that all was lost and that the clocks had been turned back irreparably on racial progress. Many right-wing types were gloating over the perceived demise of affirmative action.

I delivered the keynote address to the convention. There were more than 10,000 delegates and attendees at the Detroit meeting. I had to somehow summon the troops to fight on. I talked about the power of the ballot and our belief as a people that right ultimately prevails against might. I was speaking to many people of my generation. They had seen racial barriers fall like toy soldiers over the years. Some had spent time in jail cells in cities where blacks could not vote or serve on the police departments. Now, less than 30 years later, many of these cities had black mayors and police chiefs. For the vast majority of younger African Americans, these struggles were ancient. I knew that I had to give them some reason to sustain their faith and to renew their hope. The alternative to living by faith is cringing from fear, always uncertain, cowed to inaction by the calculation of things that might go wrong. This was not the legacy I wanted to see left by the momentary setbacks.

As the week went on, speaker after speaker, presenter after presenter cited the *Crosen* case, but offered little cause for hope. What was needed was something the troops could do to keep up their morale. We needed to demonstrate to the nation that as far as we were concerned, the fight was far from over.

On Thursday morning, the closing day of the convention, I was sitting on the stage listening to presentations and debates on a number of resolutions. We had to do something soon, something out of the ordinary, to give the NAACP legions a battle cry to take home with them. We needed something to let the racists know that the battle for affirmative action, as a tool to redress the lingering effects of racial discrimination, would go forward.

I knew that we had to do something massive, different, and bold. We would march on the Supreme Court. For more than four decades, the Supreme Court building had come to symbolize the fountain of hope for black Americans. Now it had become a bastion of disillusionment. After pondering the idea, I began to think of the tremendous costs associated with putting on a national march. The NAACP would have to shoulder the financial burden. We would also have to produce the marchers. That was the reality we had to always consider when planning major national demonstrations. Additionally, the march, if it were to be successful, would have to take place by Labor Day. Congress would return from its summer recess. School was out, and many of those in our pool of supporters could take advantage of the traditional vacation period to participate.

Washington is a strange town. Getting a peaceful demonstration covered by the venerable Washington press would be a major challenge. Nonviolent protests are an everyday occurrence in the nation's capital. If we failed to attract 50,000 to 100,000 people at our march, it could be easily overlooked by a jaded media unless there was something unusual or different about it. Equally important was the question of what else was happening that day in the capital. It is possible to have a massive turnout, but if some major international or national story broke around the same time, the event might not receive any coverage.

I conferred with our Washington bureau director, Althea Simmons, who was standing at the base of the platform, leaning on a walking stick. Althea was ill. I did not know then how sick she was. The previous year she had been in good health and moving about the convention hall with regal ease. Little did I know that this would be the last convention she would attend. Althea agreed that a march was an excellent idea—it would put pressure on the members of Congress and senators who only respond to pressure. Althea, along with a number of my other staff members, was usually in favor of some kind of bold and dynamic action when all other means had failed. A march was right up her alley. After a brief discussion, we agreed that a silent march would have a dramatic impact. The silent march would be a symbolic demonstration akin to the historic 1917 march that the NAACP held in New York down Fifth Avenue to protest lynching, segregation in the South, and discrimination in the North.

On Saturday, July 28, 1917, between 8,000 and 10,000 black men, women, and children began their Parade of Faith on Fifth Avenue at 59th Street. They marched in the stifling heat to the beat of muffled drums to 23rd Street. There they dispersed. News coverage of that event had a galvanizing impact on the black community and shamed many right-thinking whites to action.

The men in that historic march were dressed in black and the women and children in white. The marchers walked proudly down Fifth Avenue, all neatly dressed—many in their Sunday best. The children led the march; directly behind them was a row of drummers. The men came next, and in the front ranks were the redoubtable W.E.B. DuBois, a founding father of the Association and the editor of *The Crisis* magazine, and James Weldon Johnson, later to become the first black executive secretary of the Association, along with his brother, who was the creator of the Negro anthem, "Lift Every Voice and Sing." Sometimes you have to look to the past for inspiration. This is what we decided to do in this instance.

After discussing the march idea with several other key staff members, I turned to Dr. William Gibson, who was chairman of the board. Gibson was an activist himself. He had led many marches in South Carolina, where he served as the president of the South Carolina State Conference of Branches. He quickly agreed that this was something we should do. Ordinarily, decisions such as this required a degree of deliberation and additional input from those staff persons who would have the responsibility of handling the logistics.

The urgency of moving forward and ending the convention on a high note altered that routine. Traditionally, many of our convention attendees leave the convention city after the closing session. Our closing banquet, held later that day, normally accommodated somewhere between 2,500 and 3,000 people. This depended on the convention city and the size of the venue we were using. We would have to make the announcement before the closing session was over.

After the presentation of the Robert Ming Award, given annually to a lawyer for outstanding legal work for the previous year, I rose and went to the microphone for my closing remarks. Looking at the faces of many in the audience, I saw conundrum-like expressions on many of the delegates' faces. I had seen that look before when it seemed to an audience that the odds were stacked against them.

I stood behind the podium and began to speak. Words came easily for me. I felt passionately about the situation that had led us to the dilemma that we found ourselves in as a nation. I announced that the NAACP had been challenged before in our trek forward. "The present Supreme Court is more dangerous to the legitimate hopes and aspirations of black people in this nation than any Bull Connor with a fire hose; than any Jim Clark with a billy club; more dangerous than any George Wallace standing in a schoolhouse door saying they shall not pass. We will march on Washington. We will march on the United States Supreme Court on August 26 by the tens of thousands. We will, by our physical witness, say to the powers that be in America that Congress must restore the rights lost by the egregious ruling of a majority of the Supreme Court." With these simple words, we had thrown down the gauntlet. There were deafening cheers and applause from the delegates. People were excited by the thought of taking on the Goliath of the Washington establishment.

When we left Detroit for the return trip to Baltimore, I was consumed by the work that had to be done to pull off a successful march. We immediately began to reach out to other groups from the Leadership Conference on Civil Rights, the Black Leadership Forum, and labor, church, and national religious leaders. We did not have much time. We had a little over 45 days to mobilize our supporters, charter buses and trains, arrange for parade permits, prepare stage arrangements, invite speakers, arrange for security, and all of the details that go into making a peaceful demonstration successful.

The reaction from the press varied. There were those who said that the Supreme Court had spoken and marching would not change the Court's rulings. The black press was supportive. They provided excellent coverage of our process. I went on scores of television and radio news talk shows to promote the upcoming march. I met with national religious groups to solicit their support, all the while rallying our troops. I was pleasantly encouraged by the enthusiasm that I found at stop after stop. Frankly, I do not know if everyone believed that the march would accomplish the desired results, but they all felt that something had to be done. To fold our tents and go home was an unthinkable option.

Dr. Joseph Lowery, the president of the Southern Christian Leadership Conference; Dr. Dorothy Height, president of the National Council of Negro Women; and Reverend Jesse Jackson, president of the Rainbow Coalition, were extremely supportive and offered their support early. So did Dr. T.J. Jemison, president of the National Baptist Convention; Bishop William Graves of the Christian Methodist Episcopal Church; Bishop William Milton Smith of the AME Zion Church and Bishop Frank C. Cummings of the African Methodist Episcopal Church; Ralph Neas of the Leadership Conference on Civil Rights; Rabbi David

Saperstein of the American Union of Hebrew Congregations; Mayor Marion Barry of the District of Columbia; President Lane Kirkland of the AFL-CIO; Coretta S. King, president of the King Foundation; John Jacob, president of the Urban League; and Julius Chambers, president of the Legal Defense Fund—and what a great supporter he and his successor, Elaine Jones, were each and every time I called on them. Elaine continues today to be a dynamic and able head of the Legal Defense Fund. We were also joined by Marian Wright Edelman, chairman of the Children's Defense Fund; Bill Pollard; Bill Lucy, president of the Black Trade Unionists; scores of union presidents and black elected officials; and a host of others.

I conferred with our staff members, Julius C. Hope, director of religious affairs, Reverend Jerry Guess, my personal assistant, and Dr. Emmett C. Burns, and asked if they would get church support organized. Dr. Hope flew all over the country mobilizing support from our church groups and turned out thousands of demonstrators. John Johnson put all security precautions in place in Washington. Howard Henderson, my chief of staff, mobilized every available resource in our organization to assist with precautions for the march. Beverly Cole, our efficient and dynamic education director, was asked to contact national education groups from all over the country to solicit their support.

Mildred Roxborough pulled every lever to gain financial support for the march. Mildred was our most experienced staffer, and she lit up the sky with fund-raising. Bill Penn mobilized branch support from all over the country. In other words, this was a maximum effort event. Hazel Dukes and Bill Gibson mobilized and activated our board. The results were outstanding.

Mildred Roxborough was one of the most organized people I have ever met. She came from an old-line civil rights family, which was forced to leave Brownsville, Tennessee, because of bigotry. The family narrowly averted death due to their involvement in the struggle. Her mother remained a resolute fighter for justice until her death. Mildred could always be counted on for knowledge, help, support, and a devotion to the cause of justice. Even today she works hard, and her commitment to the NAACP principles has never faltered.

Bill Penn was our director of branches. He succeeded Gloster Current and served well and ably and helped us to secure the largest membership in the history of the association—more than 500,000. He also led our nationwide team as we addressed the question of police conduct in well-publicized hearings in several cities around the country.

As we came closer to Saturday, August 26, students from historically black colleges and universities announced that they would be coming by the thousands. Calls flooded our operations office in Washington from all over the country reporting that buses had been chartered from as far away as Los Angeles and the state of Washington. The momentum was building. There was excitement in the air.

The day before the march, we were plagued with the normal problems of people wanting to be listed as speakers and last-minute requests from the press corps wanting specific arrangements. In addition, emergency stations for those who might become ill or suffer from dehydration, restroom facilities, and a center to assist those who became separated or lost from their group had to be set up. Putting on a major march requires an inordinate amount of detail planning.

There was one more major consideration: the weather. Anyone who has had any experience with organizing outside demonstrations can attest to the fact that if it rains, chaos results. People do not march in downpours. We checked with the National Weather Service and were assured the weather for Saturday, August 26, would be perfect. It was to be a sunny and hot day in Washington. Even the gods were smiling on us.

On Saturday morning, I woke up and said a prayer that we would have good weather and that the march would be peaceful. I left the hotel with my wife, Frances, and headed for the National Mall, between 4th and 7th streets, where we were to assemble. We could not have asked for a better day. The sun was out early; not a raincloud was to be found in the Washington sky. As I got near the assembly point, I closed my eyes and prayed that we would have a good crowd. All we needed was a sparsely attended march, and the pundits and those in the media who were cynics would point an accusing finger and say, "The NAACP failed in its attempt to rally the nation around the issue of affirmative action. Affirmative action is a dead issue."

When we turned the corner on 4th Street, I saw a vast sea of humanity. There were people with signs and banners as far as the eye could see. I was told that there were over 2,000 buses already in the parking lots that we had reserved. Buses were being sent to lots as far as 20 blocks from the staging area. I made my way to the command area where the dignitaries and marshals were to assemble. As I pushed my way through the crowd, I saw hundreds of familiar faces, men and women I had seen in little towns at NAACP banquets in Arkansas, at luncheons in Texas, at South African demonstrations in New York, at breakfast meetings in Florida—literally hundreds of people I had met from all over the nation.

As I got near the command center, I saw the people dressed in the black and white period outfits. What a sight to behold! The drummers had covered their instruments in black cloth that would later be used to create the muffled sounds for the march.

We finally gathered those who were to participate in the formal program and began to line up the marchers. The route we were to march was north from the Mall on 4th Street to Pennsylvania Avenue N.W., then east on Pennsylvania Avenue to Constitution Avenue to First Street N.E., then south on First Street past the Supreme Court. We proceeded to East Capitol Street and walked through the Capitol grounds to the west front, where the rally was to take place.

With children leading the march, followed by the drummers, we stepped off after a brief prayer. The street was full of marchers for blocks, with thousands of others waiting on the sidewalks to join in at the end of the line of marchers. There was an eerie feeling about the march. People were uncharacteristically quiet. You only heard the rustle of thousands of feet and the rhythmic beating of the drums.

Many Americans do not realize it, but it is against the law to demonstrate on the Supreme Court grounds. You cannot carry signs up the steps or protest in any other way. What a strange dichotomous situation—the right to protest ends on the steps of the U.S. Supreme Court. We had decided earlier that we would obey the law and not allow any arrests to take place. We did not want the arrest of demonstrators to become the story. The story we wanted to tell was that the Court had made a horrific mistake and its rulings must be reversed.

When we arrived at the west front of the Capitol grounds, we had to wait for almost two hours for the last marchers to arrive. According to estimates of the U.S. Park Service, there were between 70,000 and 75,000 demonstrators. We estimated that there were between 100,000 and 125,000 participants.

Before the speeches, we had a litany, participated in by the audience. A cross-section of representatives from youth, labor, religious, educational, political, governmental, and other groups led portions of the litany. After Joe Lowery, Jesse Jackson, and Mayor Barry had spoken, I called the demonstrators' attention to the reason that we had to come to Washington—to demand that the Congress reverse the actions of the Court. I challenged the massive assembly, and those who were watching on television, to believe that we could alter the destiny of the nation if we had the will and the tenacity to persevere. I reminded them of the fact that there were nay-sayers who had proclaimed that we would not end lynching, but we did. There were those who said that we would not go to the

University of Alabama or to "Ole Miss," but we did. There were those who said that we would never get the right to vote, but we did.

When the march was over, the crowd, like that of the Silent March of 1917, dispersed and went home. You can imagine how perplexed and angry I was when I read the Sunday *New York Times* the next morning and discovered that the reporter who was assigned to cover the march reported that we had a mere 15,000 demonstrators. Based on that report, well over 100,000 people did not exist. When I challenged the publisher on the accuracy of the story, I was told that the reporter had left before the marchers even arrived at the Capitol assembly area. A correction was made about a week later in a two-inch box. This was very perplexing because *The New York Times* had traditionally been most supportive of the Civil Rights Movement.

The coverage by *The New York Times* was not an isolated occurrence. Civil rights demonstrations and activities have historically received less than objective reporting from some in the media. Old-timers in the NAACP told me that for some reason the media has, intentionally or otherwise, chosen to minimize the NAACP successes.

Black organizations are often marginalized. Some reporters with no knowledge of civil rights issues are assigned to cover major civil rights events. They do not, in many instances, know the right questions to ask to get the facts. Many come with biases or preconceived notions of how things should be, and slant their stories in such a way as to render ineffective the valiant efforts of those who struggle against the odds to bring about peaceful change. Fortunately, most of our nation's press is objective and reports events in an honest fashion.

The Silent March of 1989 was a prime example of how events over which the Association had no control forced the NAACP to spring into action. While I was executive director, I was asked why we didn't just develop a long-range plan and stick to it. Unfortunately, the confluence of events often dictated that we go in new directions. The march was also proof that we had the capability of shifting our battlefield strategy to deal with changing battlefield conditions.

In less than 45 days, we were able to set into motion a chain of events that culminated in the enactment of legislation by the U.S. Congress that reversed a number of unfavorable rulings. The Civil Rights Bill of 1991 was the fulfillment of that effort. The NAACP's Silent March of 1989 was among the largest and most effective national protests of the 1980s. It brought together a cross-section of groups who shared a common agenda and reached out to others who were concerned, but who had not been visibly involved before. It also convinced both the Congress and the President that the time had come to rectify the intolerable burden of proving discrimination on the backs of those who had been discriminated against.

Without the efforts of the NAACP, the 1991 Civil Rights Bill would never have been passed and been signed into law. I am extremely proud of the role that we played in building this bridge and helping to remove the barrier that stood in the way of racial progress.

Chapter 24
KEEPING *THE CRISIS* ALIVE

One of the greatest challenges that faced me at the NAACP was maintaining and improving *The Crisis* magazine. The magazine was 67 years old when I arrived in 1977. It was the brainchild of W.E.B. DuBois, who started the magazine in the midsummer of 1910 when he arrived in New York as the director of publicity and research for the newly formed NAACP.

According to available records, DuBois launched the magazine as an instrument to disseminate his views and that of the newly established human rights organization. According to Charles Flint Kellogg, the author of the only definitive history of the NAACP, the magazine got its name in August of 1910. William Walling has been credited as the person who actually gave *The Crisis* its name. Although DuBois did not name the periodical, he conceived it and made it one of the most powerful vehicles in the crusade for human rights of the twentieth century.

Before beginning the NAACP's publication, DuBois had edited two earlier publications. One was *The Moon*, a short-lived weekly published in Memphis, Tennessee (1906), and *Horizon,* published in Washington, D.C., from 1907 to 1910. These publications bore the imprimatur of DuBois's uncompromising philosophy that unfettered civil rights for blacks were essential.

DuBois and some of organizers of the NAACP recognized that the Association had to have an outspoken publication capable of communicating the objectives of the embryonic organization. DuBois ran into opposition by some members of the governing board because his views so dominated the content of the magazine. He ultimately won the contest of wills, and the first edition was published in November 1910 as "a record of the darker race." The first publication had a press run of a mere 1,000 copies. The magazine subsequently witnessed phenomenal growth. By 1918, the publication, now known officially as *The Crisis*, had a circulation of 100,000.

The November 1910 issue, which was 20 pages, sold for 10 cents per copy or a dollar a year. Among the features were *Along the Color Line*, an editorial, an article by Moorfield Storey entitled *Athens and Brownsville*, and a suggested list of books of interest for readers. All of the advertisements were from New York City–based firms and companies. From this humble beginning, *The Crisis* became a force to be reckoned with. There was no shortage of enthusiasm and creativity. There was, however, a paucity of financial resources.

When DuBois established what became *The Crisis* magazine, it was the only publication of its kind. There were other black publications, but none had a national subscription base or dealt with the issues that this publication addressed. It should be remembered that in 1910 there were very few mainstream publications that saw civil and human rights for blacks as an important topic to cover on a consistent basis.

The scope of the topics covered was staggering. For instance, in DuBois's column, *Along the Color Line*, he dealt with political issues, education, the church, social uplift, organizations and meetings, economics, science, and the arts. DuBois made it clear that the objective of the publication was to set forth those facts and arguments that show the dangers of race prejudice, particularly as was manifested toward colored people. It would record important happenings and movements in the world that bear on the great problem of interracial relations, and especially those that affect the Negro American.

In the early days, *The Crisis* was more a newspaper than it was a magazine. It became, and has remained to this day, the official organ of the NAACP. DuBois exercised general control over the publication, writing brilliant editorials in which he expressed his views freely and openly. Some of his fellow board members, who were instrumental in organizing the NAACP a few years previously, and who were listed on the masthead of the first volume, had problems with the manner in which DuBois's views dominated the publication. DuBois was successful, however, in resisting any board efforts to restrict him.

During the early days, the circulation of *The Crisis* was larger than the membership of the NAACP, as DuBois used the publication to recruit members for the fledgling organization. For more than 20 years, DuBois and the NAACP remained largely on the same philosophical page. He became tired and frustrated with the slow pace of progress in breaking down the barriers of racism. He became convinced that it would require black leadership exclusively to head up black freedom-fighting organizations. Further, he wrote that blacks must develop separately as a race if whites refused to accept us as equals. In 1934, DuBois published a series of editorials over a period of six months in which he advocated "fighting segregation with segregation." The position taken by DuBois caused an uproar. DuBois resigned and his resignation was promptly accepted by the board.

Roy Wilkins became the editor for the next 15 years. He was followed by James W. Ivy in 1950. Ivy was followed by Henry Lee Moon, who became editor in April of 1966. Warren Marr II succeeded Henry Lee Moon in 1974. Both Moon and Marr held the titles of editor of *The Crisis* and director of public relations.

When I arrived in 1977, Warren Marr was the editor. Much had changed since the days of DuBois. There had been a proliferation of black publications. Some of these had national circulations, large staffs, and solid advertisement bases. Also, the majority press had begun to cover civil and human rights issues in some detail. In 1977, *The Crisis* had very few advertisers. Meanwhile, postage and the cost of production had increased tremendously. For these and other reasons, advertisement revenues became more important than ever.

Circulation was essential. It enhanced the publication's ability to convince advertisers to take out ads in their magazines. In 1977, we had a circulation of less than 100,000. With the exception of special issues, there was a limited number of paid advertisements in our magazines. I discovered that *The Crisis* had two issues that received not substantial, but a fair amount of advertising. Those issues were February (Negro History month, as it was then called) and June/July, which was produced in time for distribution at our annual conventions.

The June/July 1977 issue of *The Crisis* was a tremendous book. It was a special tribute to retiring executive director Roy Wilkins. Management hired a sales consultant to market the magazine for that one special issue. *The Crisis* staff labored assiduously to produce an issue that was a fitting and appropriate tribute to Roy. They succeeded in a big way. The special tribute issue had more than 130 pages and included 35 pages of advertisements.

The May issue, which was more typical, had a mere 30 pages, including two pages of advertisements. The issue following the convention issue was August/September. It had 30 pages as well, with seven pages of advertisements.

Over the years, *The Crisis* had come to depend on the NAACP to help pay its bills. *The Crisis* Corporation was wholly owned by the NAACP. There was a conscious decision by the boards of both entities to do whatever had to be done to keep *The Crisis* alive and publishing. The hope was that one day the magazine would be in a position to pay back some, if not all, of the money that had been borrowed over the years. In the meantime, it was the best public relations tool the Association had.

I saw the magazine as more than just a significant historical relic. It was a forum that black writers, academics, poets, and others could use to express their positions. In the pages of *The Crisis* we were able to highlight and underscore the positive accomplishments of our young people. Our program thrusts and important events were publicized in the pages of *The Crisis*. It was an indispensable vehicle we used to communicate with a significant segment of our membership.

I must admit, I was unaware when I arrived that the problems the magazine faced economically were so intractable. Each potential solution was contingent upon something else being done. After we successfully jumped one hurdle, another was erected. For instance, advertisers rely on circulation as a major criterion in considering any publication. However, it was not enough to merely increase our circulation. Most advertising agencies recommended a publication to a client only if its readers matched the targeted audience of the advertiser. Therefore, it became necessary to have a demographic study of *The Crisis* readership.

There are only a few such agencies in the field capable of administering the survey, which was extremely expensive and took months, if not a full year, to complete. After our readership was surveyed to determine such factors as average age, income, gender, buying practices, geographical, and other similar data, we discovered that even this was not enough. Our circulation had to be audited by a trade group known as the Audit Bureau of Circulation. This trade organization audited magazine and newspaper circulations to make sure that circulation claims were accurate.

After all of this had been done, we were not yet home free. Most major corporations retain the services of ad agencies that actually place advertisements in the publications they deem appropriate. It is basically left up to the agency to select the publications that meet the targeted demographics of the client. A separate pool of money, referred to as a minority budget, was allocated for minority publications. We had to compete for money from that limited pool.

There were just a few more hurdles we had to overcome. *The Crisis* was controversial by its nature. We took on giant corporations, Congress, the President, the U.S. Supreme Court, and even an occasional ad agency. Advertisers dislike controversy. They want their ads to appear in an idyllic environment, one free of confusion or negative overtones. The demographic study showed that *The Crisis* had the most affluent and the best-educated readership of any black publication we competed with for advertisement revenues. Regrettably, that same study showed that our subscribers were older than those of many of our competitors. Most advertisers, for marketing reasons that I do not fully understand, targeted very young audiences.

We were caught in a constant "Catch-22" situation. It was difficult, if not impossible, for us to get advertisements without constantly having to jump through a series of hoops. All of these hurdles required the expenditure of money that was in short supply. Meanwhile, marketing experts kept telling us that we needed to update and to refocus *The Crisis*. This did not come without cost. Some suggested that we drop all significant coverage of NAACP activity, which I never seriously considered. If we had to stop covering the activities of the NAACP in order to get an ad, I preferred having the magazine published and distributed without any advertisements.

There were some reasonable steps I felt we could take to make the magazine more reader-friendly and graphically more appealing to a younger audience. I conferred with a number of people in the industry and asked them for advice and assistance. One recommendation that was almost universal was to use more color in the book and to have cover story themes that would run throughout a given issue.

A number of independent studies were conducted during the period leading up to my appointment. One such report, finished in late 1976, was the McKinsey Study. The study pointed out that *The Crisis* was responsible for 14 percent of the Association's income in 1954. By 1974, that percentage had declined to a mere 3.1 percent. The consultants suggested that the NAACP needed to seriously consider ending the publishing of *The Crisis*. Our auditors also suggested in no uncertain terms that we must cease publishing the magazine. There was also an inordinate amount of criticism of *The Crisis* by members of the NAACP's board. *The Crisis*, they pointed out, had become a drain on the scarce resources of the Association.

The thought of silencing the official voice of the NAACP, the instrument that was used to fight lynching and Jim Crow, was repugnant to me. I put together a task force of writers, marketing experts, publishers, and correspondents to advise me on what specifically needed to be done to save *The Crisis*. The magazine was the oldest continuously published black publication in the nation. Many academics and civil rights practitioners had come to view it as an indispensable resource. It was the most effective instrument that the NAACP and the civil rights community had for communicating with our leadership. Additionally, it had always published the works of talented new writers. Practically every notable black writer since 1910 had contributed to it. The National Urban League, which for years published its magazine, called *Opportunity*, had long since ceased publishing.

We began to make significant changes and modifications in the focus of the magazine. We expanded and diversified the number and types of writers we used. We added new features that would appeal to a wider audience. We established an ad department whose responsibility was solely to develop a comprehensive marketing program for selling *The Crisis* to advertisers. I put my executive assistant and director of communications and policy, Jerry Guess, in charge of the day-to-day administration of the publication.

In 1981, following the retirement of Warren Marr, I convinced Chester Higgins, a former editor of *Jet Magazine* and one of my assistants while I was at the FCC, to come to New York and give me a hand in editing and repositioning of the magazine. Chester agreed to give me six to nine months of service to get the initial restructuring work done. Fortunately for the Association and *The Crisis*, Chester stayed on for a little over two years.

Chester began redesigning the book, soliciting new writers, and implementing the cover story concept. The cover story concept involved having a series of related articles focusing on a single topic that was highlighted on the cover. Over the years, we covered topics such as The Black Family, The Black Woman, The Black Athlete, The NAACP v. Hollywood, The Housing Crisis, Black Inventors, Blacks in Mass Media, Blacks in Corporate America, Blacks in Sports, The Black Church, The State of Race Relations, The Impact of Environmental Racism on the Black Community, Educating Black Boys, Billy Club Justice, and scores of other important and interesting topics.

The magazine once again became a hard-hitting civil rights advocacy publication. It had new life and vitality. Chester was a "take-no-prisoners" type of person. He was focused like a laser beam on our mission. He knew what he wanted done and was satisfied with no less than the best. At first his demeanor posed a problem for some of the longtime staff. They soon realized, however, that Chester was a consummate professional. They learned that he was not interested in receiving kudos. He was only interested in seeing the mission through to its completion.

In 1983, we increased our membership fee structure to include a *Crisis* magazine subscription along with the purchase of all adult memberships. This quickly allowed us to increase our subscription base to over 370,000. In 1983, many multi-member households opted to receive only one copy of the magazine per household. Otherwise, our circulation would have reached more than 400,000. *The Crisis* magazine became the fourth-largest black publication in terms of circulation in 1983 and remained so until 1993, when I retired. Only *Jet, Ebony,* and *Essence* magazines had larger circulations.

When Chester Higgins returned to Washington in December of 1993, I elevated Maybelle Ward to the position of editorial director. Maybelle had been a member of *The Crisis* and the public relations department's staffs for more than 40 years. She was the assistant editor under Warren Marr and had been an invaluable assistant under the editorship of Wilkins, Ivy, and Moon.

There was very little about the NAACP or *The Crisis* with which Maybelle was unfamiliar. She was a walking encyclopedia on the history and personalities of staff members of the NAACP. Maybelle was also one of the best proofreaders the Association ever had. If you gave something to Maybelle, when you got it back the grammar, punctuation, and syntax were perfect. She was indeed an institution. Maybelle became the first woman to head *The Crisis.* I am proud to have had a hand in breaking down another gender barrier at the NAACP. During her tenure, Maybelle saw to it that every article that appeared between the magazine's covers was letter-perfect.

In 1985, Fred Beauford was hired as editorial director following the retirement of Miss Ward. Beauford taught editorial writing at colleges in California and New York. He had also edited a number of smaller publications. For the next eight years, Beauford served as editorial consultant or editorial director.

I am proud to point out that we managed, despite the shortage of funds, to get *The Crisis* out 10 times in each of my 15 years. (The June/ July and the August/ September issues had always been combined issues. The other 10 months were single issues.) We mailed as many as 426,000 copies of the magazine on a monthly basis.

Little by little, the magazine won converts. Once again legal, legislative, and other initiatives began to receive wide coverage. We addressed the crisis in the black community, education, the black family, housing, police brutality, prisons, and a host of other important topics. We covered the arts, had regular *Crisis* interviews with national personalities, and gave extensive coverage to national civil rights–related conventions and conferences. We covered international issues such as conditions in South Africa and Haiti. "NAACP Focus," a column by the public relations office, covered a variety of topics, and a column called "Along the Battle-front" covered branch activities. We also initiated a health column and a book review section.

In 1989 we published our 80th NAACP anniversary issue. That issue has become a collector's item. We received literally thousands of requests from colleges, scholars, and history buffs for copies. This special edition covered—in compendium form—highlights of the NAACP's 80-year history. It featured NAACP highlights from 1909 to 1988, a definitive history of how the NAACP was founded, and articles about most of the founders. The anniversary issue contained a complete list of Spingarn Medalists, the purpose of the medal, and the conditions for the award. It contained a special feature on Roy Wilkins, W.E.B. DuBois, Clarence Mitchell, the history of *The Crisis*, "A Message to the American Negro," by Mahatma Gandhi (reprinted from the July 1929 issue), *The Crisis* classic editorial on Black English, called "Black Nonsense," and an inter-view of me as the CEO.

Not only was the anniversary issue an editorial success, at 130 pages, but it was by far the most financially successful single issue in the history of the publication. We sold just under $350,000 in ads for the issue. We beefed up our sales staff and had finally begun to make steady progress in convincing advertisers to advertise in our magazine. We managed to have *The Crisis* show a profit for each of the last three years of my tenure. We completely reversed the trend from the magazine losing money to being profitable.

The last issue that Jerry Guess, Ken Wilson (who was by now helping out with sales), Harriet Diles, sales manager, and I produced (January 1993) had over $600,000 in advertising revenue. Ken Wilson, who had built *Dawn Magazine* into a very profitable publication, worked with us during my last few years to shore up our sales department. I cannot com-pliment Ken enough for all the great work he did in helping us under-stand the nature of magazine advertising and how to secure a greater number of advertisements. He was superb. I am also grateful for the great magazine and newspapers that covered the activities of the African American community. *Jet, Ebony, Essence,* and *Black Enterprise* are sim-ply outstanding publications. I am proud to count John Johnson and Earl Graves as two close personal friends. Our great newspapers are also to be congratulated.

Our final issue was a special tribute to me for my work as executive director of the NAACP and as publisher of *The Crisis*. After the cost of production, mailing, and commissions to the sales staff, there was a net profit on that single issue of more than $400,000.

In a real sense, I left *The Crisis*—the legacy of DuBois, Wilkins, Ivy, and Moon—well positioned not just for the short term, but for the long haul. We restored its editorial prowess, modernized and updated its format, created a meaningful advertising income stream, increased its circulation to over 400,000, and left a surplus of $400,000 in revenue.

We left the magazine in a strong position financially and a great position editorially. Regrettably, under the next administration, the magazine was allowed to fail, and it ceased publication for an entire year.

I am, however, exceptionally proud that I was able to make *The Crisis* the premier civil and human rights publication in the nation. Once more, the magazine was on the cutting edge of shaping and molding public opinion on issues of race and race relations. I was delighted when Julian Bond and the team that he put together began to republish the magazine conceived by DuBois as a weapon to be used against ignorance, intolerance, and indifference.

Chapter 25

THE CLARENCE THOMAS NOMINATION

Just 10 days before we were to meet in Houston, Texas, for our 1991 Annual Convention, one of the most important events in recent civil rights history took place. On June 27, Justice Thurgood Marshall announced his retirement from the U.S. Supreme Court. Justice Marshall, former general counsel for the NAACP, had served on the Court since 1967. On July 1, 1991, President George Bush nominated Judge Clarence Thomas for the seat left vacant by the resignation of Justice Marshall. That same day, the NAACP issued a statement that said, in part, that the NAACP would take a close look at the nomination of Judge Thomas and, based upon his record, would make a determination.

Clarence Thomas's fast rise was a result of affirmative action. Ironically, he later became a virulent and vociferous opponent of the very vehicle that led to his personal rise to prominence. Immediately after Thomas's nomination, the NAACP launched an intensive investigation of his record.

Clarence Thomas had been confirmed for a second term as chairman of the EEOC despite the NAACP's opposition, based primarily on his poor record of enforcement of the existing laws, his management priorities, and his policy-making pronouncements as chairman during his first term. Despite Thomas's record at the EEOC and the NAACP's initial reservations, the NAACP decided not to oppose his nomination to the U.S. Court of Appeals for the District of Columbia Circuit in 1990. This position was based on the recommendation of Althea Simmons, who was the NAACP's Washington Bureau director at that time.

The Court of Appeals for the District of Columbia Circuit is the court from which many Supreme Court Justices have historically been selected. Mrs. Simmons took this fact into consideration when she made the decision to recommend that the NAACP not oppose Thomas's nomination. It was her view—a view shared by many in the civil rights community at the time—that, once freed of the need for reappointment, Thomas might become a more sensitive and progressive member of the judiciary. In any event, we would watch his rulings carefully. Accordingly, the NAACP took no position on Thomas's nomination to the Circuit Court of Appeals.

As was expected, the NAACP was deluged with inquiries from the press about Clarence Thomas as the heir-apparent and the nominee for the seat on the Supreme Court held by Thurgood Marshall. I was careful in couching my public statements relative to the Thomas nomination. I emphasized the fact that the NAACP would have to look long and hard at Thomas's complete record, his public pronouncements, his opinions on the court of appeals, and such other information as could be made available.

Upon our arrival at the 82nd Annual Convention in Houston, there was an atmosphere of great anticipation and unusual tension. A special meeting of the National Board was convened on the evening of July 6 by the chairman of the board, Dr. William F. Gibson. At that meeting, members of the board had an open and frank discussion on the Thomas nomination and their perception of the importance of this particular development. By and large, the members, with a few exceptions, expressed severe reservations, if not out-and-out opposition, to the nomination. Most of the board members were familiar with Judge Thomas's record at the EEOC, even though they were unfamiliar with his opinions on the court of appeals. After a spirited two-and-a-half-hour meeting, the following statement was issued:

> We recognize the importance of this appointment and its far-reaching implications in shaping the future of the Court. Therefore, we have proceeded at a rapid pace in formulating our position, taking into full account any matter related to Judge Thomas's qualifications to sit on the Supreme Court.

At the outset, the NAACP leadership realized that there was much in Judge Thomas's public history, especially during his tenure as chairman of the Equal Employment Opportunity Commission, that gave us pause, if not alarm. His record at the Commission was not a good one in terms of his sensitivity to affirmative action and racial and age discrimination matters. Without a shadow of doubt, the NAACP's assessment of Judge Thomas and his philosophy was not favorable. The board recommended the following:

1. We invited Judge Thomas to meet with the NAACP to discuss our concerns. We asked that such a meeting be held as quickly as possible.
2. The NAACP Washington Bureau was authorized to conduct an exhaustive review of Judge Thomas's record in public office, a report to be presented on or before August 15, 1991.

At a crowded press conference on Monday, July 8, the NAACP released its statement. On Tuesday, a brigade of news reporters from around the world arrived at the convention and began to circulate among delegates in an effort to secure independent assessments of their evaluations of Judge Thomas, based on what they knew of his public record. On Wednesday, July 10, at an emotionally charged meeting, the board voted to adopt the position taken by the special Call Session held on Saturday, July 6.

This vote to formally adopt the position of the National Board was passed by an usually slim margin. A significant minority of the members wanted to go on record, at that point, in clear opposition to Judge Thomas based upon what was known of his record. A subsequent special meeting was held by the board on Thursday, July 11. That meeting, again called by the chairman, was held to select the people who would comprise the special delegation to meet with Clarence Thomas, if he would agree to meet with the NAACP. It should be remembered that until this time, Supreme Court nominees did not meet with groups or individuals concerning their nominations. Normally, they restricted their contacts to members of the Senate.

It was agreed, by common consent, that the following people would meet with Judge Thomas: Executive Director Benjamin Hooks; Chairman of the Board William F. Gibson; Vice Chairman Ben F. Andrews; Association President Hazel N. Dukes; and Washington Bureau Director Wade Henderson.

The report of the board's action was made to the Plenary Session, or the legislative body of the delegates. The announcement met with little or no opposition. There was no request from any of the more than 3,000 delegates present at that session for any special action. Any delegate could have asked for the consideration of an emergency resolution to deal with the issue. All that would have been required by anyone interested in doing so was to put the resolution in writing and submit it to the chairman of the board, the chairman of the resolutions committee, or the executive director. No delegate attempted to submit such a resolution on the Thomas nomination.

The convention was satisfied with the approach taken by the leadership. At the close of the annual convention, counsels Wade Henderson and Edward Hailes, Jr., of the Washington Bureau were authorized to assemble the necessary resource people for the purpose of preparing a comprehensive report to be submitted to the National Board of Directors on or before July 31.

At an early meeting of the Special Committee on July 19, 1991, the chairman noted that a meeting with Judge Thomas was set for 12:30 P.M. at the home of Constance Newman, director of the office of personnel management, a member of the NAACP, and a close friend of Judge Thomas. I led the preliminary discussion, which focused on the NAACP's approach to the meeting with Judge Thomas. Because of the sensitivity and the importance of this meeting, it was agreed that the NAACP would neither confirm nor deny the meeting with Thomas.

Participants at the meeting with Judge Thomas included the NAACP Special Committee members, Judge Thomas, Constance Newman, and two Department of Health and Human Services staffers: Michael Calhoun, chief of staff to Secretary Lewis Sullivan, and Vernon Parker, special assistant to Mrs. Newman. After a relatively friendly but spirited discussion, Judge Thomas addressed the following key issues:

- We questioned him about his views on class action versus individual litigation. Thomas responded by saying he supports class action, but like most Americans, he is opposed to quotas. He was hostile to the role and authority of Congress to address problems of discrimination using, for example, the Fourteenth Amendment to the U.S. Constitution.
- We asked about his views on the Great Society. He hedged and avoided answering the question directly.
- We discussed comments attributed to him that were critical of his sister for her poverty and lack of education. He was evasive and stated that his comments had been taken out of context.
- We then asked about his involvement in the political fight in the Reagan Administration on whether Executive Order 11246 on

equal employment opportunity should be modified or abandoned. Thomas answered this question, in our collective opinion, in a less than frank fashion.

- We asked about his criticism of civil rights leaders and about his position on black colleges. His answer to this question contradicted statements many of us had heard him make earlier.

The NAACP delegation returned to the hotel to briefly assess the meeting. We concluded that Judge Thomas had been both friendly and cordial, but he had failed to convince the committee that we should support his confirmation.

On July 27, 1991, a comprehensive report was prepared by the Washington Bureau, with the assistance of the following people: Dr. John Hope Franklin (the distinguished scholar who also chaired President Clinton's Race Commission), Dr. Mary Frances Berry, Professor Charles Ogletree, Cecile Counts Blakely, Caroline Johnson, Leesa Richardson, Danielle Bolden, Barbara Washington, Nyisha Shakur, and Simmone Braxton.

The report was divided thus: an executive summary and introduction, the NAACP's philosophy on judicial nominations, Judge Thomas's record at the Department of Education, his record at the Equal Employment Opportunity Commission, an analysis of his articles and speeches, a conclusion, an epilogue, and a bibliography. The NAACP had three options: It could oppose the confirmation, support the confirmation, or take no position.

On August 3, 1991, we convened an extraordinary special session of the NAACP Board in Washington. Members of the board had received the Washington Bureau's exhaustive report. Wade Henderson, Bureau director, and Edward Hailes, Jr., Bureau counsel, had done an outstanding job. The report was both comprehensive and thorough. In a meeting closed to both the press and all but a few members of the staff and the board, we debated whether Judge Clarence Thomas should, in our opinion, sit on the Supreme Court.

The climate was charged with anticipation and a sense that history was about to be made. Most members came with ambivalent feelings. On the one hand, it was difficult for them to have to consider opposing the nomination of an African American to the U.S. Supreme Court. Most were concerned with the news media's speculation that if Thomas were not confirmed, a white conservative would probably be nominated. This would mean that for the first time since 1967, we would have an all-white Supreme Court. On the other hand, how could they vote for a black man who held a reactionary philosophy on issues as vital as affirmative action, desegregation, minority set-aside programs, and the Civil Rights Acts of 1964, 1965, and 1968, and their extensions?

I had already reached my decision on the nomination. There was no way the NAACP could in good conscience support Judge Thomas's confirmation.

For the next two hours we had a very open and spirited discussion on the nomination. Each member had read the Bureau's report. When we finally took the vote, 49 members voted in favor of opposing the nomination. One member of the board abstained. There were no votes for confirmation. The board had spoken 49-0.

Dr. Gibson read the official statement announcing the NAACP's opposition to Judge Thomas's confirmation at a crowded press conference at the Washington Court Hotel. The statement said in part:

> The nomination of Judge Clarence Thomas to fill the seat of the United States Supreme Court left vacant with the retirement of Justice Thurgood Marshall has presented the NAACP with a situation unique in the 82-year history of the nation's oldest and largest civil rights organization.
>
> Only once before has an African American been nominated to the Supreme Court. That individual was Mr. Marshall, who took his seat in 1967. At that time, fully aware of Mr. Marshall's outstanding record as an attorney, U.S. Solicitor General, and Federal Judge, as well as his sensitive, philosophical approach toward the law, the NAACP gave him its unqualified endorsement.
>
> The nomination of Judge Clarence Thomas, however, brought with it a special set of problems related to his record in several government positions—most notably as chairman of the Equal Employment Opportunity Commission—and his reactionary philosophical approach to a number of critical issues, not the least of which is affirmative action.
>
> Mr. Thomas is an African American, and that fact was not ignored in our deliberations. While we feel strongly the seat should go to an African American, we looked beyond that factor and focused our attention on whether Thomas, based on the criteria we have described, should, in our opinion, sit on the Supreme Court.

In the final analysis, Judge Clarence Thomas's judicial philosophy is simply inconsistent with the historical positions taken by the NAACP.

Our primary and specific objections to Mr. Thomas's confirmation are spelled out as follows:

Judge Thomas's inconsistent views on civil rights policy make him an unpredictable element on an increasingly radically conservative Court.

Prior to 1986, Judge Thomas's comments and writings acknowledged the benefits of traditional affirmative action remedies, including goals and timetables. After his confirmation for a second term at the EEOC, his position on affirmative action shifted dramatically. This position was so hostile to the best interests of black people that the NAACP called for Judge Thomas's resignation at that time.

While we appreciate the fact that Judge Thomas came up in the school of hard knocks and pulled himself up by his own boot straps, as many other black Americans have, our concern is for the millions of blacks who have no access to boot straps—theirs or others. It is particularly disturbing that a man who has himself so benefited from affirmative action now denigrates it and would deny these opportunities to other blacks.

While heading EEOC, Judge Thomas consistently complained about the laws and policies he was required to enforce. He was particularly strong in his opposition to established federal policy requiring affirmative action remedies. The results of this caused economic hardships to thousands of black Americans whose complaints went unaddressed. Also during Judge Thomas's tenure at the EEOC, the agency failed to process over 13,000 age-discrimination complaints on behalf of older workers under the Age Discrimination in Employment Act. Ultimately, this failure to act required Congress to intervene by passing special legislation to restore the rights of the worker, black and white, under the Act.

When Clarence Thomas was Assistant Secretary for Civil Rights at the Department of Education from May 1981 until May 1982, he did little to further the cause of higher education for African Americans, and he failed to implement provisions that would have funneled millions of dollars into the historically black colleges. In sworn testimony in a federal contempt of court proceeding, Judge Thomas conceded his failure to implement the order. This had a devastating effect on the educational opportunities for young blacks. We were very troubled by having to confront the possible opposition of Judge Clarence Thomas.

We believe the importance of an African American as a replacement for Judge Thurgood Marshall should not be underestimated. Diversity on the Supreme Court is absolutely essential, and failure to confirm another African American sends a dreadful signal to our community about where we stand in the body politic. It is, therefore, with regret that we are compelled to oppose the confirmation of Judge Thomas. The NAACP and the black community must and will continue to fight until an appropriate replacement who embodies the view of the majority of black Americans is nominated and confirmed.

Following the action by the National Board, I met with my public relations director. We developed a strategy to get the NAACP's public relations machinery swung into action. I issued press statements and responded to inquiries by the hundreds. I mobilized our NAACP units to action. With the exception of the Compton, California, branch president, who announced that the branch was in support of the Thomas confirmation, no other NAACP official or unit endorsed the nomination. In short order, the Compton branch reversed itself and fell in line with the NAACP's position on the Thomas nomination.

Immediately after the announcement of the board's actions, I hit the road. There were a number of major black organizational conventions being held. Here, I reasoned, was an opportunity for me to reach a large number of opinion shapers in the black community. I spoke to the National Baptist Convention, the Progressive National Baptist Convention, and the National Bar Association, just to mention a few. I appeared on "The Oprah Winfrey Show," "Crossfire," NBC, CBS, and ABC news broadcasts, and made clear the reasons for our opposition to the Thomas nomination. I met personally with denominational leaders of church groups, heads of civil and human rights groups and associations, and community leaders across the country. In less than three weeks, I traveled over 55,000 miles, criss-crossing the nation to build opposition to the Thomas nomination.

Meanwhile, a concerted effort was being made to give the impression that the NAACP was out of step with the majority of African Americans. News polls indicated strong support of the Thomas nomination among blacks. Black conservatives appearing nightly on TV and radio programs excoriated the NAACP for its position on the nomination.

By the time the Senate Judiciary Committee convened in September, the stage had been set for one of the most bitter confirmation fights in America's history. The NAACP, joined by a number of other groups, including the Congressional Black Caucus, the Progressive National Baptist Convention, the AFL-CIO, the National Organization for Women, the Leadership Conference on Civil Rights, and others, opposed the Thomas nomination. Meanwhile, the Bush Administration had pulled out all stops to garner support for Thomas. The Urban League had taken no position, or abstained on the nomination. The Southern Christian Leadership Conference had announced its support of Thomas.

After the hearings began, it became clear that the Thomas nomination was in deep trouble. Of particular concern were his speeches and writings that showed an insensitivity to civil rights, to women's rights, and to the role of government in redressing problems faced by those who have been left out of the mainstream of American life for whatever reason.

On September 20, 1991, I walked into the ornate U.S. Senate Judiciary Committee hearing room in the Capitol Building, took my seat at the witness table, and in the full glare of the battery of TV lights, began to testify. My testimony stated:

In a purely narrow sense, the immediate business before the Committee is the nomination of Judge Clarence Thomas to be an Associate Justice of the Supreme Court. But, in the broader sweep of our domestic history, there is actually at hand a unique, transcendent moment that will significantly define America in our time—what America is; what America can be; what America shall be.

A quarter century ago, when Thurgood Marshall assumed the powerful position of a Supreme Court Justice, our hearts were thrilled and our spirits came alive in renewed hope. We believed then that we were at long last witnessing an epic transfiguration; that out of the bloody trench of collective struggle, a fellow child of bondage would help light our future with the glow of progress and the fine golden flame of human freedom. Thurgood Marshall came to personify, around the globe, an America in which liberty could be something greater than a utopian abstraction; and in which God-given freedom might someday be ours as a bedrock right, not as a conditional dispensation of privilege or majority factor. We were neither disappointed nor betrayed.

As vividly etched in the chronicles of this anguished nation, 20 generations of African Americans cried aloud vainly for the simple, decent entitlements of free men and women, and for the honest protection of the law in securing a host of the most elemental civil rights. Even in the Congress of the United States, and for one and a half centuries, this nation's people of color were an inferior and inconvenient exception to America's universal proclamation of personal freedom, of equality of opportunity, and of individual worth. We were weary; we despaired. But with an abiding faith in the American promise, we did not quit. We believed that written promise, etched by the pen of Thomas Jefferson— "We hold these truths to be self-evident, that all men are created equal"—perhaps as no other people have believed. We kept the faith. We soldiered on.

Little more than 35 years ago, Thurgood Marshall stood before this very tribunal he would later come to enrich personally, and he once again demanded for us no less, but no more, than the precise measure of the Constitution afforded all other American citizens. In the face of his eloquence, and after 150 shameful years, the Supreme Court gently yielded. Suddenly, the long, tortuous nightmare of legalized bigotry and degradation seemed—at last— to be in potential retreat.

We do not speak here of ancient folklore, but of a fractious period of time entirely within the lifetime of Judge Thomas, whose nomination to the Supreme Court we must firmly resist. The NAACP did not come to its opposition lightly, or even recently. When Judge Thomas was nominated to chair the Equal Employment Opportunity Commission, we opposed his confirmation. When Judge Thomas thereafter proved not to be a champion of equal rights at the EEOC, but hostile to the aspirations of a desperate minority, we asked for his resignation. We neither opposed nor supported his confirmation to the Appellate Court, but hoped this would have permitted him to create a record in the independence of the federal judgeship upon which he could be evaluated if he were ever nominated to the Supreme Court. We noted at the time that if he became a nominee for the Supreme Court, we would vigorously re-examine his record. His tenure on the Appellate Court has been too brief to add substantively to his record.

Judge Thomas has declared, time and time again, that he does not support the civil rights concept of affirmative action. Congress supports affirmative action; the federal courts have long supported affirmative action; and the polls show that the great majority of the American people likewise support reasonable affirmative action programs. Even the current Administration says it supports the crucial tenets of affirmative action—but not Judge Thomas. He opposes it.

As every member of this committee knows very well, affirmative action is a moderate, time-tested mechanism that seeks to ensure that all persons are at least given earnest consideration in such critical matters as school admissions and employment positions. Affirmative action is, and for the last 25 years has been, a strong, unwavering national policy of inclusion in the vital pursuit of everyday necessities: a home, an education, a job, a promotion. In other words, all that affirmative action requires is a fair break. It is not a quota system. In fact, it guards sharply against a quota system, in which minority and female aspirants are passed by, or passed over, merely because of their race or sex. Senators, these are the most fundamental guarantees of the American Constitution, and yet Judge Thomas has consistently expounded his steadfast opposition.

We are particularly concerned by Judge Thomas's opposition to class-based remedies for discrimination against African Americans. Our experience, over a long period of time, has conclusively demonstrated that dealing with discrimination on an individual basis cannot possibly erase systematic and endemic discrimination. Under Judge Thomas's approach, the tree of discrimination would never be uprooted. Instead, we would spend decades clipping off individual branches, while the tree grows taller.

Despite Judge Thomas's compelling personal story, the fact of the matter is that most black Americans over the age of 40 have faced the perils of discrimination and segregation prejudice, and millions of black Americans could attest to their rise above these obstacles. To that extent, Judge Thomas's story is not an exception but rather the rule.

It should be noted that experiences in and of themselves are neutral. What really matters are the lessons that are learned from these experiences. In the case of Judge Thomas, we do not question the fact that he has been a victim of poverty and discrimination. We do believe, however, that Judge Thomas learned the wrong lessons from those experiences—which is that although he has been the beneficiary of affirmative action and self-help, others only need a level playing field to achieve.

Unfortunately, despite protestations to the contrary, this is not a color-blind society. It is therefore obvious to us that it is impossible to eradicate race-caused conditions without taking race into account. As Justice Blackman stated in the *Bakke* case, "In order to get beyond racism, we must first take racism into account."

It is ironic, but from the record, Judge Thomas has not expressed opposition to affirmative action for veterans, or for the sons and daughters of wealthy alumni in college admissions programs, or through FHA and allied programs for middle-class homeowners. The only form of affirmative action that he opposes is that for African Americans.

For these reasons, in the strong interest of all Americans, we have put reason above race, principle above pigmentation, and conscience above color. We urge the members of the United States Senate to exercise their advise and consent authority by rejecting this nomination.

Following the testimony of supporters and opponents of Thomas, the committee voted to send the nomination to the full Senate with no recommendation. Almost immediately after the vote, the Anita Hill 10-year-old charge of sexual misconduct surfaced. Women's groups and opponents of the Thomas nomination attacked the Senate Judiciary Committee for not taking seriously the charges made by Professor Hill, who had worked with Thomas during his tenure as Assistant Secretary of Education and for a brief period during his tenure as the EEOC chairman.

Committee Chairman Joseph Biden of Delaware set into motion an extraordinary session of the committee to hear the charges. The nation was gripped by the specter of allegations by Hill and denials by Thomas of any misconduct.

On October 15, 1991, the full Senate acted upon the Thomas nomination. As the roll was called, each senator voted as the nation watched. When the roll call was completed, Clarence Thomas was confirmed as an Associate Justice by a vote of 52-48, thus becoming only the second African American to sit on the U.S. Supreme Court.

That same day, I issued the official statement for the Association. That statement read in part:

Now that the Senate has voted to confirm Judge Thomas as an Associate Justice of the Supreme Court, the NAACP expresses the hope that the weight and consciousness of his new responsibilities will lead him to revisit his views on a number of important issues. Like so many of our fellow Americans, we are impressed with Judge Thomas's odyssey from poverty to prominence. At the same time, we are ever mindful that Judge Thomas is not unique in his accomplishments—his story is a common occurrence in the black community. As a member of the High Court, we hope Justice Thomas will recall the people and the community that nurtured him—that he will recall his own struggle to overcome poverty and racism and, in so doing, will exhibit a sensitivity toward moving America to the place where all of us can enjoy full benefits of constitutional equality.

Chapter 26
THE RODNEY KING VERDICTS

On the night of March 3, 1991, a black motorist was chased, stopped, and brutally beaten by at least four police officers while he lay helpless on the ground. He was arrested and charged with a series of felonies by the police. Nothing was new about this development; after all, this scene was repeated on a daily basis in communities around the nation. There was, however, a difference this time. A concerned citizen had videotaped the whole incident. The video clearly showed that the Los Angeles police officers involved had engaged in criminal assault. They had used unnecessary and excessive force on Rodney King, who was seen lying on the ground attempting to fend off the repeated blows from the police batons.

African Americans have complained for decades about the excessive use of force and criminal assault by the police in cities, towns, and rural areas. Hardly a black living in this country does not know at least one person who claims to have been criminally assaulted by police who were sworn to protect them. I heard stories when I was growing up in Memphis about policemen who actually killed blacks and were never brought to justice. I knew from my experience as a public defender and a judge that policemen often engaged in brutality because of racism and because they knew that they could get away with it. My years of work in the civil rights arena had made it abundantly clear that police brutality was pervasive throughout the country, not just in the South. Rarely could a policeman be convicted, because they were part of an oppressive system made up of fellow officers, prosecutors, and judges who saw this as a way of doing business.

The Los Angeles Police Department had a reputation for being particularly brutal and racist. Blacks and Latinos bore the brunt of this hostility. The blue wall of silence could not be easily penetrated; police routinely fabricated stories and manufactured evidence where necessary. In 1965, the Watts riots resulted from the sense of black citizens that the primarily white police force functioned as an occupying army rather than as protectors. The same sense of bigotry was present in Detroit and Newark in 1967, when deadly riots broke out. The Miami riots in 1980 were a textbook case of police oppression leading to urban eruptions by those who felt that violence was the only way to cast off the oppressive yoke.

I hasten to add that most police officers in 1991 were basically honest and saw their mission as protecting the citizens in the jurisdictions where they worked. But there is always a core cadre of belligerent officers who saw their badges as a license to dispense justice as they saw fit and their gun as an instrument to carry out the sentence that they had individually determined in their minds. There is no definitive study published that gives a percentage or number of officers who are racist and relish the notion of brutalizing citizens. I believe that the percentage is small, but the so-called code of silence engulfs a far larger percentage who merely go along with wrongdoing and perjury.

Los Angeles had as its police chief a man whose spoken words and actions made him particularly repugnant to minorities and civil libertarians. Chief Darryl Gates was a throwback to the old Bull Connor days. He permitted violations by his subordinates that would not be tolerated by police chiefs in many jurisdictions. Following the beating of Rodney King, Chief Gates went out of his way to defend the officers involved against the indefensible. He tried to get the public to believe that Rodney King was resisting arrest when he put his arms over his head while lying on the ground to protect himself against the blows raining down on him by a phalanx of helmeted policemen.

When I first saw the clip of the Rodney King video on the evening news, I said to myself, this is a clear-cut case of the police going wild. I thought that no one who saw the film I saw could conclude otherwise. How wrong I was. I had handled a number of cases as a public defender where blacks were beaten by policemen and charged with assault and resisting arrest. These are catch-all charges that are difficult to disprove, especially when the only witnesses one had were fellow blacks, or people who some might think had a vested interest in coming to the defense of the victim. But here we had incontrovertible proof in a running videotape taken by a white man who did not know the victim or have any ax to grind with the police department. There is a Latin expression I learned in law school that summed up my feelings: *Res ipsa loquitor*—the thing speaks for itself.

When the trial began, I had ambivalent feelings about the ultimate outcome. First, the trial was moved to Simi Valley where an all-white jury was seated to hear the case. Second, a public relations campaign evolved that was designed to demonize Rodney King. His previous arrest record was used to justify the violence against him. The Los Angeles Police Department defenders and spin doctors went to work. Next, defense lawyers for the four officers tried to portray every defense movement by Rodney King, lying on the ground being beaten nearly to death, as an act of aggression. You learn after practicing law for years that juries can do strange things with what you believe to be a slam-dunk case.

I followed the trial of the officers with keen interest, as a former trial lawyer, trial judge, and as a civil rights leader. I knew that there would be an explosion of anger by the black community if for some reason the police were acquitted. If a jury could not convict, they reasoned, with evidence of criminal misconduct caught on videotape, the system was incorrigible. Hopelessness breeds contempt. Many white supporters and detractors alike cannot identify with this, because they have never had to think and act in ways that African Americans have had to in responding to law enforcement. We have had completely different experiences in dealing with those assigned to protect us.

When the trial phase was over and the jury began to deliberate, I was hoping against hope that somehow even this all-white jury could put itself in Rodney King's place. How would they feel if they had been speeding and the police made an attempt to stop them? Suppose they panicked and tried to outrun the police because they had an expired license, registration, or insurance card? Once stopped, they were ordered to lie on the ground and the police began to brutally beat them as other officers stood by doing nothing to help them. How in the name of God could they allow the perpetrators of this wanton, inhumane act to not be held accountable for their actions?

Instinctively I knew that many black Americans had come to see the Rodney King incident, and not Rodney King, as a test for our legal system. If justice as they saw it—the conviction of the four charged officers—could not be assured by videotapes clearly showing the police were out of control, then what would it take to get justice? An acquittal would reinforce the cynicism that abounds in our communities across the nation.

I have always abhorred violence. Violence, as Dr. King taught, is self-defeating. Our communities are the ones that are destroyed in urban riots; our inhabitants are the ones who will be arrested; our young men are the ones killed; and our children will witness the tragedy of man's inhumanity to man.

There was also the likelihood that angry young men would use the verdict as an excuse to engage in criminal activities that would jeopardize the lives of innocent black people. How about the seniors who have invested all of their savings in houses that would be burned or, after a riot, prove to be "unsellable"? The prospect of an acquittal was repugnant to me for these and other reasons.

I was out of town on a fund-raising trip when the not-guilty verdict was read in open court. When I heard the news I was stunned and numbed. I called the office and spoke to Jimmy Williams, my director of public relations. Jimmy was a veteran of many battles. He had been a reporter for the *Afro-American Newspaper*, served as public relations director at the National Urban League under Vernon Jordan, and was doing a splendid job for us at the Association for almost six years. Jimmy agreed with me that we had to issue a statement immediately condemning the verdict and calling for reason and restraint on the part of those who, like us, were disappointed. Within the hour, I called Jimmy back and dictated to him some ideas that I had scribbled on the back of some airline tickets.

Approximately 30 minutes later we had a final draft ready for release to the major news outlets. One of the strengths of the NAACP was our ability to respond to emergency and unanticipated situations. We were institutionally proactive as well as reactive. That is the nature of the civil rights struggle. We issued the following statement on April 29, 1992:

Statement by Benjamin L. Hooks, Executive Director/CEO, NAACP on Innocent Verdicts in the Rodney King Case

The gross injustice done by the jury in the Rodney King case ranks in infamy with that handed down in the Scottsboro Boys case of the 1930s, in which an all-white jury convicted nine innocent black boys of rape. The all-white jury has in effect said the brutal beating of Rodney King, seen by millions on videotape, was justifiable and all the officers involved acted properly.

We see little difference in injustices perpetrated against human decency in both instances. The not-guilty verdicts in the King case are outrageous, a mockery of justice. Clearly, they send an inviting sign to the other law enforcement officers so inclined, that anything goes in the name of law enforcement.

Given the evidence, it is difficult to see how the jurors will ever live with their consciences. African Americans and many others are grieved by the inexplicable miscarriage of justice that will reinforce the belief there is a double standard of justice when race enters the picture.

We are convinced that the change of venue that produced an all-white jury, and Mr. King's race, were major factors in the acquittals.

We are bitter and disappointed at the outcome, but we urge that the decision be met with calmness. Any anger felt should be directed into constructive channels, such as we have done by holding a series of public hearings to compile information on the status of relations between the African-American community and the police.

These hearings were held toward the end of last year in six cities—Norfolk, Miami, Houston, Los Angeles, St. Louis, and Indianapolis. From the information gathered, we, with the cooperation of experts at Harvard University and the University of Massachusetts, are preparing our findings, conclusions, and recommendations. We will have a preliminary report ready by midsummer, with the final report to follow in short order.

Our initial assessment is that there is a towering wall of distrust between African-American citizens and the police, built in large measure by the historical mistreatment of the former by the latter.

The King verdicts will certainly increase the height of that wall.

Within minutes after the verdicts were announced, tensions exploded in the South Central section of Los Angeles. South Central is composed primarily of working-class, minority residents. A majority of them are black and Hispanic. It is one of the poorest areas of Los Angeles, with few amenities and poor government services. Unemployment is the highest in the city and the schools are the worst, with the lowest graduation rates. Beverly Hills is as far from South Central Los Angeles, culturally and economically, as is Sarajevo. The glitz and glamour of Hollywood were in stark contrast to the poverty and despair that reign supreme in South Central.

This was the area hit hardest by the riot. There was some damage in the downtown area and some scattered rioting in other sections of the city, but by and large it was restricted to the African-American and Hispanic communities.

The riots in Los Angeles mirrored the social and political pathology of Miami, where the black areas known as Liberty City and Overtown had poor economic conditions and police tactics that were contributing factors to the domestic disorders. The Kerner Commission report in 1968 had set forth the formula for disaster, and the NAACP's report published in 1981 made clear that perceived and real abuses by police officers were the elements that ignited the 1980 Miami riots.

The first night of the riots, April 29, 1992, I watched the television coverage of billowing smoke and leaping flames against the dark night. Police sirens were wailing frantically, emergency vehicles were making their trips to emergency rooms carrying the injured, and police officers crouched behind cars and police vehicles. If one did not know better, one would think that the broadcast was originating from Beirut, Lebanon, not an American city. It was surreal and scary.

That night I called members of my senior staff and asked them to give some thought to what steps the Association could take to address the underlying issues and to expedite the end to the violence then taking place in Los Angeles. By this time, I had assembled an outstanding staff. Many were veteran civil rights advocates who had years of experience in the struggle. Others had come from allied organizations and institutions. Unfortunately, most of the staff was not widely known outside of the civil rights community. They were a multifaceted and multitalented group.

While I made my way back to Baltimore, where we were headquartered, they were meeting at the National Office: Jimmy Williams, director of public relations; Jerry Guess, director of communications and policy; Walter Morrison, director of research and a writer for *The Crisis* magazine; John Johnson, who was serving as my executive assistant as well as labor director; William Penn, director of branches and field services; Beverly Cole, director of education; Howard Henderson, director of administration and finance; Aileen James, director of our Back-to-School program; Wade Henderson, director of our Washington Bureau; and Mildred Bond Roxborough, who participated by phone.

When I walked into the office, the meeting had just broken up. It was quickly reconvened, and I received the following recommendations of the senior staff:

1. I should call the President to request a meeting to discuss the Rodney King case and the facts surrounding it.
2. I should urge the president to address the nation and call for calm and recommend the strengthening of U.S. Federal Civil Rights statutes.
3. I should go to Los Angeles to participate in the community rally and call a black community leadership meeting.
4. Call for a national day of outrage to be held on Sunday, May 3, 1992, across the country. There were to be communitywide services held in churches and community centers.
6. NAACP units should push immediately for the establishment of civilian police review boards.

After a spirited discussion, I decided that we would go through with the outlined plan. However, I added a few elements. We would meet with Mayor Thomas Bradley to determine what the city's priorities were in bringing about order and to ascertain what help he needed in securing assistance from Governor Wilson and the Bush Administration. Then we would meet with Governor Wilson to follow up on the requests of Mayor Bradley.

We made a call to the White House. The President was tied up in a meeting, so I spoke to his chief of staff, John Sununu. I was assured that President Bush would call back shortly. We resumed our discussion in a general way, exploring a series of alternatives in the event that one of the elements of our plan did not materialize or proved to be unworkable.

Approximately 10 minutes had elapsed when the telephone rang. It was the White House operator—the President was calling. People often underestimate the importance and the power the NAACP had amassed over the years. This was due to the organization's reputation for integrity and its historical nonpartisan posture. I had known President Bush since his days as chairman of the National Republican Committee. During his tenure as vice president, we had a number of meetings in which we discussed a wide range of topics. When he was elected, we met and talked on a number of occasions. He was always polite to a fault. He was one of those politicians who told you what he was thinking and what he could or could not do.

Moments later, there was that familiar voice on the phone saying, in his New England accent, "Hi, Ben. How's Frances doing?" After a little more small talk, I got to the points that I had called to discuss with him. I let him know that I was shocked and dismayed by the verdicts in the

Rodney King case. I told him that something had to be done by the national government to assure the American people that this miscarriage of justice was not sanctioned by respectable Americans, who were basically a decent people.

The President assured me that there had been many cases where juries had made mistakes, some honest and others based on their biases. He agreed to go before the nation to speak out against the evils of bigotry and the need for Americans at all levels to become less tolerant of any form of discrimination. He also agreed to consult with top-level representatives from the Administration to decide what could be done to help those who had been the victims of the riot, and to see if it was possible to have the U.S. Department of Justice bring violation of civil rights charges against the four acquitted police officers. He asked me to have my staff provide him with some language that we felt would be useful if included in his national remarks. I told him that we would have some suggestions faxed to him by 3 P.M. that day. It was a little before noon when we spoke.

After a little over five minutes, our conversation came to an end. I thanked the President and asked him to give Barbara our regards. The work necessary to carry out our ambitious task was daunting. We had to bring staff and allies up to date and make appointments with Governor Pete Wilson and Mayor Tom Bradley's offices. We had to make travel and hotel arrangements for the staff who would join us. We also had to mobilize the religious community and get back with the President in less than three hours with suggested language for inclusion in his address to the nation that evening. I organized the staff into task forces to accomplish these goals.

We had a small staff. I know that when people thought of the national NAACP, they assumed that we had a staff of hundreds. That has never been the case. In most cases, a department consisted of the director and a secretary. We had an inside joke that we used to tell friends and supporters: "We have done so much, with so little, for so long, that now people expect us to do everything with nothing." Here we were, once again, having taken on a tremendous challenge with very few staff members and severely limited financial resources. We had depth, a branch structure, and hundreds of thousands of members, lawyers on retainer in countless cities, and a track record for following up on our announced positions and planned activities.

That afternoon we called every regional director and gave them a briefing of what we planned and the help that we needed from them. We asked them to notify their branches, youth units, and college chapters to organize a "National Day for Justice" on Sunday May 3, 1992. I spent hours on the phone talking with my colleagues in the Leadership Conference on Civil Rights and the Black Leadership Forum, and with members of the NAACP's National Board and the Special Contribution Fund (SCF) Board of Trustees.

We worked at breakneck speed, each person carrying out his assignment. What was truly refreshing and uplifting to me was the manner in which my staff pitched in and helped each other. Gone were the pettiness and the office politics that are part and parcel of any office. We were one—all working on the same page. For the next few weeks, the entire staff functioned as a well-oiled machine. It reminded me of earlier days in the movement, when Jesse Turner and Maxine Smith and I were leading demonstrations in Memphis, or when Dr. King was leading demonstrations in Alabama or Mississippi. The Rodney King verdict had an unexpected consequence of bringing us together in an unusual way. I can honestly say I did not speak to one person who expressed opposition to what was planned, or who gave any indication that they would be less than totally cooperative with the effort.

We sent out 500 telegrams to key NAACP branches, advising them that Sunday, May 3, would be a "National Day of Concern," and set into motion meetings with the governor of California and the mayor of Los Angeles. Meanwhile, our Washington Bureau moved full speed ahead pressing for the enactment of every pending piece of legislation dealing with police brutality and job creation programs. Our Legal Department worked in conjunction with the Bureau to ascertain what state laws we could pass that dealt with police excesses.

On Friday, May 1, I left for Washington to appear on CBS's *Street Scenes* and for an hour-long telecast on BET. The next morning I appeared on *Good Morning, America*, and made the scheduled 9:30 A.M. meeting at the White House. This was a meeting with the President and key black leaders to discuss the Los Angeles crisis. I served as the spokesman for the group.

At the meeting with President Bush, I insisted that there be immediate proceedings to deal with the officers involved in the beating of Rodney King under federal law, Title 18, Sections 241, 242. Afterward, the entire group of black leaders unanimously endorsed the idea. The President announced later that night that he was asking the Justice Department to pursue that option. Later that day I appeared on *Crossfire*, C-Span, and then ABC, where I was interviewed by Peter Jennings. The press was very interested in the threat of further outbreaks of violence in other communities. I made it clear that black America was not interested in reacting violently to the King verdicts. The major concern of black America was the reform of a justice system that made the verdicts possible.

On May 3, I left for Los Angeles. A special NAACP task force had already arrived in the city. The group consisted of Jerry Guess, Howard Henderson, Jimmy Williams, William Penn, John Johnson, and Kip Branch. They had assessed the work that needed to be done, arranged for the meetings with the governor and the mayor, and organized meetings with the local black community, as well as the religious and political communities. We already had in Los Angeles our regional director, Shannon Reeves; our West Coast legal counsel, Nyisha Shakur; Ernestine Peters, our West Coast membership coordinator; and Pailanta Rieout-Hairston of our Los Angeles office. We received invaluable volunteer assistance from board members John Mance and Jose DeSosa. Joe Duff, an outstanding civil rights lawyer and the local branch president, was also on hand to help. We had the support of all the black elected officials in California. They answered every call, and we worked with the other major civil rights groups in the area.

Shortly after I arrived in Los Angeles, we met with Los Angeles Mayor Thomas Bradley. Mayor Bradley, the first African-American mayor of Los Angeles, had done an outstanding job in opening up opportunities for minorities and women. He was a popular elected official who was still basking in the afterglow of one of the most successful Olympics in modern history. An extremely competent and sensitive man, Mayor Bradley gave us an overview of the efforts that the city had made. He also offered us the help of his staff in our efforts to redress the grievances of local residents.

Later that evening we met with Governor Pete Wilson. The governor brought with him to the meeting a number of staff persons who had responsibilities for a variety of state departments. He was, like Mayor Bradley, extremely cooperative and helpful. Governor Wilson understood clearly that the problem in South Central Los Angeles—as well as in other areas of the state—went well beyond the Rodney King verdicts. Economic deprivation and poor educational opportunities had to be addressed. He advised us that he was working closely with Mayor Bradley to get an infusion of state funds to help in South Central. We agreed that we would explore a number of economic development possibilities, which we did in the ensuing months.

The next day, we held a series of well-attended meetings with the leaders of our 27 NAACP branches in the Los Angeles area. We also took an extensive tour of the riot-torn areas. The fires had completely devastated huge tracts. Many local grocery stores and strip malls where food could be purchased were now ashes.

The NAACP's WIN Program (Women In the NAACP), headed by my wife, Frances, had undertaken a project to secure food and supplies for many of the riot victims who were left homeless or unemployed by the devastation in South Central. They managed, in a short period of time, to have two 16-wheel trailer loads of supplies on the spot. We delivered the supplies to First African Methodist Episcopal Church and Second Baptist Church. Both of these black congregations had emergency relief efforts in place and a distribution network. There was enough food and other emergency supplies on the trucks to take care of the basic needs of 1,000 families for two weeks.

On Tuesday, May 5, we were again engulfed in meetings with a number of politicians and Administration officials, who by now had arrived on the scene. Among them were Jack Kemp, Secretary of HUD; Arkansas' Governor Bill Clinton; U.S. Representative Maxine Waters; and state Senator Diane Watson. Later that evening we were in Sacramento, where we met with our local NAACP leadership.

The next morning, I met with the Speaker of the California Legislature, Willie Brown. I also met with the members of the California Legislative Black Caucus. Later that morning, Speaker Brown introduced me to the State Assembly. Willie Brown was absolutely superb in his leadership in this matter. As was his usual custom, he was well informed and well prepared, and moved with energy and enthusiasm.

We had planned a demonstration, a march to the State Capitol Building, for Thursday, May 7. We had less than a week to plan this event, but we felt that it was necessary to have a public outpouring of support for the end of police brutality. We had given serious thought to having the march in Los Angeles, but the climate there was far too volatile for a public demonstration. To change the entrenched police force of Los Angeles—and its Police Chief Gates—would require outside intervention. So we went to the seat of power in California.

The morning of the march was bright and clear, with a cloudless sky. The conditions were ideal for an outdoor protest. The mood of the marchers was one of determination. The march was not just to protest the Rodney King verdicts, but for dignity and justice. There were people from all over the state—civil rights activists, religious leaders, labor leaders, and others from all walks of life—who joined in. We marched about a mile and a half to the Capitol Building. There were more than 20,000 people, black and white, young and old, and even some in wheelchairs.

When we reached the stage, I could see the thousands of people who by now had filled the Capitol Mall area. It was a beautiful sight. Following the invocation by the Reverend Yardley N. Griffith, of the Greater Faith Baptist Church in Sacramento, and the statement of purpose by Dr. Willie Ellison, president of the NAACP's Sacramento branch, Willie Brown, Speaker of the Assembly of California, reminded the marchers of the seriousness of the injustice in the King decision.

"Blind bigotry begets blind rage. They're one and the same, and they have no place in society. There must never again be an opportunity for a Rodney King case to happen," he said.

California Assemblyman Art Torres assailed the Bush Administration and its policies, and also called for a revamping of the Los Angeles Police Department.

"We're never going to give up the fight for justice," he said, referring to the verdicts in the King case. "This state must not be ruled by police officers; this state must be ruled by justice. This isn't a white, yellow, black or red California—this is our California."

An especially moving part of the program occurred when Carisha Ables, president of the Sacramento NAACP Youth Council, told the audience that what she had witnessed in the King beating had diminished her faith in America's system of justice.

"I don't understand how anyone can be beaten like that," she said, fighting back tears. "Society has compromised our civil rights," she added. Still, she said that "it is up to today's young people to lead the fight for justice. The youth who marched today will carry on," Ables said. "Youth led this assemblage, and we will lead you to the right place."

Marcia Levy of the American Civil Liberties Union credited the NAACP with being in the forefront of the efforts to remove Los Angeles Police Chief Gates from his position, and she said that no longer can the police not be held to the same standards as ordinary citizens. "We cannot allow the police to continue policing themselves," Levy said. "We want police review boards now."

Donald Northcross, deputy sheriff of the California Black Deputy Sheriffs' Association, told the crowd that African-American police officers have a special role to play in changing the perception of African-American police officers in light of the turmoil that occurred in Los Angeles. "If we are ever to effect change, we must get inside the system," Deputy Northcross said. "Now is the time for African-American officers to become more visible in the African-American community in a positive way."

Then came my time to speak. I knew that I was speaking to two audiences—those who were assembled at the State Capitol and a wider national audience. It was important that I call the attention of the nation to the fact that the Rodney King verdicts were the catalyst that brought us together, but the systemic causes of the problem were racism, economic deprivation, and injustice. We had to address these issues openly and honestly if our society was ever to be healed. With that in mind, I delivered the following address:

We come today to Sacramento, to the seat of government of the Golden State of California, to raise our voices and to express our outrage at what has become a national pattern and practice of injustice in this nation. We come not merely to speak to the obvious injustice in the Rodney King case, but to express our consternation at the hundreds and thousands of instances, not recorded on videotape, where those who are sworn to uphold the law see themselves as an army of occupation operating under the codes of war and not the rule of law.

We come to Sacramento today in the tradition of peaceful protest, which has been the hallmark of the civil rights movement, amidst the simmering smoke springing from the ashes of the massive devastation that has engulfed much of the city of Los Angeles.

We come to Sacramento to share the grief of the more than 50 families who lost loved ones, those who this week are burying their dead—to say that we care. In the words of John Donne, "... the death of any man diminishes me .... Never send to know for whom the bell tolls; it tolls for thee."

There are those who ask the question today, why do we march? We march in the tradition of the nonviolent movement to raise the consciousness of the American people and to call on our beloved nation to confront the pressing urgency of the moment and to bring about much-needed change before it is too late.

We march today because for too long the voices of reason and the shrill cries for help from those trapped in the countless cycles of poverty, despair, and hopelessness have not been heard.

Why do we march? We march because there exists today in our land the notion on the part of many (in the words of the *Dred Scott* decision) that blacks have no rights that whites are bound to respect. The mentality of racists and bigots in Selma, Alabama, in 1965 are echoing today in Simi Valley, California.

We march because we are fully aware of the fact that despite the momentary concerns expressed by the media with the plight of the poor and oppressed and those left out of the sunlight of opportunity, soon the smoke will clear up; soon the debris from the senseless rioting will be swept up; soon the TV cameras will withdraw from Los Angeles's inner city; soon the news reporter will be off on some other mission; and those who are trapped by a vicious cycle of poverty will become yesterday's news and a concern of a bygone time.

We march today to say by our presence that we cannot afford to accept a "business as usual" posture. We simply will not accept the continuing saga of joblessness, crime, police brutality, and the rampant destruction of the aspirations of so many of our young people.

We march to tell Chief Gates in 1992, as we told Chief Bull Connor in the '60s, that we shall not tolerate the mentality and the mind-set that says that it is permissible for law enforcement officers to beat African Americans with impunity and to treat us with disdain, contempt, and utter disrespect.

We march to say to the status quo that while we were appalled by the violence which followed the verdicts in the Rodney King case, while we have condemned the lawlessness and wanton disregard for life and property from day one as being self-defeating, senseless, and inexcusable, we are cognizant that there exists another form of violence that we find equally repulsive and revolting. It is the violence that so many of our people face every day of their lives. I am talking about the violence of the economic looting of our communities by those who reap the benefits, but do not reinvest in our community or show respect for our people.

I am talking about political violence by politicians, both Democrats and Republicans, who come into our communities, sing "We Shall Overcome" in our churches, and express concern for our needs, pick up our votes, and forget about those who are like boats stuck on the bottom until the next campaign for office. The looters of the trust of those who possess so little hope are no better than the thugs and malevolent individuals who sacked stores in Los Angeles.

I am talking about the educational violence against so many of our young people who must attend overcrowded classes, be taught by inexperienced and underpaid teachers who, in many instances, do not believe that these young can be taught or that they are capable of learning.

Yes, my friends, there other forms of violence that are just as pernicious, just as devastating, and just as rampant as the looting, the killings, and the burnings that we abhorred in Los Angeles last week.

Why do we march? We march to say to the members of the California State Legislature that they must reject the "rogue cop protection bill," AB 2067. This frightening piece of legislation introduced by Gardena's assemblyman, Richard Floyd, gives law enforcement officers the right to refuse to answer any question that might lead to disciplinary actions. Even officers who are not targets of investigations but who witnessed misconduct or have information about fellow officers could not be required to answer questions.

If enacted, this bill would encourage the code of silence and give law enforcement officers rights not accorded to the ordinary citizen. If enacted, this bill would be a license for law enforcement officials to obstruct justice.

We march to support Charter Amendment F, a part of the Christopher Commission reforms that limits the term of the L.A. Police Chief and would create much-needed checks and balances—thereby making the chief of police a public servant, not a lifetime, Old West-style public tyrant.

We march in solidarity with our brothers and sisters, black, white, yellow, red, and brown, those who have known no peace, those who struggle from day to day for the basic necessities of life. We march for the basic necessities of life. We march for those who cannot find the dignity of work, a basic job from which self-respect and self-esteem are enhanced and spirits lifted; those who are unskilled, through no fault of their own; those who live in substandard housing; and those who are homeless.

We march in solidarity with those who hold two part-time jobs and yet can't afford health care insurance for their families; those who have been laid off and cannot afford to take their children to see a doctor; those who live on a battlefield of our nation's streets every day which are more dangerous than the terrain on which our troops who served in Operation Desert Storm fought and died. We march for those who must live in the shadows of the sale of crack and other drugs; those who hear daily the sounds of gang weapons being fired; and those who have already attended too many funerals of our young children. We march to say to our brothers and sisters trapped in the prison of drugs—don't give up hope, don't give up dignity. We say to those embroiled in violence end crime, or crippled by ill health, don't give up hope, don't give up dignity.

We march to say we cannot let dope, violence, crime, and poor health destroy us, even as we struggle against racism. We must call on the strengths within to push us forward.

We march to say to our leaders of government, at all levels, that the time has passed for the hurling of the Molotov cocktails or the incendiary rhetoric of blame and recrimination. The time has passed for tired old excuses for ignoring the plight of those who are caught in the valleys of poverty, and ignorance, and despair.

We march to send a message to Marlin Fitzwater that we do not believe for a single moment that the programs of the Great Society had anything at all to do with the disorders in Los Angeles or any other place.

This charge turns the truth on its head; makes day into night; rewrites history.

It is not enough to talk about the national debt or the current deficit. If we can find hundreds of billions of dollars to bail out the savings and loans fleeced by the greed of the rich and the infamous, if we can afford to grant credits to the former Soviet Republics, if we can afford to spend billions to defend the Emir in Kuwait and the oil sheiks of the Mideast, why can't we afford to invest the money necessary to rebuild our nation's cities, to ensure adequate education for our young, health care for the more than 37 million people who do not have health insurance, and job opportunities for the millions of unemployed citizens in this land?

Unless America deals with these problems soon, she will have spent her valuable capital of good will, she will have exhausted her deep wells of the patience of her people, and like those who once yearned for freedom behind the iron curtain, those so long oppressed, they will rise up and revolt, and our system of government as we know it today might be in jeopardy.

There simply must be justice and opportunity for all or there will be justice and opportunity for none. Our courts must protect the powerless as well as the powerful if respect for the judicial system is to survive. Law enforcement officers must themselves obey the laws that they have sworn to uphold. To that end, we will demand the development of civilian police review boards in every city where there are none—to strengthen those that do exist.

We will also insist that every police jurisdiction in the country implement psychological screening for all prospective employees, and periodically screen those on duty.

We will also demand that all police training include sensitivity training, and that there be more racial, ethnic, and sexual diversity on police forces.

We are glad to note that the Attorney General appears to be moving forward by invoking Title 18, Section 241-242 of the Federal Code to ensure that the officers in the Rodney King case face the possibility of federal charges. We are insisting that this be done. We must realize that the statutes in question were enacted over 100 years ago to deal with just this type of situation where the state refused to render just verdicts.

We come, finally, to give voice to the millions marooned in the distressed and dying communities across America, white and black, red, brown, and yellow. We speak on behalf of those muted by lost hope and the lack of opportunity, for the 30 million Americans mired in poverty, by our own government's count. We come to speak for those struggling to make it against the odds. We cannot solve our problems as a nation by building more jail cells at the cost of $150,000 per cell, and spend up to $25,000 to keep a man in jail. We must expand the educational horizons of our young, rebuild the wastelands that are our urban centers—and let them know that they count, that their future matters. We must expand our economic base and provide jobs for every man and woman in this nation seeking employment.

America, now is the time to stand up and throw off the yoke of bankrupted policies, worn-out slogans, and racial, group, and class divisiveness.

Now is the time to focus our primary attention on Los Angeles, not the Russian Republic; San Francisco, not the Middle East; Sacramento, not Saudi Arabia. A nation is only as strong as her people.

Now is the time to close the chasm between the rich and the poor of this land—not by taking from the rich to give to the poor, not by giving additional tax cuts to the richest 1 percent of our citizens, but by expanding the economic pie and giving every American a reasonable portion of economic justice.

If we do this, we will become the land of promise. If we do this, we will be worthy of the title "the leaders of the free world." If we do that, we will reach our potential, and in the words of the prophet Amos, we will speed up the day when "Every valley shall be exalted, end every mountain and hill shall be made low; and the crooked shall be made straight, and the rough places plain; and the glory of the Lord shall be revealed, and all flesh shall see it together."

The Sacramento march received wide-scale coverage on TV and in newspapers across the nation. It help to set in motion a series of interventions in South Central Los Angeles. The Department of Housing and Urban Development, the U.S. Department of Education, and the Department of Human Services provided emergency and long-range assistance to residents and small businesses. The NAACP, under the direction of Fred Rasheed, Our Fair Share director, negotiated many agreements with Los Angeles-based companies. This led directly to more blacks and minorities being hired at entry-level positions. Minority vendor opportunities were enhanced, and blacks and minorities were promoted to middle- and senior-management positions.

Our regional director, Shannon Reeves, along with our Los Angeles branches, worked with emergency relief agencies to ensure that residents who had lost their homes and their jobs because of the disaster received assistance. We invigorated our education efforts and implemented additional Back-to-School efforts.

On June 22-24, 1992, we conducted a retreat at the University of California, Los Angeles campus with experts in the field, government officials, and community-based organizations. We agreed on a number of approaches to help the people of Los Angeles.

The problems that were at the root of the riots in South Central in 1991 stemmed from a growing feeling of hopelessness and powerlessness by many residents of the inner city. The Rodney King verdicts were merely the sparks that ignited an already incendiary mix of social pathologies—high unemployment and underemployment, teenage pregnancies, poor housing, inferior schools, drugs, and high crime.

These problems did not lend themselves to quick fixes. They were too entrenched. The NAACP's role was to serve as an agent of change. Our job was to force the apparatus of government to become responsive to the crisis—and to take the necessary remedial steps to correct it. There was no other entity in the nation that had the collective experiences we had in dealing with similar situations. There was no other national organization with the breadth and scope or the credibility to help bring together the resources of the federal, state, and local governments to address the critical issues in Los Angeles. In less than a week, the National NAACP, working with its vast network of contacts, was able to do what no other group in the nation could do.

I wish I could say that we were able to realize the utopian dream of justice, economic parity, and social equality in South Central Los Angeles. Unfortunately, we could not. We can, however, take solace in the role we played in reshaping the political and social landscape, not just in Los Angeles, but also in cities across the nation.

Chapter 27

UPSTAIRS AT THE WHITE HOUSE

Because the NAACP is the most important secular black organization in North America, its leader has always had tremendous access to the most powerful and influential figures in this country, especially our presidents. I served as executive director during the terms of three presidents, Jimmy Carter, Ronald Reagan, and George Herbert Walker Bush.

My closest relationship was with Jimmy Carter and his vice president, Walter Mondale, who were in office when I took the helm of the NAACP. During his presidency, from 1977 to 1981, Mr. Carter sent me on two overseas trips as one of his representatives. One was to attend the funeral of the president of Kenya. On that trip, I accompanied Supreme Court Justice Marshall, Coretta Scott King, and Andy Young. He sent me on another trip as a special ambassador to the island of Fiji for an independence celebration. Frances and I had the privilege of being the American representatives at that affair, and we had dinner with Prince Philip of England.

On numerous occasions I had the opportunity to visit the White House along with other leaders of the civil rights community to confer with President Carter. One of the real thrills of my life was an occasion when Roslyn Carter and President Carter invited Frances and me up to the second floor of the White House for lunch. As you perhaps know, not many people get the chance to see the second floor, and we were able to see the Lincoln bedroom and the upstairs of the White House. I must confess that, like the average American citizen, I am overjoyed and even intimidated by the White House, which is an astonishingly beautiful place. President Carter, in my judgment, was one of our greatest presidents. Americans no doubt appreciate him more now than they did when he was in office, and I am glad to have had the opportunity to work with him.

I also had an enduring friendship with Vice President Mondale, whom I visited each year that he was in office. He invited me to accompany him on a special tour he made of Africa, where we visited seven nations. Standing out in my mind was the stop we made in Cape Verde, that peculiar island where it had not rained in some seven years. We also had a tremendous tour of Nigeria.

I was the director of the NAACP during the eight-year term of President Reagan and the four years of his successor, George Bush. I did not have a chance to see President Reagan often, but he did come and address our convention. Most of my dealings were with Vice President Bush.

When Bush became president in 1989, I asked him to hire a black person in a position similar to that held by Robert Brown, who had served under President Nixon, or Louie Martin, who served under President Lyndon Johnson. During these administrations, black leaders could call either Brown or Martin and have their concerns relayed quickly to the President. But President Bush told me, "Ben, if you need to talk to me just pick up the phone and call me. I will get right back to you." And I must say that he did.

But one of the great disappointments I had during the Bush presidency came one night when the President called and wanted to see Vernon Jordan, William Coleman, and me to discuss the Civil Rights Bill. I was in Baltimore and could not make it in time, and Vernon Jordan was out of the country. He met with Coleman, and that night the three of us conversed via telephone. Despite our efforts to the contrary, President Bush did veto that bill.

Frances and I also had a relationship briefly with President Ford. I was invited to attend a National Broadcasters Association meeting in Las Vegas, Nevada, when Ford was President. I was attending a reception with Frances and my sister Julia. I shall not forget the evening because President Ford and his wife were especially gracious in their conversations with Julia and Frances. Julia is a hardcore Franklin Roosevelt Democrat, but she was very impressed with Ford and his wife, as was Frances. I had a chance to also meet with Vice President Dan Quayle and he addressed our convention, as did George Bush during his vice presidency. I made it a point when I was at the NAACP to be nonpartisan in my approach, and we invited people from both the Democratic and Republican parties to speak at our conventions.

I did not have a chance to serve long with President Clinton in the White House. He took office in January of 1993, and I left the NAACP in May. I had known, of course, Vice President Al Gore and his family for many, many years before my tenure at the NAACP. I had the honor of supporting his father for the Senate the first time he ran, and I've been a strong supporter of Al Gore, Jr. for many years. I delivered the eulogy at the funeral services for Senator Al Gore, Sr.

In fact, my association with presidents spans several decades. In 1960, I was still a member of the Republican Party and was serving as vice chairman in Shelby County when Vice President Richard Nixon came to Memphis. I was part of the official host committee, as I had been for the Dwight Eisenhower visit back in 1952. Since 1964, however, I have been consistently voting in the Tennessee Democratic primaries.

I also had a chance to hear Nixon make a private speech to the National Broadcasters Association in 1974. He chose to speak about the very bad way that white America had treated its black citizens. It was rather surprising that he made what was to be a very fine speech on that day. Strangely enough, as I looked around at the meeting, I think that Frances and I were the only black people in that meeting room of between 500 and 600 people. Nixon did not know that I was there until the speech was over. Later, in the reception line, he made a point of having a picture taken with Frances and me.

But the experience I recall and value the most with presidents occurred when President Carter invited me to Camp David to attend a meeting to address problems in his administration. Traveling to Camp David is a riveting experience. I had heard and read of it, but had never expected to be there. But there I was among some 50 people drawn from the ranks of labor and civil rights organizations and other leaders from education, business, industry, and politics. The media had focused hard on the perception that Carter was failing to get the country moving.

As we gathered around the table that morning with President Carter presiding, he said to the assembled group, "I want each of you in two to four minutes to tell me where we are and what we should do." He then asked three people present to sum up the thoughts expressed by the group. He asked me to be one of the three summarizers. I was thrilled, astonished, and flabbergasted. I grasped my pen and note pad to record the thoughts and then to express my view as to what had been said. I summed up as follows.

Mr. President, thank you for inviting us here. Thank you for your concern and thank you for soliciting our views. The participants here have expressed various views [and I attempted to summarize them]. Mr. President, you are a great Bible scholar and you recall the words of Apostle Paul—"If the trumpet gives forth an uncertain sound, who will prepare for the battle?" This alludes to the fact that a call of the trumpet must be clear and loud to prepare for battle. The sound cannot be soft or shaky or indistinct. Mr. President, the conclusion reached here is that the country is facing now, as often in the past, a battle for economic strength, for justice, for inclusion of all, for strong, moral imperatives, and for leadership. Mr. President, you have summoned us here to Camp David, you have asked for our thoughts, our views, our hopes, our plans, our advice. Mr. President, gather this advice, study it, weigh it, measure it, assess it, judge it, and then, sir, leave this mountaintop place and come down with a clear message. Tell the nation we are going up, not down, forward, not backward; our nation will be stronger, not weaker.

And after a few more words, I concluded:

Mr. President, give forth a loud sound, a steady sound, a clear sound, a certain sound—a sound that sends the call for battle, that summons the troops. For I hear the words, Mr. President, and you know them better than I. If the trumpet gives forth an uncertain sound, who will prepare for the battle? Thank you, Mr. President, and leave here giving forth a certain sound, a clear sound, a leadership sound, and prepare the people for the battle.

Chapter 28
MY LIFE AND THE CHURCH

For as long as I can remember, the church has been an integral part of my life. First Baptist Church is the beginning of my church experience. My religious experience, of course, was present every day of my young life. Before we went to bed every night we got on our knees, and I mean all of the sisters and brothers, but particularly my two younger sisters, Bessie and Mildred, because they were nearer my age and we went to bed about the same time I did. I was born in 1925, Mildred in 1927 and Bessie in 1932. Every night, 7 nights a week, 365 nights a year, "now I lay me down to sleep. I pray the Lord my soul to keep. If I should die before I wake, I pray the Lord my soul to take. God bless Mama, God bless Daddy, God bless grandma, God bless all my sisters and brothers. We pray in the name of Jesus, amen." Then we would jump up and go to bed.

My mother was a devout member of St. Andrews AME church. In my youth my father was not a regular member of any church. Not until I was a grown man, in fact, not until I was pastoring a church, did he attend church on any sort of regular basis.

First Baptist Church St. Paul (later known as First Baptist Church Lauderdale, but officially called First Colored Baptist Church) was located one-half block from my house. My older sisters and brothers took me to Sunday school for as long as I can remember. Oh, how I remember that Sunday school department located in the basement, whose main feature was a huge coal-burning furnace. In 1928, many churches were still heated by the stove located in the sanctuary, where various members brought coal and wood, started a fire, and kept it going. First Baptist on St. Paul had a big furnace and the church was heated by radiator heat. Because of the proximity of First Baptist to my home, I attended Sunday school at that church. I am convinced now of the importance of Sunday school for church membership growth because I joined church, as did most of the kids in my neighborhood, at the place where we attended Sunday school. Our Sunday school teachers were, among many others, Dr. T.O. Fuller, my pastor; Mattie Porter, public school teacher and superintendent of the children's department; J.E. Rhodes, U.S. postal employee and superintendent of the Sunday school; Carrie Nabors, schoolteacher; and Mr. Savage, Mr. Burton, Mr. Glover, Mr. Stroud, Dr. Taylor, Mrs. Hudson, and Mr. Pully.

First Baptist was a somewhat non-traditional Baptist church. Most black Baptist churches of my day were great but were highly emotional. There was a great deal of shouting and public praise. First Baptist was a so-called "blue stocking church"—intellectual, not much given to shouting. Dr. Fuller, my pastor, was a college graduate (unusual for that time). He had served a two-year term as a member of the North Carolina state legislature. And in fact, he was the last black man to serve as a state senator in North Carolina during the Reconstruction period. His term was 1898 to 1900. It should be noted that he introduced the bill that created the North Carolina Mutual Life Insurance Company, the largest black-owned business for many years in America.

Dr. Fuller became pastor of First Baptist Church in 1900 and served for 42 years until his death in 1942. Somewhere around 1908 or 1909, he built a beautiful brick structure with a full basement and upper sanctuary, stained-glass windows, and elegant brick construction. We never had a large membership. I suspect at its peak our membership did not exceed 400 people. Dr. Fuller was an excellent preacher, an outstanding orator, and a historian. I think it important to note that he was the author of several books: *20 Years in Public Life*, *Flashes and Gems of Oratory*, *Banks and Banking*, *History of Negro Baptists of West Tennessee*, and *Pictorial History of the American Negro*. How inspiring it was to me to be able to look into my home library and find books written by a Negro author who happened also to be my pastor.

The habits of older brothers and sisters can be very influential on their younger siblings. Somehow or the other, Robert, Charlie, Julia, and Raymond never stayed to attend church service after Sunday school. Sunday school was 9:30 to 11:00. Church service was 11:00 until, maybe 1:00, 2:00, or 2:30. Because my older brothers and sisters did not attend church, neither did Mildred or Bessie or I. Each Sunday after Sunday school ended, we came home. I think now that I missed a lot. Nevertheless, I also gained a lot because I have loved the church all my life.

In those days, every church had a revival that usually lasted for a two- or three-week period. During that time a more visible, concerted effort was made to encourage people to accept Jesus as their savior. We had what is known as a "mourners' bench," which was a first seat in the middle aisle. That seat always remained vacant, and during revival those who had never accepted Christ were invited to sit on that particular bench. During the revival season at the Sunday school review hour, the older members and teachers would gather up the youngsters who had not been baptized and escort them to the front seat. Special appeals and prayers were made for their salvation. I must confess that somehow the devil got hold of me and I did not much like the idea of going on that front bench. I felt demeaned, humiliated, insulted—my privacy invaded. It was a very strong feeling. It was so strong that if I became aware that revival season was on, I did not go to my Sunday school but would go right across the street to the Tabernacle Baptist Church. It is difficult to express even today how strongly I felt about that. I somehow feel now that I was wrong, but it has always influenced my life as a pastor and how I approached salvation.

I came out of the Baptist tradition, and in that tradition you had to publicly confess your faith in Christ and make a statement. Unfortunately, during my childhood days many young people were guilty of making up elaborate statements. On the other hand, I am certain that some people had a genuine supernatural experience. If one reads the Bible closely, there is more than one way cited on conversion. We hear today much talk of born-again Christians. There was a day when that term was not very much used. I believe that conversion can be a dramatic, riveting, soul-shaking experience or it can be a gradual growth into the knowledge that Jesus Christ is Lord. My conversion experience was not a soul-shaking, sun-rising-at-midnight type of thing, but rather a growing awareness that God exists, that Jesus Christ is His only begotten son, and acceptance of him in my life as Lord. And that is how I was converted.

And so, during those weeks of revival time at First Baptist, as I mentioned, I would move across the street and attend Tabernacle. Tabernacle had once been the largest black church in Memphis, had fallen on hard times and lost its sanctuary, and was now conducting worship as a small group in the assembly hall of Howe Institute.

Howe Institute was a school where Dr. Fuller served as president. In the early days, right after slavery, and until the 1920s, church groups worked exceedingly hard to maintain educational institutions. All over the South there were small schools. They called themselves colleges and institutes, and tried to give an education to black children. That educational experience spanned first and second grade subjects and continued on to and Greek and Latin. When Dr. Fuller served as president of Howe, he did a marvelous job of building an institution that had a dormitory, classrooms, teachers' cottages, academic facilities, and some four or five well-built brick buildings on perhaps a 10- or 15-acre site. This college was located directly across the street from the church he pastored, First Baptist Saint Paul. The official name was First Colored Baptist Church, and now it is First Baptist Church-Lauderdale.

One Sunday morning in 1939, I stayed at church after the Sunday school hour. I was sitting in the last pew of the middle aisle, which is some 15 pews back from the pulpit. My pastor, Dr. Fuller, was out of town, and our guest speaker that morning was a Reverend Mr. Walker, who was employed by the Post Office as a letter carrier. Dr. Walker was preaching that morning, and at the end of the sermon I felt moved to join church. And in fact the church sang a song that was then and is now my favorite. The words are,

> "I heard the voice of Jesus say come unto me and rest, lie down thy weary one, lie down thy head upon my breast. I came to Jesus as I was, weary, wounded, and sad. I found in Him a resting place and He has made me glad."

That song spiritually lifts me up, exalts my spirit, and magnifies in my perception the goodness of God.

I remember that Dr. Walker did what we call "open the doors of the church." This is an expression meaning he extended the call for Christian discipleship. With his arms out raised he appealed to those of us who did not belong to the church to come down to the front and give our hand to him but give our hearts to God and become a member of the church and to accept Jesus as our personal savior. I recall now some 60 years later that he had the choir and people sing that song three or four times and he reissued the invitation. I was lifted, I was moved, and had tears streaming down my cheeks. I walked down that aisle that Sunday morning and indeed publicly gave my life to God.

I always rejoice when I think of that moment in my life and I shall always be grateful that I am a born again Christian. In my mind even today I can feel the tension in the church, the rejoicing in the congregation, the spiritual ecstasy that the church felt because I was a Hooks—one of seven Hooks children who attended that Sunday school each Sunday, and I was only the second of the seven to make a public profession of my faith. Raymond, the brother next to me, had confessed his faith in Christ a few years before and had been baptized.

On the second Sunday in July 1939, I was baptized at Old First Baptist. My friend to this day, Charles Graham, was baptized also. I remember Dr. Fuller baptizing me. I remember putting on my baptizing clothes and walking into that pool in the basement of the church, a pool that frightened me almost to death to look at. Even though I was 14, I had never learned to swim (and never have). I guess the water was around four feet deep, and the pool itself must have been 5 feet wide and 8 feet long, and I remember Dr. Fuller standing there with that black robe on, waiting to take me beneath the waters of baptism. Baptism is a unique thing, and I am fascinated by it even now. I shall never forget the chanting of the congregation, "Take me to the water." I shall never forget the baptism songs and how my soul was moved strangely by the words and the sound of those great hymns of faith. Even today I shall never forget that beautiful time of my life.

And then my first partaking of the Lord's Supper—I can see that table draped in white. Beneath the white cloth were the elements of the communion: the grape juice in small glasses, the bread baked without leavening by the mothers of the church. I can see Dr. Fuller and the deacons standing around the communion table in their dark suits and white gloves and the church singing, "Were you there when they crucified my Lord," and the old uplifting spiritual, "Let Us Break Bread Together on Our Knees," and how the tears unbidden ran down my cheeks. As I participated in my first Lord's Supper experience, I can hear and see Dr. Fuller now leading us through that ceremony. I never in the 65 years since then have forgotten how I felt then and how I feel mystically moved even now as I stand around the Lord's Supper table. I know that one day around the great communion table on the other side of this journey, at that place where the wicked shall cease from troubling and where the weary shall be at rest, I will join with my brothers and sisters, those who have gone on before, and with my blessed Lord and savior partake of one last communion supper.

The church has been vital in my life. I remember old St. Andrews AME church where my mother attended and quite often, even though I did not stay to attend church services at First Baptist, on my way home from Sunday school or shortly after I got home, my mother and I would join up and would walk together to St. Andrews. It was located four or five blocks farther away from my home than First Baptist. My mother was not a shouting, that is to say a publicly shouting, Christian, although she did shout in her heart and mind. But I could tell by the tapping of her feet, by the tears that ran down her cheeks, and by the nod of her head that religion was real, and that it gave her the courage to carry on in a very difficult time.

The AME church had what we call the "decalogue"; it was a chant. The pastor I most remember was the late Reverend J.W. Hall, who must have been about 6 feet 5 inches tall, with a booming voice, as he would step up to the pulpit, wearing a little prayer cap on his bald head and what I call a preacher's coat—that is to say, a suit coat that you could wear anywhere but that was really longer than most ordinary coats, cut to hang below his knees and yet not what we would call a Prince Albert. I can see Dr. Hall now stepping up to that pulpit crying out, "I am the Lord thy God that brought thee out of the land of Egypt, out of the house of bondage. Thou shalt have no other gods before me." And the people would chant, "Lord have mercy upon us and incline our hearts to keep these laws." And then as Reverend Hall would recite the rest of the Commandments, the people responded, "Lord have mercy upon us and write these laws upon our hearts." Then they would chant "Nearer my God to thee, nearer to thee, even though it be a cross that leadeth me." I can hear them now chanting in response. My spirit literally moves as I look back at old St. Andrews and see those hundreds of worshipers on Sunday morning drawn together by a common thread that leads all the way back to the God of our creation. And how my mother hated the thought of missing the decalogue. To her that was the highlight of the Sunday morning service. I love it today, and sometimes in bed at night I sing it to myself.

The experience of the church has been the most challenging, the most pervasive, the most important thing in my life. Whatever else I have done—the practice of law, sitting as a judge, being a businessman, serving on the Federal Communications Commission, serving as a banker, or whatever else I may have done, the church is first and foremost in my life. My religious beliefs have dictated what I have tried to accomplish. I can hear the songwriter say, "I love the Lord, He heard my cry, pitied every groan; as long as I live, when trouble rises, I will hasten to His throne."

I can see old man Butler at First Baptist Church Lauderdale, as soon as Sunday school was out and as we transitioned into the morning service, fall on his knees praying and I can hear deacons across this land and country—Chicago, Los Angeles, wherever you go, praying on Sunday mornings as I travel across the nation. And there was a certain kind of sameness to their prayers, a timeless quality that still shines. I can hear some of the words and phrases now, "Lord we thank you that things are as well with us as they are. We thank you for a reasonable portion of health and strength." Little did I recognize or realize as a boy what that meant. But today that has a special meaning, as I suffer now from the aches and pains of arthritis and rheumatism.

I know what the old folks meant when they said thank you for a reasonable portion—not a whole lot, not all life had, but a reasonable portion of health and strength. And then I can recognize they were praying at a day when there was not enough food on the table to go around, when clothes had to be saved. I can see them now in those shiny black suits they saved for Sunday morning, as they said, "We thank you that things are as well as they are." What a marvelous insight. How my life has been changed for the better as I have taken the time to analyze the prayers, the prayer service of the people who very seldom had enough to eat, who lived in difficult circumstances, who were called "boy" long after they were men, who were called Annie and Mary even though the people who called them that were young enough to be their grandchildren. But on Sunday mornings they were kings and queens; on Sunday mornings they were in their power; on Sunday mornings they were transported beyond the cares and troubles of the days that had preceded and were given what it took to make it.

Those of you who read this book may make fun of me. You may think that I'm foolish and have lost my sense of bearing, but I know what it was to ride on the back of a streetcar, or the front end of the train where the cinders would wear you out. I know what it is to have to go into that segregated lunch counter to buy a hamburger, to walk up to a simple Dairy Queen and ask for a frozen custard and to be told I had to go to the back door. I know what it is to walk into a restaurant in the North thinking I could be waited on and be told, "The law may require it but we will not do it willingly."

It has been my faith, our faith, in God that sustained us. I remember one particular occasion when I was traveling with my wife, Frances, across the country. We were going to Wilberforce University, where she attended college, to the little town of Xenia, Ohio. Oh, how Frances wanted to go by there, and finally we went out of our way to go to this little restaurant she thought she had patronized as a student. We went into the restaurant and noticed how long it took them to come over. We took our seats and we sat, and sat, and sat. I think it was Frances and I and our daughter, Pat, and two or three of my nephews and nieces. Finally the owner, I suppose, came and put a written sign in front of us, about the size of a typewritten sheet, which said, "Ohio public law so and so demands or requires that we serve you but we would like for you to know that we do not wish to do so." They set the sign up; it was like a menu, but it had a back on it. It was set on the table so you could read it easily.

Here we were in Xenia, Ohio, which probably would not have existed if not for the college, the largest employer in the county, and we were told they didn't want to serve us. Now we were sitting there on the horns of a dilemma: I'm a Christian and trying to decide what to do. Finally, somebody came back around. I knew the awful stories of how people spit on your burger or polluted your food. When the waitress came back, I said, "I know you do not want to serve us, but we want to order," and we all ordered something. We waited maybe 45 minutes and finally they came back. When they put food on the table, we all got up and said, "but since you don't want to serve us we'll not force you to do so." And then we walked out of the restaurant, which was our small way of trying to maintain some human dignity and yet not completely submit to the laws of segregation.

I love the great hymns of the church, great hymns of faith that tell a story. I must confess, I am not too much in love with all these new, jumping songs. I know they have their following, but I love the songs that have a message: "Jesus savior pilot me over life's tempestuous seas, unknown waves before me roll, hiding rock and treacherous shoal, wondrous sovereign of the sea, Jesus savior pilot me." "Trust and obey, for there is no other way to be happy in Jesus but to trust and obey." I listen to the words of the songs, on the plane I hum them, in bed at night I sing them to myself, and if a song does not say something, I don't want to hear it. I like to think about "Amazing Grace, how sweet the sound, that saved a wretch like me. I once was lost but now am found, was blind but now I see." Later in my life I attended the church service in the army. While my church was being rebuilt in 1942, I attended Metropolitan Baptist Church, pastored by Reverend S.A. Owen, and Mississippi Boulevard Christian Church, pastored by Elder Blair T. Hunt. I attended Second Congregational Church, famous with me because the service lasted only one hour. And from time to time I would go back to St. Andrews.

In college I became a member of the choir, and I attended chapel service every week. My father was a photographer, and in that capacity, we had much work to do at churches for funerals, weddings, church anniversaries, and other affairs. So I came to understand and appreciate worship services at various churches while working with my father. And always my love for the church grew.

Dr. Fuller died in 1942, and my grandmother died in April of 1942 just a few days before her 90th birthday. Dr. Fuller preached her funeral sermon, and I was the one who called him and informed him of my grandmother's death. Little did I know that he would be dead within two months.

I was always moved by my religious experience. When I came back from the service, my pastor then was Reverend H.C. Nabrit, and he remained so for the next 21 years. Dr. Nabrit was not only my pastor but my friend, my brother, my mentor, my trainer, and my supporter. When I became judge and was called to straighten out the jury system, I appointed Reverend A.C. Nabrit as assistant jury commissioner to carry out this assignment. Later on, Reverend Nabrit attended law school, passed the bar exam in Ohio, and became a practicing lawyer in the early 1970s.

As Baptists, we subscribe to the theory that preachers are divinely "called." It is difficult perhaps to explain, but it means that you really feel that God has specifically and personally called you or asked you to be a minister of his gospel—that without that call you would never be a preacher, and with it you would never be happy unless you answer it. I had felt from my early days that God had called me to preach. There are stories told quite often among my sisters and brothers and others how as a little boy I would preach to the chickens and cats and make the other children sit down on the porch steps while I preached a sermon, and that we would duplicate the baptizing services.

Most of us were Baptists, which meant we believed in the deep-water baptism in water that would come up to your waist and the minister dipping you beneath the water. Methodists had been often baptized by sprinkling; they simply had the preacher pour water over their head. I was a deep-water Baptist. And it is said by my brothers and sisters that I would make them listen to my preaching, and quite often I would put a box up in front of a mirror and preach. I do know that I felt strangely called to preach as a kid of 14 or 15.

In my father's office building, there were also offices for a dentist, a doctor, a lawyer, and a room where the Baptist ministers met, called the Baptist Ministers Alliance, so I was exposed early on to a variety of black professionals. My father was pious in the sense that he believed in God, believed in the power of prayer, but did not for some reason follow the organized church too well. Later, he joined my church, Middle Baptist, and I had the blessed privilege of baptizing him. He sort of discouraged me from preaching by simply saying, "If you want to preach, all right. But be sure that you are prepared to lead the life of righteousness the preacher ought to lead, no half-stepping." I did not announce my call to the ministry until I was 30 years of age.

After I returned to Memphis to practice law in 1949, I embarked on a career of public speaking. And I do believe in miraculous experiences in life. I recall very well my introverted nature, how I could not stand to speak after I was about 12 to more than one person at one time. When I finished grade school, in the eighth grade, we had a salutatorian, who was the number two person in the class, and the valedictorian, who was the first person in the class, make a speech at graduation. As salutatorian of my eighth-grade class, I recall how, even though I had learned my speech, I cried all the way through it, and was not capable of public delivery. After the seventh grade I simply could not talk before a group of people. Many times when I was in law school, and we thought about lawyers as depicted in the movies, making great orations to the jury and being great speakers, I would ask myself, how are you going to practice law when you can't talk to more than three people at a time? How could you ever convince a jury of anything?

It is strange how we thought about lawyers in those days primarily as public speakers and not as tax lawyers and non-litigators who didn't go to the courtroom to argue cases. Nevertheless, I persevered, and I recall vividly that in law school we had professors who would call on me to say something and I was really incapable of responding. I could not stand up in my law class with 40 students and give a review of a case. Every now and then I would ask myself, "Are you losing your mind? How do you plan to practice law?"

Shortly after I came back to Memphis, I was asked by Reverend Alexander Gladney, who was a member of the Saint John Baptist Church of Douglas, to come over to his church on a certain Sunday morning and deliver an address for young people. I agreed and started preparing the address. And the longer I worked on it, the more I wondered, "What are you thinking about? You know you can't stand before people. You know when you stand up tears will well up in your eyes and you will never get beyond reading the first three sentences!" And yet I kept on working.

I was practicing law, but I had not been called on at this point to make any public proclamations to the court. I had not, in that early stage of my career, ever argued before a jury or had much to say to a judge. Now I was preparing to be a full-time lawyer and, more immediately, had agreed to give a speech before an audience of perhaps 200 or 300, and was unable to keep myself cool enough to speak to 10 people.

I had tried to address one or two little civic organizations where there were 20 or 25 people and had failed dismally. Now here I was getting ready for this speech at what we called Young People's Day. I prepared the speech. I worked on it. I thought I had some good material. And I wondered what in the world was going to happen.

That Sunday morning, bright and early on a June day in 1949, I went to the Saint John Baptist Church in the Douglas neighborhood. I had my little prepared speech neatly written up in a folder. When they were ready to present me, Reverend Gladney got up, introduced me, and turned the pulpit over to me. There were about 200 people present, more or less, and I presented my speech without any nervousness, hesitation, or fear. And since that time I have delivered thousands of speeches to varied groups as large as 100,000 people, from legislative bodies to corporate assemblies. I was the first and only black person to make a major address in the same year to both the Democratic and Republican National Conventions in Detroit and in New York City. *The Detroit Free Press* commented that my speech to the Republican Convention was extremely important and well delivered. And God has fixed it so that never in these 50 or more years have I suffered from fear or shame. I call this divine intervention.

After law school, when I came back do Memphis, I immediately started attending church on a regular basis and spoke as a Sunday evening speaker nearly every Sunday. These were addresses given by a layman to the church but which led me further and further into the field of the ordained ministry. From time to time I discussed this with my pastor, and we finally concluded that I had been "called" to preach and I had a simple decision to make: Answer the call or try to ignore it. In May of 1955, I stood up in the First Baptist Church, by then no longer First Baptist Church Colored but First Baptist Church Lauderdale (the street where we were located), and announced to the congregation that I had been called by God to preach his gospel. Reverend Nabrit, my perceptive, kind friend and pastor, recognized what I was doing and immediately that morning put it to a vote to license me as a minister of the gospel.

I was called to pastor my first church, Middle Baptist Church, a few months later. In the Baptist tradition, when a church is "vacant," that is, without a pastor, it is up to the congregation to "call" a minister. That usually consists of the presiding deacons inviting visiting preachers in to speak. Finally, the congregation by vote extends the "call."

There is a church in Memphis called the Middle Baptist Church that was pastored by the Reverend E.W. Williamson. It was a relatively small congregation, perhaps 350 or 400 members, and not a great shouting church, but more intellectual. In 1956, its pastor, Reverend Williamson, was "called" to the Olivet Baptist Church in Memphis. When he informed his congregation that he would be leaving, they began seeking a pastor.

Strangely enough, this was early 1956. In 1955, during the Thanksgiving season, Reverend Williamson had asked me to preach a three-night youth revival on the Monday, Tuesday, and Wednesday night before

Thanksgiving. I agreed to this. When the time came, my wife made plans for us to go to Beaumont, Texas, where her sister, Anita, lived to spend the Thanksgiving holiday with them. Her plans called for us to leave town on Wednesday. If I had done as my wife had wanted, I would not have been able to preach the Wednesday night service at Middle Baptist. I would only have preached Monday and Tuesday night. From my perspective, the spirit of God led me to say to my wife, I have to fulfill my obligation, I have to stay in Memphis and preach this Wednesday night, and then somehow we will go to Texas very late on Wednesday night. My wife was very much opposed, but I followed what I conceived to be the calling of the spirit of the Lord and remained, and Frances stayed with me and I did preach that Wednesday night.

I was led by the spirit to deliver a sermon on that night called "Songs in the Night." The principal message of that sermon was that in times of trouble, God gives us songs in the night. And that in the dark night of slavery, God gave us songs. "I am so glad trouble won't last always." That message gives hope in times of hopelessness. Quite often we hear the lyric "Swing low sweet chariot, coming for to carry me home," but we did not realize that the song was not always simply about death, or that there is life after death, or there is resting in the arms of Jesus, but it also meant Harriet Tubman coming with the freedom train, to lead the slaves from Mississippi to Ohio and then to Canada. So, these songs held us together.

It was that sermon that lived at Greater Middle Baptist even until today. Why am I saying all of this? Because when Reverend Williamson a few months later decided to leave Greater Middle Baptist Church to become pastor of Olivet Baptist Church, the leadership of the Greater Middle Baptist Church, Deacons Fred Eddins and Charles Turner, came to me to ask if I would consider becoming pastor. I agreed, and preached my first sermon as pastor on the third Sunday in March 1956. It is now 2003 and I am still pastor. I have had a loving, marvelous relationship. I shall never forget what that church has meant in my life and in the lives of hundreds of good people that have stood by my side.

At that time, the budget for Greater Middle Baptist Church was $17,000 a year. My salary was $75 a week. The budget of Greater Middle Baptist Church now approaches $1 million a year. One of the strange things about my pastorate, and one about which many people ask me, is that for 30 years I pastored two major churches, one in Memphis and one in Detroit. Black people in America who lived in rural areas were accustomed to the early church pattern, where one pastor may have four churches. He would pastor one church on the first Sunday and a second church on the second Sunday.

But by 1956 when I started pastoring, these churches were more inclined to have one full-time pastor. What happened? How did I end up with two major churches in two major cities and remain there for 30 years? Well, it was rather simple from my viewpoint. I was considered strongly for Olivet Baptist Church in Memphis in 1956, but I made an arrogant assumption—that I was not strong enough to be accepted. In later discussions with outstanding ministers, I was warned that this was arrogance on my part and if extended an invitation, I should go and let the people make the decision. So, I decided then that if offered an invitation to preach at a vacant church, I would accept it.

One of the beautiful things that happened at Middle Baptist Church is that Reverend Williamson preached his last sermon on the second Sunday in March 1956, and I preached my first sermon as pastor on the third Sunday. So Middle Baptist was never without a pastor. This is unusual, to say the least, in most church circles. I was elected and took over on the third Sunday in March 1956, and thereafter we had a marvelous relationship at Middle Baptist Church.

In 1963, the chairman of my deacon board, Charles Turner, lost his father, who had quite a personality. He belonged to a church in Detroit called Mount Moriah Baptist Church. My deacon, Charlie, had belonged there for three or four years. Charlie Turner asked if I would go to his father's funeral with him. The pastor of Mount Moriah Baptist Church was Reverend Craig. At the funeral, he asked me to make a few eulogistic remarks. This was in 1963, toward the end of the year.

Mount Moriah Church had a registered membership of some 1,700 members. When Reverend Craig resigned in February 1964, it was traumatic and unexpected. During this period, the elders of Mount Moriah decided to ask me to come to Detroit to preach what we called a trial sermon. I went knowing deep in my heart that I had no intention of accepting the appointment if I got it, but also knowing that I had promised God I would never turn down the opportunity. So I accepted the invitation to return to Mount Moriah to preach.

To my utter surprise, that congregation extended me a "call" to come pastor that church. That was a church with a congregation four times larger than my church, and with a budget of $50,000 a year. They were planning on building a brand new building and had architectural plans already drawn up. Although this was an opportunity to go to a large church with tremendous potential, I decided to remain in Memphis. I was in love with Memphis and with Middle Baptist Church. So I told the people at Mount Moriah that I did not feel I could answer their call.

On my visit to Detroit, I also discovered a split in that church. The trustees were planning to build a large, expensive church, and tear down the present facility, without a pastor. The deacons did not want to build without a pastor. I sensed this disagreement would create turmoil. When I turned down the pastorate and told them I could not serve, I put in my letter what has come to be known as the famous postscript, a famous "P.S.": "Even though I could not come to your church as pastor, if you feel that you would like me to come to your church to pastor you during the time that you are building a new church, and I would be able to come two Sundays a month, then I would answer that call and come and stay with you on that basis until you have completed your building."

I had no expectation whatsoever that this large, prosperous congregation—perhaps the third or fourth largest in the city of Detroit, a city renowned for its great black Baptist churches—would ever consider this. Having made this compromise with myself, I went to sleep very happy knowing they would not extend me the call and I would not have to deal with this. To my utter surprise, a few weeks later on the first Sunday morning in July, the chairman of the deacon board of Mount Moriah Church called me on the phone. They had met the night before and had agreed to accept my offer to go and serve them on a limited basis. When the call came—and it's providential and ironic that some great things in my life have happened with my wife taking over and getting involved much more than she should have been—I had a sneaking suspicion the news was not what I wanted to hear.

I was still in bed because it was only 7:00 A.M. in Memphis. Frances looked at me and said, "Deacon Bolden is on the phone and wants to talk with you." "Tell him I can't get to the phone, I haven't gotten up," I said. "I'm not telling him that. You're in this mess now. Take the phone and answer it." I said, "Frances, I can't talk now." "But you are going to talk now," she said and she put the phone in my hand. I couldn't do a thing about it but take the call. I said good morning. He said "Reverend, this is Deacon Bolden. Mount Moriah has decided to accept your P.S." You could have bought me with a nickel's worth of peanuts. I was now called upon to make a decision whether to follow through. I then went to the Middle Baptist Church here and told them Mount Moriah wanted me to come. I told them the circumstances and said that I would like to go and do this. I said, "It is your choice to make. You can tell me no, I can't go and stay here. If you say that to me, then I have to make a decision whether to resign this church and go to Detroit or tell Detroit I cannot make it and stay in Memphis."

The church in Memphis, again to my utter surprise, voted in favor of me taking both churches. The vote was 108 to 4 that I could go. This was almost unheard of in 1964. So, I went to Detroit and I stayed there 30 years. The record will also reveal that I had great, some would say phenomenal, success at pastoring in Detroit and that the church went from a membership of 1,800 to more than 3,500 at a time when we registered every year. Had I been counting my members loosely, as some did, I could have claimed a membership of 10,000 because we had people join every Sunday. Look at what happened in the 30 years. This was 1964.

Later on in that same year, Governor Clement appointed me to become a judge in the fourth division of criminal court in Memphis. At that time there was not a single black person who was a judge of record in the South. The fact of the matter is there were very few black judges anywhere. In the great city of Detroit in 1964 there were only three black judges, and very few anywhere else. I accepted the appointment as judge in Memphis, which meant that many Friday afternoons when I closed my docket in Memphis, I would get on the plane and fly to Detroit, spend all day Saturday and Sunday there, catch a plane back to Memphis at 2:00 Monday morning, and be on the bench at 9:30. Many days I would preach in Memphis, deliver the Lord's Supper at the 11:00 A.M. service, catch a plane, fly to Detroit, and have the Lord's Supper in Detroit at night service, at 8:00 P.M.

In those days, churches had night services, and that was a common practice of black Baptist churches all over the nation. I also had the privilege of building for Mount Moriah a brand new church that seated 900 people and cost close to $400,000 in 1964. We paid that debt off in less than 18 months. We had the distinction of doubling the size of the church a few years later. When I left, there was a church that was almost brand new that would seat 1,800 people. That church cost more than $1 million to build. And at that time, we received a bank loan of $600,000, the largest amount a black church had ever been able to borrow.

When I went to Mount Moriah Baptist Church, it was one of the best organized churches I had ever seen. Reverend Craig was a great preacher and organizer. I thank God I have always had the ability to give other people, my predecessor or successors, praise if they have done well or if they do well. At Mount Moriah, we built the largest missionary society in the state. One Sunday we had 58 people join on a single morning, which was strange because the speaker was a layman. I had invited Governor Frank Clement of the state of Tennessee to come to Detroit and deliver a lay sermon. He did, and he was a great lay speaker of the Methodist church.

When I began at Mount Moriah, they had a male chorus called "Voices of the Thunder" with a membership of about 50. We became the wonder of the nation when the chorus developed into an active membership of over 135 men. And the Holy Ghost reigned supreme. Souls were saved. Lives were directed, and the blood-stained banner of our Lord was raised high. In Memphis our congregation continued to grow, and while we did not build a church in Memphis, we did purchase a modern and spacious facility at 2445 Lamar.

When I left Mount Moriah in Detroit, I left more than $500,000 in the treasury and every bill paid, and a growing, progressive church of some 3,500 in place. My successor, Reverend Kenneth Flowers, has moved ahead very well at that church, and today the annual budget of Mount Moriah Baptist Church in Detroit exceeds $1 million a year. We were blessed to have great musicians in both churches, including Herbert Pickard, Robert Nix, Jack Folsom, Elma Newburn, and, in Memphis, George McGowen, Nancy Bradshaw, Beula Fritz, Audrey Hall, Louise Turner, Arlene Yarborough, Ron Williams, and Delores Wade.

Some 200 members from Mt. Moriah of Detroit and Greater Middle Baptist of Memphis attended my swearing-in to the FCC on September 1, 1965 in Washington. I had a good friend, Mori Griner, who was vice president and general manager of WMCT-TV, the largest television station in Memphis. Mori had come to be with us at the swearing-in ceremony. Just prior to the ceremony, Mori said, "You are having a reception for all these people at your apartment and it is too much for your nephew Robert to handle by himself. I will stay and help him." And he did assist greatly. One of the church members from Detroit, a little lady about 80 years old, came bouncing in and whispered to another member, "Reverend has gone too far now. He has hired a white man to be his butler."

The rules of the FCC prohibited me from receiving outside compensation during the years I served the churches. Five years later, the NAACP also insisted that I not pastor a church, so from 1977 to 1993, I served these two churches without any financial compensation. I requested and was granted a leave of absence as pastor and was elected chairman of the official board of each church. I have absolutely no regrets about this. I lived comfortably and Frances accepted it. Above all, in the words of the song, "I love Thy kingdom, Lord, the house of Thine abode, the church our blessed redeemer saved with His own precious blood."

I enjoy the work of the church. Of all the things I have done in my life—student, teacher, lawyer, judge, community activist, banker, businessman, executive director, fraternal leader—I consider preaching and pastoring first and foremost in my life. When I resigned the NAACP in

1993, I remained with both churches for one year. In June 1994, I resigned Greater Mt. Moriah, having completed 30 years. I then settled in comfortably at Greater Middle Baptist Church. The Detroit church was one of the most active in the political affairs of the city, with mayors, governors, senators, and other elected officials routinely dropping by.

Had I been interested in pursuing a political career in Detroit, that probably was an option. Alberta Blackburn, one of the most astute political forces in Detroit, David Akins, Macie Wright, Donald Walton, William Brock, Tom Turner, Sharon McPhail, Dr. Claude Young, and a whole host of people, I believe, would have helped me. I chose not to go that route, however. In the 20 years that I pastored, I would not have been able to make it except for the assistance of the Reverend Robert Joe Page, who served as co-pastor of Mt. Moriah from 1972 to 1993. He and his wife, Maude, did indeed "make a difference." I had other able assistants—Reverends Grimes and Caldwell—and I also brought in from Tennessee Reverend Jim Holley, who now pastors Little Rock Baptist Church. Jim served several years as my youth minister. I look at the list in Memphis . . . Reverends Rainey, Middlebrook, Whalum, Pleasure, Dinkins, Jones, Pinkney, all of whom served ably and well. Then there was the Reverend Ralph Jackson, who served faithfully. He was an AME minister who was known as the AME co-pastor of a Baptist church.

While in Detroit, we did not choose to buy a house. We lived for 10 years with the Hendersons (Oliver and Pearl) and the next 20 years with the Brock family (William and Lyndall, their children Yvonne, Rickey, and Randy, and their granddaughter, Sommer). It was a little taxing on Frances because she did not have a house to call her own. The treatment afforded by Pearl and Linda, assisted by friend Macie Wright, was wonderful, however. What these wonderful ladies did was indeed motivated by Christian friendship. We lived together as if we were blood-related brothers and sisters.

While it is true that Frances never had a house in Detroit, she did have a home. Greater Middle Baptist Church continues to move forward, and the challenge of the pastorate continues to inspire me. We now have a beautiful sanctuary and modern chapel, a 20-room educational building, a full-size gym that doubles as a banquet hall, and two modern and spacious day care centers. Recently, the church bought a 9-acre site a few blocks from our current location that has a beautiful sanctuary, and we are developing the grounds with a softball field and other park features such as swings and slides. We also operate a senior citizens' center and own three modern vans. We love Greater Middle Baptist Church with all our heart and strength and are mindful of the words of another great song, "We have come this far by faith leaning on the Lord."

Some time ago, I was in the St. Louis Post Dispatch Building in St. Louis calling on some of the editors. As I was leaving, I ran into a young man who knew me and started a conversation. He said, "Reverend Hooks, you will not remember this, but the year I finished high school you conducted a revival at my church, Mt. Moriah in Orange Mound. I was on the mourners' bench all five nights, Monday to Friday. On Friday night you preached, and my soul opened. I accepted Christ as my savior, was baptized, and became a member of the church. Reverend Hooks, thanks."

This young man's statement reinforces and reaffirms that, of all the things I have done or am doing, preaching is first and foremost, and in the end I know that only what I do for Christ will last. I have been with Middle Baptist 47 years and with Greater New Mt. Moriah for 30 years—a total of 77 years.

Thank you for the memories, for comradeship and companionship, and for officers who have been like brothers and sisters. Memphis, I will always be grateful to you. I was born and first saw the light of day here. When it is time to leave these mundane shores, I hope my death will occur here in Memphis, where I met Frances, and for 53 years we have been together. Memphis, I hope to sleep in your blessed soil until God, the Righteous Judge, shall sound the gavel in glory, and I will arise with all the saved of God and go home to meet Him.

Chapter 29

FRATERNAL ORGANIZATIONS AND POLITICAL ACTIVITY

One of the great joys of my life has been my civic, social, and fraternal activity. As a child, after the sixth-grade experience of being promoted a grade level, I became very introverted. And reading books or going to the movies, or later watching television, were solitary activities. While in Chicago I spent a great deal of time at the churches. One of the great churches was the First Church of Deliverance, pastored by the Reverend Clarence Cobb. Reverend Cobb's choir exceeded 300 members and he had the largest audience of anybody at that time. I attended that church every Sunday night. And since it was only eight blocks from my house, I walked home most nights. There were a number of neighbors who would walk together for the eight or 10 blocks from 47th and Wabash to where I lived at 38th and State.

In Chicago, I also attended the movies regularly. Some movies not only had a double feature, they had a triple feature, which meant if I had the time, I could spend six hours watching the movie, eating popcorn, and sleeping. In Memphis, the minute I came back from law school I became immersed in civic and political activity. There was a great fraternal organization known as Knights of Pythias. I joined that organization and belonged to Griffin Lodge Number Ten. At that time we had fewer than 100 black Pythians throughout the state of Tennessee, scattered in about six lodges ranging in membership from five to 20. Eventually I became grand chancellor (state president) of the group. Later, I became supreme worthy counselor (national president) of the women's division, Court of Calanthe. After the death of the supreme head, I became national president, supreme chancellor. My predecessor as supreme chancellor was R.A. Hester of Dallas, Texas. I succeeded him and have been the head now since about 1982. It is very small. We control practically no money, and our membership is more or less scattered among 25 states, with 100-200 members in each state.

The states are in a sense sovereign, and the national order really does not run them. In their heyday, the Knights of Pythias had 150,000 national members scattered in 30 states, with most states having from 4,000 to 10,000 members. Tennessee alone had 10,000 members among the men and 10,000 members among the women. And during the period 1910 through 1930, when the Depression depleted their ranks, they may have had a national membership of close to 300,000 men and women. We have never been anywhere near that since I have been involved. Nevertheless, one of the interesting things was that the women in the state of Texas managed to hold on to 10,000 members. Today I serve as supreme chancellor (national president) of the men's organization, and we meet in our convention once every two years. We have a possibility someday of regaining some of our membership but certainly never again will be as strong as we were in the early period.

I enjoy working with these men and women. I enjoy it because I still believe that somehow we have got to be at the grassroots level where everybody can be somebody. In the Masonic organization we have some 7,000 or 8,000 members in the state of Tennessee. We are Prince Hall affiliated. I served as grand secretary (that is, state secretary) of this organization for 30 years. Three years ago, I was elected grand master (state president). And this organization still has a membership close to 7,000 and a treasury close to $600,000. It is one of the most concerned and affable groups in America. And we have great plans for the future. In this regard, we are most concerned about the youth and have some interesting prospects for increased and expanded youth membership. What a joy it is to work with these two groups. The women's group with the Masons is known as the Order of Eastern Star ("We have seen his star in the east and we have come to worship Him"). The national membership of the Masons and the Order of the Eastern Star approximates 300,000. My local lodge is Eureka Lodge #3. Before World War I, my grandfather, Charles A. Hooks, served as secretary of this lodge and my wife's grandfather, Samuel Graves, was a member.

I also belong to an organization known as the Elks. It has been a joy being a part of them for some years. I was a chaplain for Bluff City Lodge Number 96. And there is another group known as the Knights and Daughters of Tabor. This group originated in Mississippi and for many years operated a first-class hospital in the all-Negro town of Mound Bayou. P.M. Smith was a leader of this group. I served for one term as international treasurer, but at the present time my schedule makes it impossible for me to be active.

I have often been asked why I remain active in the of fraternal organizations. It is primarily because they represent the grassroots aspirations of many African Americans who strive to push our community forward, to see our community excel, who reach out with well-worn but well-used tools of love, charity, friendship, and concern to make life better for others. They are unselfish and seek reward only in doing for others. The many people with whom I meet are people I respect and admire, people with whom I love to work, and I look forward to many more years of continued blessings—not material blessings, but blessings of community, brotherhood, and fellowship.

Our Greek letter organizations are all membership-oriented at the college level. The collective membership exceeds 700,000. During my years at the NAACP, all of them contributed heavily in money, time, and talent to the work of the NAACP. The organization to which I personally belong is the Omega Psi Phi Fraternity, and I have served as the equivalent of the Memphis Chapter president.

When I returned to Memphis, I enjoyed becoming a part of the expansion of black political power in Shelby County. The Democratic Party nationally was a party of Strom Thurmond, Theodore K. Bilbo, Jim Eastland, Ross Barnett, Fielding Wright, Russell Long, and many other unreconstructed rebels of the South. Of course, it was also the party of Hubert Humphrey, John Kennedy, Lyndon Johnson, and other great and outstanding people.

Locally, in Memphis, blacks could not belong to the Democratic Party because boss Ed Crump ran the town, and with a coalition of the bosses of Nashville and Chattanooga, they ran the state. Crump had to produce a big voting block. So, routinely he would poll 60,000 voters in Shelby County for his candidate. The opponent would receive fewer than 1,000 votes. The only way to reach 60,000 was to have black people involved. So, in the whole South, Memphis was one of the few places where blacks could vote in the Democratic primary. But they could not be a part of the Democratic Party machinery. That was reserved for white Democrats.

There had been a great black leader in Memphis, R.R. Church, who exercised tremendous influence over the Republican Party both locally and statewide. When I came back to Memphis, therefore, it was not difficult for me to join up with the Republican Party. George W. Lee at that time was a local black Republican leader, and he did a simply out-standing job. One of the things we did to increase voter registration was to encourage black people to run for office. Crump had had a run-in with the governor, Gordon Browning. And Browning, in order to "fix" that, had the state pass a law to purge the voter registration rolls of Shelby County and remove every voter, black and white, from the voter roll. We started with zero. By the time I came back to Memphis in 1949 to practice law, there were only 7,000 blacks registered to vote. I became a part of the movement to increase black voter registration. Every time we had a campaign, we were trying to increase that number. The number of black registered voters has now increased to over 200,000.

I ran for the state legislature. I ran for juvenile court judge. I ran for city court judge. I supported Dr. Walker as he ran for the board of educa-tion. We simply turned this town upside down and started the move-ment that eventually resulted in a black voter registration moving beyond 200,000. This made possible the election of Harold Ford to the Con-gress, Willie Herenton to the mayor's office, A.C. Wharton to the county mayor's office, and blacks to many other positions. Those elected in-cluded my nephew, Michael Hooks, as Shelby County tax assessor, at the time the highest job ever attained at the county-wide level by a black person. Politics, when practiced right, is an effective mechanism for moving forward.

In the meantime, after the Barry Goldwater situation, I left the Re-publican Party. Even in the years that I was supporting the Republican ticket nationally, many times I supported the best Democratic candidate for senator and governor. (There were no Republicans running at this time.) So I supported great people like Estes Kefauver, Al Gore (senior and junior), Frank Clement, Gordon Browning, and many others.

In 1959, we fielded "The Volunteer Ticket." Four of us ran for public office. H.C. Buntyn, pastor of Mt. Olive CME Church and later a bishop of the church, ran for the school board. Roy Love, pastor of Mt. Nebo Baptist Church and president of the Baptist Pastor's Alliance (which had some 150 members), also ran for the school board. Russell B. Sugarmon, Jr., a brilliant, Harvard-trained lawyer and astute politician, ran for Com-missioner of Public Works. I ran for election as a juvenile court judge. At that time, Memphis had a commission form of government with five commissioners elected, one of whom would be mayor. We ran together as a team and galvanized the city of Memphis. Never before had there been such enthusiasm—50 to 60 rallies a day, appearances on television and radio. During this campaign the total registration of black voters went above the 60,000 mark, as compared to 7,000 just 10 years before. It was an exciting, marvelous, never-to-be-forgotten time. None of us won the office we sought, but the lessons learned, alliances forged, voters registered, the spirit of enthusiasm engendered live on even today. Later, it led to the election of Harold Ford, Sr., to Congress. What an unforgettable victory that was. It also led to the election of Willie Herenton as mayor of Memphis and A.C. Wharton as mayor of Shelby County. In addition, it led to the election of numerous black people to the city council, county commission, board of education, state house, and senate, and some 17 elected judges and many other elected positions. Memphis, in 1959, became one of the most progressive political cities in the nation.

I think of Memphis and the many changes that have occurred here over the years. All my life I read about Ed Crump, who, I believe, had the longest-living political machine anywhere. From 1909 until 1954, the year of his death, he ran Memphis ruthlessly, singlehandedly, and on his own terms. He decided where new stop signs would go, where schools would be built, tax rates, what dog catchers would be paid, which streets would be paved and which would be patched. Strangely, however, he did many things for blacks—he built swimming pools and new schools, paved streets, and put up stoplights in black neighborhoods. Many years of studying political science and witnessing Crump's activities *changed forever the way I look at politics*. I have been a fanatic to ensure that I would never again live under such a dictator.

I think of my grandmother, a musician extraordinaire, who tried in vain to teach me to play. In my mind's eye, even now, I can see hundreds of people she trained, taking their seats at the piano bench, sitting up straight, raising their hands just so, and as they play I can see Grandma all over again. I hear her talking about assisting W. C. Handy with some musical theories, and I remember Handy as the man who forever *changed the way we view music with the introduction of the Blues*.

Memphis—I remember reading of Clarence Sanders, founder of the Piggly Wiggly stores and the man who introduced the supermarket concept, which eventually wiped out the traditional corner grocery. I will forever think of him as a man who *changed the way we buy groceries*.

I am grateful to have known Horace Hull, founder of Hull Dobbs Ford Company, the world's largest Ford dealer, who always provided assistance when I called on him to support black charitable causes. My deacon, Charles Turner, worked for Mr. Hull. I will always think of Mr. Hull, who introduced innovative financing, as the man who *changed the way we bought cars*.

Memphis—where I think of Lt. George W. Lee, the man who ran the Lincoln League. The Lincoln League was the political mechanism developed by R. R. Church, an outstanding black Republican politician, and the last of the old-time black political bosses of so-called lily-white Republicans. George Lee was another who forever *changed the way we approach politics*. He believed that a candidate must support the people who supported him. He also insisted, "If you can't call me Mister, don't call me George—call me 'Lieutenant,' my army title." So everywhere he went, he was known as Lieutenant Lee. Very few people, black or white, ever called him George.

Memphis—where I met Dr. J. E. Walker, the man who started Universal Life Insurance Company and led it to become the fourth largest black business in America by 1948, and who in 1956, at the age of 65, founded and organized the Tri-State Bank of Memphis, aided by his son, Maceo. Tri-State Bank, which I now serve as a director, is a $100 million institution that has helped thousands of people with loans they otherwise might never have gotten. Dr. Walker founded a church, the Mississippi Boulevard Christian Church, and ran for the school board in 1951, when it was physically dangerous to do so, and he spent countless hours in community work. Dr. Walker *changed the way many people look at public service and forever inspired me to remain involved.*

Memphis—where I met Dr. L. G. Patterson, a pioneer black doctor who ran, until his death, the Tri-State Fair—an event that attracted thousands to the fairgrounds and gave blacks a place to exhibit our talents in farming, canning, and homemaking. Dr. Patterson forever challenges me to keep moving.

Bishop Charles Harrison Mason, founder of the Church of God in Christ, was a legendary preacher and religious leader who built a denomination from a handful of members in 1907 to more than 1 million members at his death. Today, that church is the fastest-growing denomination in America and has over 4 million members. Bishop Mason *changed forever the way millions practice their religion.*

Memphis—where I had the chance to meet with Kemmons Wilson, founder of Holiday Inn, and his friend, Wallace Johnson. These men *changed forever the shape, size, and price of hotel rooms in America.*

Memphis—where I met Ira Lipman, president of Guardsmark, who *changed forever the nature of America's private security and guard system*, and made it fair, workable, and affordable.

Memphis—where I met, knew, and worked with Dr. R. Q. Venson and his wife, Ethel, who founded the Memphis Cotton Makers' Jubilee.

These two looked with disdain at the role (or lack of one) that blacks played in the Memphis Cotton Carnival, the city's premier social event. Seeing blacks in jumper overalls, leading the horses that often drew the floats, influenced the Vensons to start the Cotton Makers' Jubilee. In its heyday, this organization gave honor and dignity to the role blacks have played in the development of cotton as an economic resource. We had our own kings, queens, and floats in a parade. Dr. and Mrs. Venson *changed in a positive way the African American image of self.*

Memphis—where I met Lucie Campbell, my teacher in the ninth and eleventh grades at Booker T. Washington High School. A great musician, songwriter, and composer who wrote great songs that are still very often sung today—songs such as "Footprints of Jesus," "Just to Behold His Face," and "Something Within . . . ." It was a blessing to serve as her pastor at Bethesda Church for a number of months in 1955 and 1956. Lucie Campbell *changed forever, in a beautiful way, the music in our churches.*

Memphis—where I met Blair T. Hunt, my high school principal, who stamped and molded me forever to believe in discipline and order as a prerequisite for teaching in our public school system and *changed for the better the attitudes of the thousands he taught.*

Memphis—where I met Fred Smith, founder and president of Federal Express, a business employing nearly 125,000 people. The name FedEx has become synonymous with fast, efficient mail delivery. Fred Smith is a man who *changed forever how we deliver our mail.*

Memphis—where I met Jed Dreifus, a retail jeweler; Mori Griner, general manager of Channel 5, WMCT; and Lester Rosen, an insurance salesman. These men became my friends, helped me, and in so many ways *changed, in a positive way, the way I view race relations.*

Memphis—where I practiced law for 16 years, from 1949 to 1965, before I went on the bench. During this time, I was never addressed as "Mr. Hooks" or "Lawyer Hooks." In the courtrooms, however, in which the bailiff, clerk, judge, and most of the juries were white, never once was I mistreated or misused because of my race. Every judge of the court of record, without exception, was fair and square and otherwise courteous to me. I shall always cherish this and forever be grateful, for I understand that unfairness and outright prejudice prevailed in many other courts throughout the South at that time.

City court with Judge Beverly Boushe was different, however. Judge Boushe allowed police officers to use racial epithets openly in his court and permitted them to provide hearsay testimony about what happened at crime scenes before the police ever arrived. Yet, even in Judge Boushe, I saw signs of change. Often, on Saturdays, he would drive to my house and ask me to pray with him and for him.

One climactic day, we had a big sit-in hearing in his courtroom and the place was packed. After court opened, he asked me to pray. I did, and it was the talk of the courthouse for days. Judge Boushe died shortly thereafter during a hotly contested campaign, and yet in death he received the most votes. Judge Boushe placed in my heart forever the knowledge that *people can and do change.*

Memphis—where I met at various rallies and functions *four men who changed my life:* Governor Frank Clement, who appointed me to the bench; John Hooker, who introduced me to the fast-lane business world; Howard Baker, whose influence placed me on the FCC, where I helped *change forever the minority position in telecommunications;* and Governor Sundquist, who appointed me a special justice on the Tennessee Supreme Court. The case before the court involved the constitutionality of a statute authorizing the election of appellate court judges based on their record, rather than by running against an opponent. There were five justices, and the court voted 3 to 2 to uphold the statute providing for the so-called "Missouri Plan" as a method for electing appellate judges. I voted with the majority. I thus kept the *change in the law that governs elections of appellate judges in Tennessee.*

Memphis—where I met John Tigrett and his lovely wife, Pat. They lived in the building where I now live. We were there together about six years. I read his book, and quite often I had the chance to talk with him. They came to my church, heard me preach, and discussed my sermons with me. Thank you for helping me keep an open mind and for encouragement in the dark days.

Memphis—where I was born and raised by my mother and father, who taught me reliability and stick-to-itiveness, honesty, integrity, and dependability. They passed this on to their family. They did not *change us; they molded us.*

At one time, I may have been a male chauvinist. Momma, my three sisters, my wife, and my daughter have changed this absolutely and positively for the better.

Religion has always played a pivotal role in my life. I am happily, gladly, proudly a born-again Christian with great concern and respect for the religion of all. A special thanks to Middle Baptist Church and Mount Moriah Baptist Church.

Thanks to all of my family—Frances, Pat, Mildred, Julia, Raymond, and all of my nephews and nieces, aunts and uncles, cousins and in-laws, surely Anita, Arlie, John, Barbara, and Eurline. To my brothers and sisters, the Masonic, Eastern Star, Pythian, Calanthe, Elk and Daughter Elks, and my brothers in Omega Psi Phi, thanks. Thurgood Marshall at the end of his life said, "I did the best I could with what I had." May that be my epitaph.

Afterword

I come now to the close of this volume, which has been a labor of love. I think of Jerry Guess, above all others, for he labored so hard to bring this together. I thank Frances for reading, Adrienne for her efforts, Debbie Peeler, my secretary, and Reece and Xernona. Thanks to all.

I glance back now briefly at the events I have tried to cover in this book. How fitting it was that my grandmother died peacefully and comfortably in the very rest home that she had founded some 30 years before, The Hooks Edwards Rest Home.

Surely her roots are deep. Her two sons were productive and successful businessmen; 10 grandchildren are and were teachers, activists, government workers, and lawyers; Henry Sr.'s children are Henry Jr., Maude, and Charlie, and Robert Sr.'s children are Charles, Julia, Robert, Raymond, Ben, Mildred, and Bessie. Her grandchildren included lawyers, teachers, government workers, businessmen, and the executive director of the NAACP. The tradition of public service continues through Ronald Sr., who is regional director of the National Labor Relations Board. Michael is a member of the Shelby County Board of Commissioners and former elected tax assessor. Great-grandsons and -granddaughters include teachers and government workers. The great-great-grandsons, Carlos and Carlton, are successful mortgage bankers and real estate investors. Carlton also played football in the NFL for eight years. Michael Jr. serves as president of the Memphis Board of Education and Ronald Jr. is manager of a franchise drug store. And as I look at the generations, they keep coming.

I grew up in Memphis, and that was a remarkable experience. My school years were years of learning and growing and understanding the nature of giving and receiving.

I suppose that most soldiers did not want to go into the Armed Services; I did not. But once in, I did my best, and the lessons I learned live with me now. Concentrating on the civil rights mystique had been my boyhood preoccupation. The names of all of the great women and men who changed the face of American history ever marched before me. I am glad that I had the opportunity of being the first black public defender in Memphis. I'm glad to have had the opportunity to be the first black judge of a court of record, not only in Shelby County but in the entire South, since the Reconstruction period. I am glad that history will report that we made some fundamental changes in the court system.

To know Martin Luther King, Jr., to work with him, to have walked with him, to have sat down in counsel with him scores of times was a great privilege that very few people enjoyed. There is an old black spiritual that says, "I wouldn't take nothing for my journey here." Well, I wouldn't take anything for my knowing King. He was a great, gallant, honest, unimpeachable leader.

I have always believed that it was necessary for black people to break the barriers that have kept them out of the top echelons of business achievement. I know full well the hurdles thrown our way, the slippery sticks, the changes in rules, the difficulties of learning the system, but I also have a joy of having participated in two marvelous business ventures. And in my retirement I have had the opportunity of utilizing some of these experiences. I serve as the chairman of the board of Minact, Inc., the largest minority business venture in the operation of job corps centers. Under the able direction of Booker T. Jones and Dr. Aaron Henry, co-founders, Minact operates seven job corps centers, employs over a thousand people, is training some several thousand students, and contributes greatly to giving a second chance to those who need it most. I have also come to meet, know, and appreciate the contributions of Dr. Robert Smith, an outstanding physician and pioneer civil rights leader in Mississippi, and a member of the Minact Board.

Since leaving the NAACP, I have served on the boards of the Chapman Company (a minority financial institution), TV station WLBT, the Maxima Corporation (a computer back-up service), and as chairman of the board of MINACT, founded by B.T. Jones and Aaron Henry, the largest minority-owned company in the job corps field, operating seven centers throughout the U.S. Aaron Henry was one of the truly great and legendary civil rights leaders of the nation, springing from the heart of Mississippi. It was a joy to work with him. I also was a member of the board of directors of Tri-State Bank, a $100 million bank owned by the minority community and served as chairman of the Tennessee Human Relations Commission. In addition, I am ex-director emeritus NAACP and first vice president of the Memphis branch. I also serve as president of the National Civil Rights Museum, which is located at the site of the old Lorraine Motel, where Dr. Martin Luther King, Jr. was assassinated in 1968.

It is here that I have come in contact with Pitt and Barbara, Jeanie, Beverly and Carla, Jim and Herb, Willie, Rose, Theresa, and a host of others. Pitt Hyde is one of the most dedicated men I have ever met. He has not only contributed large sums of money to the museum, but he has given heavily of his time, talent, and energy. Without him I am sure we would not have been able to continue to present to the world the most dramatic and vivid collection of material and exhibits depicting the civil rights movement.

I also serve as a distinguished adjunct professor at the University of Memphis, to which I have donated my papers. Doug Imig and David Madlock worked with me to develop a comprehensive presentation of civil rights history at the research center, called the Benjamin Hooks Institute for Social Change, at the University of Memphis. Thanks to President Raines and former President Rawlins, Provost Faudree, and Doctors Haddock and Black for their continued interest and concern. Due to the efforts of Congressman Harold Ford, Jr. and U.S. Senators Fred Thompson and Bill Frist, we recently secured over $1 million in funding for the Institute. Much work remains to be done to finalize this project. A Benjamin L. Hooks Chair has been established at Fisk University, and much credit goes to Francis Guess, executive vice president of the Ray Danner Corporation and a former member of the U.S. Commission on Civil Rights, and Howard Henderson for their efforts to ensure its success.

I still serve in the fraternal world as Supreme Chancellor (president) of the Knights of Pythias and Grand Master (state president) of the Prince Hall Masons of Tennessee. I continue as pastor of the Greater Middle Baptist Church. In my retirement I have served on so many nonprofit boards, agencies, and institutions that I shall not attempt to name them all. I am thankful for the memories, grateful for the challenges of the present, and look forward to the opportunities of the future. In the words of the great, black spiritual, "I don't feel no ways tired, I've come too far from where I started from. I don't believe He brought me this far to leave me."

In 2002, I joined the law firm of Wyatt, Tarrant & Combs, LLP, to establish their Diversity Services Practice Group. As chair of the group, I lead a team of lawyers who provide counseling and government relations advice to companies and organizations committed to attracting and retaining diverse employees and customers. It has been most rewarding to get to know Tom Dyer, who serves as chief operating officer of the Mem-

phis office. I shall not forget sitting in a restaurant eating lunch one day
and running into Hal Gerber, a brilliant criminal defense lawyer in Memphis who was then engaged in general practice.

We began a conversation that resulted in him asking me to consider
becoming a part of his firm. I said I would definitely consider the offer.
Hal called me several times and encouraged me to seek association with
his firm. I gladly accepted the offer. While there, I also met J. Michael
Brown, a minority partner of the firm who worked in the Louisville,
Kentucky, office. He is the former city attorney for Louisville. I have
worked closely with Mr. Brown in developing the Diversity Services
Practice Group. Thank goodness I found another great administrative
secretary, Debbie.

I have also formed a public service group known as the Children's
Health Forum, co-founded with Secretary Jack Kemp. We work on issues involving improving children's health, particularly in the area of lead
paint poisoning.

Also in my retirement I served as president, chairman, and CEO of
the Universal Life Insurance Company, the nation's fourth-largest black
insurance company. When I assumed the job, Universal was on the verge
of being taken over by the State Insurance Commission, with the stockholders receiving not a penny and the policyholders being dispossessed. I
was able to lead the company successfully and, in winding down its affairs, placed the policyholders safely in other companies and paid to the
stockholders close to $9 million. I thank men and women like Lawrence
and Cecelia Wesley, Frederica Hodges, Charles Jackson, Robert Johnson,
Eldridge Williams, Alvin Jackson, George Johnson, Robert Gholston,
Charles Dinkins, Harold Shaw, Jr., and J.W. Payne, and fellow members
of the board of directors for the aid, counsel, and leadership in bringing
this matter to a successful close. A special thanks to John C. Parker,
former personnel director of Universal, and Jessie Turner, Jr., president
of Tri-State Bank, for their particular help.

My service on the Federal Communications Commission brought
about a mammoth change in the role that blacks were able to play in the
media. I look back particularly at Tony Brown, with whom I worked to
help establish a school of communications at Howard University. During my tenure at the FCC, the number of radio stations owned by blacks
increased from 13 to more than 200, and I was able to help the splendid
media personalities Robert Johnson, Kathy Hughes, Percy Sutton, Ragan
Henry, Dorothy Brunson, and hundreds of others.

My service in the NAACP does, upon reflection, speak for itself. I am particularly indebted to the print media giants like Earl Graves, John Johnson, Robert Maynard, Ken Wilson, Carl Rowan, and Vernon Jarrett, without whom we would not have survived. Thanks to the millions of NAACP board, staff, and volunteers for your persistence. It was during these days that I had a chance to work with Al Sharpton, who is shooting for the top. I'm thankful for the opportunity to have worked hand in glove with Vernon Jordan, John Jacob, Coretta Scott King and all of the King children, Ralph Abernathy, Hosea Williams, Elaine Jones, Wade Henderson, Joe Rauh, Ralph Neas, Bill Taylor, Julius Chambers, Joe Lowery, Joe Madison (who led the now-legendary voter march and Trail of the Slave march), Paul Brock, and our inexhaustible Jesse Jackson.

I shall not here name all of the Congress people and senators, but let me particularly lift up the black mayors such as Maynard Jackson, Coleman Young, Tom Bradley, Harold Washington, David Dinkins, Richard Hatcher, Ernest Morial, and Richard Arrington. In fact, I could name them all. How can I forget the invaluable contributions of Ed Brooke, first black senator of the modern age and an invaluable ally and leader in the thrust for full citizenship; Doug Wilder, governor of Virginia; and Carol Moseley Braun, first black Democratic senator of the century. I think of the invaluable contributions of those blacks who have served as cabinet officers.

I have talked about it in the book, but let me just repeat, hats off to the scores of athletic stars and radio and movie personalities, and talk-show hosts, who have been supportive above and beyond the call of duty.

I close with this story about how God has blessed me beyond measure throughout my life. As a 12-year-old boy, I sat many nights on the back porch of my father's studio at 164 Beale Street in Memphis. I would look up toward the north and see the Peabody Hotel two blocks away. On warm summer nights, I could see tiny figures of dancers, and would read later in the newspaper about the parties they were attending. I could see white coats the men wore in the Skyway. I remember even now The Peabody's slogan: "The South's finest, one of America's best hotels." I remember even now wondering whether I would ever have a chance to be up there on that roof top, not as a musician or waiter or bus boy, but as a guest.

Fast forward to 1978, and I am being honored by the Memphis branch of the NAACP. The affair is being held, you guessed it, at The Peabody Skyway. I walk around and start looking south. All of a sudden it hits me. I am looking down at my father's old studio. I am looking down south at that little back porch where for so many years I looked up north at The Peabody. Tears unbidden start to flow, and one or two people came by and ask what is wrong. I answered, "nothing is wrong, I am just shouting and rejoicing and saying, 'Praise God from whom all blessings flow.' I have made it from there to here, may I forever be grateful and worthy."

That back porch on Beale Street forever changed and stamped my life.

Index

ABA LAWYER BIOGRAPHY SERIES

THE LAWYER BIOGRAPHY SERIES, published by the American Bar Association, is a new series about lawyers who are visionaries, who inspire, or who are role models – in short, who work to make a positive contribution to society and the legal system.

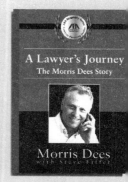

2004 384 pages 6 x 9	2003 297 pages 6 x 9	2002 367 pages 6 x 9	2001 365 pages 6 x 9
Hardback with dust jacket	Hardback with dust jacket	Hardback with dust jacket	Hardback with dust jacket
Product Code: 1610025	Product Code: 1610022	Product Code: 5310309	Product Code: 1610021
Regular Price: $39.00 + S/H	Regular Price: $39.00 + S/H	Regular Price: $39.00 + S/H	Regular Price: $39.00 + S/H
ABA Member Price: $34.00 + S/H	ABA Member Price: $34.00 + S/H	ABA Member Price: $34.00 + S/H	ABA Member Price: $34.00 + S/H

PURCHASE ALL 4 BOOKS IN THE LAWYER BIOGRAPHY SERIES AND SAVE 25%

Product Code: 1610026P
Regular Price: $117 + S/H (Regularly $156)
ABA Member Price: $102 + S/H (Regularly $136)

ORDER TODAY!
Visit our web site to learn more about this and all our other publications.

AMERICAN BAR ASSOCIATION

www.ababooks.org
Phone: 1-800-285-2221
Fax: 1-312-988-5568

Defending Liberty
Pursuing Justice

Publications Orders
P.O. Box 10892
Chicago, IL 60610-0892